# INFORMATION, FREEDOM AND CENSORSHIP

## The ARTICLE 19 World Report 1988

**ERRATA**

The map on page 128 is drawn incorrectly and should be disregarded entirely. In the map on page 246, Tehran and Baghdad have been transposed in error. The publishers apologise for these errors and would like to emphasize that the maps were intended only as sketches to indicate the location of the countries covered in the various reports.

This book is dedicated to Zwelakhe Sisulu, editor of *New Nation*, detained without trial in South Africa since Dec. 12, 1986.

Zwelakhe Sisulu was elected to the international board of ARTICLE 19 in November 1986.

# INFORMATION, FREEDOM AND CENSORSHIP

## The ARTICLE 19 World Report 1988

Prepared by the staff of
ARTICLE 19

Longman

INFORMATION, FREEDOM AND CENSORSHIP
The ARTICLE 19 World Report 1988

Published by **Longman Group UK Limited**, Longman House,
Burnt Mill, Harlow, Essex CM20 2JE, United Kingdom

ISBN 0-582-02624-5 (Longman)

**British Library Cataloguing in Publication Data**

Information, freedom and censorship: the Article 19 world report 1988.
1. Freedom of information. International political aspects
I. Boyle, C.K. (C. Kevin)  II. Piette, Matthew, *1963-*
III. Article 19.
(*Organisation*)
323.44'5

ISBN 0-582-02624-5

Computer typeset by SB Datagraphics, Colchester, Essex, England
(An Ician Communications Group company)
Printed and bound by Mackays Ltd of Chatham

# CONTENTS

EUROPE—contd.

MIDDLE EAST AND NORTH AFRICA

OCEANIA

# PREFACE

## by William Shawcross

*Assassination may be the extreme form of censorship. It is not so extreme, however, as to be unusable; even that form is employed all too frequently in the world. There are, of course, all the less 'extreme' but effective forms that are used daily, widely, constantly. Detention, arrest, imprisonment, torture, threats, the use of the law to prevent freedom of speech and expression. More often, the law is abused to do the same. All these are commonplace, as ARTICLE 19's timely and essential World Report makes clear.*

*And why? Because, fundamentally, almost everyone is in favour of some sort of censorship. Almost everyone believes that there are some things, personal or otherwise, which he or she would rather were left unsaid. Censorship is not an issue on which many people take an absolutist position. It is this that makes freedom from censorship such a hard cause to fight.*

*It is not to denigrate Amnesty International to say that combating torture is a simpler cause. To eradicate torture is obviously hard. But there are not many people—outside the apparatus of dictatorships—who would be seen or heard defending torture or even the detention of political prisoners. On the other hand many of those who decry torture or imprisonment find it easy enough to invoke 'restraint' or 'the national interest' or 'national security' as reasons for limiting freedom of expression and the right to know. Censorship, unlike torture, does not seem to be a black and white issue.*

*Yet the essential point which Roderick MacArthur grasped, and for which he founded ARTICLE 19, is that the abuse of power which is embodied in censorship can lead to all the other abuses of power. Censorship is essential to tyranny. Not all tyrants torture but all tyrants censor.*

*Freedom of speech is the essential right if all others are to be sought. It is the fundamental defence of the individual against government. Perhaps it cannot always be an adequate defence, but it is vital nonetheless.*

*ARTICLE 19 is a new organization. It has a long way to go in trying to combat censorship. But of one thing we are certain. Freedom of speech is indivisible; we are here to defend it, wherever and whenever—and we are here to oppose those who seek to infringe upon this right. For, once that freedom is lost, all other freedoms are lost with it.*

London, 1988.

ARTICLE 19 is an international human rights organization established in 1986 to promote the right to freedom of opinion and expression and the right to seek, receive and impart information and ideas through any media regardless of frontiers. It takes its name from Article 19 of the Universal Declaration of Human Rights, which proclaims these rights. ARTICLE 19 has established an international research and information centre on censorship in London to document and combat censorship on a global basis. The Chairman of ARTICLE 19 is William Shawcross and its director is Kevin Boyle.

ARTICLE 19 wishes to acknowledge and to thank the many individuals and the other human rights organizations that have contributed to the production of this Report. Special thanks to all those who helped in the preparation of this report, its editors Kevin Boyle and Matthew Piette, and the rest of the staff of ARTICLE 19; Friederike Knabe, Robin Bonner, Elizabeth Cleary-Rodriguez, Susan Hay, Annie McMorris, Ann Naughton and Lene Johannessen. Thanks also to Timothy Westcott and Kristi Rudelius.

Most of the material was written by individual contributors and special support was given by the following organizations: Americas Watch, Asia Watch, Amnesty International, International PEN Writers in Prison Committee, PEN American Centre and Writers and Scholars International (*Index on Censorship*). ARTICLE 19 also acknowledges the support of the J Roderick MacArthur Foundation. Thanks are also due to Ciarán Ó Maoláin for his careful correction of the text, to Nicola Greenwood of Longman for copy editing, to Allan Lamb of Longman for the maps and to Alison Cowan for the index.

# INTRODUCTION

This is a Report on the right to freedom of expression in the world and how that right is denied through censorship. It is a contribution by a new human rights organization, ARTICLE 19, established to combat censorship and to secure proper recognition and protection throughout the world for this fundamental right of the individual.

The core of the book is an account of the state of freedom of expression in fifty countries representative of all regions and of different political and ideological systems. The countries were not chosen to represent best or worst cases but to document the diverse issues and challenges that the right to freedom of expression and its protection from censorship gives rise to in all parts of the world. No attempt is made to rank or classify countries. In subsequent reports, the range and number of countries will be more comprehensive.

Freedom of expression is not the property of any political system or ideology. It is a universal human right, defined and guaranteed in international law. ARTICLE 19 is committed to the task of ensuring that its international definition and full guarantee are recognized and respected by the governments of all countries.

As an international human right, freedom of expression means that every individual has the right to hold opinions and to express them without fear and it includes the right of everyone 'to seek, receive and impart information and ideas' of all kinds through any medium of choice, regardless of national frontiers or state boundaries. Freedom of expression therefore entails press freedom and freedom of all media as one of its principal guarantees. Censorship is any interference with the individual or a means of communication that denies these basic rights and freedoms or arbitrarily encroaches upon them.

The book also represents a contribution towards marking the 40th anniversary of the adoption of the Universal Declaration of Human Rights. This historic human rights text was adopted by the General Assembly of the United Nations on Dec. 10, 1948 and has inspired all efforts since that date to secure human rights worldwide.

The Preamble of the Universal Declaration records that 'the advent of a world in which human beings shall enjoy freedom of speech and belief and freedom from fear and want has been proclaimed as the highest aspiration of the common people'. It is an advent that has not yet come. But the aspiration to be free from hunger and from the risk of war has never been stronger. Among the more hopeful advances have been the actions of the 'common people' which have forced governments to address hunger and famine in the world and to confront the threat to all represented by nuclear weapons.

To date, however, little has been achieved with respect to the other ideals described equally in the Universal Declaration as the highest human aspiration—freedom of speech and belief. This World Report is concerned with freedom of speech, a right intimately linked with freedom of belief. The systematic disregard for both deserves greater attention from the world community.

Over the forty years since the adoption of the Universal Declaration of Human Rights there has been enormous and exciting progress in the technical means of expression and communication, both within and between countries. But the satellite images flashed around the earth hide another and shameful reality. In varying degrees and many forms, rule through censorship is in fact the global norm. As this World Report amply demonstrates, freedom of expression is blatantly and often brutally denied. Every day, individuals are dismissed or imprisoned for holding opinions deemed unacceptable by governments or other powerful groups. Writers are attacked and imprisoned; literature, art and film is suppressed as dangerous or seditious; journalists are intimidated, detained, deported and not infrequently killed, often because they expose abuses of power by those who rule. Newspapers, periodicals and books, local and foreign, are seized or banned; radio and television stations are jammed, silenced and shut down.

But the Report also illustrates that attacks on these fundamental rights are not always overt. The objective of controlling the individual's right to speak can also be pursued through more subtle means. It is this combination of direct and indirect violation that makes censorship a complex and difficult issue to confront and defeat.

The victims of censorship are not only the creative, the dissenter and the media. If the struggle against censorship is to be a truly popular one, then the common people invoked by the Universal Declaration must come to realize that all can be victims. The right to be informed is equally a feature of freedom of expression. Chernobyl and earlier nuclear accidents and the spread of AIDS throughout the world have contributed to the realization that full freedom of information is not a luxury but may be literally a matter of life and death. The denial of information vital to health, such as arises from the dumping of unlabelled pesticides and pharmaceuticals in the developing world, for example, is censorship to be opposed just as much as the more classic manifestations of censorship in book banning, radio jamming or the destruction of printing presses. In the name of state secrecy or national security, people everywhere are routinely denied access to information they have a right and need to know. Governments surround their administrations in secrecy, to insulate themselves from criticism and to limit their accountability. These issues are also reported upon in the book. ARTICLE 19 supports campaigns to reduce administrative secrecy, to have 'freedom of information' laws requiring openness or *transparence* from governments, and generally any measures which strengthen the right to know.

Freedom of expression and freedom of information are not only basic to the development of the human personality, but are essential for full democratic participation in society. Without full information, the citizen cannot criticize policy. Without a voice and the right to put forward views, the citizen cannot contribute to polical and social change. It is because the media are the chief vehicles of communication and publicity that their freedom and independence is vital.

If there is a hopeful side to this Report, it is the overwhelming evidence that the individual everywhere identifies with these rights and the justifications for them. Those who suffer for their views, such as the hundreds of thousands who have supported the recurrent human rights movements in China, the theatre actors in Chile threatened by death squads, or the many writers mentioned in this book who sit in prison cells all over the world, raise precisely the demand that governments recognize their freedom to express opinions and criticisms. The movement for *glasnost* and *perestroika* in the Soviet Union is the most recent and significant recognition of the centrality of freedom of expression to social progress.

Freedom of expression and its corollaries, freedom to hold opinions and freedom of information, are as complex as they are fundamental to human existence. Interference by governments with these freedoms is achieved through a wide variety of means. Any attempt to oppose censorship must seek to understand both the nature of these freedoms and the techniques and justifications invoked to deny them. Michael Scammell's essay in the first section of the book is a sustained analysis of the concept of censorship and its historical roots by a distinguished writer and former editor of *Index on Censorship*. In the final section, following the Country Reports, an attempt is made to build on this analysis and to index and comment on the many facets of the subject raised in the countries surveyed.

The struggle for the maximum freedom of expression must explain the fact that it can never be an absolute right. The international standards admit of limitation or restriction; few rights are absolute in these terms. But experience teaches that denials of human rights are invariably justified by reference to limitations arbitrarily invoked and applied. The international standards make it clear that, in invoking limitations, governments must put the right to expression first, and not submerge it under the guise of its balance with other rights of the individual or interest of the state. It is in the abuse of restrictions that most censorship occurs, and the campaign against censorship must monitor closely these restrictions. At the same time, ARTICLE 19 is committed to reducing to a minimum all restraints on freedom of opinion and expression.

The country reports, which have been written with the help of expert consultants and other human rights organizations, are not simply a record of incidents such as the arrest of dissidents or the closure of newspapers, but an attempt to provide a reasonably detailed picture of how freedom of expression in general is respected in the country in question. In broadly similar format, these essays detail the legal standing of rights to expression and information, the structure of the media and limitations on them and how censorship, if it is practised, functions and is justified. Current issues of interest are highlighted, such as *glasnost*, in the USSR entry; official secrecy in Britain and the government's efforts to suppress the Spycatcher book; the use of censorship to stifle reports of human rights abuses in South Africa; concentration of ownership of the media in France, USA and Britain; and the status of freedom of expression in proclaimed emergencies in Central and Latin America. The starting point and the guide for this report is the language of the Universal Declaration of Human Rights, Article 19:

'Everyone has the right to freedom of opinion and expression; this right includes freedom to hold opinions without interference and to seek, receive and impart information and ideas through any media regardless of frontiers.'

ARTICLE 19 was named following this article as an international human rights organization, independent of all governments and ideologies, to campaign globally for the greatest possible protection of these rights and freedoms. It is supported entirely by donations. ARTICLE 19 takes no stand on particular political systems, but upholds the right of everyone to their own views, the right to express them and the right to be informed.

*This Report has been prepared to assist those already engaged in the defence of freedom of expression and to interest others not yet involved. ARTICLE 19 seeks to build an international movement for these fundamental rights and in defence of those who are victims of censorship. It can only succeed if it generates worldwide support and international action. If you wish to join us or to give financial support, write to ARTICLE 19, 90 Borough High Street, London SE1 1LL, United Kingdom.*

Kevin Boyle

# CENSORSHIP AND ITS HISTORY - A PERSONAL VIEW

*Michael Scammell was editor of Index on Censorship from 1971 to 1980 and is currently Professor of Russian Literature at Cornell University in the United States. He is the author of 'Solzhenitsyn, A Biography' (London, 1984).*

'Censorship' is one of the popular catchwords of our time, and like most catchwords is peculiarly difficult to define. The ultimate form of censorship, according to George Bernard Shaw, is assassination, a proposition for which there is even more evidence in today's world than there was in Shaw's. At the other extreme it has been argued that all editing is a form of censorship, and that writers who anticipate editing by tailoring their work to suit a particular audience are practising 'self-censorship'. There is an element of truth in both these propositions, but if both extremes are true, and the same word is employed to describe them both, the very width of the definition becomes self-defeating. The word 'censorship' loses its usefulness as a descriptive tool and ends by obfuscating rather than clarifying the matter it seeks to define.

One reason for this state of affairs is that 'censorship' belongs to that category of words describing apparently simple, but in reality highly complex social mechanisms that have been the subject of impassioned dispute in modern political life, as a result of which they have become subject to selective definitions or even outright distortion, and have been turned into slogans. Most people experience a negative reflex on hearing the word 'censorship', and if asked to produce a snap judgement, many would almost invariably vote against its use, or feel queasy if obliged by conscience to vote the other way. 'Censorship' is a handy word to throw at political opponents when one wishes to discredit them, producing quick results on the mind of the listener or reader. Consequently it is bent, twisted and distorted to suit the immediate needs of whoever happens to be using it and is applied to situations that do not merit this description.

Yet it was not always so. Censorship started out as an accepted component of good government and was so regarded for over a thousand years before it was perceived differently. Even today, certain forms of what is called 'censorship' are more widely practised and receive broader assent than its baleful reputation would seem to indicate. If we wish to understand what it is all about, therefore, our task would seem to be twofold: to ascertain how and why the idea of censorship was transformed from a positive good to a negative evil; and to discover what constitutes censorship in the modern world. If we can do this, we may, perhaps, be able to restore a little meaning to this abused and mistreated word.

1

# CENSORSHIP AND ITS HISTORY

## The origins of censorship

Curiously enough, neither the *Oxford English Dictionary* nor Webster's *New International Dictionary* (the standard American work) give much information on the word 'censorship'. Indeed, the Oxford does not give it a main heading at all, simply listing it as a derivative of the word 'censor' and describing it cryptically as 'the office or function of a censor', while Webster adds 'the action of a censor' to the Oxford definition. This perhaps testifies not only to the general vagueness surrounding this concept, but also to its remoteness from Anglo-Saxon ways of thought.

The word 'censor' is better served, with three practical definitions in the Oxford dictionary and a fourth more specialized one as follows: '1. One of two magistrates in ancient Rome, who drew up the census of the citizens, etc., and had the supervision of public morals. 2. An official whose duty it is to inspect books, journals, plays, etc. before publication, to secure that they shall contain nothing immoral, heretical, or offensive or injurious to the state. 3. One who censors private correspondence (as in time of war). 4. A power within the soul which represses certain elements in the unconscious.'

If we take these as our starting point we find that for our immediate purposes a systematized censorship began with Rome, where the function of the censor was to 'supervise public morals'. The Romans found nothing inconsistent in the fact that officials whose duty it was to establish people's whereabouts and income for taxation purposes should also concern themselves with how those people behaved, nor did they doubt that this was the proper business of the state.

The second definition brings us closer to the heart of the matter, for it includes all the elements of what we have come to recognize as a fully developed system of censorship, indicating both the targets: books, journals, plays, etc.; and the censor's prophylactic role—as a guardian against public 'immorality', 'heresy' and matters 'injurious to the state'. The clue to what happened after the Romans is to be found in that one word 'heresy', which takes us at once to the Christian religion and the rise of the Christian church. It is above all with the rise and decline of the Church that the European practice of censorship has been connected.

The Church itself, of course, had suffered persecution and suppression in its early days, and that experience left an indelible mark on its future development. Once established as the official religion of Rome, the Church itself made haste to consolidate its position by suppressing all competing views and dissent, which it labelled 'heresy' (it is interesting to note that the Latin—and English—words are cognate with the Greek word for 'choice'). This meant, among other things, strict control over the dissemination and interpretation of the Holy Scriptures, which entailed censorship. Throughout the Dark and Middle Ages, the problem was not great. 'Books' were handwritten, and were produced laboriously and slowly by a small number of initiates. Even after the Inquisition had been founded in the 13th century, censorship as such did not bulk large among its concerns. The big change in attitude came in response to a stimulus

2

from outside—the invention of the printing press by Gutenberg round about 1450. All of a sudden, the production and dissemination of books was revolutionized. 'Choice' was automatically available, and on a scale never before dreamed of. And 'choice' was tantamount to heresy.

A mere thirty five years after the invention of the printing press, in 1485, the Archbishop of Mainz (where Gutenberg had lived and worked) requested and obtained the establishment of the first secular censorship office. In 1493 a revitalized Inquisition in Venice issued the Church's first list of banned books, and in 1501 the Pope attempted to make censorship universal throughout Christendom. At that first attempt he failed, but fifty years later, in 1559, one of his successors established the *Index Librorum Prohibitorum* (*Index of Banned Books*), which was made binding on all Roman Catholics (i.e. the entire population of Europe, apart from the English). The office of the Inquisition, which administered the *Index*, survived until 1774 in France and 1834 in Spain, while the *Index* itself has remained in force for Roman Catholics up to the present day, though its role is nowadays advisory.

## Church and state

The Church's role in the development of European censorship was paramount, but not unique. 'Matters offensive or injurious to the state' were also part of the censor's concern, and for many centuries church and state were so close that what was injurious to the church was automatically regarded as injurious to the state. In fact, it was only when church and state began to separate that views on censorship began to change.

In Rome, Christianity was eventually adopted as the official state religion and this was the position when the Holy Roman Empire split in two at the end of the 14th century, with the Eastern Roman Empire based on Byzantium and the Western one based on Rome. The distinguishing feature of Byzantine Christianity soon became the complete subordination of church to state and the consequent fusion of spiritual and temporal power under a monolithic governing elite, a situation that persisted until the fall of Byzantium in 1453. The distinguishing feature of the Western and Roman church, on the other hand, was its independence of the state and the division of temporal and spiritual power. This worked to the Western church's advantage in the early centuries of its history. Right up to the end of the 12th century, rulers like Charlemagne and Barbarossa claimed their power in the name of the Holy Roman Church and derived their legitimacy from the Church. Indeed, the Holy Roman Empire survived, under the aegis of the Hapsburg dynasty in Austro-Hungary, until 1806, if only in name by this time. But paradoxically, the Western church's strength, its independence, was also its weakness, for once its ascendancy had been broken, secular rulers in turn claimed independence from the Church and its power went into inevitable decline.

It is tempting to think that censorship began to decline with it, but it is more complicated than that. In fact, systematic church censorship got

3

under way only **after** the Church's monolithic power had been broken by the rise of the secular nation state, that is, when the Church began to feel threatened. And the new secular states were not immune from the practice either. On the contrary, they exercised their own censorship, parallel to that of the Church. Henry VIII, the first monarch to break with Rome altogether, was also the first European monarch to issue an official list of banned books—in 1529, thirty years before the Roman Catholic *Index* was established. In Germany, the famous Frankfurt Book Fair, founded at the end of the 15th century, was eventually killed stone dead by censorship. It is true that much censorship continued to be exercised at the instigation of the Church and in concert with it, but it also suited the secular authorities to have the instrument of censorship to hand for their own use and to be able to deploy it for political as well as religious purposes.

Nevertheless, the split that Henry VIII brought about in the Roman church and the impact of the Reformation that followed did prove to be decisive in determining attitudes to the institution of censorship. Censorship derived its authority—and therefore received the assent of the people—from its role as an instrument for reinforcing revealed truth, one and indivisible, as interpreted and expressed by Rome. Once that truth had been seriously questioned, and the 'heresy' of choice introduced, it became impossible to maintain that there were no possible alternatives to the Roman way. The cat was let out of the bag and there was no way of getting it back inside again.

While the English state still felt threatened by Rome and the continental powers it had every reason to maintain and continue its own form of censorship, but once its independence, and the independence of the Anglican church, had been fully established, these reasons were less compelling. To get rid of the censorship was not easy, however. Governments are ever jealous of their prerogatives and never give them up without a struggle.

In England the decisive battle took place in the 17th century. At that time, the chief instrument of censorship was the Licensing Law 'for preventing abuses in printing seditious, treasonable and unlicensed pamphlets, and for the regulating of printing and printing presses'. In 1644 John Milton published his essay, *Aeropagitica*, the first and still most powerful broadside against censorship ever written, in which he set out, with unrivalled eloquence, most of the arguments that have since become standard among opponents of censorship: 'Truth needs no licensing to make her victorious. Who ever knew truth put to the worse in a free and open encounter?' Milton was a deeply religious man and turned the tables on his opponents by citing religion in defence of his plea against censorship, just as early thinkers had invoked religion in its favour: 'As good almost kill a man as kill a good book. Who kills a man kills a reasonable creature; but he who destroys a book kills reason itself, the image of God.' But Milton was also a Puritan and therefore in dispute with the Church of England. He knew that there were now many versions of 'the truth', and that the free exchange of ideas was essential to Dissenters, like himself, if they were to have any chance of propagating their views.

As a matter of historical record, Milton's essay had virtually no visible political impact at the time it was written. At the end of the 17th century, however, the debate about censorship entered the foreground of political life. Milton's arguments were taken up by pamphleteers with motives less lofty than his, but they were successful where he had failed, and in 1695 the Licensing Law was annulled.

Similar developments took place in Holland, where the Reformation was also influential. In France and Germany the struggle took longer and was harder fought. With the growth of Absolutism in the 18th century there was even a backward movement, with kings and governments clamping down wherever possible. The French Revolution of 1789 seemed to have reversed this trend, with Clause 11 of the Declaration of the Rights of Man enshrining freedom of 'speech, thought and expression' in terms very much modelled on Milton's, but after the failure of the Revolution, censorship was again introduced. The infamous Metternich introduced a scheme for Germany and Austria that allowed for a centralized organization to be set up, under strict government control, to administer and direct the entire German-language book trade. Fortunately it was never put into effect and censorship in Germany was officially abolished in 1848. In France it was abolished in 1872.

Of prime importance to this story is also the example of the USA. The founding fathers of America had been Puritans, like John Milton, and the Puritan free-thinking tradition played an important part in encouraging the colonists' disaffection with Britain. When the American Revolution took place at the end of the 18th century it embodied a synthesis of English constitutional and French Enlightenment ideas that completely coincided on the subject of free speech, and this was enshrined as one of the fundamental principles of the new American constitution: 'Congress shall make no law ... abridging the freedom of speech, or of the press, or the right of the people peaceably to assemble and to petition the government for a redress of grievance.' America henceforth became a bastion of free speech, equalling and in some respects outstripping the mother countries in Europe.

## Censorship as an instrument of power

It will be seen from this rudimentary summary that the notion of censorship is intimately connected with the notion of power, and its exercise with the exercise of power. Indeed, censorship is the handmaiden of power, without which it is inconceivable. It is an instrument to assist in the attainment, preservation or continuance of somebody's power, whether exercised by an individual, an institution or a state. It is the extension of physical power into the realm of the mind and the spirit; and the more centralized the physical power and the more total its claims, the more intolerant, wide-ranging and complete the censorship will tend to be.

The history of Western Europe shows a steady diminution in the centralized power of the Holy Roman Empire, and subsequently, in the multiple secular states that replaced it, a steady diminution in the power of their monarchs and central governments over their peoples. How this was achieved politically is beyond the scope of this article, but in the realm of censorship it was associated with an extremely important conceptual development that originated with the Reformation. This was the separation of the two concepts of 'action' and 'expression'.

Up to the 17th century, 'action'and 'expression' had been held to be virtually one where religious heresy and political crimes were concerned. To advocate unorthodox or dissenting religious views was tantamount to a physical attack on church members or property (in fact worse), while to advocate political change or express hostility to the prevailing order was 'sedition' and equivalent to treason. What Milton and his successors did was to demonstrate that 'expression' was in a different category from 'action'. While Milton was not of the opinion that **all** forms of expression should go unpunished, he saw the injustice of regarding political and religious dissent as a crime, and he perceived the abuses to which it gave rise. A ruling power might reasonably be expected to take measures against **actions** hostile to its existence, but it should tolerate the expression of hostile **opinions**. The accusation of 'sedition' should be restricted to those who advocated the overthrow of the entire political order or state, rather than of a particular government, party or ruling group.

No government or ruling power has ever been prepared to go all the way with this proposition. Rulers have always succeeded in establishing certain areas of national life in which open criticism is curtailed, but the basic premise that the expression of political and religious opinion, even violent opinion, is of a different order from starting a revolution, eventually won general consent. It depended on the premise first enunciated by Milton: 'We can never be sure that the opinion we are endeavouring to stifle is a false opinion; and if we were sure, stifling it would be an evil still.' This was sharpened by Voltaire when he supposedly said 'I detest what you say, but I will defend to the death your right to say it', and received its fullest expression in the 19th century in John Stuart Mill's famous essay *On Liberty*: 'If all mankind minus one were of one opinion, and only one person were of the contrary opinion, mankind would be no more justified in silencing that one person than he, if he had the power, would be justified in silencing mankind.'

Mill's principal concern in his writings was the establishment of good and just government, and he realized that freedom of expression was vital to the achievement of peaceful and orderly change in government. Seen in this light, freedom of expression becomes a utilitarian mechanism for ascertaining the views of the governed and helping to effect that change, as well as for enabling the rulers to govern with the consent of their people. Acceptance of this proposition in turn depends on the acceptance by governments and rulers of the desirability and necessity of peaceful change, in other words on the acceptance of a democratic order. Conversely, governments that do not believe in parliamentary democracy or regular political change, and whose main interest is in clinging to power, can be expected to be hostile to freedom of expression and in favour of maintaining censorship.

## Censorship by consent

Given that the general development of Western Europe and countries under its influence has been away from systematic censorship, there are still times and situations in which censorship is regarded as normal and justified even in parliamentary democracies. These are when not merely the governing group but the entire social and political order feels itself fundamentally threatened in some way. The classic instance is in time of war. During the second world war, for example, all the combatant powers introduced censorship, and all with the consent of the overwhelming majority of their populations. Hence definition number three in the Oxford dictionary: 'One who censors private correspondence ...( in time of war).' In fact, the censorship in European countries went far beyond the mere surveillance of letters during the war, but even then it was not as extensive in, say, England, as it is even in times of peace in the average communist country.

By extension of the above principle, censorship is usually practised, and frequently accepted, in time of revolution, civil war and civil emergency, such as during a rebellion or a *coup d'état*. Such things may not be very desirable and perhaps should not come to pass in a genuinely democratic state, but the fact is that when they do occur and censorship is introduced, it frequently meets with understanding on the part of the population. Of course, it is then, as always, being employed as an instrument for preserving or obtaining power, but the very gravity of the struggle guarantees its acceptance. Such was the case in the Soviet Union in 1918, when Lenin reintroduced censorship within months after it had been abolished by the freely elected Constituent Assembly (which Lenin dissolved). It was announced as a temporary emergency measure to protect the infant Bolshevik regime against hostile propaganda, though of course it has since survived for 60 years without material alteration. In Portugal in 1920 censorship was also proclaimed as an 'emergency measure' after a coup and survived until the Portuguese revolution of 1975, while Franco introduced censorship to Spain during the Civil War and maintained it until his death.

In these cases censorship accompanied or followed a military upheaval, but on other occasions it precedes or anticipates it. For instance, it is commonly introduced at the same time as martial law or a state of emergency. This occurred in Turkey in 1971 and 1980, in Sri Lanka in 1979, in the Philippines in 1972, in India in 1975, and is the case now in Iran (although some form of censorship has always existed in Iran). In these instances the declared aim of the censorship has been to avert civil or military strife, to preserve order and maintain calm. The present situation in Northern Ireland provokes comparison with these examples. Since 1984, the British government has sought to contain the conflict with individual emergency regulations, rather than by re-introducing a state of emergency, but these regulations as yet have never included formal censorship. Nevertheless, the campaign of the IRA has thrown considerable strain on the country's democratic institutions and the issue of censorship has repeatedly arisen in debate about the measures to be taken. There is little doubt, for instance, that some members of the government, the civil service and the military authorities have exercised a degree of censorship over the reporting of events from Northern Ireland, and where pressure can be brought, as on the government-financed and regulated television networks, it has sometimes been done, with limited results in the authorities' favour.

## The self-concealment of censorship

One thing the above situations have in common is that they are exceptional. Censorship is regarded as abnormal, an emergency measure (in theory at least), which will be removed as soon as the danger has passed and order has been restored, and this has a peculiar consequence whenever, for some reason, censorship is institutionalized and becomes permanent. This is that the censorship hides itself. One of the first words to be censored by the censors is the word 'censorship'. A few years ago a full-time professional censor from Poland defected to Norway, bringing with him a complete copy of one of the Polish censorship manuals. In it one can read of the incredible lengths to which the Polish censorship went to conceal any reference to its own existence, despite the fact that it employs thousands of civil servants and is well known to every writer, journalist, broadcaster and performer in the country. This concealment is endemic to communist countries and is based on the Soviet model established under the bureaucratic and euphemistic title of 'Central Board for Literature and Press Affairs', known as *Glavlit*, for short, in Soviet parlance. Khrushchev's son-in-law, Adzhubei, brought its name slightly closer to reality in 1964 by renaming it the 'Central Board for the Safeguarding of State Secrets in the Press'. But it is not permitted to refer to the existence of this board, let alone that it is in reality for the purpose of censorship, despite the fact that not a single matchbox label or theatre ticket can be printed without its imprimatur.

Furtiveness about the fact of its own existence can be seen as in some ways a healthy sign—another token of the obeisance that vice makes to virtue. And in the topsy-turvy world where censorship reigns, 'virtue' in this area is simultaneously loudly proclaimed. The Soviet Constitution contains explicit guarantees of freedom of speech and expression modelled on the language of the French and American constitutions. In Portugal after the 1926 coup the very law that proclaimed the abolition of censorship went on to codify it in every last detail. In short, where censorship is loudly denied, its existence is almost inevitable.

Another approach to censorship is to call it something else. In South Africa most censorship is carried out not by the body overtly responsible for it, namely the Publications Control Board, but through the use of such laws as the Suppression of Communism Act and other laws designed to protect 'national security', which allow, among other things, for the 'banning' of undesirable individuals and everything they write or say. In practice, virtually all forms of serious political discontent with the present regime are subsumed under the general heading of 'Communism', which is merely another way of using the emergency concept to justify censorship. The alleged Communist threat is also the classic argument that has been used by the military dictatorships of Latin America, notably in Chile, Argentina, Uruguay, Paraguay, Bolivia and in the countries of Central America (with the exception of Nicaragua, of course). And it has been the rationale for censorship in much of Asia—in Saudi Arabia, Malaysia, Singapore, Indonesia, Thailand and Taiwan. Communist states have their own version of the external threat. The Soviet Union, despite (or perhaps because of) the fact that it constitutes one-sixth of the globe, saw itself as 'encircled' by hostile imperialist forces dedicated to its physical destruction. Internally the corresponding threat was thought to come from 'counter-revolutionary' forces or even a hostile bourgeois class that had somehow survived three generations of Communist rule. At all events, an essential component of all Communist demonology has been the existence of a virulent and never-sleeping threat to the revolutionary power.

A common phenomenon is thus the government that protests that censorship is not practised within its country, while simultaneously justifying that censorship, albeit under the name of unspecified exceptional measures, on the grounds of an external (or internal) threat to national security. And from the point of view of the study of censorship, there is little to choose, in principle, between Communist countries with their counter-revolutionary phobias and 'anti-communist' countries with their phobias about a Communist plot. It must be conceded that many of these countries **have** suffered, or do still suffer, from some sort of internal or external threat, or rather, and this is the crucial distinction, that their current rulers do. The question to be asked is to what extent the threat is self-created, either as the result of revolution or *coup d'état*, or simply by institutionalized repression. Many of the rulers of these countries have come to power, or clung to power, by what are essentially illegal means. They have reason to feel threatened. Their rule is illegitimate, they lack the support of a majority of their populations and that is why they find censorship essential to them.

Similarly, one must examine the situations in which a state of emergency or martial law is proclaimed. I have said that censorship on such occasions is usually 'acceptable', but of course the test of acceptability must be whether the emergency is justified. In India in 1975, for instance, Mrs Gandhi was unable to carry a majority of the population with her, and India's democratic traditions and institutions proved to be sufficiently robust to take the strain and reject the introduction of an authoritarian system of rule. A somewhat analogous development may be taking place in South Korea at the moment, where martial law was

9

suspended to allow a general election to take place. The lifting of martial law was accompanied by a significant relaxation of the censorship, and it is clear that these moves will be successful in the long run only if South Korea has developed a sufficient attachment to democratic procedures (including freedom of expression) to deter any backsliding.

## Towards a definition of censorship

Until now I have used the word 'censorship' as a blanket term to cover all kinds of restrictions on freedom of expression, with the unspoken proviso that whether I refer to censorship existing in a given country or not, I am referring to an organized system, rather than individual measures. This suggests the need for at least a working definition, and I would propose the following. Censorship, for all practical purposes, is the systematic control of the content of any communications medium, or of several or all of the media, by means of constitutional, judicial, administrative, financial or purely physical measures imposed directly by, or with the connivance of, the ruling power or a ruling elite. It may or may not be accompanied by violence, it may or may not be total, it may or may not include propaganda. But the concept of a **systematic** imposition of controls is, I think, essential to determining whether or not censorship is being practised in a given country, just as is the concept of intent. To establish just what sort of censorship it is we must examine what methods are in use. Where a systematic control of **all** the communications media is in force, we may properly speak of 'total' censorship. Where the control is less than total and exercised selectively, we may speak of 'partial' or 'selective' censorship; and where it is capricious and arbitrary we may perhaps call it 'random' censorship, intended to intimidate and inhibit, but not to put a total ban on undesirable expression.

## Methods of systematic censorship

The next question to consider is that of the methods themselves. If a government wishes to impose censorship there are two broad categories of information that have to be brought under control: internal sources of information and external sources of information. To take care of the former the government has to control (i) the press; (ii) radio and television; (iii) book publishing; and (iv) education. To take care of external sources the government has to control (i) postal, telephone and telegraph communications; (ii) external radio and television broadcasts; and (iii) emigration, immigration and travel.

Generally speaking radio and, where it exists, television are the first to come under government scrutiny and control. This is both easy to effect and usually quite direct and unsubtle, being achieved either by placing the broadcasting systems under direct government or party control, or packing the management with government nominees, or by passing stringent fiscal or legal regulations under which the systems are obliged to answer to the government. There are good reasons for the high priority usually assigned to broadcasting. In many countries where censorship flourishes there is a high degree of illiteracy combined with poor conventional communications, so that the importance of radio far outstrips that of the written word. Radio is also more vivid and direct, with greater impact on unsophisticated minds, and this applies even more to television, of course, where it exists.

In the case of the press, governments that are capable of exercising subtlety can often be a little more liberal. When the literacy rate is low (keeping it deliberately low is another form of censorship, of course), and the press is read only by a narrowly based educated elite, and when that elite has already been cowed and bullied into submission by a one-party government or a military dictatorship, the press may be allowed a certain latitude for restrained criticism, provided it is not specific and does not probe too deeply. This was the position until recently in Brazil, and is the situation in a number of African countries, such as Zambia and Tanzania. Alternatively, as happened in Spain towards the end of Franco's rule, the mass circulation press may remain muzzled, but latitude may be granted to highbrow, small-circulation magazines that are read only by a tiny intellectual minority. This seems to be the kind of arrangement that countries like Hungary and Poland are groping for, and it may even be the point to which Gorbachev's reforms ultimately bring the Soviet Union.

There is also a greater variety of methods available for controlling the printed media. They can be as direct as for radio and television, i.e. nationalization and direct government control, or they can be indirect and more discreet. In 1973, for instance, the Sri Lankan government established a Press Council 'to ensure the freedom of the press in accordance with the highest professional standards'. The Council was supposed to be independent of both the government and newspaper owners and was purportedly based on similar bodies in England, India and elsewhere. But its detailed clauses setting out what the government regarded as 'free, responsible and professional' were so restrictive as to ensure the opposite of the Council's alleged aims, and interpretation of them was handed over to government-controlled courts.

Another method, particularly effective in poorer countries, is to withhold government and official advertising. Since advertisements are the only guarantee of financial independence in many countries, newspapers that are deprived of them by their primary source can quickly be brought to heel or driven out of business. Mrs Gandhi employed this tactic in India after her declaration of the State of Emergency in 1975. She ordered that no government advertising should be placed with the *Statesman* or *India Express* groups of newspapers, or with the *Tribune*. An alternative to this is to place restrictions on the import of newsprint. Newsprint has become prohibitively expensive in recent years and no one can deny that poor countries have to be most careful about their import bills, nor that there are more urgent priorities than newsprint (which can also be shown to benefit only a tiny privileged minority). Consequently it is most difficult to demonstrate that import quotas are being used unjustly or demonstrate that import quotas are being used unjustly or are another form of censorship.

Yet another variant is to manipulate the tax laws. In Greece publishers traditionally used to get a proportion of their newsprint duty-free, but the colonels saw to it that certain newspapers, unfavourable to their coup, were deprived of this privilege and therefore financially penalized. Lastly, of course, the government may simply buy up part or all of the press, or arrange for it to be bought by its supporters. The South African government tried to employ a variant of this a few years ago by financing a supporter to set up his own English-language newspaper favourable to the government, but it failed to buy out any of the established newspapers and therefore to silence some of its critics.

Book publishing is rather a different matter. Like some of the intellectual magazines, books are perceived to be directed at an educated elite and for that reason are often not as strictly controlled as the mass media. Book publishers, too, of course, can be subjected to discriminatory taxation and paper quotas, but it is here that we most often find formally constituted censorship procedures operating. The two main methods are pre-censorship and post-censorship. Pre-censorship is the method universally employed in Communist countries and also in a number of others that can afford it. It involves having all manuscripts submitted to the censor before permission is given for publication and making publication dependent upon that permission. Without the censor's stamp the presses are simply not allowed to roll. Post-censorship is the method preferred in most other countries where books are subject to control. In Iran and South Africa, for instance, no decision is ever reached until a book has actually been printed. This seems, on the face of it, to be more liberal than pre-censorship, for at least the book gets into print. And in the past, a traditional way of outflanking the censor has been to go ahead and publish a controversial book in the knowledge that perhaps thousands of copies will be sold before a banning order is passed. Complacent and liberal censors have frequently aided and abetted this, as in France in the years leading up to the Revolution, and at certain periods in 19th century Russia. In South Africa today it is often possible for a book to sell many copies before the Publications Control Board has had a chance to ban it. The hazards of this system in a private enterprise economy, however, can be very great. A publisher can go to the expense of paying his author an advance, and having the book set, printed and bound, perhaps in tens of thousands of copies, only to find that he can sell very few or maybe none at all. After one such experience the publisher is liable to become much more cautious. After two or three—bankrupt.

Education is also in a special category. Many rulers are aware that habits of free and independent thought begin in the schools and are fostered by the universities. If they intend a system of censorship to be really effective, they must extend it to all branches of information and make it reach back as far as possible—to the very beginning of the learning process. They may also reason that if a really efficient educational system can be devised, together with an effective censorship, and made to last long enough, the censorship should in time become superfluous. This was the reasoning behind the Bolsheviks' reform of the entire Russian educational system, and it was behind the attempt of the Greek colonels to restructure Greek education with a view to inculcating 'Christian Hellenism'. In many of the countries of Latin America it is the universities that have borne the brunt of pressures on education, while struggles have taken place in the universities of Turkey, Iran, Kenya, South Korea and many other countries over the content of the curriculum. In Czechoslovakia during the 'Prague Spring', Charles University was one of the spearheads of the Communist reform movement and consequently was heavily purged and restructured after the Soviet invasion.

Having gained control of all internal sources of information, a censoring government is still faced with the possibility of undesirable information reaching its subjects from outside. To prevent this it must first take steps to control the mail. Under modern conditions it is physically impossible to monitor all correspondence flowing in and out of a country, but usually it is sufficient to control the letters of a selected number of individuals and to make it widely known that **any** letters are liable to be intercepted and opened. This will act as a virtually insuperable deterrent to foreigners with their correspondents' welfare at heart. The same applies to telephones, which can be tapped, and to the use of the telegraph.

External radio and television broadcasts present a different problem, but the usual technique is to jam them, as the Russians have been doing virtually continually since the Second World War. The difficulty with this method is that it is extremely expensive, and also difficult to do with television. Moreover, the impending introduction of satellite broadcasting may make all technology in this field obsolete. Much of the steam behind the frantic efforts going on at international negotiations over satellite broadcasting at the moment to introduce strict controls is fuelled by the fear of certain governments that this form of broadcasting will conform too closely for comfort to Milton's plea for 'free and open debate'. It is true that few desire to be exposed to an uninterrupted stream of advertisements for pepsi-cola or General Motors, as critics of unimpeded satellite broadcasts insist, but pepsi-cola is not the problem (being drunk in censored and uncensored countries alike). Rather it is the news and opinions that will accompany the advertisements.

The unhampered travel of individuals or groups across borders is also a hindrance to censorship and must be curtailed if perfection in this field is to be attained. This means that formal emigration and immigration must be virtually stopped, and travel permitted only under conditions of close surveillance and control, particularly where the government's subjects are concerned.

The question of information exchange with outside countries raises an additional problem for the government that practises censorship, namely, how to control the flow of information from inside the country to the outside world. The crude banning of foreign correspondents is too naked and provokes too much unfavourable comment. Besides, it is a hindrance in getting out information that the government wants to get out. A better way is to allow the correspondents in, then restrict their movements and sources of information and exercise control over the instruments (telephone, telegraph, teleprinter, etc.) by which they send their information abroad. That this subject is of burning interest to a growing number of countries is attested by the recurrent discussions in UNESCO about how to assure the control of national governments over the flow of news, though it now appears impossible to gain international sanction of this form of censorship.

In this review of methods I have tried to be systematic in covering all the ground, but there is one form of censorship that is not susceptible to this form of analysis. It may be combined with other methods or it may stand alone, but in either case it is highly effective. What it comes down to, in brief, is the institution of a kind of controlled terrorism. At first glance such terrorism may appear as random and indiscriminate, and part of a larger campaign of terrorism that has nothing to do with the communications media or education. But soon it emerges that only certain kinds of reporters, television producers, writers, playwrights, university professors and performs disappear or are killed, while others survive and prosper. Perhaps not all of one kind disappear, while not all others survive—this is important to support the façade of randomness—but the ultimate message is clear: keep off, keep quiet, it may be your turn next. In a sense it is an extension of the method described by Bernard Shaw—assassination. Its main practitioners are in South and Central America. Argentina was once the outstanding example, with Chile, Uruguay and Brazil not far behind. Today it is Guatemala and El Salvador. While defying specific analysis, it is undoubtedly a most deadly and efficient form of censorship.

## Other forms of censorship

I have indicated that some sort of intentional system should be the criterion by which we determine whether a country practises censorship or not, and this certainly stands us in good stead when examining authoritarian government. However, it creates certain problems when we come to other systems. Can it safely be said that no censorship at all exists in the parliamentary democracies of Western Europe and North America? Obviously not. And yet the word in its strict sense, or in the sense in which I have defined it, does not really describe what happens in those countries. The difficulty is that we have no other word to describe collectively the various limitations that can be, and frequently are, placed on freedom of expression in those countries, and this is one of the sources of that confusion I referred to at the beginning of this essay.

Generally speaking, the position in a democracy is that freedom of expression, although an important and highly prized civil right, is only one

14

of a number of rights that sometimes come into competition. The most obvious instances of competing rights are those like the right to a fair trial, unprejudiced by prior publicity, the right to personal privacy, and the right not to have one's reputation traduced by malicious or untrue gossip, all of which may conflict at times with the right to freedom of expression. In England, for example, these rights are protected by laws on contempt of court and the law of libel. A few years ago, these individual rights were enlarged in two particulars: the right not to be defamed on grounds of race or colour (enshrined in the Race Relations Act), and the right not to have past criminal activities referred to in print after the passage of a certain number of years (the Rehabilitation of Offenders Act). In each of these instances where it is now possible for an alternative right to come into conflict with the right to freedom of expression, the issue is decided by the courts. Quite frequently this results in an abridgement of the right to freedom of expression, but it is questionable whether this can properly be called censorship.

More problematical are what one might call the 'relics' of an earlier age of censorship. These are notably official secrets acts, sedition acts, and laws on blasphemy and obscenity. Official secrets and sedition acts clearly represent a continuation of that old concern with 'matters ... offensive or injurious to the state'. The difference between the way they operate in a democracy and in a state sporting the entire panoply of censorship regulations is not so much one of principle as of degree. One may suppose, from mere observation, that the innate disposition of all rulers is to extend their power to its utmost. The crucial distinction to be made, however, is between those whose power is limited by custom, law and consent and those whose power is unbridled, or is limited to a very minor degree. In the case of sedition, the touchstone is whether criticism of a particular government, leader or group of leaders is automatically regarded as criticism of the political order as such, and therefore seditious, or simply criticism of the political order's servants.

Official secrets are a different matter. Their vast extension over so many areas of national life is commonly justified by the national security argument and by the sheer size and technological complexity of modern government. The 'right' of governments to a degree of secrecy is generally acknowledged in democratic societies, but the ways in which that right is used, or just as frequently abused, vary from country to country. Generally speaking, Western European states are more restrictive in this area than those of North America or Australasia. British governments in particular, of whatever political persuasion, have been obsessed with secrecy throughout most of the 20th century, and it is probable that the present government's heavy-handed attempts to suppress Peter Wright's book *Spycatcher* have done more to damage freedom of the press and advance the cause of censorship in Britain than any single political policy since the Second World War.

These cynical manoeuvrings have prompted many British politicians and commentators to look longingly across the Atlantic at the American practice of drastically reducing the scope of official secrets and of introducing a Freedom of Information Act (as in Sweden) to guarantee greater government disclosure. Indeed, the American model of freedom of expression, based firmly on the rock of the First Amendment, has come increasingly to be regarded as the goal to which Western European reformers aspire. Their instinct is probably sound, but we should not blind ourselves to the fact that it was precisely the openness of the American government to scrutiny, and the consequent fear this provoked in certain influential officials, that provoked the Irangate conspiracy, which the American media were powerless to stop in the beginning (though they were instrumental in bringing it to a halt). In other words, important as they are, institutions and legal provisions are rarely sufficient in themselves: the price of freedom remains, as always, eternal vigilance.

As for blasphemy and obscenity laws, these generally refer back to traditional questions of immorality, heresy and the power of the church. In Roman Catholic countries these laws tend still to be strong, especially where the government has signed a concordat with the Vatican. But even in Protestant England there have been modern convictions for blasphemy (for example when the newspaper for homosexuals, *Gay News*, was fined in the 1970s for publishing a homosexual poem about Christ by James Kirkup, although the poem's alleged 'immorality' played a role in the judgement).

Immorality is, in fact, much the strongest censorship issue in all West European countries and in North America as well, as is evidenced by recurrent debates about pornography and the formation of several Presidential commissions to examine the subject. It is also, traditionally, what the general public first thinks of when it hears the word 'censorship' mentioned. This is not to say that this preoccupation is exclusive to the democracies. On the contrary, I can think of no country practising a strict political censorship that does not also exercise strict controls over public morals and the expression of sexual subject matter. Nor of any country anywhere that does not take this matter seriously, though the Scandinavian countries of Sweden and Denmark, followed by the United States, have pioneered a much more liberal attitude to it. Remembering the concern the Romans showed, one must conclude that the 'supervision of public morals' will always be with us in some form or other. And it is generally accepted even now that the public display of sexual matter should be curtailed in the interest of protecting the citizen's right to privacy, and that minors should be protected from exploitation by traffickers in corruption.

There are also new and disquieting questions being raised about the nature and effects of pornography, by activists in the Women's Movement, and there may well be moves to handle this issue in line with the procedures of the Race Relations Act, i.e. to ban pornography on the grounds that it incites hatred of, or contempt for, women. In general, however, the trend in Western societies has been to exercise less and less overt control in these matters and leave them more and more to the choice of the individual.

# A PERSONAL VIEW

## Self-censorship

A word should be said about the fourth definition of 'censor' in the Oxford dictionary, if only because it is the source of some of the confusion about censorship referred to earlier. The definition in question, 'a power within the soul which represses certain elements in the unconscious', was coined by Freud to describe certain operations of the unconscious mind. Its use for this purpose was both poetic and apt, and its meaning was carefully defined by Freud to fit his theory of psychoanalysis. Like many of Freud's theories, however, it caught the public imagination. What better image to express the unconscious workings of the mind of a bigot, a tyrant or a prude? And there is undoubtedly a connection. The true censor, the person who carries out his censorship duties with zeal and conviction, almost certainly experiences Freud's psychological form of censorship working inside him. This is the psychological basis for all forms of censorship. But the 'born' censor, deprived of the mechanism of an organized censorship, may never exercise censorship of others in any meaningful way. He may feel he would like to do so. He may yearn for such a mechanism. He may even, if he lives in the right place at the right time, have the opportunity to construct such a mechanism. But without it he cannot be an active censor.

One must also be careful with the concept of 'self-censorship', in the discussion of which a crucial distinction needs to be made. There is a form of self-censorship that is a direct product of systematic, external censorship. This comes about when a writer or journalist is faced with a brutal choice in case of disagreement with the views of the censors: either he remains silent, thus disqualifying himself from his proper work and condemning himself to helplessness and penury, or else he suppresses or disguises those of his views and ideas that he knows will not pass the censor—in other words, he indulges in 'self-censorship'. Self-censorship in this form is properly a sub- category of 'censorship' in its primary sense. In its Freudian form, however, it is the product of internal fears and pressures, and no matter how urgent or debilitating these may be, they are not related to any social form of censorship.

Another common delusion runs as follows. If an author writing for, say, a conservative audience, adjusts his views or his vocabulary in order to 'accommodate' that audience, or if in writing for women or foreigners or some other well-defined audience he suppresses certain things he might like to have said and writes others, he is said to be practising 'self-censorship'. If, in doing so, he further claims to be anticipating the kind of editing he is going to receive from the editor of a particular newspaper, book or magazine, this may be quoted to support the notion that 'editing is censorship'. Neither view, to my mind, has any validity. Provided the author has freedom of choice and is able to write what he likes, there is no 'self-censorship' or 'censorship' involved. He may, of course, mystify his audience, or insult them, or find his work rejected by the editor to whom he has submitted it. But if no one is forcing him to write for that particular audience, or forcing him to write in a particular way, and if he may offer his work to other editors, he is not obliged to do violence to his conscience but is merely experiencing the normal risks of his trade. It is the resort of weak minds and vain egos to cry censorship whenever editorial judgement is being exercised, whether consciously or unconsciously, and whether by the author himself, or by an external editor.

## Conclusion

I have attempted in this brief survey to touch on some of the main problems raised by the practice of censorship in the modern world, and to set them in some sort of rudimentary historical context. The very idea that censorship is a social evil to be opposed is a relatively modern one, and received its greatest impetus from the thinkers of the Enlightenment. Even so, it was not until after World War Two that the idea gained more or less universal acceptance by being embodied in Article 19 of the Universal Declaration of Human Rights (itself a notable product of the Enlightenment tradition), and it has not been until the last thirty years that a variety of nongovernmental organizations have come into being with the express aim of securing international adherence to the ideals embodied in the Declaration.

The problems they face would appear to be of two main kinds. In three-quarters of the world, it is a matter of encouraging and assuring adherence to a system of law that approximates at least somewhat to the principles embodied in the articles of the Universal Declaration. This would supply some kind of standard by which to judge the different states and to which to try to hold them in matters of expression. When this has been achieved, the problem becomes one of striking a balance between competing rights, competing benefits and competing claims (as well as competing duties). There will always be debate and disagreement about where the balance is to be struck, and there will always be pressures and forces pushing and pulling in different directions. These skirmishes, in my view, are but the usual expressions of competing forces and opinions within a healthy society, as are most of the pressures described in the last section of this overview. They are tokens of energy and life, rather than of sickness and decline. We should bear in mind that a society that is totally safe and tranquil, in which there are no controversies over freedom of expression, is a society that is dying or dead.

# COUNTRY REPORTS

This section of the Report contains studies on the state of freedom of expression in 50 countries representative of all regions and of the different political and ideological systems. The countries were chosen to reflect the diverse issues and challenges raised by the rights to protection and by the violation of freedom of expression and information in all parts of the world. Countries are not rated or classified. The cut-off date for these entries was Jan. 1, 1988.

Where information has been available and where it does not place an individual at risk, we have included particulars concerning a sample selection of those writers, journalists and media workers against whom action has been taken during the course of 1987 or who are still in prison.

Statistics for the Reports were taken from *The Europa Yearbook 1987*; *UNESCO Statistical Yearbook 1987*; *United Nations Statistical Yearbook 1985*; and from ARTICLE 19's International Centre on Censorship. The abbreviation 'est.' indicates that a statistic covers the period 1980-1986. Countries that have not ratified the International Covenant on Civil and Political Rights are marked 'no'. For other countries the year of ratification is given.

# COUNTRY REPORTS—AFRICA SOUTH OF THE SAHARA

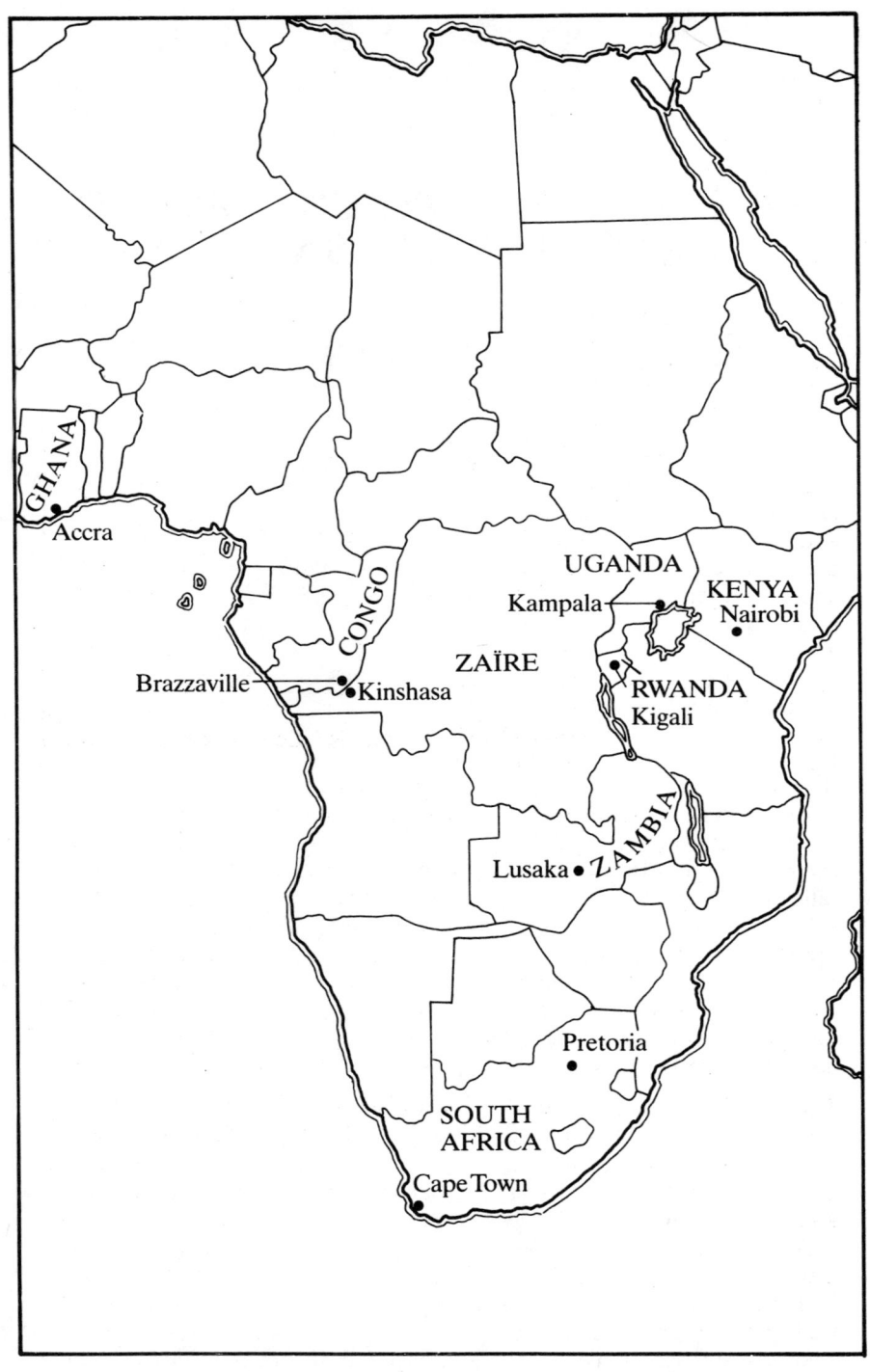

# CONGO

In January 1972 the People's Republic of the Congo was officially declared a Marxist-Leninist state. State power is exercised through its single political party, the *Parti congolaise du travail* (*PCT*), the 'supreme form of political and social organization', which rules through directives.

The government of the Congo has ratified the International Covenant on Civil and Political Rights and the African Charter of Human and People's Rights. Freedom of expression, of the press, of association and of demonstration are guaranteed by Article 16 of the Constitution. However, these rights are limited by 'conditions laid down by law'. In practice the Party exercises direct control over the content and means of all communication within the country.

|  |  | Year |
| --- | --- | --- |
| Population | 2,000,000 | 1985 |
| GNP ($ per capita) | 1,120 | 1984 |
| Illiteracy % | 37.1 | 1985 |
| Daily newspapers | 1 | 1984 |
| Non Daily newspapers | 2 | 1984 |
| Periodicals | 10 | est |
| Radio stations | 1 | est |
| Radio receivers | 100,000 | est |
| TV stations | 1 | est |
| TV sets | 5,000 | 1984 |
| Press Agencies: Agence Congolaise d'Information (ACI) | | |
| Covenant on Civil & Political Rights _____ 1983 | | |

Article 29 of the 1979 Constitution makes it a criminal offence to challenge the authority of the single-party state while Article 18 forbids the use of religion for political purposes and proscribes a number of religious groups such as the Jehovah's Witnesses.

The opposition parties, the *Mouvement patriotique du Congo* (MPC) and the *Rassemblement démocratique congolais* (RDC) are banned, along with their publications, and operate from France.

Since the election of the country's President, Denis Sassou-Nguesso, to the chairmanship of the OAU Committee of Heads of State in 1986, there have been signs of a relaxation of official censorship.

**The National Censorship Commission:** A National Censorship Commission has functioned since 1972. Its staff is made up of Party cadres. The Commission is the principal instrument for controlling the media as well as writers, theatre and artists. It meets every three months and lists of banned publications are regularly published.

A recent example of censorship in practice arose from a proposed article on human rights due to appear on Dec. 10, 1986, International Human Rights Day, in *La Semaine Africaine*, which is owned by the Catholic Church and is the only independent newspaper in the country. The article was submitted by the Congo's first and only human rights lawyer, Maître Maurice Massengo-Tiasse.

The authorities objected to the article's reference to freedom of worship and religion and the 'right to freedom of thought and conscience'. Maître Massengo-Tiasse was told by the censors that he had gone 'too far'. He claimed, however, that the fact that he had afterwards appeared on radio and television discussing human rights was a positive development: 'I was the first to do so; and one hour on radio and forty minutes on television is a lot in a country where it is unpopular to talk about such things. Instead they prefer talking about apartheid.'

A Zaïrean journalist, who has lived as a refugee in the Congo, expressed misgivings about the lawyer's assessment. 'It depends on how one discusses human rights. It is easy to talk about human rights from a purely pedagogic angle; but to discuss concrete cases... that I don't believe possible. There are many cases of human rights violations in the Congo which are never mentioned.'

## The Media

In addition to the five daily newspapers, all of which are government-owned—*Courrier d'Afrique*, *L'Eveil de Pointe-Noire*, *Le Journal de Brazzaville*, *Journal Officiel* and *Mweti*—the Party publishes a weekly organ, *Etumba*, and, since 1985, a monthly journal, *Congo Magazine*.

In 1967 a decree by the Council of Ministers made all media personnel civil servants. Journalists, presenters, comperes and announcers were invited to act as revolutionaries and become Party watchdogs. A set of guidelines produced by the Party defined the concerns which journalists were expected to address.

Mild criticism of policies by the domestic press is tolerated as long as the issue is not sensitive. However, more serious issues either fail to be brought to public attention or are only reported once they have appeared in the international press. This was the case when a number of students were killed by Congolese soldiers during the student demonstrations of 1985 and 1986, and *La Semaine Africaine* had one of its issues seized by the censors after publishing 'a Christian Reflection' on the Third Ordinary Congress of the PCT in July 1984.

People who have criticized public officials and government departments have had their articles published but they have suffered reprisals. In 1982 a Zaïrean refugee, Michel Eke Akanga Nkoy, was repatriated to Zaïre in spite of protests by the then Foreign Minister of the Congo, Pierre Nze. According to one Zaïrean journalist, there have been other cases which went unmentioned by the Congolese press, of journalists being expelled without any reasons being given.

Foreign publications are vetted by the National Censorship Commission for critical articles. The many banned publications include novels such as Ian Fleming's 'The Spy Who Loved Me', Marchenko's 'Karl Marx' and Mario Pomito's '*La cinquième évangile*'.

Guy Menga, former Head of Programmes at *La Voix de la Révolution*

*Congolaise* and a well-known writer, has described the restrictions facing both local and foreign journalists. Local journalists have to wait for a foreign news agency's report before writing about an event, even if they are aware of it, while their foreign counterparts have to wait for an official communiqué before dispatching their articles. In July 1987 approximately twenty army officers were arrested, yet no mention was made in any Congolese dispatch. 'The news filtered through only after travellers coming from Brazzaville gave word of the events in Paris. It was only after the foreign press ran the story that people became aware of what had happened. Yet the local journalists knew what had happened. Even the foreign correspondents knew. They were waiting for the government communiqué. The journalist who takes the risk to relate an event without the Party's intervention risks expulsion or arrest.'

**Foreign journalists:** On Oct. 29, 1987 the Congolese security services detained the correspondent of the French News Agency *Agence France-Presse*, Jacques Lumbwele Boy Buta, together with eleven other people, all of them Zaïrean refugees, and opponents of Mobutu Sese Seko's government in Kinshasa. According to the Congolese authorities the Zaïreans were held for 'verification of their activities'. The Congo's Minister of Information, Christian Gilbert Bembet, told *AFP* on Nov. 19—four weeks after the men's detention—that Boy Buta, (who is also Zaïrean), had 'not been sentenced, nor charged, but simply interrogated over his activities'. All the detainees are being held without visiting rights.

**Radio and television:** Radio remains the most important source of information for the majority of the population. There is one radio station, *La Voix de la Révolution Congolaise*, which transmits programmes in French, English, Portuguese, Lingala, Kikongo and Subia. In 1984 there were an estimated 97,000 radio receivers and approximately 4,800 television receivers in use.

Television began transmission in 1963. Although there are programmes in Lingala and Kikongo, French programmes predominate.

The overall responsibility for electronic media is exercised by the Ministry of Information, Ports and Telecommunications. In June 1986 the Party Training School was incorporated into a government department, the Department of Ideology and Political Development. The former Director of the Party School, Jean-François Obembe, became Secretary of this Department with responsibility for the press, propaganda and information.

**Writers and artists:** Signs of a changing climate in the Congo include the fact that the ban on Guy Menga's play '*La marmite de Koka-Mbala*', which the authorities deemed too critical of the post-revolutionary society, has now been lifted. But there has been no mention of the play's author, still banned as a person though not as an artist. His other books are freely available in Brazzaville. In an interview in Paris in November 1987 Menga stated that the works of other Congolese writers have also been banned, citing Sony Labu Tansi's '*La vie et demie*' as an example.

Not all artists whose works are banned find themselves in conflict with the authorities. Emmanuel Bomdzeki Dongala, a well-known Congolese writer, retained his post as Professor of Chemistry at Brazzaville University in spite of his short story collection '*Jazze et vin de palme*', which was banned for satirizing party members and the official 'scientific Marxist' ideology of the State.

A number of artists have had songs banned, like Pamelo Munka who composed a song condemning corruption among public officials. The song was in Kikongo. The popular group Muyidika's song, '*Simba Nsakala*', was also banned in 1985. Its theme centred on the 'suspicious' loss of a football championship. The song was regarded as a provocation against the Party and anyone who sang it risked imprisonment. Records are reviewed by the State Censorship board and certain artists are prevented from giving performances in their mother tongue.

## Current detainees

Included among those writers, journalists and media workers against whom action has been taken during the course of 1987 or who are still in prison: Jacques Lumbwele Boy Buta, journalist, in detention since October 1987.

# GHANA

With the exception of the short-lived period of government under Dr Hilla Limann (1979-1981) most organs of communication in Ghana (the press, television and radio), together with the film industry, the news agency and two training institutions in film and journalism, have always been owned and controlled by the State.

The various governments of Ghana since independence (in 1957) have exercised control through what is now the Secretariat for Information. The Secretariat appoints and dismisses editors of government papers and other senior media personnel and holds regular meetings with the *Daily Graphic, The Ghanaian Times*, the *Weekly Spectator*, the *Ghana Broadcasting Corporation, The Mirror*, the *Ghana News Agency*, the National Film Training Institute and the Ghana Institute of Journalism, all the meetings being chaired by the Secretary for Information.

|  |  | Year |
|---|---|---|
| Population | 12,000,000 | 1983 |
| GNP ($ per capita) | 350 | 1984 |
| Illiteracy % | 46.8 | 1985 |

| | | |
|---|---|---|
| Daily newspapers | 4 | 1984 |
| Non Daily newspapers | 13 | est |
| Periodicals | 34 | est |
| Published books | 350 | 1983 |
| Films produced | 1 | 1975 |
| Radio stations | 2 | est |
| Radio receivers | 2,500,000 | 1985 |
| TV stations | 1 | est |
| TV sets | 140,000 | 1985 |

Press Agencies:
Ghana News Agency

Covenant on Civil & Political Rights _____ NO

Since 1981 there has been no legislation outlining the relationship between the government and the media. Provisional National Defence Council (PNDC) Law 42 (1982), the proclamation which established the present military regime, was silent on the structure of the media, or on the relationship between executive and media. The dissolution of the Press Commission by this decree came as a blow to press freedom in Ghana. The Press Commission, made up of representatives of the public, had been established under provisions of Ghana's third republican Constitution (in 1979), and was designed to draw some of the government's power away from the state-owned media.

The machinery of control has now been added to by the Castle Information Bureau, officially the press unit of the Office of the Head of State. The general manager of the Ghana News Agency in an interview published in *West Africa* said journalists were not permitted to acknowledge the Castle Information Bureau but that it regularly issued instructions on what could and could not be published in the newspapers.

27

## The Media

The Secretariat for Information has control over the supply and allocation of almost all media equipment and facilities from newsprint to telephones and typewriters. This has the effect of rendering all journalists dependent on government approval. Supplies can easily be cut to any critics of government policy.

**Newspapers:** The Secretariat for Information controls registration of all newspapers and can thus exert considerable powers over the limited private press. The regional newspaper, *The Pioneer*, in the past one of Ghana's most respected independent press organs, has had its circulation greatly reduced through the government's refusal to supply newsprint. The *Ghanaian Voice*, after suffering a temporary ban in 1985, was resurrected as a quasi-governmental organ. The only privately owned papers that seem to flourish in Ghana today are a dozen sporting newspapers which avoid controversial issues.

The last two years have seen severe action against two other private newspapers, the Catholic weekly *The Standard*, and the *Free Press*. *The Standard* was banned and had its licence withdrawn in November 1985 for writing editorials which the Secretariat for Information described as 'unpatriotic'. The *Free Press* was forced to close down in April 1986, following the detention of three of its journalists for over a year and the subsequent five-month detention of its managing editor, John Kuglenu. One of its jounalists, Kweku Baako, was arrested in April 1986 and detained for four months. The paper has since been resurrected.

**Radio and television:** Radio and television were recently overhauled with the help of Japanese technicians, but it is generally recognized that Ghanaian broadcasting facilities are still greatly underdeveloped.

**Self-censorship:** A high degree of self-censorship operates in Ghana. The media are not known to report on any arrests and detentions, demonstrations or statements critical of the government. No formal censorship machinery exists but it is well known that editors are dismissed at the fiat of governments and stay or fall with governments. This has led to a gate-keeping role being adopted by junior reporters through to sub-editors and editors which ensures that all critical or unfavourable news that could possibly be a source of political embarrassment is suppressed.

Reporters quickly learn that reports on modest official gatherings may be printed whereas large demonstrations which attack any aspect of government policy cannot. In addition, reporters who wish to investigate a sensitive story must do so at their own expense which has major consequences given the low level of salaries for journalists in Ghana.

**Sedition:** The law on sedition makes it a crime to report on any event or statement that could bring the government into disrepute or contempt or cause disaffection. The colonial government invoked the law to charge and convict T. A. Wallace Johnson and Nnamdi Azikiwe of the pre-independence newspaper the *African Morning Post*. The same law was invoked against a journalist on *The Pioneer*, Kwabena Gyimah, who in 1969 wrote that the country's border guards were corrupt. In May 1987, the law on sedition was again applied to detain three prominent political figures, Kwasi Adu-Amankwaah, Kwesi Pratt, and Akoto Ampaw.

A further cause of reticence on the part of journalists is the PNDC's overall powers under a preventive custody law, PNDC Law 4. This led to arrests and detention without trial of at least three journalists from the *Free Press* between 1982 and 1985.

This environment of intimidation has resulted in either the resignation or departure from the country of respected journalists with critical pens. In 1986 two columnists of the weekly *The Mirror*, T. A. Ofori-Mante and Ajoa Yeboah-Afari (also the deputy editor of the paper), resigned. The two had established reputations for the quality of the critical commentaries in their columns. The departure of senior journalists of quality is likely to have long-term effects on the Ghanaian media. One consequence is that young journalists do not receive adequate training. An acceptance of mediocre standards is evident among Ghanaian photo-journalists. Long accustomed to simple stand-up photos of ministers and others delivering speeches, they can provide little of greater quality.

## Restrictions on freedom of opinion and expression

Since January 1982 there has been a ban on the reporting of opposition political activity. Although there are repeated calls for national discussion of political issues, the columns of the media, with the exception of *The Mirror*, do not reflect any serious debates. One-sided views are always published with the state-owned media in many cases refusing to publish the views of groups opposed to the government. It is common, for instance, to find editorials condemning workers in industrial conflicts and failing to offer the public any information on the specific grievances voiced by the workers involved.

The Ghana Bar Association, the National Union of Ghana Students and the Trades Union Congress have all complained about the refusal of the media to report their views. Organizations which owe their existence directly to the government or support it, such as the June 4 Movement, the 31 December Women's Movement and the Committees for the Defence of the Revolution, find that their statements are regularly published, while groups like the Kwame Nkrumah Revolutionary Guards and the New Democratic Movement, opposed to policies of the government, are denied access to the media.

With the demise of *The Standard* and the *Free Press* and the reduced circulation of *The Pioneer*, the alternative forum for political debate is beginning to disappear. This means that most major government policies, such as the decision to hold district council elections in 1988, are imposed without debate.

The overall effect of such measures is a general reluctance on the part of most Ghanaians to express their opinions on political issues. Ironically, for reasons of its own, it is the government itself that has recently drawn attention to the ill effects of this tendency. In 1986 a campaign was launched to break what the government's National Commission of Democracy has called a prevailing 'culture of silence'.

E. A. Haizel, executive secretary of the National Commission of Democracy, said recently that silence has so trapped the Ghanaian people that 'there is now a lot of murmuring and passivity around instead of positive declarations of opinion'. This is an accurate summary of the state of health of free expression in Ghana.

## Current detainees

Included among those writers, journalists and media workers against whom action has been taken during the course of 1987 or who are still in prison: Kwesi Pratt, journalist, detained since May 17 1987: Kwame Korikami, journalist, detained since July 15 1987; Ben Ephson, journalist, detained for interrogation since September 1987.

# KENYA

In June 1982, the National Assembly passed a constitutional amendment making Kenya a one party state under law. Since then the KANU (Kenya African National Union) has come into increasing conflict with the Assembly in terms of its role and position in the hierarchy of government. In November 1986, President Daniel arap Moi proclaimed that 'the party is supreme' over parliament and the judiciary, because as he said, 'I appoint High Court judges, provincial commissioners, district commissioners, the Vice-President and others'.

He proclaimed 1987 'a year of discipline' and increasing use has been made of emergency powers under the 1967 Preservation of Public Security Act (PPSA) to detain without trial any potential opposition from within or from outside the party. Since March 1986 over 70 people have been imprisoned for alleged participation in *Mwakenya*, a clandestine opposition group. Many others have been imprisoned for 'seditious offences'. There have been repeated allegations from human rights groups of torture of detainees.

|  |  | Year |
|---|---|---|
| Population | 20,000,000 | 1985 |
| GNP ($ per capita) | 300 | 1984 |
| Illiteracy % | 48.0 | 1983 |
| Daily newspapers | 5 | est |
| Non Daily newspapers | 6 | est |
| Periodicals | 67 | est |
| Published books | 235 | 1983 |
| Radio stations | 1 | est |
| Radio receivers | 2,800,000 | 1984 |
| TV stations | 1 | est |
| TV sets | 140,000 | 1984 |

Press Agencies:
Kenya News Agency

Covenant on Civil &
Political Rights _____ 1972

The rights and freedoms of individuals guaranteed by the Constitution of 1963, as amended, have come to mean very little. The Constitution itself has never been readily accessible as a public document. It is believed that its publication and circulation are now prohibited.

Section 79 of the Constitution guarantees freedom of opinion and expression, as well as the flow of information and ideas and passing of correspondence. Under powers in the PPSA the President can suspend such rights and has instituted extensive censorship.

## The Media

**Newspapers:** There are three national daily newspapers in Kenya. Two are owned by multinationals: the *Daily Nation* published by the Aga Khan Group (based in Paris) and *The Standard* published by the Lonrho group (based in London). Both English-language papers have been published in Kenya since before independence. The Daily Nation also publishes a

31

daily Kiswahili edition, *Taifa Leo*, shorter and more locally focused than the English edition. The third Kenyan daily, the *Kenya Times*, published in English, was founded in 1983 by the KANU. It also publishes a Kiswahili edition, *Kenya Leo*.

Only a small percentage of the population can read English and afford a newspaper. The English press caters for the foreign aid élite which remains aloof from politics, and a local élite, which favours the status quo.

A celebrated confrontation took place in 1982 when George Githii, editor of *The Standard*, wrote a blunt editorial attacking the increase in detentions without trial which was immediately denounced by the government. Lonrho, *The Standard's* owners, responded by sacking Githii and printing an unreserved apology to the government of Kenya on the front page of its next edition. Since then it has had few problems with the government.

**Self-censorship:** One of the most difficult aspects of Kenyan journalism is that limitations on reporting are not written down, and are largely dependent on the mood or whim of the President, who does not hesitate in taking *ad hoc* measures against journalists. Day-to-day editorial control of content and perspective is exerted by the Office of the President either through direct censorship—telephone directives, or written instructions, backed up by the threatened or actual arrest and imprisonment of individual journalists—or through threatened or actual withdrawal of government advertising. Journalists trained at the University of Nairobi are made well aware that certain subjects must not be covered, including any criticism of the President or his policies. In addition, those below the President often seek to prove their loyalty and enhance their standing in the KANU by acting on the President's behalf and will often take a harsher, less tolerant line than the President himself. It is difficult to judge what might be deemed 'unsuitable' on any given day. The most successful Kenyan journalists, like Hilary Ng'weno of the *Weekly Review*, develop an acutely-honed sense of the shifting political mood and are able to shift emphasis accordingly, but this is a difficult and dangerous achievement and few succeed for long. Lavish praise is given to President Moi on the front pages of newspapers—no event is too minor in this respect.

Fear is engendered by abuse and detention of journalists. One journalist, Otieno Makonyango, had been detained in Kamiti prison without trial from 1983 until his release on Oct. 20, 1987. Even those at the highest levels are vulnerable—the Deputy Chief of Information of the UN office for Emergency Operations in Africa, Salim Lone, who once ran a magazine— *Viva*—in Kenya, was detained in July 1986.

The unpredictability of presidential attitudes is such that civil servants up to the level of permanent secretary are unwilling to comment on even the most mundane matters or to provide basic information for news stories for fear of reprisal. The Office of the President becomes the sole source of information for anything from political events to the size of Kenyan livestock herds.

# KENYA

**Foreign correspondents:** Between 100 and 150 correspondents, representing predominantly, but not exclusively, the Western European press, mass media and news agencies, are based in Kenya, and from this vantage point cover the entire East and Central Africa region, as well as Southern Africa. The foreign press has been reluctant to jeopardize its position in Kenya by publishing critical news and analysis. Unique facilities for transmitting news and information exist in Nairobi, including the fact that the international airport provides good links with other African capitals. Foreign press-owners are therefore often co-operative in ensuring that news unfavourable to President Moi does not make the headlines. Of the wave of detentions of journalists without trial only those of Lindsay Hilsum and Paul Amina (see below) were widely reported. Stories of corruption circulate freely within the country, but little appears in the foreign press.

The Kenyan leader has nevertheless increasingly found occasion to warn the foreign press corps, privately and through the Kenyan media, against negative coverage of Kenyan affairs.

Foreign correspondents have been expelled, but more frequently only threatened with expulsion. Recent cases include that of Blaine Harden, the *Washington Post*'s correspondent in Nairobi, who was arrested and ordered to leave in June 1987 after publishing a three-part series on Kenyan human rights abuses coinciding with President Moi's visit to Washington in March.

The arrest and detention without trial on Aug. 4, 1987 of Paul Amina, a freelance Kenyan journalist who worked for *Reuters* and *Agence France-Presse* as well as Kenyan news organizations, gained particular international attention. Amina was arrested at the Nairobi law courts while reporting on the case of Stephen Mbaraka Karanji, a farmer who was shot dead while in police custody and whose body had disappeared. While Amina's detention was not acknowledged by the authorities for sixteen days, his disappearance was reported by foreign correspondents in Nairobi. No coverage was given to the event by the three local Kenyan dailies. In November 1987, Lindsay Hilsum, a correspondent for several Western organizations, received spinal injuries when she was beaten by police while covering disturbances at the University of Nairobi. The University was subsequently closed.

In 1987, the Kenyan administration has issued revised rules pertaining to the accreditation of foreign journalists. In addition to more stringent visa requirements, which have led to the refusal to issue or renew visa applications, foreign correspondents must supply accrediting letters from their respective professional associations, labour unions, and embassies of their nationality to the Kenyan government. Foreign journalists must also be approved by the Kenya Union of Journalists in order to practise in the country.

The Kenyan government does not hold regular press briefings. Statements and directives relating to government policy are issued by the Presidential Press Unit through the *Kenya News Agency*. The foreign press corps has no access to this material.

33

**The foreign press:** Several Western European daily newspapers and periodicals are received in Kenya, either through private subscription or for mass circulation in urban centres. A government censor is stationed at the international airports to vet the contents of all incoming publications for mass circulation. On direction from the Office of the President, the General Post Office vets pages containing articles or news items critical of Kenya, particularly those addressing issues of human rights violations or critical of government practice, which are removed at the airport. Occasionally, but not consistently, private subscriptions are intercepted and not delivered to subscribers. All incoming international news transmitted by international wire services must pass through the *Kenya News Agency* where it is vetted before relay to the Kenyan press and mass media.

**Radio and television:** Kenya has one broadcasting authority for both radio and television, the *Voice of Kenya* (*VOK*), established under the Ministry of Information and Broadcasting with transmitters in Nairobi and Mombasa and relay stations near other urban centres. No private radio or television transmitters have ever been approved for operation in Kenya, although applications have been filed.

Radio and television programming is strictly controlled in terms of political content and perspective. The *Voice of Kenya* has a censorship board which vets both foreign and locally produced material prior to going on the air. Fifty-three per cent of television programming is locally produced—by the *Voice of Kenya*, the Kenya Institute of Education, the Kenya Institute of Mass Communications, and small private production companies. 47 per cent of television programming comprises foreign material which Kenya buys, predominantly from Britain or the USA.

Much radio programming is allocated to government news broadcasts and the speeches by the president, and to a lesser extent coverage of parliamentary or other government business. Creative local programming has been discouraged. Music on one of the three radio services, the *General Service*, is predominantly popular and foreign whereas music broadcast on the *National Service* and the *Vernacular Service* is mostly Kenyan. However, songs containing provocative or political lyrics are censored, thwarting a rich oral narrative tradition.

**Books and periodicals:** Issues of periodicals may be easily withdrawn on an *ad hoc* basis if they contain articles critical of the government. In July 1987, for instance, the government recalled the August issue of *Beyond*, the monthly publication of the Kenyan National Council of Churches, for publishing an open letter from former Vice-President Oginga Odinga criticizing the KANU.

**Seditious publications:** Section 57 of the Penal Code makes it a criminal offence to utter 'any words with a seditious intention', or to print, publish, sell, offer for sale, distribute or reproduce any seditious literature. Possession of seditious literature can bring up to seven years' imprisonment. There is no functioning or legal definition of 'sedition' or 'seditious publication'. A 'seditious publication' would appear to be any publication or written document (persons have been convicted and served maximum sentences for possessing notes in their own handwriting) which the State determines to be seditious at any given time or circumstance. It is sufficient that the State informs the courts that a particular publication is seditious. Since the publication is usually deemed seditious in every word, it is not permitted to admit the publication as evidence in open court. The increasing number of persons arrested under Section 57, many of whom 'disappear' before coming to trial is a matter of great concern in the country.

**Prohibited publications:** Under the Prohibited Publications Order (Penal Code Section 52), it is prohibited to import 'any publication depicting or containing any symbol, emblem, device, colours, slogan, motto, words or letters signifying any association with or support for a political object or political organization', or 'to have in one's possession or under one's control a prohibited publication'. The latest list of banned periodicals includes: *Voice of Africa, Revolution in Africa, Sauti ya Wananchi* (published by the Kenya Socialist Group), *Suauti Ya Urafiki, News* (a German Democratic Republic illustrated monthly), *Africa and the World* and *World Revolution*. Banned books include 'The Uganda Crisis 1968', 'Two Years After the Battle of Mengo Hill', 'The Reds and the Blacks—a Personal Adventure', '*Cheche Moja Yaweza Kuanzisha Moto Mbugani*' by Mao Tse-Tung, 'Quotations from Chairman Mao Tse-Tung'; all publications by the Beijing-based Foreign Languages Press; *The African Communist, Adam* magazine, *Cavalier* magazine and *Men Only* magazine.

While the country's foremost writer—novelist, playwright, essayist and political commentator, Ngugi Wa Thiongo—has been forced to live in exile since mid-1982, his books are still readily available, not only in urban bookshops but on many of the street corner book stands, with some titles still included in the schools syllabus. To a lesser extent this is true of the work of other exiled, detained or imprisoned Kenyan writers. Kenyan publishers, unlike foreign publishers, dare not publish these writers' works.

**Film:** Licence to film and approval of film scripts must be obtained from the government through the Office of the President and the Ministry of Information and Broadcasting. There is a Film Censorship Board, appointed by the Ministry of Information and Broadcasting and composed of lay citizens and ministry officials. This body reviews films intended for commercial screening, as well as films distributed by various foreign and indigenous interest groups—embassies, cultural institutes and religious organizations. Political content is the primary focus of scrutiny and censorship.

**Public performances:** Theatre companies performing outside of educational institutions must be registered as commercial companies or societies, the scripts for theatrical productions must be approved by the

35

district or provincial administration, and licences thus obtained for public performances. Licensing regulations from colonial times were little enforced during the latter years of the Kenyatta Administration, until it became evident that a dynamic, nationalist theatre movement as an avenue for freedom of expression was emerging and gaining popularity in rural areas as well as in the urban slums. The government then tightened up censorship, but in an *ad hoc* manner. The result is that a play allowed public performance at one time and place, is banned in another.

The highly popular Kamiriithu Community Educational Cultural Centre (KCECC), whose first production had been banned in 1977, had another production banned in 1981. Armed police were dispatched to bar the group's entry to rehearse at the Kenya National Theatre. The group then moved to the theatre at the University of Nairobi, where a licence from the government is not required for the staging of a theatre production. After ten days of open rehearsals, which attracted full-house audiences, the government ordered the university theatre to be locked and sent armed police. Two weeks later, a lorry full of administration police were sent to Kamiriithu and destroyed the KCECC's amphitheatre.

## Freedom of opinion and expression

**Electoral queueing:** A proposed amendment to the national election law endorsed by the KANU in August 1986 seeks to abolish the secret ballot. In the preliminary elections for nomination of parliamentary candidates, a system in which the electorate (registered KANU members) will queue behind their choice of candidate on election day, will replace the secret ballot. This proposal was endorsed in a pre-emptive move by President Moi in August 1986. It subsequently generated expression of grave concern as to its implications for freedom of political expression from bodies outside the KANU and the national assembly, notably from the National Council of Churches of Kenya (NCCK). The government responded to these criticisms by launching an 'investigation' into the connections between the NCCK and '*Mwakenya*' (the underground opposition movement).

## Current detainees

Included among those writers, journalists and media workers against whom action has been taken during the course of 1987 or who are still in prison: Paul Amina, journalist, detained since Aug. 20, 1987 under the Public Security Regulations; Maina wa Kinyatti, lecturer and author, sentenced to six years' imprisonment in 1982.

# RWANDA

The Constitution of the Rwandese Republic guarantees freedom of expression, thought, conscience and religion. It does not guarantee the separate freedom to hold opinions without interference, a right declared in the International Covenant on Civil and Political Rights which the state has ratified.

Rwanda is a single-party state. The *Mouvement révolutionnaire national pour le développement* (MRND) is the sole political organization, outside of which no political views can be expressed or political activity exercised, and to which all Rwandese citizens are deemed automatically to belong. A government representative has described the MRND as a popular movement which in seeking a better life for all Rwandese calls for the unreserved adhesion of the entire nation in a single unified mould so that no individual or group can escape the social control of the MRND. The need for this political system is justified historically; Rwanda went through very difficult periods before and after independence following ethnic conflicts between minority Watutsi and majority Hutu tribes.

|  |  | Year |
|---|---|---|
| Population | 6,000,000 | 1987 |
| GNP ($ per capita) | 270 | 1984 |
| Illiteracy % | 50.0 | 1987 |

| | | |
|---|---|---|
| Daily newspapers | 1 | est |
| Non Daily newspapers | 2 | est |
| Periodicals | 6 | est |
| Radio stations | 1 | est |
| Radio receivers | 250,000 | 1986 |

Press Agencies: Agence Rwandaine de Presse (ARP)

| | |
|---|---|
| Covenant on Civil & Political Rights _____ | 1975 |

People known to have been in conflict with the authorities for exercising their rights to freedom of opinion and conscience have been charged under the Penal Code with offences related to their religious beliefs. The relevant laws have been interpreted by the courts so as to make the expression of beliefs by non-violent means punishable by imprisonment.

In October 1986 a major trial took place in which 296 defendants were charged with offences related to their activities as members of religious sects. According to the authorities they 'preached incitement to civil disobedience' because they refused to participate in political activities organized by the MRND. In their defence many defendants claimed that their religious views did not allow them to participate in the activities of any political party; some specifically stated that they did not regard themselves as members of the MRND. They were sentenced to up to twelve years' imprisonment. Most of them however were among the 4,000 prisoners released under a presidential amnesty on July 1, 1987.

# RWANDA

## The Media

Radio is a particularly important means of communication in Rwanda, where the illiteracy rate is around 50 per cent. The national radio broadcasts daily in Kinyarwanda, Rwanda's national language, and in Swahili and French. It is used by the government as an education and entertainment medium. There are an estimated 250,000 radio receivers in Rwanda. There is no television.

**Newspapers:** No press code nor any other legislation regulating the press currently exist. In November 1987 the government stated that a new law governing the press was in preparation. The printed press is limited: Rwanda has no daily newspaper. There are two main newspapers: a weekly, *Imvaho*, which is state-owned, has an estimated circulation of 23,000 and a second paper, *Kinyamateka*, a fortnightly which has been published since 1933, has a circulation of 11,000. Both are published in Kinyarwanda. The government also publishes a French-language weekly *La Relève*. The national press agency, *Agence rwandaise de presse*, issues a daily bulletin in French. The official languages are Kinyarwanda and French, but only a small percentage of the population read French.

In the 1960s *Kinyamateka*, which appears to be close to the Catholic Church authorities, had serious problems and was suspended several times. In recent years it has not suffered any major incidents of censorship.

At the university level, the journal *Le Dialogue* is published bi- monthly in French. It is a forum for intellectual discussion and debate. *Le Dialogue* has its main financial support from the Catholic Church.

There is no record of the arrest of any journalists in recent years for what they have written. On occasion, the press has been cautioned; editors have been called in by the government to ensure that the press concentrates on efforts to promote development in the country. The official position was expressed to the Human Rights Committee in 1982 : '... although there was no censorship, extensive collaboration existed between the private and official press.'

Over the last eighteen months there has been more openness and flexibility regarding freedom of expression. A certain amount of criticism of government actions and administrative performance can be found in the newspapers, including the government media such as *Imvaho*. During 1986, for example, a debate developed in the media about the impending rise in the price of beans, a staple food in Rwanda. The government was criticized in the media for its pricing policy, which resulted in changes in government action. Newspapers also discuss corruption problems and mismanagement by government officials. In April 1987 the Minister of Health, Dr François Muganza, was one of three ministers replaced. He was criticized in the media for refusing to acknowledge the problems of AIDS in Rwanda and to act accordingly. A comprehensive education programme on AIDS has since been introduced in Rwanda. The main exemptions from any criticism by the media appear to be the constitutional system, the role of the MRND and the status of the president. Nevertheless self-censorship is pervasive. Nine out of ten professionals are employed by the State. Professionals and intellectuals have a clear understanding of how far the discussion of critical issues can be taken and what can be printed.

**Foreign media:** There appear to be few restrictions on access to foreign media by Rwandese citizens. This, however, has to be seen in the context of the small percentage of Rwandese people who communicate in French and of foreigners who can communicate in Kinyarwanda.

## Freedom of expression of minorities

The largest minority in Rwanda are the Watutsi. There are also some 2,500,000 Watutsi living outside the country. Claims have been made that there are restrictions on the freedom of expression of the Watutsi population. Difficulties are placed in the way of Watutsi wishing to return to Rwanda. Within Rwanda the authorities have been criticized for a strict quota system in the allocation of positions, employment and training to members of the Watutsi ethnic group.

# SOUTH AFRICA

In South Africa it is an offence to quote Oliver Tambo, President of the African National Congress (ANC) in the newspapers, but not to publish his photograph. It is not an offence, however, to quote Nelson Mandela, but it is to publish his photograph. Such peculiarities are the by-product of a legal system which comes close to total regulation of the freedom to seek, receive and impart ideas and information, proclaimed in the Universal Declaration of Human Rights, a Declaration on which South Africa abstained at the United Nations in 1948.

Dr Stoffel van der Merwe, Deputy Minister and Chief of the Bureau for Information, recently stated that South Africa is engaged in an unconventional war in which the weapons are words and thoughts. Although the Minister was speaking in the context of the current State of Emergency, his remarks are hardly novel. Control of words and thoughts in circulation has been a central objective since the National Party government first came to power in 1948. Over many years, the means have been perfected to circumscribe rights to opinion and expression when these were exercised in any fashion considered seriously to challenge apartheid policies. With few exceptions, those South Africans who have held or proclaimed opinions considered hostile, and who might command attention or influence, have been victims of virtually every conceivable mode of repression—including political trials, detention, internal exile and prohibitions on their writings or on otherwise communicating their views.

At the same time, voluminous regulation has been directed at determining what people can read, view or hear. Censorship extends to everything capable of conveying information, ideas or messages— books, magazines, newspapers, films, radio, television, videos, music and plays, and even T-shirts, key rings and posters.

From 1948 up to the present time the thrust of restrictions on freedom of expression has been twofold: first, to insulate South Africans against ideas and information, both internally and from abroad, which the government regards as undesirable; second, and increasingly of late, to prevent the world knowing what is happening inside the country.

|  |  | Year |
|---|---|---|
| Population | 25,000,000 | 1984 |
| GNP ($ per capita) | 2,260 | 1984 |
| Illiteracy %: Whites | 7 | |
| Asians | 29 | |
| Coloureds | 38 | |
| Blacks | 68 | |
| Daily newspapers | 23 | 1977 |
| Non Daily newspapers | 104 | est |
| Periodicals | 325 | est |
| Radio stations | 23 | est |
| Radio receivers | 10,000,000 | 1986 |
| TV stations | 4 | est |
| TV sets | 2,700,000 | 1986 |
| Press Agencies: South Africa Press Association | | |
| Covenant on Civil & Political Rights | NO | |

**The State of Emergency:** The current State of Emergency was declared in June 1986 and renewed in June 1987. The Emergency has sought to silence and cut out large sections of thought and behaviour—mostly that aimed at ending apartheid from outside the parliamentary parties and structures. An estimated 15,000 people, including thousands of children, have been detained over the emergency to date. There are believed to be over 1,500 still detained. The only white person known to be detained is Raymond Suttner, a law lecturer at Witwatersrand university and author of a book on the Freedom Charter. In addition to extensive powers given to the security forces to detain people without trial, the combined effect of a number of the emergency regulations (replacing earlier reporting restrictions imposed in November 1985) is to impose a virtual news and information blackout on matters connected with 'unrest situations' and with measures taken by the authorities to counter them. Press freedom in relation to the security situation has been brought almost to an end. The emergency measures have made it impossible for the national and international media to present independent information and comment about unrest and other current events affecting the (black) majority of the country or about the activities of the security forces. The Bureau of Information is the only authorized source on information relating to and arising from the state of emergency. Regulations on the reporting of 'subversive' activities, which were redefined in very broad terms, were strengthened in December 1986, although a subsequent court case forced the revision of the orders. In August 1987 Proclamation R123 introduced a further phase of censorship aimed at local independent publications which includes the power to install a government censor at the editor's elbow.

**Internal Security Act:** Legislation attacking freedom of opinion and expression dates from the enactment of the Suppression of Communism Act, 1950. The law was rapidly used to restrict the freedoms of speech and association of anyone who was too vigorous in opposing the government. The law was renamed the Internal Security Act (ISA) and strengthened in 1982. It gives the government wide-ranging powers to 'ban' individuals, organizations and publications and to use administrative measures to silence people and suppress information.

The decision to ban a person is taken by the Minister of Law and Order, acting on the advice of the Security Police. No reasons are given for the decision. Once a banning order is served, the victim cannot be quoted in any way, whether in newspapers, books, or on radio and television. He or she is not allowed to prepare any statement for publication. A variety of other restrictions go with banning, from prohibitions on attending meetings, entering schools, universities and factories to being ordered to remain at home within set hours. A further device involves persons being 'listed', which means that it is a criminal offence to quote them in the media, and they are disqualified from standing for parliament or engaging in legal practice among other disabilities. Bannings and listings have silenced many hundreds with the effect that an entire spectrum of political opinion has been eliminated from public debate. It has been calculated that approximately 1,500 people have been affected by these orders since the 1950s. There are fewer cases today. Winnie Mandela's ban was allowed to lapse and the Rev. Beyers Naude was 'unbanned' in 1984. However, in December 1987, seventy-seven year-old Govan Mbeki, who was released five weeks earlier from a life sentence which he was serving with Nelson Mandela, had a banning order imposed which confines him to Port Elizabeth. He may no longer be interviewed or quoted in the press.

The banning of an organization means that it ceases to exist legally. Over twenty organizations have been banned, most of them before the 1982 Act came into force.

**Other legal restrictions:** The ISA is only part of the story; other laws affecting freedom of information—one calculation is at least 100 statutes—into all aspects of South African society. They represent a highly complex network of restrictions with different departments and services often running parallel systems.

The duplication not only enables the government to pick and choose its vehicle of attack on dissenters but can also act as a smokescreen to conceal the true extent of control: lifting of the State of Emergency will not alter the fact that the government can exercise much of the same stringent powers through other existing laws.

**The Publications Act:** The main censorship system is applied under the Publications Act of 1974, supplemented by the Publications (Amendment) Act 1986. This basic law deals with censorship of all 'publications or objects' except newspapers published by members of the Newspaper Press Union, which have their own control mechanism in the Media Council. It includes therefore the newspapers outside the mainstream, also called the 'alternative press', journals and pamphlets, and in addition films, music, posters and other visual objects.

At its heart is an immensely wide and intimidating definition of what can be deemed 'undesirable'—and therefore open to being declared illegal and banned.

The decision to declare a publication 'undesirable' is taken by an anonymous committee, the Publications Control Board, but can be challenged by appeal to the Publications Appeal Board. The names of the members of the committee were published for the first time in July 1987. The Board has developed an independent and increasingly liberal approach in recent years. One reason fresh censorship restrictions were introduced in 1987 was alleged to be concern by the government over the Publications Appeal Board, which had unbanned a number of newspapers, journals and books.

## The Media

**Newspapers:** There is a considerable newspaper industry in South Africa, with over twenty dailies and a similar number of weeklies and fortnightlies. Newspapers are published in the major regional centres;

some reach national audiences. Several newspapers are closely linked to or published by the ruling National Party, and are regarded as the government voice, such as *The Citizen* and *Die Burger* (in Afrikaans) with circulations of 70,000 and 80,000 respectively.

In general, the English-language press takes a more liberal and independent line in reporting than the Afrikaaner press; English papers include *The Star* with a circulation of some 180,000 and the *Cape Times* with around 75,000 readers. The *Rand Daily Mail*, one of the most famous and outspoken critics of apartheid, closed in 1985. The majority of newspapers are members of the Newspaper Press Union and operate a self-regulating Media Council. The Council was established in 1974 (as the South African Press Council) when the government threatened state regulation, and it has the power to impose heavy fines (up to R10,000) on newspaper editors. Outside the Newspaper Press Union, there are a number of other newspapers, such as the *Sowetan* (daily) with a circulation of around 110,000, and the *Weekly Mail* and *New Nation* with circulations of more than 30,000 each. Newspapers in South Africa are subject to registration. Under the 1982 ISA, a bond of R40,000 is to be deposited with the Minister in case he believes it may be necessary to ban the newspaper in the future. This does not affect newspapers established before 1982. However, it is known to have prevented at least ten new newspaper ventures which could not or would not make the deposit.

**Radio and television:** Radio and television are operated by the South African Broadcasting Corporation (SABC). Both services are considered to be subject to government direction. The Board of Governors is appointed by the State President. The radio operates twenty-three services in ninteen languages including external services. Television has four channels including two for African-language broadcasts. Television is subject to the Publications Act 1984, but most programmes are exempted. *Bophuthatswana Broadcast Television* (*BOP-TV*), the television station of the 'independent' homeland of Bophuthatswana can be received in parts of the Witwatersrand.

**Foreign journalists:** About 200 correspondents, photographers and television personnel are accredited to foreign news organizations. By the end of November 1987, eleven foreign journalists had been expelled from South Africa since the beginning of the Emergency in 1986. The most recent case was David Turnley, an American news photographer, who was accused by the authorities of sending 'biased photo material' overseas. In May 1987 three journalists were expelled within two days of one another, Michael Buerk, *BBC* television news correspondent, Peter Sharpe, *Independent Television News* (UK) correspondent and Steve Mufson, a former staff correspondent for the *Wall Street Journal*. In each case the authorities refused to renew work permits. Also in May, two Australian television journalists were expelled after being accused of distorted reporting of events there. According to the authorities they filed a report on the white elections which was 'riddled with blatant untruths'.

These expulsions were seen by the Foreign Correspondents Association as a sign of the 'government's intention to end independent coverage of South Africa's social conflict, because it believes that secrecy will help it win'. In 1986 four resident correspondents were expelled from South Africa, including Richard Munning, *Newsweek's* Bureau Chief. In September 1985, a *Newsweek* reporter's permit was cancelled following what the Minister of Home Affairs claimed was a series of one-sided articles in the magazine. In the latest move, the authorities have revised and tightened the accreditation rules. Most foreign correspondents can stay on three-month visas only, followed by application for renewal. Foreign news agencies and newspapers have been discouraged from appointing South African journalists as correspondents.

**Detention of journalists:** The large-scale detention of journalists is a feature of the present State of Emergency in South Africa. As far as is known, about twenty journalists, all of them black, have been detained for varying lengths of time, some for over a year without charge. Although the South African government has denied detaining journalists simply because they are journalists, both the government's actions and words point firmly in that direction. Among those still detained on Jan. 1, 1988, are Zwelakhe Sisulu, editor of the *New Nation,* who was arrested and detained without charge on Dec. 12, 1986. In mid-November 1987, he lost a legal application to be released. Others still in detention include: Brian Sokutu, freelance journalist of the independent *Veritas* news agency, who has been detained since June 1986; Dan Thobejare, executive member of the Mahwelereng branch of the Azanian People's Organization who was arrested in August 1986; and Mbulelo Grootboom of a small community paper, *Saamstaan,* in the Southern Cape. She spent thirteen months in emergency detention, was released and then re-detained on Sep. 11, 1987. Almost all the staff, contributers and associates of *Saamstaan* have been detained at some time.

Under the Emergency Regulations, it is a crime for journalists to be present at a scene of unrest; if any trouble erupts and the police or army are involved, journalists must immediately get out of sight. It is frequently reported that photo journalists in particular are taken into police custody prior to a 'security situation', such as demonstrations or actions in the townships, and later released. No photographs or television pictures are possible. Maximum penalties for non-compliance are a heavy fine and/or ten years' imprisonment, the same penalties as for publishing or distributing 'illegal' news.

**The media restrictions of August 1987:** Until now, restrictions have been applied either by specific prohibition or by leaving it to the media to decide what they can safely publish within the limits of the law. However, the government's latest action is to give those it views as offenders notice that they are publishing reports to which it objects. If they do not mend their ways, government censors can be put in to check material prior to publication or the periodical can be banned for three months at a time.

The minister responsible, Stoffel Botha, explained to South African editors that the purpose of the new powers was to act against newspapers which 'fostered and promoted a climate of violent overthrow of the state'. To co-ordinate the task, a directorate of media relations had been set up by the Ministry of Home Affairs. A system of 'scientific evaluation' would be applied to judge newspapers, following the advice of a panel of experts. The names of the members of the panel of experts had to remain secret in order 'not to subject them to criticism and ridicule'. He emphasized that the censorship powers already available had 'not allowed the government to deal with the sort of "propaganda" it had in mind'.

It is generally understood that the 'alternative media' are the main target of these new restrictions; the *New Nation*, the *Weekly Mail* and the *Sowetan*, as well as the research journal *Work in Progress*, have all received the official warning letter under Proclamation R123. In the case of the *New Nation*, the Minister's letter identified twenty-six items in three issues of the paper—advertisements, reports, photographs and a poem—which were variously considered a threat to public order, promoting revolution, stirring up hatred against a security force or 'promoting the public image or esteem of an unlawful organization'.

**Banning of books:** The number of 'banned' books is estimated at more than 18,000. Independently compiled lists are available of which books, pamphlets, etc. are banned (as notified weekly in the *Government Gazette*), those held up by the customs authorities and which cannot be distributed until the censors have passed judgement. It also lists those which can be possessed but not distributed, and what material has been 'unbanned'.

**Cultural censorship:** Although the criteria for censoring are zealously applied, a significant amount of liberalization has occurred, in particular in the cultural and social sphere. This shift in thinking is a recent development and appears to be linked to the government's policy of racial reform: the reforms are limited and have not satisfied demands for a non-racist, unified, democratic society; but they do exist and a ripple effect is noticeable.

For a long time, publications which contradicted Afrikaner views on race—such as a set of Unesco booklets on race and science—were not allowed. These days, academic books containing the views of banned organizations and differing political views are permitted. Books such as 'Detention and Torture in South Africa', or 'The War Against Children: South Africa's Youngest Victims', by the US Lawyers' Committee for Human Rights, can be published and sold although in the case of the latter, with restrictions on the outlets where it may be sold. University libraries are not as strict as they were in keeping academic books about Marxism locked away, giving access only to *bona fide* students and recording their names.

An assessment of the likely readership and the potential impact is part of the decision-making process whether to ban or not to ban. A collection of poems by a black South African poet could appear in book form;

however a periodical which contained one of his poems was banned because of it. Plays by Athol Fugard can be put on stage but a television screening of one of his plays was cancelled at the last moment in July 1987.

**Film and theatre:** The change in movies and related fields is even more dramatic. No longer are films showing inter-racial physical contact rejected out of hand. American sitcoms such as 'The Cosby Show' projecting a prosperous black family are prime-time television viewing. Serious movies suffer far less mutilation from the censors and much of what the world sees can be presented, albeit perhaps to restricted audiences at film festivals. At the *Weekly Mail* Festival of South African Films in August 1987, two films were shown which had recently been 'unbanned' on appeal: Sharon Sopher and Kevin Harris' 'Witness to Apartheid' (unconditionally) and Elaine Proctor's 'Sharpeville Spirit' (restricted screening).

Plays which satirize government leaders or savagely attack apartheid have become a regular feature of theatre, at least in a few cities, and only occasionally do the censors interfere as a result of complaints.

The combined restrictions have ensured that the government is in large measure able to dictate how much, or how little, South Africans know about the unrest in their country. They know extremely little. The curbs have also proved successful in reducing the international media focus on apartheid. Government leaders are gratified by these successes: their belief that unrest and rioting go hand-in-hand with the dissemination of news and the taking of pictures is confirmed. There is every reason to believe that the South African government will continue to do its utmost to conceal news about black resistance as much as the details of its repressive response.

## Current detainees

Included among those writers, journalists and media workers against whom action has been taken during the course of 1987 or who are still in prison: Zwelakhe Sisulu, editor, in detention since December 1986; Brian Sokutu, freelance journalist, in detention since June 1986; Robert Tendamudzimu Ratshitanga, poet, in detention since July 1987; Jaki Seroke, editorial director, in detention since September 1987.

# UGANDA

'We have no intention of introducing censorship...', Prime Minister Samson Kisekka declared in a speech in March 1987 to the National Press Club in Washington DC, 'but we intend to resist journalistic injustice ... by the journalists who publish falsehood, exaggerations and create sensationalism which may be intended to destabilize'. The Prime Minister said this would not be done by repressing the news media, 'but by informing our nationals and the international public what the true situation is in Uganda'.

With the formation of the new government by the National Resistance Movement (NRM) in January 1986 and the replacement of the previous army by the

| | | Year |
|---|---|---|
| Population | 12,000,000 | 1980 |
| GNP ($ per capita) | 230 | 1980 |
| Daily newspapers | 5 | est |
| Non Daily newspapers | 4 | est |
| Periodicals | 5 | est |
| Radio stations | 1 | est |
| Radio receivers | 600,000 | 1986 |
| TV stations | 1 | est |
| TV sets | 90,000 | 1986 |

Press Agencies:
   Uganda News Agency (UNA)

Covenant on Civil &
   Political Rights _____ NO

National Resistance Army (NRA) human rights abuses did diminish. The NRM's expressed commitment to human rights is corroborated by international human rights groups. As of October 1987 there were, however, consistent reports that the situation in the Northern and Eastern regions of Uganda was still characterized by civil strife and human rights violations including some by the NRA.

Freedom of expression in Uganda today has to be seen in the context of recent history and periods of traumatic human rights abuses by previous rulers. Guarantees were enshrined in the Constitution of 1967 but political conditions prevented their implementation. Proposals for a new Constitution are being debated and new laws are in preparation including laws on the press.

## The Media

From the mid-1950s to the early 1960s several newspapers and periodicals were produced, sponsored by the colonial government, the nationalist political parties and other institutions, but by the late '60s their number had greatly declined as a result of government interference.

The situation worsened during Idi Amin's administration which lasted from 1971 to 1979. His period of government was in general characterized by the persecution of anyone who expressed dissenting views.

*The Uganda Argus*, later renamed *The Voice of Uganda* and popularly

47

known as 'The Voice of Amin', was the government newspaper and unquestioningly printed his personal views and disinformation. Other newspapers that still existed did not dare speak out but had to go along with the 'official' version of events.

Amin even used the paper to 'warn' the public before a public figure was made to 'disappear' which meant his almost certain death. Such was the case with the Chief Justice, Benedicto Kiwanuka. *The Uganda Argus* of Aug. 21, 1972 quoted Amin: 'A few Ugandan Africans, including some high officials, are in the pockets of the outgoing Asians and the imperialists and are opposed to the move to expel them. One such official holds a very high position in the government and is known to be prime mover of this small pocket of opposition. The person concerned is known to the government and the government has already lost confidence in him as a result of his dirty activities.'

In an open letter to Amin, published by the International Commission of Jurists in 1972, Amin's brother-in-law and former Minister of Foreign Affairs, Wanume Kibedi (now ambassador to the United Nations), wrote: 'The person you were referring to here was Benedicto Kiwanuka, the Chief Justice; and "government" meant Amin and nobody else. A few weeks after you spoke those words, Kiwanuka was arrested at the High Court by military personnel in civilian clothing. That was on Sept. 21, 1972.' Kiwanuka was killed soon after his arrest. The same treatment from Amin and his newspaper mouthpiece was given to Frank Kalimuzo, the Vice-Chancellor of Makerere University. Just a matter of weeks after Amin had expressed his criticism, Kalimuzo was arrested. He was later killed at Makindye barracks.

After Amin and during the three short-lived administrations of Yusufu Lule, Godfrey Binaisa and Paulo Muwanga that followed until December 1980, the Ugandan press was described as 'the freest and most prolific in Africa'—there were between thirty and forty journals and newspapers, reflecting every political and ideological hue. Following the election in December 1980, which brought the Uganda People's Congress (UPC) party led by Milton Obote to power, the situation deteriorated. By the end of 1984, the number of papers that could be defined as representing views different from those of the government had been reduced to a handful, all appearing only in stencilled editions. They were *The Star*, the only English language daily, its Luganda edition *Ngabo*, the Democratic Party paper *Munnansi* (*The Citizen*), the long-established Roman Catholic paper, *Munno,* and the independent journals *Weekly Topic*, *Equator* and the *Ugandan Pilot*.

During 1983 and 1984 a number of journalists working for these newspapers and periodicals were arrested, among them two senior journalists of *The Star*, who were detained from November 1984 until January 1985 apparently without charge. It was reported at the time that the reason for their detention was that they had printed 'publications meant to spoil the name of the government'.

# UGANDA

The continued existence of *Munnansi* was surprising since it courageously provided weekly accounts of the excesses of the government and of the then Uganda National Liberation Army. In cases where stories could be cross-checked, the paper maintained a high standard of accuracy. There were accounts of illegal detentions, lists of bribes and charges payable to soldiers manning the various roadblocks around Kampala, the names of people murdered since 1980 (between fifty and seventy-five per issue) and details of army massacres and corrupt activities by ministers and UPC officials.

The paper was allowed to survive but it was banned several times in 1981, and its printing press was smashed. *Munnansi's* journalists and directors were detained on occasions, and either charged with sedition or served with detention orders under the Public Order and Security Act of 1967.

The foreign press did not fare any better: the last resident foreign correspondent had been expelled by February 1982 and only favoured reporters and other 'non-controversial' journalists were allowed entry visas. Some journalists were reluctant to publicize the worst aspects of life in Uganda, while others had come to know and befriend Milton Obote in his years in exile in Tanzania from 1971 to 1980. Some independent reports were produced including one by a television crew but few atrocities were brought to international attention. Obote's second administration had a good international press largely because his party was regarded as having been elected through democratic means. The full scale of atrocities was not known until the regime was overthrown in July 1985.

Since the NRM came to power in 1986 a new diversity in the newspaper industry has developed. An encouraging number of newspapers and journals are being published. Among them is *Munno*, established in 1911 by Roman Catholic missionaries. Before Amin banned it in 1976, it was perhaps the most influential and most popular local language paper in Uganda. *Munnansi* is the weekly newspaper of the Democratic Party; *The Star/Ngabo* (which resumed publication in 1984) is close to Baganda monarchists. *Weekly Topic* is an outspoken independent journal, which has been criticized by the government for false and exaggerated reporting. It takes a nationalistic line. The government newspaper *New Vision* has taken over from the *Uganda Times*.

**Censorship:** Newsprint is available only in limited supply and is very expensive. Most papers have to use very poor quality printing paper. Officially it is stated that there are serious financial problems and that papers which can find the financial support can print their newspapers. It has been suggested, on the other hand, that it is easier for some newspapers to buy newsprint than it is for others.

There is no formal system of censorship operating in Uganda today. A diversity of issues and problems can be discussed in the media. However, the President and members of his government have warned the press to refrain from 'exaggerated and false' reporting. *Munnansi* effectively ceased publication for some time after its editor was arrested for treason in October 1986. During 1987 editors and journalists of newspapers such as the *Sunday Review, Munnansi* and *Focus* have been seriously attacked by the authorities. In February 1987 President Museveni warned that he would revive wide-ranging powers of detention to deal with journalists who in his view distort the truth about rebel actions in the north. This reflected a retraction of some of the promises given earlier in 1986 to the media, when, for example, the Minister of Information and Broadcasting assured journalists of their freedom to report. He also appealed for their co-operation to assist the NRA/NRM to develop the country and to bring peace. Media reports relating to the actions of the NRA in the north of Uganda have drawn the most criticism. Since it is practically impossible for journalists to visit the area, reporting on the war in the north remains a dangerous undertaking.

In June 1987 the Ugandan Prime Minister accused journalists of exaggerating issues affecting the relationship between Uganda and Kenya. He felt that journalists should concentrate on positive reporting instead of 'blowing up negative issues'.

During 1986 to '87 the media in Uganda and Kenya have attacked each other and their respective governments. Some refer to a 'media war' being staged. Various underlying issues have been reported, including frontier transgression, protection of rebels, smuggling, and in particular the Ugandan government's decision to change over from the use of road transport to the cheaper, publicly-owned railway system. High-ranking Kenyan officials allegedly have important financial interests in the road transport business.

## Commission of inquiry

In May 1987 the NRM government established a commission of inquiry, headed by a High Court judge, to investigate violations of human rights from independence in 1962 until the NRM came to power. The government also established the post of Inspector-General of Government whose terms of reference include investigating complaints of human rights abuse.

Following investigations by the commission of inquiry, a police official, Charles Tindyebwa, who was deputy head of Idi Amin's anti-smuggling unit, was arrested and charged with killing four European journalists shortly before Amin was overthrown in 1979. The journalists, two West Germans and two Swedes, were in Uganda to investigate reports of atrocities.

**Uganda Human Rights Activists:** This group, established in Sweden in 1982 and launched in Kampala in the summer of 1985, is the most outspoken human rights group in the country. It monitors human rights issues and regularly publishes its findings. The group also plays a vital role in human rights education through dissemination of material.

On Feb. 28, 1987, its secretary-general, Lance Sera Muwanga, was arrested and he has been in detention since that time under the Public Order and Security Act of 1967. This act was often invoked by Milton Obote's government to detain political opponents. In contrast, the government of Yoweri Museveni has rarely applied the act. The apparent reason for the detention of Lance Sera Muwanga is an interview which he gave to *Africa Concord* in February 1987 describing human rights violations by the NRA in Northern Uganda. It was alleged that the government was also concerned about lack of accuracy in the group's reporting. Appeals from local and international human rights groups for his release have not, so far had any effect.

# ZAÏRE

Article 18 of the Zaïrean Constitution of February 1978, as amended, guarantees freedom of expression. Other provisions in the Constitution, however, impose serious restrictions on its enjoyment. Zaïre is a single-party state governed by the *Mouvement populaire de la révolution*, (Popular Revolutionary Movement, MPR). The *Manifeste de la N'Sele*, which contains the fundamental principles of the MPR, declares that 'the enjoyment of human rights is not possible other than in a "politically structured state" and that 'the freedom of the individual cannot be allowed to lead to anarchy of the State'.

Article 33 of the Constitution

|  |  | Year |
|---|---|---|
| Population | 30,000,000 | 1985 |
| GNP ($ per capita) | 140 | 1984 |
| Illiteracy % | 38.8 | 1985 |
| Daily newspapers | 7 | 1984 |
| Non Daily newspaper | 4 | est |
| Periodicals | 14 | est |
| Radio stations | 2 | est |
| Radio receivers | 525,000 | 1986 |
| TV stations | 1 | est |
| TV sets | 15,000 | 1986 |

Press Agencies:
Agence Zaïre-Presse

Covenant on Civil &
Political Rights _____ 1976

describes the political system in Zaïre: 'The MPR is the Zaïrean nation organized politically. Its doctrine is Mobutism. Every Zaïrean is a member of the MPR.' 'Mobutism' has been officially declared as the state philosophy—in practice it means total control of the political system by the President, Mobutu Sese Seko. There is no political debate possible outside the MPR, while inside a system of direct and indirect pressure is applied so that no change within the Constitutional system can occur.

The Constitution prescribes that every Zaïrean has responsibility for the progress of the MPR and 'has a duty through constant vigilance to support the Revolution, to defend its gains, and to safeguard national unity and territorial integrity'. Political comment is actively discouraged, and criticism of the President impossible. On the basis of the Constitution it is argued that the president of the MPR, who is by law the President of the Republic and the 'incarnation of the nation', requires immunity from criticism in order to give him complete freedom of action.

The right to express opinions and feelings through speech, writing and images is subject to 'public order and morality' (*bonnes moeurs*). The term *bonnes moeurs* (standards of good behaviour or morality) is used pervasively to justify legal limitations on freedom of expression and is often used to stifle opposition views.

# ZAÏRE

## Freedom of opinion

Efforts by groups and individuals over recent years to introduce new ideas into the existing political system including proposals for an opposition party, although advocated by peaceful, non-violent means, have been consistently suppressed. The individuals involved in such attempts have been detained and many charged under Articles of the Penal Code regulating actions to destroy, change or attempt to 'overthrow the constitutional system'.

Between mid-October 1985 and the end of January 1986 more than 100 people known to be critics of the government were arrested in Zaïre. By the end of 1986 Amnesty International had taken up the cases of seventy prisoners of conscience, although the true figure of political detainees in this category was deemed to be much higher. The individuals concerned were suspected of supporting an opposition political grouping, the *Union pour la démocratie et le progrès social* (UDPS) formed in 1982 by ex-members of the National Legislative Council to campaign for the legalization of a second political party. Support for any political party other than the MPR is considered an offence. Individuals have been convicted of 'trying to change the Constitution' and have been sentenced to up to fifteen years' imprisonment. Two leaders of the UDPS were arrested in October 1985 for insulting the head of state but were released in February 1986. Other supporters of the UDPS were forced to leave the country.

In September 1985 Roland van der Gogaert, a Belgian national, was charges with possession of allegedly seditious documents and cassettes and helping UDPS supports to bring into Zaïre a number of documents allegedly intended to discredit the Zaïrean government. He was sentenced to ten years' imprisonment but was released in February 1986.

It is consistently claimed that President Mobutu applies a 'carrot and stick' policy towards his opponents and encourages them to return to the MPR fold. On Oct. 31, 1987, Mobutu appointed seventeen new members of the MPR's Central Committee. Among them were two longstanding opponents of the MPR and members of the UDPS who had been imprisoned and banished for years—Kibasa Maliba and Ngalula Mpandandjila—as well as two other UDPS activists and another two opposition figures.

## The Media

Given the all-pervasive presence of the MPR, information control is almost complete. The current Press Law came into force in 1981 after extensive debates in the National Press Union, which reviewed in 1980 the state of freedom of the press in Zaïre and the statutes of journalists. It was the general view at the time that the situation of the press needed major improvement and that information was not circulating effectively. Access to sources of information for journalists was one of the new provisions. The Press Law is part of the Penal Code of Zaïre.

Article 1 proclaims the 'freedom to print, publish and disseminate written material subject to the press laws and relevant regulations in force', but Article 19 prescribes 'that all writings published by a newspaper or a periodical must not undermine public order, morality and good standards of behaviour (*bonnes moeurs*), or the honour and dignity of individuals'. In July 1987 a government representative told members of the UN Human Rights Committee that information was categorized into two types and that all information which 'touches in any way upon party doctrine' is always subject to prior censorship.

The production and management of newspapers and periodicals are regulated in great detail in the Press Law. In substance the law requires prior authorization to publish newspapers and periodicals. In addition the proprietor-editor is subjected to personal scrutiny. Applications to start a new periodical have been refused on several occasions, and periodicals banned after initial authorization.

**Newspapers:** The major newspapers are privately-owned. There are four dailies and twelve periodicals printed in Zaïre. They are believed to be heavily dependent on the government for financial support. The two main national papers, *Salongo* and *Elima*, published in Kinshasa, have a circulation of some 10,000 copies each. They are known to represent important financial and political interests of the MPR. Their directors are militants in the party. Editorial and managerial personnel of most newspapers are believed to be activists in the MPR.

Journalists must be members of the National Union of Journalists. Without the press card issued by the union, journalists cannot work professionally. The total dependence of journalists on the press card results in extensive self-censorship. The MPR sees the role of the media as in the forefront of the struggle to develop the country and journalists have a specific responsibility to the state and the party.

**Prohibition of publications:** Without recourse to judicial proceedings each Regional Commissioner can prohibit the sale and distribution of publications and issues of periodicals if they are 'contrary to good standards and of a nature to compromise public peace and order'.

In April 1985 *Les droits de l'homme*, an independent bi-monthly journal, reappeared after a nine-year absence. It had been published between 1962 and 1976 and ceased to appear, under indirect pressure, according to the proprietor-editor, Malenge Ilunga. No further issues are known to have been published and the circumstances of the second discontinuation of the journal are not known.

In February 1986 another journal, *le Passeport africain*, was banned and the proprietor-editor, Tchamala Mulembwe, detained for eight months, shortly after the publication of the first issue. The paper had received authorization in November 1985. Two main reasons for his detention were suggested: the paper had changed its title (*le Passeport*) to *le Passeport africain* and its scope had broadened from the initial mainly economic focus. Secondly, an article had appeared in the first issue that criticized the First State Commissioner (Prime Minister). In January 1987 Tchamala Mulembwe returned as director of *le Passeport*; it is not known whether another issue has appeared.

The national press agency, *AZaP*, is run by government officials. It is the main information source for the media in Zaïre, although there is an independent Catholic news agency.

The main independent publishers are the Christian publishing houses, of which there were two in 1985. It was reported in 1986 that the publication of manuscripts was occasionally refused on the grounds that there was a serious shortage of paper.

**Radio and television:** Radio and to a lesser degree television are important communication media in Zaïre. In 1983 there were an estimated 500,000 radio receivers and some 12,000 television sets in use. More recent statistics are not available. Both radio and television are state-owned and controlled. *La Voix du Zaïre* broadcasts in French and five local languages. *Zaïre Television* is a government-run commercial station broadcasting five hours a day (ten at weekends).

**Foreign media:** Under the Press Law 'it is prohibited to introduce, circulate and offer for sale in Zaïre newspapers, journals or written materials, periodical or not, published abroad, in whatever language, which are of a nature to disturb public order or are contrary to... *bonnes moeurs*'. The government admits to controlling the circulation of foreign publications by use of this law.

Foreign journalists require prior permission from the Department of Information to operate in Zaïre. Several journalists have been refused visas. In late 1985 a journalist representing *Agence France-Presse* was briefly detained and expelled after he allegedly received information from a supporter of the UDPS concerning an assault by a member of the security forces on a number of UDPS leaders.

It appears that the press is not only muzzled effectively within Zaïre but that efforts are made to minimize the number of critical media reports on the President and his policies outside the country. Members of the unofficial opposition who live as exiles abroad also speak of harassment and persecution.

In an interview in September 1987 in Brussels, President Mobutu heavily criticized the Belgian media for 'deliberately avoiding objectivity' and publishing reports that distort the truth about Zaïre and its head of state. In a similar vein, he ridiculed Zaïrean opposition groups in exile during an interview in Switzerland in November 1987.

**Censorship of music:** Music in general and songs in particular are perceived by the Zaïrean authorities as such an important communication factor that a special set of laws regulate the performance and recording of music. The laws prescribing censorship of music and establishing a Censorship Commission of Music were passed in 1967. The Commission monitors the conformity of songs to *bonnes moeurs* and public order. All songs performed in publicly-accessible places or recorded for reproduction are covered by the regulations. Only songs previously authorized and listed in a central register in Kinshasa can be performed or recorded.

Wide-ranging powers are given to the Censorship Commission to monitor the application of the laws. For example, the Commission has to ensure that the songs are not of a nature as 'to provoke racial or tribal hatred, nor to include anything that contains insults, strong dislikes, slanderous or damaging claims'. Despite the authorities' efforts to police music-making it apears that this popular method of sharing informal information and news continues to flourish.

# ZAMBIA

Zambia became an independent Republic in October 1964. In December 1972 the National Assembly voted unanimously (after a walk-out by members of the opposition) to approve a constitutional amendment bill banning opposition parties whilst establishing President Kenneth Kaunda's United National Independence Party (UNIP) as the sole legal party. The official political ideology is 'Zambian Humanism', a concept of national brotherhood drawn up by President Kaunda in 1967 and expanded in his 1974 manifesto.

According to government representatives the single-party system and philosophy should be understood within the context of

| | | Year |
|---|---|---|
| Population | 6,000,000 | 1983 |
| GNP ($ per capita) | 470 | 1983 |
| Illiteracy % | 24.0 | 1983 |
| Daily newspapers | 2 | est |
| Non Daily newspapers | 8 | est |
| Periodicals | 29 | est |
| Published books | 454 | 1983 |
| Radio stations | 1 | est |
| Radio receivers | 1,000,000 | 1983 |
| TV stations | 2 | est |
| TV sets | 240,000 | 1983 |

Press Agencies:
Zambia News Agency (ZANA)

Covenant on Civil &
Political Rights _____ NO

Third World countries and is designed to enable a speedy programme of development unhindered by internal conflict. 'We want everybody to join in and use their criticism within and improve the single party, rather than making opposition outside it' (J. L. Kanganja, Permanent Secretary in the Ministry of Legal Affairs).

Zambia ratified the African Charter and the International Covenant on Civil and Political Rights in 1984. A Bill of Rights is embodied within the Zambian Constitution; Article 21 guarantees the right to freedom of conscience and belief while Article 22 guarantees the right to hold opinions, receive and communicate ideas without interference and the right to freedom of expression.

There is no other legislative provision confirming freedom of expression and, in particular, freedom of the press in Zambia. Such legislation as is relevant concerns restrictions. Laws governing defamation (libel and slander) establish both civil and criminal responsibility. Defamation in publications containing material likely to injure reputation or expose the subject to hatred, contempt or ridicule, extends to persons both living and deceased. The penalty for such action is three years' imprisonment. It is also an offence to defame the President whether orally, in print or any other form with the same penalty applicable.

Although laws governing sedition, which date back to the colonial period, were contained in the Penal Code there is little information on their current use. Prior to independence the laws of sedition were directed at independence movements. Concern has been expressed that given the prohibition on opposition groupings the law on sedition could be used to repress freedom of opinion and expression within Zambia.

Article 53 of the Penal Code empowers the President to prohibit publications which in his opinion 'are contrary to the public interest'. The prohibition orders are published in the *Government Gazette* and relevant local newspapers. Prohibition can apply to any publication or newspaper, foreign or local, and may be retrospective.

Any person wishing to obtain a prohibited publication may apply for a permit to import it. In the event of the request being turned down an appeal can be made to the President. These presidential powers to ban publications are supported by penal sanctions under Section 54 of the Penal Code.

Other powers include those that censor foreign publications, songs and films. A Censorship Board exists which may vet materials 'inimical to the nation', although it is unclear how this body is composed or its source of authority.

Government representatives claim that there is no general prohibition on the receipt of foreign newspapers or magazines but rather that due to economic constraints, it has become difficult for booksellers and newsagents to procure these publications.

## The Media

**Newspapers:** There are currently two daily newspapers in Zambia. *The Times of Zambia*, owned by the UNIP, has a daily circulation of approximately 57,000 copies, and the government-owned *Zambia Daily Mail* which has a circulation of 45,000 copies. Both these newspapers were initially owned by foreign enterprises and were established before independence. There are at least twenty-nine periodicals published in a number of local languages including English, and which encompass a wide spectrum of commercial and non-commercial publishers.

**Press Council Bill of 1980:** In 1980 the government decided to create a press authority in Zambia which would be a party organization. This was considered by journalists at the time to constitute a press censorship board. Republished in 1984, the Bill proposed disciplinary powers over journalists, including powers to order dismissal. The Press Council would recommend to the party and government the banning of any publication that published information 'likely to incite or cause alarm or despondency', and the prosecution of the journalists responsible. Although the Bill has not been proceeded with to date, it represents a continuing threat to freedom of expression and the rights of journalists.

**Incidents involving the press:** In recent years there have been a number of incidents which raise concern for freedom of the press in Zambia. Both before and after the government took control of *The Times of Zambia*, action was taken or threatened against editorial staff.

Before the UNIP bought *The Times of Zambia*, it was able to hire and fire senior staff. Deputy editor-in-chief William Saidi was dismissed by President Kaunda in November 1975 because his performance as a journalist was considered 'inconsistent with the philosophy and spirit of the paper which must be the mouthpiece of the party'. (*The Times of Zambia*, Nov. 5, 1975.) Saidi was reinstated in January 1977.

In 1983, the then editor of *The Times of Zambia*, Naphy Nyalugere, was prosecuted for 'publishing false news with the intent to cause fear and alarm to the public'. The newspaper had reported that a truckload of weapons had been stolen from Arackar barracks outside the State House in Lusaka. Nyalugere and Josiyas Mbuzi, a reporter, were convicted and fined 500 kwacha each.

In 1983 the news editor of the *Zambia Daily Mail*, Shadrack Soko, was detained for questioning without any reason being given.

In 1981 the then Minister of State for Information and Broadcasting, John Banda, commented to graduating students of journalism 'Don't bite the hand that feeds you in the name of a free press. You may end up without a job... there is no such thing as free press, it is an illusion, a creation of journalists' (*The Times of Zambia*, Sept. 26, 1981).

Although the government disassociated itself from the remarks of the Minister it would appear that there are pressures on journalists to conform to a particular perspective, at least from some officials.

Self-censorship may result especially in view of the relationship between the government, the Party and newspapers. A former editor of *The Times of Zambia* is the press secretary of the President and a former press secretary is now Minister of National Guidance, Information and Broadcasting Services.

**Foreign journalists:** A report in *The New York Times* in June 1987 alleged that visas were denied to journalists seeking to report on Zambia's economic crisis. In December 1986 the *Associated Press* Southern Africa correspondent, John Edlin, was detained for six days in a Zambian prison. Edlin was on his way to the Copperbelt province to report on the aftermath of the food riots in which at least fifteen people were killed.

**Radio and television:** Zambia Broadcasting Services incorporate radio and television; both are state-owned and funded. There are an estimated one million radio receivers and 240,000 television receivers in use. Radio programmes are provided in English and seven other Zambian languages. There are seventy-three languages in Zambia and the difficulty in spreading information effectively within the country is apparent. Attempts are being made to surmount the problem through educational and literary broadcasts. Of the two existing television channels one is dedicated totally to educational and in-school services. The news bulletins for both radio and television are prepared by the *Zambia News Agency* (*ZANA*) which is a government-created service.

# COUNTRY REPORTS—AMERICAS

# ARGENTINA

The Constitution presently in effect, promulgated in 1853, affirms 'freedom of the press' and the right to publish one's ideas in the press without prior censorship (Articles 31 and 14). Court decisions have interpreted this language to cover other forms of expression, including artistic expression. However, since 1930, the rights and guarantees of the Constitution have frequently been suspended in Argentina, both by military governments that took power through *coups d'état*, and by elected governments that resorted to the state of siege provisions of the Constitution in times of internal turmoil. Declaration of a state of siege does not automatically impose prior censorship, but its effect on free expression has generally been strongly negative.

|  |  | Year |
|---|---|---|
| Population | 31,000,000 | est |
| GNP ($ per capita) | 2,230 | 1984 |
| Illiteracy % | 4.5 | 1985 |
| Daily newspapers | 191 | 1982 |
| Non Daily newspapers | 3 | est |
| Periodicals | 32 | est |
| Published books | 4,216 | 1983 |
| Radio stations | 112 | est |
| Radio receivers | 16,000,000 | 1983 |
| TV stations | 71 | est |
| TV sets | 5,910,000 | 1983 |

Press Agencies:
TELAM SA, DYN, NA

Covenant on Civil & Political Rights _____ NO

**The Junta**: The military regime that governed Argentina between 1976 and 1983 did not impose censorship through any formal legal mechanism. However, some books and theatre presentations were banned, and there was at least one incident of public burning of books, in Córdoba in 1976. Newspapers and magazines which voiced criticism of the repressive methods used by the regime were punished with partial closures. In the case of *La Opinión*, the newspaper's owner Jacobo Timerman was jailed and his paper was confiscated. The worst attack on freedom of expression was the targeting of more than 100 journalists for 'disappearance' or extra-judicial execution. The victims included some of the best-known writers and investigative journalists in the country, such as Haroldo Conti and Rodolfo Walsh. Many of the country's best theatre actors and directors and most popular singers were forced into exile.

**The Alfonsín government**: The situation began to change dramatically after the defeat of the Argentine military in the Falklands/Malvinas war. It has remained very different throughout the government of President Raúl Alfonsín, who took office on Dec. 10, 1983. Open and free debate has flourished and the period has been marked by the resurgence of the country's rich cultural traditions.

Nevertheless, Alfonsín has had to tread carefully, faced with support for the military in the media, an open rebellion at the Campo de Mayo base in Easter week 1987, and suspicions that the military intelligence services are involved in bugging the telephones of politicians and union leaders, and with a spate of recent bomb attacks. The government has been denounced as the 'radical synagogue', an anti-semitic reference (Alfonsín's party is the Unión Cívica Radical). Such attacks from supporters of the old order have often been accompanied by violence. Offices of the ruling party have been bombed.

In October 1985, following a series of bomb attacks, President Alfonsín imposed a forty-day state of siege, and ordered the arrest of twelve persons suspected of conspiring to destabilize the government. One of those arrested was journalist Horacio Rodríguez, who writes a column under the pseudonym Daniel Lupa and is openly supportive of the former military regime. He and the others were eventually released without charges. To make it known that he was not being punished for his views, the government allowed Rodríguez to continue publication of his column while in prison.

In contrast, the government response to the Campo de Mayo insurrection of April 1987, was for ministers to appeal to the press not to interview its leader, Col. Aldo Rico, nor to report on the mutineers' claims that the rebellion was spreading to units not, in fact, affected.

## The Media

**Newspapers**: Either as protection against terrorist attack, or because of their own political preferences, major newspapers engage in selective censorship. The established, large-scale circulation newspapers in Argentina now take positions openly hostile both to President Alfonsín and to measures taken to investigate the abuses of the past. Following promulgation of the 'Due Obedience' law in June 1987, which bars prosecution of most of the military officers who committed grave crimes against civilians during the period of military rule, a lawyer tried to publish a paid advertisement pointing out that the law prevented the prosecution of navy officers accused of kidnapping two French nuns who worked with relatives of the 'disappeared'. The nuns' fate has never been established; they are thought to have been thrown into the sea from a navy aeroplane. Argentina's largest daily, *Clarín*, refused to publish the advertisement, which was eventually run by *Página 12*, a smaller newspaper.

In May 1987, a federal judge issued a restraining order against the publication in three major newspapers of a paid advertisement on the national holiday of May 25, in which some 5,000 citizens praised Gen. Jorge Rafael Videla, the first President of the military regime, for his contribution to ridding Argentina of 'subversion'. The order was prompted by a petition from journalists' trade unions and other newspaper workers, and was supported by the central labour federation. The judge found that the text of the paid advertisement constituted *apologia del crimen* ('public praise for crime', an offence under the Penal Code), since Videla had been convicted on dozens of counts of murder, torture and false arrest for his role in the 'war against subversion'. The proponents of the advertisement did not appeal, but its text was widely publicized.

At President Alfonsín's initiative Congress passed a law in 1984 called *Derecho a Réplica* ('Right of Reply'), obliging newspapers and other media to provide those who think they have been maligned in commentary or in news articles with the opportunity to respond. Although there was some opposition from the management of journalistic enterprises, the bill was passed with a comfortable majority.

**Magazines and books**: Periodicals of all ideological colours circulate freely, including some that criticize the government from a leftist point of view, as well as those that defend the old military order. The Catholic hierarchy has campaigned against the profusion of sexually explicit magazines and television comedies that have emerged in the period since the restoration of democratic government in 1983. Taking up that theme, suporters of the military criticize the present state of affairs as a 'pornographic democracy'.

The book industry is plagued by the economic problems that beset all of Argentina, but there is no restriction on the sale of any book. In 1976 the Junta imposed a ban on the publication, distribution and export of anti-semitic literature, halting the activities of the *Editorial Milicia* publishing house; such material is, however, circulating freely at present.

**Television**: News programmes and talk shows continue to be run by commentators who were avid supporters of the military, though some new programmes have also entered the scene. Right-wing critics have accused the government of manipulating television coverage of certain climactic events, like the military rebellion of Easter week 1987, to rally popular support for its policies. Although most TV stations are government owned or controlled, there is no evidence of undue interference by the government with their reporting. A bomb was placed in the building of the *Canal 13* TV station in Buenos Aires on July 4, 1984 when the station presented a programme called '*Nunca Más*' ('Never Again'), prepared by the National Commission on the Disappearance of Persons.

**Radio**: Radio has made a very successful comeback as a medium for political debate. Several talk shows now feature very lively discussions on all the issues of the day.

**Film and theatre**: Even without a centralized policy of restriction, some institutions of the state continue to exercise controls on the media. A judge recently banned the showing of the controversial French film '*Je vous salue, Marie*' after the Church called it blasphemous and vowed to use every means to prevent its public exhibition. The judge cited legal precedents preventing publication of material considered offensive to religion. Simultaneously, unknown groups threatened to bomb the cinema where it was due to be shown. In the end, the distributors withdrew the film, which has still not been screened in Argentina. In 1975 a right-wing group had carried out a similar attack which led to the destruction of one of Buenos Aires's finest theatres. The attack was aimed at preventing the theatre from presenting the musical 'Jesus Christ Superstar'.

**Human rights groups**: In spite of the progress in the tolerance of ideas and expression, some restrictions have proved hard to abandon. Lower-ranking administrative authorities have been responsible for some restrictions of free expression. In June 1987, the Jewish Movement for Human Rights organized a round-table discussion about the youth of the 1970s and the radical movements in which they participated. One of the guests was going to be a former leader of the *Ejército Revolucionario del Pueblo* (ERP) who is now active in non-violent politics after spending ten years in prison. The conference was scheduled to take place in the *Centro Cultural Gen. San Martín*, a government-owned and operated theatre and arts complex in Buenos Aires. When right-wing publications criticized the event, the management of the *Centro Cultural* cancelled it, giving no reason.

In cities in the interior of Argentina, similar restrictions are more frequent. One of Argentina's largest human rights groups, the *Asamblea Permanente de Derechos Humanos* (APDH), has weekly slots assigned to it on local stations of *Radio Nacional*, the federal government's cultural radio network. Following changes in local management, APDH progammes have been taken off the air in Bahía Blanca, Córdoba and other cities.

There is no doubt that freedom of expression in Argentina will depend on the country's future stability. The disturbing presence of paramilitary organizations composed of former and current agents of military and police services has created a tense climate which menaces attempts to break with the past.

# CANADA

Freedom of speech and of the media in Canada has been preserved more by tradition than by state or judicial protection. The press is independent of the government and there is no censorship of political discussion in public meetings or in radio and television broadcasts. Scathing political satire is commonplace.

Section 2(d) of the Canadian Charter of Rights and Freedoms guarantees 'freedom of thought, belief, opinion and expression, including freedom of the press and other media of communication'. This section applies to the Federal Government, and to the governments of the ten provinces and two territories. Anyone may invoke it to challenge legislation or administrative practices.

|  |  | Year |
|---|---|---|
| Population | 25,000,000 | 1985 |
| GNP ($ per capita) | 13,140 | 1984 |
| Daily newspapers | 112 | 1984 |
| Non Daily newspapers | 1,085 | 1984 |
| Periodicals | 144 | 1984 |
| Radio stations | 210 | est |
| Radio receivers | 8,756,000 | est |
| TV stations | 892 | est |
| TV sets | 8,681,000 | 1984 |

Press Agencies:
The Canadian Press

Covenant on Civil &
Political Rights _____ 1976

## Language rights

The right of anglophones and francophones to express themselves in either official language is protected by the Constitution. Sections 16-22 guarantee equal status for French and English in all institutions of Parliament and government of Canada, and those of New Brunswick, the only officially bilingual province. Related language rights are protected for certain judicial proceedings and educational purposes. There is an active programme to promote language equality in the federal sphere, overseen by the Commissioner of Official Languages.

Problems remain, however. Although technically Canadians have the right to express themselves in either official language, for francophones this is largely limited to federal buildings in parts of the country with French majorities. Recently in Alberta, a member of the Legislative Assembly was disciplined for speaking French in the Assembly.

In Quebec, on the other hand, the francophone majority has asserted French language rights in law and practice to enhance the formerly inadequate opportunity to communicate in French. This has led to a diminution of the opportunity for non-francophones to work, carry on business, or advertise in English or to have children educated in that language. During the 1970s, there was a resulting exodus of anglophones

67

from Quebec. A 1987 judgment that considered a law restricting the use of English in Quebec said that manufacturers had a constitutional right to advertise in English. A proposed constitutional amendment, known as the 'Meech Lake Accord' and approved by a majority in the House of Commons on Oct. 26, 1987, will (if ratified) recognise Quebec as a distinct society within Canada, thus strengthening francophone language rights in Quebec.

Language rights for Canada's indigenous peoples are affirmed under the Constitution. Section 27 requires that Part I of the Constitution be interpreted 'in a manner consistent with the preservation and enhancement of the multicultural heritage of Canadians'. Section 14 guarantees the right to an interpreter 'in any proceedings', for anyone who cannot understand or speak the language used. Until 1984, the government of the Northwest Territories had English and Inuktitut ('Eskimo') as its two official languages, and has been endeavouring to make greater official use of other aboriginal languages. The imposition (by the federal government) of French as an official language in 1984 was not welcomed by territorial peoples.

## The Media

While the government does not seriously inhibit freedom of the media, there are two constraining factors: oligopolistic ownership of the press, and cultural domination by the United States.

**Ownership**: Television stations and newspapers are highly profitable businesses. Concern over the lack of real competition led to two extensive federal reviews, a Senate Study on the Mass Media (1970), and the (Kent) Royal Commission on Newspapers (1981). The Kent Report found that eight organizations controlled about 75 per cent of Canada's newspapers, with two chains alone controlling about 60 per cent of English language circulation. One family controlled all English language dailies in New Brunswick (as well as owning many broadcast outlets). The press opposed the Kent Commission recommendations which were designed to ensure greater competition, and the Report had little eventual impact.

Under the 1968 Broadcasting Act, radio and television frequencies are considered to be public property in Canada, and owners of stations and networks (including the publicly-owned *Canadian Broadcasting Corporation, CBC*) must obtain and periodically renew licences to broadcast. A broadcast licence, issued by the Canadian Radio-television and Telecommunications Commission (CRTC), is accompanied by conditions. Licence approval hearings are public, and enable consumer organizations to seek to have conditions attached that benefit their communities.

Private broadcasters have generally shown a desire to maximize profit by purchasing cheap and popular United States shows for which to sell advertising time. Two areas of CRTC overview that are spurred on by consumer groups are rules requiring the use of more Canadian productions, and policies designed to ensure that both programming and advertising reflect the increasingly diverse nature of Canadian society, and do not exhibit stereotypes of women or of minorities.

Newspapers, books and magazines are not subject to similar supervision. Complaints concerning stereotyping or unfair representations may be made to 'press councils', but these are voluntary bodies with no teeth.

**Cultural protection**: Governmental efforts to ensure the existence of a healthy cultural sector are considered a necessity, because of the scale of the American entertainment industry. Only 20 to 30 per cent of films distributed to cinemas are Canadian. Tax concessions, lower postal rates, and government grants have been employed to assist Canadian publishing and film production. 'Canadian content' quotas require that a high percentage of Canadian produced programmes be broadcast on television. Similarly, a high ratio of Canadian music must be played by radio disc-jockeys. Although this has led to some strengthening of Canadian content policies there are continuing problems. Broadcasting outlets get around the quotas by playing Canadian films or music late at night or early in the morning when audiences are small. Strong vocal opposition has been voiced by cultural nationalists to the Free Trade pact signed by Canada and the United States in October 1987 which will allow US publications to compete directly with Canadian ones. Preferential postal rates available for Canadian magazines are to be extended to US magazines merely printed in Canada and a tariff protecting the Canadian record and tape industries will be removed.

**Defamation laws**: In all parts of Canada, traditional ('common') laws apply that seriously restrict free speech in order to protect honour and reputation. In most provincial and territorial jurisdictions, these non-criminal statutes provide monetary compensation for damage to reputation. Offending words defame a person once they are published or communicated to a third person, and tend to cause the subject of them to be exposed to hatred, contempt, shunning or ridicule, or to lower the esteem of the subject in the eyes of reasonable members of society.

There are four standard defences to a defamation action. *Absolute privilege* exempts statements made in parliamentary, judicial or quasi-judicial proceedings. *Qualified privilege* protects those who report or publish such statements. *Fair comment* rests on the notion that everyone has the right to comment fairly and honestly on matters of public interest; it applies only when the assertions relied upon are true. *Justification* requires that the offending statements themselves be true; it applies even if the words were published with malice.

In additon to these laws, there is a Criminal Code of Canada offence of 'defamatory libel'. It is almost never resorted to; the Law Reform Commission of Canada has said that it should be abolished.

**Discrimination and 'hate' messages**: Each Canadian jurisdiction has a statute prohibiting adverse discrimination on named grounds, as well as a mechanism for enforcement, usually a 'human rights commission'. The prohibited grounds are race, colour, religion, gender, age and physical disability, and the areas of activity covered include employment, education, housing and access to public services. Advertisements are covered, and usually any notice, sign or message. In most laws, there is a specific statement guaranteeing that in non-discriminatory cases, freedom of expression continues to apply.

In the (federal) Canadian Human Rights Act (CHRA), there is a section outlawing 'hate' messages. The CHRA prohibits telephone communication likely to expose people to hatred or contempt on the basis of a prohibited ground of discrimination. This section has been tested in a series of cases dealing with anti-semitic taped messages played through the telephone by one organization. After repeated violations of an order by a tribunal to cease, the main perpetrator, John Ross Taylor, was sentenced to a prison term. In appeal proceedings, it was argued by the defence that the CHRA 'hate message' section violated the 'freedom of expression' protection in the Constitution. Section 1 of the Constitution allows a government to impose reasonable limits, however, and the judges ruled that the section in question and the manner of its enforcement were justifiable, reasonable and fair.

**The criminal code**: There are four offences that relate to hate propaganda: advocating genocide; publicly inciting hatred against an identifiable group, where such incitement is likely to cause a breach of the peace (harm to a person or to property); wilful promotion of hatred against an identifiable group; and wilful publishing or false news or statements which the publisher knows to be false and which could or does cause injury to public interest (Section 177).

The sensational trial of Ernst Zundel involved Section 177. Zundel had distributed pamphlets worldwide denying that six million Jews had died in the Nazi holocaust. The seven-week trial provided Zundel with extensive exposure for his theories. His conviction was overturned on appeal, and a new trial ordered. The appeal court found, however, that Section 177 does not violate the Constitution, holding that 'the maintenance of racial and religious harmony is certainly a matter of public interest' and that 'spreading false news is the antithesis of seeking truth through the free exchange of ideas'.

The Zundel case has bolstered the longstanding arguments by civil libertarians, newspaper editors, and the Law Reform Commission of Canada for removal of Section 177, seen as an unnecessary and troublesome restriction on free speech. Other commentators have said that an important public service has been performed by the prosecution of Zundel. Canadians have had a chance (through expert testimony) to see just how baseless Zundel's 'holocaust fraud' theories are.

**Obscenity**: Provincial administrative bodies classify films as being suitable for certain age groups, and may require advertisements to include warnings as to their contents (e.g. 'violence and coarse language' or 'some nudity'), or may ban a film from distribution. The standards vary considerably from province to province.

Such censorship is opposed by civil liberties groups, cinema owners and members of the artistic community. Regimes of censorship have been challenged in court. In a leading case, the Ontario courts decided that the province was justified in having a board of censors, but that its terms of reference were too vague and, therefore, violated the Constitution.

Federal legislation permits customs officers to censor imported books and magazines, but there is little monitoring of publications. Video rental businesses and the tapes which they offer are also virtually unregulated. Nevertheless, an important constitutional case testing Criminal Code provisions on obscenity concerned a rental business called Red Hot Video Ltd (1985). The Code outlaws distribution of obscene material, 'a dominant characteristic of which' is the 'undue exploitation' of sex, or of sex linked with violence or cruelty. The judges ruled that the degrading treatment of women portrayed in the offending video tapes was 'unacceptable by any reasonable Canadian community standard'. The court found that the restriction on freedom of expression was acceptable, given growing community concern over exploitation of women and children in some publications and films.

**Official secrets**: The principles surrounding governmental secrets are based on United Kingdom precedents. They have not been seriously challenged until recent years. In addition to federal law on state secrets, there are federal and provincial laws that forbid the release of information held on individuals (personal privacy) and on business corporations (to keep information away from competitors and employees). There has been a gradual movement toward greater openness and improved public access to official information.

In a case that attracted much attention, the Supreme Court of Canada upheld the dismissal of a federal employee for criticizing aspects of government policy. It was decided that he had displayed a lack of loyalty incompatible with his public service duties.

**Access to information**: The federal and other jurisdictions have procedures for members of the public to obtain unpublished government information. The key federal statutes are the Access to Information Act and the Privacy Act. The former allows (with many exceptions) citizens or permanent residents to seek access to any documentary or computer record under the control of a government institution. The latter allows individuals to have access to information or opinions recorded about themselves and to have any errors corrected.

Under the Access to Information Act, there are many categories of data not available for public scrutiny: most commercial data; information originally obtained by a foreign government or by another domestic one; information that could harm defence, diplomatic or trade interests or that pertains to law enforcement; and records connected with the operation of the federal Cabinet. This has meant in effect that Canadian access law is very weak, and has resulted in very little material coming to light. Several newspapers, including the *Toronto Star*, the *Globe and Mail* and the *Ottawa Citizen*, have journalists who have become specialists in seeking information through the access law. However, the most they have discovered are moderately embarrassing stories on such matters as the cost of refurbishing the Prime Minister's official residence.

**USA and Canada compared**: The Canadian access law is essentially the opposite of the US law, under which officials must justify any decision *not* to release information. In Canada officials can hold back information on any number of broad, subjective pretexts, and it is up to the journalist to appeal, and to prove his right to the material. Although there is an access commissioner with the power to order the material to be turned over, the commissioner must follow prescribed, laborious procedures which have the effect of dragging out the decision for months or years. Because the US government often holds important information on Canadian companies, policies and environmental issues on file, many Canadian journalists resort to seeking such information under US access law, even though this information remains secret in their own country.

In March 1987, a parliamentary committee suggested 108 reforms to liberalise the Acts. One suggestion was to remove the government's right to withhold information if there were any harm to national security or foreign relations or federal-provincial relations, and to require instead a balance of the public benefit of releasing information versus the harm from disclosure. The committee also suggested that a senior judge be allowed to examine material claimed to consist of Cabinet confidences, to ensure that it truly warranted secrecy. In a report released on Oct. 15, 1987, the federal government rejected most of the 108 recommendations.

# CHILE

Gen. Augusto Pinochet Ugarte has ruled Chile in conjuction with the commanders of the four armed services since the military coup of 1973. Following the coup, publications sympathetic to the deposed Allende government were forcibly closed, printing equipment was destroyed, and personnel affiliated with the press and media were jailed, deported, 'disappeared' or killed. Radio and television stations were taken over by management appointed by the military so that news and opinions were disseminated in compliance with the wishes of the new regime. This radical transformation was based on the ideological concept that free speech allowed the inculcation of 'alien principles', and that national security required all institutions to work for the goals of the military government.

|  |  | Year |
| --- | --- | --- |
| Population | 12,000,000 | 1986 |
| GNP ($ per capita) | 1,710 | 1984 |
| Illiteracy % | 5.6 | 1983 |
| Daily newspapers | 37 | 1982 |
| Non Daily newspapers ⎫ Periodicals ⎭ | 128 | 1986 |
| Published books | 1,653 | 1984 |
| Radio stations | 321 | 1986 |
| Radio receivers | 14,000,000 | 1986 |
| TV stations | 6 | est |
| TV sets | 2,500,000 | 1986 |
| Press Agencies: Orbe Servicios | | |
| Covenant on Civil & Political Rights _____ | | 1972 |

**The 1980 Constitution**: In 1980 the military government promulgated a new Constitution which was approved in a plebiscite. Article 19, clause 12 provides for freedom of expression and private operation of the press and media. The State is prohibited from establishing a monopoly over the mass communication media, and prior censorship is allowed, but only to uphold 'general norms' concerning 'artistic activities'. This freedom is, however, further qualified by Article 8 which bans activity 'intended to propagate [ideas] of a totalitarian character or based on class warfare'. Anyone who acts with the intention of spreading such concepts is ineligible for numerous positions 'related to the broadcast or dissemination of opinions or information' for a period of ten years following each violation.

Freedom of expression is also qualified by Article 41 (emergencies) and by transitional Article 24. The latter is one of twenty-nine transitional articles of the 1980 Constitution which are to remain effective until 1989, during the nation's 'transition' from a military to a democratic form of government. Under the Constitution a plebiscite is to be held by 1989 in which a single candidate proposed by the military junta may run for an eight-year term as President. Article 24 permits the President to 'restrict the right of assembly and the freedom of information, the latter only with

73

reference to the founding, editing or circulating of new publications' if 'acts of violence, designed to disturb public order, occur, or should there be danger of disturbance of internal peace'. The law provides that violators may be fined heavily. The Supreme Court has ruled that it cannot review executive actions under the authority of transitional Article 24.

Article 41 permits suspension and restriction of the rights to freedom of information and opinion during a declared state of emergency. The President has the power to declare a state of national emergency and thereby to establish censorship at any time. He may punish the dissemination of any material which he deems to be harmful to 'national security' by suspending publications or broadcasts for a specified period. For example, during a state of siege imposed from November 1984 to May 1985, a reporting prohibition was announced which banned all news that might 'create alarm' and all political news except that released by the government. Six weekly magazines were shut down during this period and only one opposition publication, the Christian Democratic weekly *Hoy*, was allowed to publish. It was subjected to strict prior censorship.

**Slander and insult**: Statutory provisions also restrict information that reaches the public. Article 417 of the Code of Military Justice makes it an offence to slander the armed services. A journalist was prosecuted under this law when, on the cover of the weekly *Análisis*, the word 'assassins' was printed across a photograph of military personnel at the site where three Communist Party members were found murdered. Another journalist was prosecuted in 1985 under a statute that punishes those who insult the President and the armed forces. Legislation which broadly defines slander as a violent political offence is also used to prosecute journalists for accusing military officers of repression. Photo-journalists whose equipment has been smashed, and who have been beaten with clubs and dragged into police vans by uniformed personnel, have subsequently been charged with 'aggression against the police'.

**Privacy law**: A law promulgated in May 1984 (Law 18.313) makes it punishable to publish 'material concerning the private life of an individual which damages or could damage the individual'. In the 1980 Constitution, Article 19, clause 12 already permits officials 'offended or unjustly alluded to' to have rectification disseminated gratis in the offending medium. The 1984 law provides for a jail sentence and does not allow truth as a defence. It has been suggested in Chile that the 1984 law was designed to protect Pinochet from allegations involving illegal landholdings.

**The Law for Internal Security**: This is probably the law most frequently used to repress free expression. This makes it a crime to call for disruption of public order and for the illegal paralysis of national activities. No reporting is permitted which may 'disturb internal order'. In 1984, it was used by the government to bring charges against opposition publications for reporting on planned protests. In February 1986, the leader of an opposition group, the *Intransigencia Democrática*, was charged under the Internal Security law with incitement to disrupt public order and to overthrow the established government. This law was also used to prosecute the director of the independent weekly magazine *Cauce* for publishing a series of exposés on a political prisoner's alleged torture.

**The opposition press**: Despite harsh legal restrictions, including another four-month state of siege from September 1986 to January 1987 with the shutdown of several opposition publications; despite severe (and often violent) repression in practice, including the September 1986 death squad murder of a leading journalist, José Carrasco Tapia; and despite frequent jailings and prosecutions, the Chilean press has been remarkably resilient. In this sense, Chile presents a contradiction: it is simultaneously a country that treats dissent with extreme harshness and one in which, under duress, the expression of dissent flourishes.

Aided by the skill of the country's strong Church-backed human rights movement in focusing international attention and pressure on Chile, the opposition press has been able to publish information and ideas that are anathema to the government regime. In 1987, significant steps were taken to enhance diversity of expression when two opposition daily newspapers began to publish. On March 18, 1987, *La Época,* which is modelled closely on the Madrid daily *El País*, started to appear. Four weeks later, on April 14, 1987, *Fortín Mapocho*, previously a weekly that had been closed by the government during the 1984-5 and 1986-7 states of siege, began appearing as a daily.

The tenuous nature of the freedom to publish these papers was demonstrated by the imprisonment shortly thereafter of Felipe Pozo, editor of *Fortín*, and a reporter for the paper, Gilberto Palacios, on charges of insulting the armed forces in a 1986 article criticising compulsory military service. Because the article dealt with the military, their case was subject to the jurisdiction of the military courts. In another case a leading journalist, Juan Pablo Cárdenas, editor of the weekly *Análisis*, was sentenced after appeal on May 28, 1987 to eighteen months' night-time imprisonment on charges of slandering the President in a series of articles which had appeared in his magazine the previous year.

Around thirty people were being prosecuted for 'offences' against the military or the President at time of writing. The editor and assistant editor of the weekly *Apsi* were arrested and jailed in August 1987, and a satirical issue of the magazine was confiscated. They were released on bail on Oct. 22, 1987.

**Propaganda raids**: The media are also vulnerable to guerrilla attacks. The Manuel Rodríguez Patriotic Front (FPMR) and other groups have conducted raids on radio stations and forced staff to broadcast political statements. The International Press Institute reports that in March 1987 the FPMR simultaneously took over nine radio stations in Santiago and the provincial cities of Rancagua and Coquimbo. Staff were tied up and forced to broadcast a prepared tape of music along with a political statement. One man was killed at *Radio Tropical*, a local pirate station in northern Santiago, whilst attempting to prevent the raiders' getaway. The *Associated Press* offices in central Santiago were also entered by FMPR agents, who held up staff at gunpoint and sprayed slogans on the walls of the office before leaving.

## Freedom of opinion and expression

The Chilean government employs many different methods in punishing the expression of dissenting views. On Nov. 28, 1986, 14,000 copies of the latest book by Colombian novelist Gabriel García Márquez were burned on arrival at the port of Valparaíso under the order of the naval admiral in charge of enforcing in the area the state of siege then in effect. Peaceful street demonstrations have been frequently dispersed by military and police attacks on demonstrators that include shootings, clubbings, tear-gassings and the extensive use of water cannons. Known dissenters have been killed in supposed armed confrontations (*enfrentamientos*) which are widely believed to be staged executions. In one episode, in 1985, three prominent Communists were kidnapped on the same day at separate locations in Santiago. Their bodies were subsequently found together, all three with their throats slashed.

In October 1987 the opposition Christian Democratic Party criticized a bill approved by the junta which aims to ban Marxists from access to the media, to remove their civil and political rights, to bar them from holding public office and to refuse them positions as journalists or teachers. News organizations publishing Marxist views may face a fine of up to US$17,000.

Many Chileans have been imprisoned for peaceful dissent and, over the years, torture of detainees has been pervasive. Chile has forcibly exiled tens of thousands of political dissidents, though the number known to be now excluded by the government was down to about one thousand by September 1987. Typically, exile has been by administrative decree rather than as a consequence of judicial determination. The same is true of internal exile, a sanction which was used extensively in former years but seldom recently.

Although there has been some softening of the Pinochet government's tyrannical methods since the events of 1973, there is always the prospect that it could again suppress dissent through the exercise of arbitrary power. The Chilean opposition press is well-organised, resilient and experienced in challenging the government.

## Current detainees

Included among those writers, journalists and media workers against whom action has been taken during the course of 1987 or who are still in prison: Juan Pablo Cardenas, editor, sentenced to 541 nights' imprisonment; Diane Aaron, journalist, arrested November 1974, disappeared.

# COLOMBIA

Colombia has ratified the International Covenant on Civil and Political Rights and the American Convention on Human Rights. Both of these contain guarantees on freedom of expression. Each is incorporated into Colombia's domestic law. The Constitution cites war, social instability and public disorder as conditions which may abrogate this freedom. These 'conditions' have plagued Colombia longer than any other Latin American country.

Colombia is reputedly the most violent country in Latin America. Homicide is the fourth-ranking cause of death for the entire population; over 11,000 people were murdered in 1986 alone. A count by *El Siglio*, a Bogotá newspaper, puts at 1,754 the number of deaths associated with the conflict between the military and a half dozen guerrilla movements in 1986. The *Miami Herald* reports that fifteen Colombian journalists have been assassinated since 1984. A state of siege, which was in effect for most of the past thirty years, was lifted in 1982 and reimposed in 1984 when the Minister of Justice was murdered.

|  |  | Year |
|---|---|---|
| Population | 28,000,000 | 1985 |
| GNP ($ per capita) | 1,370 | 1984 |
| Illiteracy % | 14.8 | 1981 |
| Daily newspapers | 31 | 1984 |
| Periodicals | 30 | 1984 |
| Radio stations | 486 | 1985 |
| Radio receivers | 25,000,000 | 1985 |
| TV stations | 3 | est. |
| TV sets | 4,500,000 | 1985 |
| Press Agencies: | | |
| Ciep – El País, Colprensa | | |
| Covenant on Civil & Political Rights _____ | | 1969 |

Though there are few formal restrictions, a number of aspects of life in Colombia have contributed to restrictions on freedom of expression. First, the politics and economy of Colombia were for decades and to a large extent still are in the hands of the ruling 'five families', who headed both the Liberal and Conservative parties. Almost all the country's print and broadcast media are closely linked to these two parties, whose interests and viewpoints they articulate. Second, the power of the military, which the civilian government relies upon to control dissent, is also an important factor restricting freedom of information.

**The 'Peace Process'**: Initiated by President Belisario Betancur (1982-86), the 'Peace Process' succeeded in securing ceasefires between the military and several guerrilla movements. Many members of the military, and conservative factions of society, opposed the goal of bringing the leftist guerrillas into the mainstream of Colombian politics. They were able to undermine the 'Peace Process' by withholding information or providing inaccurate information to the government and the press. The absence of objective information was most critical with respect to the initiation and conduct of armed operations between the military and guerrilla organizations, and the identification of those responsible for criminal actions and alleged human rights violations by the military. There was initially extensive coverage of guerrilla statements, but this coverage came to be seen as aiding the guerrillas' cause, and a process of self-censorship in the media ensued. It is rare today to find stories in major newspapers referring to the guerrilla version of events. A related problem is that because communication with certain rural areas is extremely difficult, both because the country is divided by major mountain ranges and because some areas are entirely militarized, the military is the only source of information for the media.

A number of journalists, and Colombians sympathetic to the 'Peace Process', have complained of the military's 'disinformation'. Debate on this issue was heightened when the press published a story, later proved false, regarding a brutal murder by guerrillas. President Betancur's willingness to believe the charges led to the collapse of negotiations with that particular guerrilla group.

**Cocaine**: Another factor which has had its effects on freedom of expression is the growth of the Colombian cocaine industry. Some 80 per cent of the world cocaine supply originates in Colombia. Cocaine now provides Colombia with more export earnings than coffee and has created a new, unrestrainedly brutal class of billionaires. Corruption and fear created by the drug money has reached into nearly every Colombian institution, including the judiciary, military, police, the legislature and the guerrillas. The press practises some self-censorship on cocaine, but there are many journalists who speak out against the traffickers. They suffer the consequences. President Virgilio Barco, who took office on Aug. 7, 1986, launched a much publicized counter-attack on the drug dealers in December 1986, but so far it has produced few results.

## The Media

**Newspapers**: In 1975, the Liberal government of Alfonso López Michelsen passed the current Press Law, which stipulates that journalists must have a journalism degree from an institution approved by the government, and should carry a press card or face fines.

Under this law, the Ministry of Education may suspend or cancel a licence if a journalist breaks laws regarding journalism or if the journalist is convicted of damaging third parties in his work. A National Council of Journalism was created to consult with the government about press freedom, union freedom, protection of journalistic interests and ethics. This body includes three representatives from the government.

A similar law in Costa Rica was held to violate the American Convention on Human Rights. The Inter-American Court of Human Rights held that the licensing of journalists was an impermissible interference with freedom of expression (the Schmidt case).

# COLOMBIA

In a March 1986 report, the Inter-American Press Association complained that several new laws threaten press freedom. Among those mentioned were a Narcotics Law passed to combat drug trafficking which limits the free flow of information on the subject; a law dealing with the legal character of political parties which hinders the publication of political advertising, and the continuation of an 8 per cent import tax on newsprint which has had a particularly serious effect on smaller newspapers.

One of the two largest daily newspapers, *El Tiempo*, is strongly conservative, although a Liberal Party paper. Its editorial stance pervades its news reporting to such an extent that it labels the victims of many crimes as 'subversives'. The paper is accused of accepting the military version of events uncritically and either ignoring reports of human rights violations by the armed forces or repudiating them as part of a campaign to attack their prestige. The other major newspaper, *El Espectador*, is considered somewhat less biased in its news reporting, although it is also aligned with a Liberal faction.

**Radio**: There are two Conservative Party radio networks: *Cadena Radial Colombiana Caracol* and *Radio Cadena Nacional*. The smaller, Liberal Party *Circuito Todelar* network is acknowledged as a source of generally more balanced coverage.

**Television**: Television is owned by the State, but it leases time to private companies with some guidelines to ensure equal time for political candidates. During the 1986 congressional campaign, three leading candidates appeared in a televised debate, and during the presidential campaign, the government ensured that each of the four announced candidates received equal time in a series of national television appearances. An electoral reform bill currently under discussion aims to guarantee access to electronic media for all political parties.

## Attacks on journalists

**Political reporting**: Courageous journalists who speak out on such issues as military injustice and government corruption face harassment, threats and death.

On Feb. 21, 1986, *Circuito Todelar*, the station to which Juan Guillermo Ríos moved his news staff after being fired from the programme *News at Seven* for denouncing a section of the Colombian military code, was bombed.

In July 1986 three Colombian journalists were arrested, fingerprinted and interrogated in Medellín after attending a press conference held by guerrillas in a secret location. Notes and cassettes were reportedly confiscated.

On Feb. 23, 1987, political commentator Carlos Julio Rodríguez was badly wounded by submachine gun fire as he was leaving home for his job at *La Voz de la Selva*, a *Caracol* radio network station in Florencia. Rodríguez had been denouncing local political corruption in his broadcasts.

79

Paramilitary groups are responsible for the deaths of many journalists. In August 1987 Colombian newspapers published a list of twenty-two people 'condemned to death' by a presumed anti-communist group. The list included the names of six journalists and several political and labour leaders. An updated list increases the number to thirty-five and includes human rights activists.

Guerrilla groups have also been implicated in attacks on journalists. According to a story by *Agence France-Presse*, on Feb. 11, 1987, a bomb exploded at a radio station in Medellín, destroying part of the transmitter tower and injuring two station employees. An anonymous caller claimed responsibility for a guerrilla group.

Foreign journalists are also subject to interference. In January 1986, three journalists from a French television station, *Antenne 2*, were detained for five days for questioning after reporting on guerrilla activities. Two days later army units attacked a rebel news conference in Alto de Paramillo, Cauca Department. The guerrillas had freed three captured soldiers who were being presented to foreign correspondents. In February authorities removed three British journalists, representing the *Independent Television* network, from a combat zone in Miranda, and detained them for questioning. The reporters were released the next day and advised to leave the country.

No foreign correspondents are known to have been killed so far, although two—Joyce Holmes and Timothy Welch—have disappeared and several have been threatened. Lore Croghan, a stringer for the American magazine *Newsweek*, left Colombia in 1985 'because all my sources were getting killed'. These included a Minister of Justice, a press secretary in the Colombian Attorney-General's office and Croghan's contact in the National Police.

**Reporting on drugs**: The rise in narcotics traffic over the last decade has led to 27 unsolved murders of Colombian journalists. Three murders in 1986 finally succeeded in capturing the attention of the nation. On July 16, Luis Roberto Camacho, a part-time correspondent for *El Espectador*, was murdered after investigating the activities of suspected cocaine dealer Evaristo Porres. On Sept. 17, Raul Echavarria, the deputy editor of *Occidente* in Cali, who had applauded a call in the US Congress for the death penalty against drug traffickers, was shot. On Dec. 17, Guillermo Cano, editor of *El Espectador*, was gunned down outside the newspaper office after signing a series of editorials demanding extradition of drug traffickers to the United States.

After Cano's death, the press organized a 'day of silence', without newspapers, radio or television broadcasts; journalists joined in a six-mile march through Bogotá to demand stronger government action. In mid-January, every newspaper in the country published on its front page a declaration of principles which was also broadcast by all radio and television stations. Calling for a 'united front', the media said they had 'decided to mount a permanent guard to demand that the government, the political parties and Colombian society unify solidly behind effective actions to win the war against narcotics criminals'. The federal government immediately announced special measures to expedite the capture and conviction of drug dealers. In the months that followed, the police and armed forces reported that they made 1,862 arrests and seized 321 kilos of cocaine. The numbers were more impressive than the results, however. 'Much noise, few bosses', said the news weekly, *Semana*.

Journalists are now exercising varying degrees of self-censorship when reporting drug-related stories. Stories on drugs are still big news, but articles are unsigned. In Medellín, the centre of the cocaine business, two papers, *El Colombiano* and *El Mundo*, did not participate in the anti-drug press campaign because their editors feared for their lives. Editors have begun to use bullet-proof cars and armed bodyguards.

More recently, journalists have co-ordinated certain news stories in an attempt to insure against attacks on individual reporters. The US-based *Columbia Journalism Review* reported that in March 1987 a group of reporters joined to put together an account of the November murder of Col. Jaime Ramírez, a narcotics officer. The article ran in 19 papers and on radio and television. Although some reporters complained that the article skirted the subject of police involvement in the murder, others were pleased that the story survived. 'We hope that this kind of collaboration will allow us to continue covering the story, but you never know', said one. 'We're always waiting for the next murder.' The fear of reprisals has had a significant effect on freedom of expression in Colombia. Unless and until measures are taken to redress the situation in any meaningful way this freedom will remain no more than a notional right.

# ECUADOR

Ecuador's current Constitution dates from 1979, when a civilian government was returned to power after seven years of military rule.

Widespread concern has been expressed at the way in which President León Febres Cordero, who took office in August 1984, has used the Constitution to flout its guarantee of freedom of expression. The Constitution guarantees 'the right to freedom of opinion and the expression of thought by any means of social communication' (Art. 19.4), along with freedom of conscience and religious belief (19.6) and of association (19.13). Only in situations of national emergency properly declared by the President can prior censorship of any media be permitted (78.5).

|  |  | Years |
|---|---|---|
| Population | 10,000,000 | 1986 |
| GNP ($ per capita) | 1,220 | 1984 |
| Illiteracy % | 6.1 | 1982 |

| Daily newspapers | 18 | est |
|---|---|---|
| Periodicals | 18 | est |
| Radio stations | 320 | est |
| Radio receivers | 1,900,000 | 1985 |
| TV stations | 10 | est |
| TV sets | 600,000 | 1985 |

| Covenant on Civil & Political Rights _____ 1969 |
|---|

Otherwise, the Penal Code stipulates penalties for obstructing the freedom of expression and information. Article 178 states that any authority who by arbitrary or violent means inhibits the capacity to express thought freely shall be liable to one to five years' imprisonment and deprivation of political rights for a time equal to that of the sentence. Article 179 states that anyone who prevents or obstructs the free circulation of any book, magazine, or journal, provided that it is not published anonymously, shall be liable to between six months and two years in prison.

**'Unconstitutional' laws**: On several occasions, the President has used the expedient of not publishing legislation properly passed by Congress in the Official Gazette, the *Registro Oficial*, but instead publishing his own proposals, in contravention of constitutional procedures.

The President has refused to accept, publish and give effect to amnesties granted by both the national legislative and locally-elected authorities. One of these amnesties involved the Air Force general, Frank Vargas Pazzos. He led a rebellion in March 1986 against what he alleged was corruption by the Minister of Defence and the Army Commander-in-Chief. Both of those men resigned, but Vargas was kept in custody in the capital, Quito. In October 1986, Congress voted in favour of granting Vargas an amnesty. This was opposed by the President and the chiefs of the armed forces, who argued that the legislature could not grant an amnesty for a military matter. Instead of resubmitting the question to Congress, however, the President maintained that, as the amnesty had not been published in the *Registro Oficial*, it did not have any force in law.

The President used a similar tactic in the case of an old political opponent, Abdalá Bucaram. Bucaram fled the country in September 1985, a few days before he was due to face charges of slandering the President and the armed forces in a radio broadcast. Congress amnestied him from these charges in October 1986, but the President again refused to allow this ruling to be published in the Official Gazette, so it never became legally effective.

In these cases, Congress has appealed to the *Tribunal de Garantías Constitucionales* (Constitutional Guarantees Tribunal), which is meant to be a non-partisan body having the final say in all matters which involve an interpretation of the Constitution. Febres Cordero has accused the Tribunal of being politically biased, and has refused to abide by its rulings.

## The Media

**Radio**: In a mountainous country such as Ecuador, with a high illiteracy rate, radio is perhaps the most important form of mass communication. There are over three hundred stations, the vast majority of them local commercial ones, based either in the capital, Quito, or the main port, Guayaquil.

Independent radio stations critical of Febres Cordero's government claim to have been the object of a campaign to silence them at critical moments in recent Ecuadorean history.

In April 1985, the *Dinámica* and *Victoria* radio stations in Guayaquil were temporarily shut down after broadcasting allegations of official corruption. When Gen. Vargas rebelled in March 1986, the government used its emergency powers to shut down eight radio stations in Guayaquil and Quito. A particular target has been the *CRE* (*Cadena Radial Ecuatoriana*) chain, headed by Rafael Guerrero, a strong opponent of the government. One of the stations closed in March 1986 had its central installations destroyed by a gang of five or six men in January 1987 during the kidnapping of the President by Air Force personnel trying to secure the release of Vargas. Guerrero put the blame for the incident squarely on the authorities, claiming the intruders were in the pay of the local governor.

The government again intervened to close three radio stations in March 1987, when there was a general strike throughout the country. The closure of three stations, *Democracia*, *Éxito* and *El Sol*, for two weeks, led to widespread protests by other media, which culminated in a march for freedom of expression on 31 March. The directorate of the independent Ecuadorean Radio Broadcasting Association met with government officials, and the ban was lifted.

**Television**: Critics of the government point to a large number of dismissals of television journalists as evidence of Febres Cordero's desire to silence

83

dissenting voices in the media. The worst case of suppression has been that of *ORTEL Canal 5* of Quito. A group of young journalists was granted a franchise to set up this new television channel in the days between the end of Osvaldo Hurtado's term of office as President, and Febres Cordero's assumption of power. The new government argued that the contract was invalid, since the frequency that the station was to operate on was reserved for use by the State. Both the National Congress and the Constitutional Guarantee Tribunal ratified the contract with *Canal 5*, and the company went ahead with its preparations to go on the air. Within a few hours of doing so, however, on April 22, 1985, troops were sent to close the station down. Despite strenuous efforts since then, again backed by Congress, *Canal 5* has been unable to operate.

**Press**: There are periodic complaints about the physical maltreatment of journalists trying to carry out their professional duties. During the Vargas uprising, and the later kidnapping of President Febres Cordero, journalists were denied access to news sources. In general, however, the written media are allowed scope to criticize the government, within limits that are known though unspoken. The government has been accused of removing two journalists, Juan Cueva and Simón Espinoza, from public sector posts, for 'writing in an opposition magazine'. It has countered the charge by arguing that, according to the Constitution, public officials cannot hold more than one job.

Another form of government control has been through the placing of official advertising. The proprietors of *Hoy*, a new Quito daily, and *Nueva*, a monthly left-wing magazine, both complained in 1985 that the government had deliberately cut its advertising with them. They also suggested that the government was trying to persuade commercial companies not to advertise in their pages, and was putting pressure on the private banks which had loaned the publications money. This situation had apparently improved by 1986, when the National Secretary for Public Information was changed. More recently, however, *Hoy* alleged that the authorities were delaying supplies of newsprint in an effort to control its content.

**Guerrillas**: It has been claimed that the authorities also restrict the information journalists receive and can publish about operations against Ecuador's main guerrilla organization, *Alfaro Vive, Carajo*. In 1986 several of its leaders, including Arturo Jarrin, were killed by the security forces, but journalists were only given official versions of how they had died, and had no opportunity to verify their truth. Concern was also expressed by local human rights groups that relatives of suspected guerrilla sympathizers face constant police harassment, have their telephones tapped and their mail opened. The same happens to the human rights groups, it being alleged that the government is attempting to equate their work and that of legal opposition parties with the activities of armed groups.

The guerrilla groups themselves have used the tactic of abducting journalists or taking over media outlets to gain themselves attention. In May 1986, Enrique Echeverría, a journalist for the newspaper *El Comercio* and presidential adviser on constitutional matters, was held for five days by the small *Montoneros Patria Libre* group. They claimed to be holding him to highlight President Febres Cordero's abuse of the Constitution. They eventually surrendered peacefully to the police. In June 1987, the same group held radio reporter Iván Oña captive for two days until his station, *Radio Quito*, agreed to broadcast a political message putting forward the group's ideas.

Restrictions on freedom of information and expression in Ecuador tend to be personal and arbitrary decisions by the President and his supporters rather than a concerted effort to suppress news and ideas in the name of national security. The situation has worsened considerably over the past few years, and with an election due in 1988, when Febres Cordero's four-year term ends, political pressures on the media are bound to increase.

# EL SALVADOR

On June 1, 1984, José Napoleón Duarte took office as El Salvador's first elected civilian president in fifty years. His inauguration was accompanied by hopes of a political opening for opposition views, expectations that until mid-1987 at least remained largely unrealized.

Despite his party's achievement of a Legislative Assembly majority in 1985, President Duarte has consistently failed to safeguard such fundamental civil liberties as the rights of free expression and assembly. Until January 1987, the provisions of the 1983 Constitution were suspended by the state of siege, which had been in effect, almost without interruption, since 1980. All restrictions on constitutional guarantees were then lifted when the state of siege lapsed, due to a legislative strike called by a right-wing coalition hostile to Duarte's economic policies.

|  |  | Year |
|---|---|---|
| Population | 5,000,000 | 1985 |
| GNP ($ per capita) | 710 | 1984 |
| Illiteracy % | 30.2 | 1980 |

| Daily newspapers | 6 | 1982 |
|---|---|---|
| Non Daily newspapers | 1 | est |
| Periodicals | 7 | 1982 |
| Radio stations | 75 | est |
| Radio receivers | 2,000,000 | 1985 |
| TV stations | 5 | est |
| TV sets | 350,000 | 1985 |

| Covenant on Civil & Political Rights | _____ | 1979 |
|---|---|---|

## The Media

**News coverage**: Although no formal system of prior restraint exists, there is a widely perceived need for self-censorship, given government mechanisms for exerting pressure and the all-too-recent history of violence against reporters and news offices. With the closures of *La Crónica del Pueblo* in 1980 and *El Independiente* in 1981, following a campaign of brutal repression by security forces, El Salvador lost the two major newspapers critical of the Salvadorean military. Since then, the Salvadorean printed press, with the exception of *El Mundo*, has either supported the government or challenged it from a right-wing perspective.

**Television**: In the past year, television stations, particularly *Channel 12* and *Channel 6*, have been at the forefront of a movement to provide more open coverage of the range of political opinion in El Salvador. Controversial events which once would have gone unmentioned increasingly receive coverage by both television and radio stations.

In June 1987, for example, *Channel 6* covered a death squad threat issued against student leaders at the National University, the trial of civil defence members for the killings of several civilians, and the machine-gunning by guerrillas of a police squad car.

# EL SALVADOR

**Radio**: Given the country's widespread illiteracy and extreme poverty, radio remains the most important mass medium, although television is rapidly catching up. There are several commercial stations, owned mainly by private companies or individuals; however, the government retains the right to revoke a radio or television station's operating licence at any time. *Radio Sonora* and *Radio Yaesu* carry frequent news broadcasts. There is a radio station run by the Armed Forces, *Radio Cuscatlán*, and a clandestine station, *Radio Venceremos*, operated by the rebel Farabundo Marti National Liberation Front (FMLN). Although balanced, in-depth reporting of the country's civil war remains largely absent, the commercial stations have continued their practice of conducting telephone interviews with the exiled leadership of the Democratic Revolutionary Front (FDR), the political allies of the FMLN. In addition, for the past year the commercial radio stations have repeated information initially broadcast over *Radio Venceremos*.

**Newspapers**: There are five major dailies. *La Prensa Gráfica*, a mass circulation paper, provides strident right-wing opposition to government policies and takes an unfavourable stance toward trade unions and co-operatives. This daily characterizes the FMLN as a terrorist organization and reproduces without changes the releases from the Press Committee of the Armed Forces (COPREFA). The only other paper with a mass circulation, *El Diario de Hoy*, vehemently opposes the policies of the Duarte administration also from a right-wing perspective, including any government intervention in the economy. Like *La Prensa Gráfica*, *El Diario de Hoy* reproduces only those Western news service cables that do not conflict with government or military accounts. Advertisements appear in its pages from the Arena party (the main right-wing opposition), the Chamber of Commerce and the Association of Coffee Growers. Both *La Prensa Gráfica* and *El Diario de Hoy* are owned by traditional oligarchic Salvadorean families, whose interests tend to coincide with those of the business sector. Accordingly, the editorial policies of both papers reflect their owners' deep conservatism.

The *Diario Latino* once strongly supported the Salvadorean extreme right, but since its 1986 purchase by the Rey Prendes family, it has provided pro-government coverage. The newcomer *Noticiero* appears to specialise in sensational news coverage.

*El Mundo* remains El Salvador's most moderate newspaper. Although traditionally conservative, pro-business, and pro-US government, the paper has demonstrated a growing openness. *El Mundo* publishes international wire service cables that report the Salvadorean civil war in terms differing from the Army's communiqués. It prints the statements of opposition groups—even, on occasion, those broadcast by the guerrilla-operated station, *Radio Venceremos*. Like the commercial radio stations, *El Mundo* carries paid announcements from trade unions, student groups, political groups on the left and right, and human rights organizations, which in effect supplement the news. It sells advertising space to peasant co-operative associations, unlike *El Diario de Hoy* and *La*

*Prensa Gráfica*; unfortunately, this smaller-circulation daily rarely reaches the rural areas. Unlike the other newspapers, *El Mundo* is owned by a shareholders' group, rather than by a single prominent family, which may account for its greater editorial freedom.

**Restrictions on reporting**: Compared to the international media, the Salvadorean press is largely conservative and passive. The subsistence wages paid to Salvadorean journalists, who tend to be self-taught, encourage corruption, such as pay-offs from business associations and municipal governments in return for favourable reporting of their press conferences and statements. Investigative reporting remains a foreign concept, with battle coverage largely restricted to information disseminated in the capital from the offices of the armed forces representative. Although this information is not always accurate, there are no subsequent retractions by COPREFA or the news medium publicizing its account. In an effort to balance coverage, some of the media published FMLN claims regarding the number of army casualties for the month. As a rule, however, foreign journalists are viewed by their Salvadorean counterparts as better able to take risks and to report on such sensitive topics as paramilitary death squad activity and military wrongdoing.

Although events in mid-1987 suggest a loosening of the tacit restrictions on freedom of expression, until recent months there appeared to be unwritten limitations on what the Salvadorean press could report. In September 1986, when Salvadorean radio journalists broadcast telephone interviews with FDR leaders Rubén Zamora in Nicaragua and Guillermo Ungo in Panama, the government responded with stern admonitions, warnings all the more meaningful as past threats to withdraw advertising revenues had prompted the dismissal of the responsible radio journalists.

The Salvadorean government employs a variety of measures to control press coverage, including restricting access to conflict areas, regulating the entry of foreign journalists into the country, threatening reporters with lawsuits, and detaining and interrogating journalists.

**Foreign journalists**: The Army requires foreign and domestic journalists to obtain official permission from both its high and local command before entering zones of conflict. By denying or limiting access, the military makes the verification of reports of killings and bombardments difficult. In northern Morazán, reporters who have obtained army permission to enter the conflict zone may nonetheless be denied access by the FMLN. As a result, the Salvadorean press almost invariably accepts the military's version of events as the main source of information on inaccessible war-torn areas.

Foreign reporters have been both threatened with prosecution, and actually prosecuted, for criminal defamation over stories that implicate military leadership in wrongdoing. In 1985, *UPI* correspondent Michael Drudge was forced to leave the country after reporting that an army commander had embezzled US economic aid designated for his province. A Salvadorean court sentenced Drudge in absentia to three years in

## EL SALVADOR

prison. On May 7, 1986, *AFP* correspondent Ana Cristina Hasbún was interrogated by the armed forces, after publishing FMLN allegations on the involvement of two army officers in a kidnapping-for-profit ring. At her detention, both military men were present and threatened lawsuits.

The recent decision to enforce a 33-year-old law requiring US citizens to obtain visas, which went into effect on Nov. 25, 1986, is ostensibly an attempt to control the entry into El Salvador of people sympathetic to leftist rebels. It could provide a means of barring or restricting foreign journalists. US journalists who are critical of the Salvadorean armed forces are now being denied visas.

**Physical attacks**: Extra-legal repression peaked in 1980-1984, a period which claimed the lives of eleven Salvadorean and ten foreign reporters—some of them in circumstances which indicated that they were targeted because of their reporting. But journalists, especially foreigners, continue to face physical peril.

On April 8, 1986, the Salvadorean army bombed and strafed the village of Arcatao in Chalatenango Department. The 'foreign mercenaries' they intended to capture turned out to be three fully accredited foreign journalists. The reporters were detained for eleven hours, their film, tapes and notes confiscated. After Army intelligence photocopied the notes and transcribed the tapes, these items were returned. In September 1986, three European journalists, also travelling within Chalatenango Department, were detained and their cassettes, notes and film confiscated by the military. The reporters were then turned over to the Treasury Police, who 'advised' them to leave the country.

On June 21, 1987, French journalist Lucas Mouzas, on assignment for *Radio Canada*, was arrested by armed forces in Chalatengango Department. The reporter had been accredited by COPREFA and granted permission to enter Chalatenango by the military's high command.

From August 1986 to June 1987, the military arrested some six foreign journalists, including the three Europeans already mentioned, and advised them to leave the country. An Italian photographer was held for five days without being permitted to eat or to speak to anyone.

### Freedom of opinion and expression

At present, the margins of freedom of expression appear to be tentatively and cautiously widening. When the Vice-Minister of Communications, Roberto Viero, visited the United States in early 1987, his agenda included the study of the relationship between the national media and the government; how the press reinforces the democratic process through its adversarial relationship with the government. But the Salvadorean government, seconded by the US Embassy and the State Department, has decried the bearers of bad news, be they the press, human rights organizations, or other groups, imputing to them a bias in favour of guerrillas fighting the government. These denunciations are all the more disturbing, given El Salvador's history of death squad activity against government critics.

The months of May and June 1987 were marked by reports of brutal army repression directed against peasants and union leaders suspected of leftist sympathies as well as the re-emergence of one of El Salvador's most notorious death squads, following an increase in political activity at the National University. The government's toleration of the media coverage of these events, which would once have gone unreported, is itself an important and encouraging development. Still, as of June 1987, there were more than 700 political prisoners in El Salvador, most held without trial, and many imprisoned solely for the non-violent expression of their political beliefs. Frequently, extra-judicial confessions are extracted through coercive interrogation, often including physical torture. In some cases, the government has broadcast these confessions, in effect conducting a trial by public opinion through the dissemination of false, biased, or unsubstantiated information.

**Restricted information**: The operations of the Ministry of Culture and Communications attempt to control freedom of expression and opinion. In 1985, President Duarte created the office and appointed his closest aide, Julio Adolfo Rey Prendes, as minister. The Ministry acts as the propaganda arm of the government, issuing communications to local newspapers, radio and television stations. The office concerns itself with managing the news, promoting the government's position and pressurizing its detractors.

When FDR criticisms of President Duarte's economic package were aired on a local radio station—a particularly sensitive political issue since the government's measures entailed hardships for the peasantry and working classes who formed the traditional basis of Christian Democratic support—the Ministry was quick to act. At January and February 1986 press conferences, Rey Prendes issued a call to self-censorship: the press could avoid stricter government measures later by judicious self-regulation, for 'faced with a war situation, we could take [measures] to a point where it's difficult to know where the limits are'.

Behind this threat loomed not only the prospect of overt government action under the then-existing state of siege, but also the withdrawal of government advertising, which constitutes 30 to 40 per cent of all advertising, according to statistics presented to the Association of Central American Newspapers (ARCA). *El Diario de Hoy*, which is antagonistic to the governing Christian Democrats from the right, has been particularly vocal on the use of government advertising as a restraint on speech, enlisting the support of the Inter-American Press Association in its efforts to obtain what it considers a fair share of government advertising.

Like the Ministry of Culture and Communications, the Press Committee of the Armed Forces engages in the practice of disinformation. A typical example occurred in January 1987, when, according to local inhabitants, seven civilians died in an Air Force bombing and strafing raid on an isolated peasant village. The Army Press Office denied both the attack and the loss of civilian lives. As evidence accumulated, however, the press office admitted the attack and the possibility of civilian casualties.

Such official conduct has become part of everyday life in El Salvador. Salvadoreans are denied an accurate picture of the most fundamental events that shape their futures. Although the increasing openness of the press is a reassuring development, the freedoms of expression and of opinion remain precarious.

## Current detainees

Included among those writers, journalists and media workers against whom action has been taken during the course of 1987 or who are still in prison: Edgar Mauricio Vallejo, journalist, disappeared; Cesar Najarro, journalist, disappeared; Jaime Suarez Quemain, journalist, disappeared; Amadeo Mendizabel, journalist, disappeared.

# HONDURAS

Freedom of expression is relatively untrammelled in Honduras compared to other Central American countries. The Honduran Constitution provides for free expression of thought disseminated through any medium and without prior censorship (Art. 72). Moreover, means for the broadcast or communication of information may not be seized, confiscated, closed, or interrupted for any misdemeanour or offence relating to the dissemination of thoughts and ideas (Art. 73). Freedom of thought and expression may not be restricted through indirect means of censorship, such as the abuse of government or private controls over newsprint and radio broadcasting frequencies (Art. 74).

|  |  | Year |
| --- | --- | --- |
| Population | 4,000,000 | 1985 |
| GNP ($ per capita) | 1,700 | 1984 |
| Illiteracy % | 40.5 | 1985 |
| Daily newspapers | 8 | est |
| Non Daily newspapers | 12 | est |
| Periodicals | 17 | est |
| Radio stations | 209 | 1985 |
| Radio receivers | 20,000 | 1985 |
| TV stations | 4 | 1985 |
| TV sets | 140,000 | 1985 |

Press Agencies:
  Asociacion de Prensa Hondurena

Covenant on Civil &
  Political Rights _____ Yes

However, prior censorship may be allowed to protect the ethical and cultural values of society as well as the rights of persons, especially children and young people (Art. 75).

The Honduran Constitution also guarantees freedom of association, provided its exercise is not 'contrary to the public policy or to public morals' (Art. 78). Individuals possess the right to peaceful assembly, without arms, in public demonstrations on behalf of their 'common interests of whatever nature', without the need for special permission (Art. 79). Despite these provisions, which are not without troubling qualifications, individuals have been detained and imprisoned for exercising their constitutional rights of association and expression.

**Licensing of journalists**: There are no statutory restraints on freedom of expression, such as prior censorship laws. Journalists are subject only to the Honduran press law on *Colegiación Obligatoria*, the requirement that reporters belong to a professional guild. In practice, however, the law has been employed in an effort to harass and silence domestic and foreign journalists, an effort in which both the government and the Honduran College of Journalists (CPH) have collaborated. A newspaper found liable for employing a non-licensed journalist may be subject to heavy fines, and its editors risk the loss of their accreditation. The outspoken *El Tiempo* has frequently faced prosecution under this law. Although it is by no means evident that the law was ever intended to apply to foreign journalists, the

# HONDURAS

May 1983 expulsion of *UPI* correspondent John Lantigua, who had publicized the existence of houses of torture and contra bases within Honduras, was justified on the grounds of his non-accreditation, as was the exclusion of the outspoken Juan Antonio de Lua, correspondent for the Spanish news agency *ACAN-EFE*.

Other Honduran laws have been invoked to quiet dissent. Anti-Terrorist Law 33, enacted in 1932 in reaction to heightened guerrilla activity, has been brought to bear against Honduras' active union movement. Peasant leaders have been especially hard hit by accusations of terrorism and sedition. Individuals failing to comply with the 1984 law requiring national identification cards have been treated by police as potential subversives.

## The Media

Despite the absence of formal censorship mechanisms, Honduran reporting on such sensitive issues as government policy and military corruption is often guarded. Criticism of the contras once aroused great controversy; it has recently become more acceptable, given the Honduran government's growing reluctance to continue providing a contra base. In the all-too-recent past, government retaliatory measures have forced the dismissal or expulsion of responsible journalists considered to have probed too deeply beneath false official accounts.

Even as reporters practise self-censorship out of caution, the ideologies of the various newspaper owners further narrow the range of public expression. As one dismissed reporter put it: 'Freedom of the press here belongs to the owners of the newspapers. They decide what gets printed.'

**Newspapers, radio and television**: Most news organs are owned by individuals with strong ties to the government or the military, and harsh criticism is rare. Carlos Flores Facusse, former Minister of the Presidency to the then President Suazo, owns *La Tribuna*. The paper is the voice of the conservative centre-right of the Liberal Party. *La Prensa* has the largest readership of the dailies with over 40,000. Along with *El Heraldo*, it is owned by Jorge Larach, who has strong ties to the military right wing and the Nationalist Party. Both papers are stridently anti-communist. *El Tiempo* is Honduras' most independent newspaper, with a tradition of reporting human rights abuses by the Honduran military and by the security forces (FUSEP) and their investigations bureau (DNI). The paper has the smallest circulation (20,000-25,000) and is owned by Honduran Vice-President Jaime Rosenthal.

The four papers combined reach a daily circulation of 150,000. The country's widespread illiteracy and extreme poverty contribute to these small newspaper runs. Given these conditions, radio is the primary source of news for many Hondurans, especially those living in rural areas. But here again the pressures exerted by the government and conservative owners invariably infringe upon the public's right to information. Three television stations and the largest radio network are owned by Manuel

Villeda Toledo and José Rafael Ferrari, men with strong ties to the military. Moreover, the government's control of licensing and broadcasting frequencies enables it to affect not only the content but also the range of radio news.

**Corruption**: The economic realities of journalism in Honduras make corruption routine. Salaries are so low that one publisher acknowledged that he assumed his reporters worked second jobs as a matter of economic necessity. Gifts and cash may be offered discreetly under the table, or more openly, as in the lavish Christmas presents bestowed by political leaders, gifts that would cost a Honduran reporter a month's salary. Such financial inducements inevitably affect coverage, quietly contributing to self-censorship as surely as pressures by newspaper owners or economic coercion by government advertisers. Moreover, given the government's past history of retaliatory action, the fear of dismissal operates as a form of financial repression. In Honduras, for every two to three positions that open yearly, whether in government, public relations, or with the press, the School of Journalism at the University of Honduras graduates ten to twenty students.

**Restrictions on journalists**: A number of means are employed to restrict journalists: access to press conferences, military bases, and emergency zones is denied; foreign journalists are expelled on immigration technicalities; newspaper and radio owners are pressurized into firing outspoken reporters; and journalists are bribed to print news favourable to the contra cause.

The Honduran Army restricts public access to border areas by military roadblocks. In addition, the public relations office of the armed forces issues the permits that authorize reporters' travels throughout the country.

The government cordons off whole areas as part of a strategy of information control (especially concerning contra bases) and also selectively restricts access based on reporter coverage. For example, in December 1986, the name of Gustavo Palencia was deleted from the list of journalists allowed to enter a sealed-off zone along the southern border. Palencia, an award-winning reporter for *El Tiempo*, is known for his hard-hitting questions on the contra and US presence. The military explained that the exclusion was based on the content of Palencia's reporting. When pressed further, Gen. Regalado, Chief of the Armed Forces, denounced Palencia as 'a Sandinista spy', a label routinely applied to journalists, foreign and domestic, whose coverage displeases the authorities. In response to the growing public outcry over the contra presence, the April 1986 issue of the military monthly *Proyecciones Militares* warned that the local press corps had been infiltrated by terrorists.

**Foreign journalists**: In the past the Honduran authorities have resorted to technicalities in the immigration laws to expel foreign journalists who report on embarrassing or sensitive topics perceived as denigrating the image of the country. Gillian Brown, a British journalist who heads *Insite*

*Video*, was detained by immigration officials on Aug. 14, 1986, and expelled the next day. Brown's expulsion followed the release of 'The Pentagon Republic', a controversial documentary she had produced on US involvement in Honduras.

Between 1982 and 1984 at least five dismissals of journalists occurred in circumstances suggesting official involvement. More recently, in September 1986, Laura Brooks, a stringer for the *Voice of America*, was fired without explanation. There are indications that Brooks was fired on the recommendation of officials of the National Security Council after it received reports that Brooks had Sandinista sympathies.

**Disinformation allegations**: In an affidavit to the International Court of Justice in 1985, Edgar Chamorro, a former contra spokesman, stated that he had served as paymaster, receiving and disbursing CIA funds to ensure reporting favourable to the contras and hostile to the Sandinistas. Chamorro claimed that some fifteen Honduran journalists and broadcasters were on the CIA payroll, and that its influence extended to every major newspaper and radio station. A former State Department policy-maker has described the CIA activities as 'psychological operations', disseminated by the local media and calculated to excite fears of a Sandinista invasion and life under communist rule. These allegations, however, remain otherwise unsubstantiated.

## Restrictions on freedom of opinion and expression

Until the ousting of Gen. Álvarez as Chief of the Armed Forces in March 1984 extra-legal restraints sharply curtailed the exercise of fundamental rights of dissent and association. From 1980 to 1984, the Army High Command appears to have maintained a network of secret cells, special interrogators, and kidnapping teams; assassinations and disappearances rose to levels unprecedented in Honduran history, with the Committee for the Defence of Human Rights in Honduras (CODEH) reporting 147 disappearances between 1979 and 1984. Nicaraguans and Salvadoreans with left-wing ties and Hondurans suspected of collaboration were targeted; however, the Nicaraguan connection also provided a convenient pretext for the repression of reform-minded Hondurans, including students, trade union activists, political leaders and attorneys. Harassment of the independent *El Tiempo* was particularly severe, with its reporters and photographers subjected to detentions, physical assaults, raids and confiscations.

Although the campaign of abductions, torture, and executions conducted by official death squads has come to a near end, illegal detentions and abusive interrogations continue. On Jan. 26, 1987, Vicente Aaron Carrera Iturralde, the Panamanian writer and editor of the magazine *Diálogo Social*, was detained, subjected to psychological torture, then deported the following day. The Honduran government claimed he was detained for attempting to smuggle subversive literature into the country.

On May 31, 1987, members of the Seventh Infantry Battalion arrested Rosa Dilia Rivera, leader of the Peasant Women's Joint Development Committee, a private group which seeks to promote the development and welfare of women in rural Honduras. According to the armed forces public relations office, Rivera was detained because she was carrying a large number of subversive documents and communist indoctrination literature, 'material which goes against our republican and democratic lifestyle'.

**Death squads**: A limited form of death squad activity resurfaced in 1986 and 1987. Victims included a leading radio journalist, a prominent labour activist, and a conservative major daily. On Aug. 4, 1986, Rodrigo Wong Arévalo, the popular liberal commentator on *Radio America*, was the target of a car bombing. Wong is well known for his sharp commentaries on government and military corruption, the US and contra presence, the Sandinista government, and human rights abuses. On Jan. 14, 1987, Leonora Meza was subjected to a bombing attack, preceded by anonymous death threats. The incident followed the publication of a double-page advertisement in a local newspaper, placed by Meza's union, which announced that during her visit to the United States she had called for the withdrawal of US troops from Honduras. On two different dates, bombs were placed at *La Prensa*, a Tegucigalpa daily that pursues a conservative editorial line. The newspaper carries a weekly supplement edited by Nicaraguan journalist (and now contra leader) Pedro Joaquín Chamorro. No group claimed responsibility for these bombings, and no pattern is evident.

In August 1986, an unsigned death list denouncing the 'Honduran revolutionary leadership' circulated, the first of its kind in years. Some seventeen left politicians, human rights activists, journalists, academics and labour leaders were named, including Victor Meza, a prominent intellectual, *El Tiempo* columnist and human rights activist, and Guatama Fonseca, a *La Tribuna* reporter. Both reporters have objected to the contra bases in Honduras. Jorge Arturo Reina, one of the political party leaders named, stated his belief that the list had been drawn up by a faction within the military to encourage private rightist groups to attack critics of the government's foreign policy. The army denied any knowledge of the list. Though none of the named individuals has been physically harmed, the prospect of political violence may well silence the expression of opposition views and so limit the range of public opinion and debate.

Freedom of expression and opinion in Honduras cannot truly be enjoyed until the government and the military recognize the right of the public to be fully and fairly informed. Given the economic circumstances under which Honduran journalists work—the low pay and the scarcity of positions—the fear of financial reprisals and the lure of financial inducements operate nearly as effectively as formal censorship mechanisms in restricting and shaping the news that the public receives. The result is a complementary system of self-censorship and official disinformation, whose subtlety makes it all the more difficult to challenge.

# HONDURAS

In the light of these conditions, Honduras's constitutional provisions provide a hope for the future rather than reflect the practice of the present. 'Those who by direct or indirect means restrict or limit the communication and circulation of ideas shall be liable before the law', according to Article 72.

# MEXICO

Freedom of expression and of the press are guaranteed by the federal Constitution, but such legal guarantees are sidestepped by the systematic and conscious use of economic and political mechanisms.

Article 6 of the Constitution states: 'The expression of ideas will not be the object of any judicial or administrative inquisition....'

In 1977 ten words were added to this Article, stating that 'the right of information will be guaranteed by the State'. Attempts to introduce enabling legislation in the early 1980s failed due to the opposition of media owners and editors, who opposed wider access to information. There is a virtual monopoly of ownership of mass media. In 1984 there were 118 television stations, of which over 100 were controlled by *Televisa*, the private television monopoly.

| | | Year |
|---|---|---|
| Population | 79,000,000 | 1986 |
| GNP ($ per capita) | 2,060 | 1984 |
| Illiteracy % | 9.7 | 1985 |

| | | |
|---|---|---|
| Daily newspapers | 52 | est |
| Non Daily newspapers | 46 | est |
| Periodicals | 50 | est |
| Published books | 4,505 | 1984 |
| Radio stations | 868 | 1984 |
| Radio receivers | 2,150,000 | 1986 |
| TV stations | 128 | 1984 |
| TV sets | 8,021,000 | 1986 |

Press Agencies: Notimex

| | |
|---|---|
| Covenant on Civil & Political Rights | 1981 |

Article 7 declares against censorship: 'The freedom to write and publish on any matter cannot be violated. No law or authority can establish prior censorship ... nor can it violate the freedom of printing....' These guarantees are nevertheless limited by the Printing Law (*Ley de Imprenta*), and are subject to the protection of privacy, private life, public health and morals.

Miguel Angel Granados Chapa, Deputy Director of *La Jornada*, observes: 'There has not been a single case in which [the Printing Law] has been applied, due perhaps to the particular relationship which exists between the government and the press, a relationship based on an understanding which makes its application unnecessary. It is not even used in cases of obscene publications.'

Instead, 'clean-up campaigns' take place. A few magazines go out of circulation only to appear later under different titles and with new boards of directors. This does not occur when the material that offends government is regarded as political; when a critical journalist is called to appear in court, the imputed crimes generally bear no relation to his work as a journalist. The media are also regulated by the Organic Law of Public Education, 1951, which regulates *modesta* (decency) in publications and illustrated magazines.

# MEXICO

A much-debated provision of the Constitution (Article 130) stipulates that religious orders are prohibited from publishing on national political issues and from criticizing national institutions. Those taking religious orders also lack the right to vote or to be elected.

## The Media

The Ministry of the Interior is the government's main media watchdog, and has been criticized as a potential Orwellian Ministry of Truth because of the scope of its powers and activities, carried out either directly or through agencies under its control. It has the monopoly on the production and distribution of newsprint; it formulates, regulates and implements the communication policy of the federal government, and of the state governments for the print and electronic media; it oversees the printed media—newspapers, magazines and books—through the *Comisión Calificadora de Publicaciones y Revistas Ilustradas*; it issues printing certificates; it grants permits and monitors national and provincial broadcasting; it produces, distributes, shows and censors films; it is responsible for liaison with the mass media. Its brief 'regarding the orientation, supervision and evaluation of the printing media, be it national or international' is 'to make sure that information meets the estabished norms'.

**Censorship and advertising**: Censorship is exercised through a number of channels. Among the most powerful are advertising, and the subsidy and distribution of paper.

Since newspapers obtain their profits mainly from selling advertising, both commercial and political, it is a direct mechanism with immediate effects. Advertisers exercise censorship on the media through the withdrawal of advertising. This is usually done in conjunction with other companies as a form of boycott bringing the 'guilty' newspaper to a situation in which its commercial standing is open to question.

An example of this is the action taken by *Televisa* and other commercial enterprises against *Excélsior* between 1972 and 1974. The same newspaper suffered a similar fate in 1976 when commercial interests withdrew their advertising because of *Excélsior*'s alleged left-wing stance.

It is on government advertising, however, that the press is particularly dependent. It constitutes two-thirds of all available advertising. Miguel Angel Granados Chapa suggests: 'Newspaper profitability does not lie in the number of copies sold. On the contrary, it lies in printing the least number of copies as the main souce of income is publicity, especially government publicity, which does not bear any relation to the prestige and/or influence of a given newspaper.' This, says Jesús Cantú, Director of *El Porvenir*, a Monterrey-based newspaper, has given rise to 'the proliferation of dailies as all of them are sure that the government will give them publicity, credit, exempt them from tax duties, erase their debts, grant them favours, and in some cases will include them in its payroll, regardless of the size of their readership' as was the case with *El Periodico*.

99

Newspapers bent on incurring the government's wrath can expect no such privileged treatment. In 1982, the government of López Portillo withdrew official advertising from the magazine *Proceso*, saying it would not finance the battering that the magazine was giving it. The publicity boycott quickly led to the closure of *Proceso*'s associated news agency *CISA* (the only independent news agency in Mexico).

Nevertheless there is a tolerated critical press. The PRT (Trotskyist) newspaper is partly subsidized from government funds (under the law on political parties) and opposition press organs are sometimes covertly subsidized (like *Sucesos* and the scurrilous *Porqué* in the past).

**Censorship and newsprint**: Censorship in Mexico is institutionalized through the *Productora e Importadora de Papel, S.A.* (PIPSA). Its creation and continued existence is full of ironies. Due to the relative scarcity and high cost of newsprint, which has always troubled the newspaper industry in Mexico, newspapers proprietors approached President Lázaro Cárdenas in 1935 to suggest the creation of a company (in which the state would have 90 per cent of shares) that would guarantee them a regular supply of newsprint at stable prices. PIPSA was soon being used to put pressure on newspapers to change their editorial policy.

Through PIPSA, the state is able not only to pressurize a newspaper into changing its editorial policy, but also to provoke its disappearance by not supplying it with paper or by not supplying it on time. The growth of a newspaper can also be controlled by reducing the amount of paper supplied. In these circumstances, many newspapers, big and small, faced with the danger of closing down due to lack of paper, prefer to correct their ways.

But toeing the line may bring some 'privileges'. PIPSA can supply newsprint on credit or at lower than average prices; if unable to pay, a newspaper's debts may be forgotten for as long as it does not become known as an organ of social criticism. To act as a social critic was *Proceso*'s brief when it was first launched in November 1976. As a result, its first issue could not be produced with paper supplied by PIPSA. This constituted a government attempt to kill this new venture at birth.

Paradoxically, the government has attempted to close down PIPSA on two occasions, but desisted due to requests by newspaper editors. One such occasion was after the tragic events of Oct. 2, 1968, when President Díaz Ordaz dissolved PIPSA. But he re-established it on April 1, 1970 for another thirty years. Consequently, no newspaper, with the exception of *Excélsior*, mentioned the massacre of Tlatelolco ever again, attacking instead the image of the university student.

Alejandro Junco de la Vega, Director of the Monterrey- based newspaper *El Norte*, points out that due to Mexico's recently acquired membership of GATT, newsprint will be freely imported into Mexico from the summer of 1988, presumably giving newspapers the choice of two suppliers and thus greater freedom vis-à-vis the state.

**Notimex**: The national press agency *Notimex* has a significant role in determining the news content of provincial papers. Originally established as the National Information Agency, it has now become the vehicle which distributes government advertising among the provincial newspapers. A provincial newspaper which wishes to acquire government publicity has as a prerequisite to subscribe to *Notimex* and adopt its line of information.

**New technology**: Further means of exercising censorship include the granting or withholding of permits to import machinery, the certificate of legality as well as the considerable number of prerogatives granted to newspapers by political and economic groups. Thus towards the end of the Echeverría administration, *El Universal* acquired, thanks to government support, the latest newspaper technology, as well as extending its premises.

In 1984, the General Communication Law was amended to give the state 'exclusive control over satellite technology, which includes the installation and operation of the spatial artefacts as well as of land- based stations with international links for communication via satellite'. The press and television have been affected differently by this action. Independent newspapers are in practice denied access to the Morelos satellite as the state allocates hours of use and has the right to vet the personnel in charge of operations. *Televisa*, under an agreement signed with the Transport and Communication Ministry during the López Portillo administration, has access free of charge and the right to exploit this new technology commercially through producing and selling satellite dishes.

**Newspaper circulation**: The government's concentration on the press is all the more surprising when one considers that in a country of eighty million people, total national newspaper circulation is less than one million a day. Circulation claimed by newspapers is known to be wildly exaggerated to attract advertising revenue. There are no exact figures but there is evidence to suggest that seemingly influential 'national' newspapers like *Novedades* or *El Sol de México* have a circulation of less than ten thousand. A newspaper like *Excélsior*, established seventy years ago and today considered to be the most influential newspaper in Mexico, does not sell more than five thousand copies in Guadalajara and Monterrey, the two main cities after Mexico City itself. Newspaper circulation in Mexico is extraordinarily low even when compared to other Latin American countries. This contrasts with the fifteen to twenty million people who watch the television news every night, the great majority of whom watch *Televisa*'s main news programme '*24 Horas*'.

## Journalism

**Bribing of journalists**: The government's obsession with the press is perhaps most clearly seen in its government's 'informal' dealings with journalists and editors. Journalists are almost all freelance and paid by the line; for staff journalists, pay scales are low ($120 per month starting salary in Mexico City, less in the provinces) and this, coupled with poor and weak trade union organization, has given rise to a custom of accepting

101

bribes from politicians, officials and businessmen in exchange for favourable coverage.

Fernando Cantú, Editor of *La Opinión*, estimates that 90 per cent of all Mexican reporters accept some kind of pay-offs on the side; 'a reporter who rejects bribes is called stupid by his colleagues'. A front page story favourable to a Ministry can mean cash for the reporter. Alternatively, journalists can sell advertising for commissions of 10-15 per cent to supplement their salaries.

If the offer of payments fails to produce the desired results, a discreet telephone call from the Interior Ministry may result in the omission of disagreeable news, or brief or soft treatment. Unco-operative editors may just be banned from Los Pinos, the President's official residence. At present Julio Scherer García, *Proceso*'s Director, is out of favour at Los Pinos.

**Attacks on journalists**: The National Centre of Social Communication, Cencos, stated in a recent report that there were 152 cases of attacks on journalists between 1984 and 1986, including twelve murders. Susan Benesch, who monitors Latin America for the New York-based Committee to Protect Journalists, observes that 'the number of journalists killed in Mexico in the last few years is really much higher than anywhere else in Latin America except Colombia'. Forty-two journalists were killed in Mexico between 1971 and June 1987, twenty-five of them since the December 1983 inauguration of the de la Madrid administration, which promised a 'moral renewal of society'. It is often difficult to determine the motive behind the crime—whether the journalist was killed in connection with his professional activities or for some other reason. Nevertheless, no one has ever been convicted.

In March 1985, the political magazine *Contenido* ceased publication, allegedly because of government warnings that its political coverage was offensive and dangerous to the public interest. Notable among the articles in the last issue was extensive coverage of former President López Portillo's claim that he had profited personally from his term in office. As Janette Becerra, a reporter for the newspaper *Unomásuno*, says: 'We learn how far you can go. There are sacred cows you have to avoid. Going too deeply into some subjects can even be dangerous.'

The Cencos report details inexplicable accidents, physical aggression, threats, persecutions, hostile campaigns, economic boycott, cancelled programmes, staff sackings, break-ins, arrests, thefts, kidnappings and torture and other measures. The overwhelming majority of these incidents have occurred in the provinces, affecting national newspapers only occasionally. This may be explained by a characteristic of the Mexican press cited by Jesús Cantú: its centralism. As most of the national press activity is focused on the figure of the omnipotent President, provincial newspapers gain a degree of freedom vis-à-vis the federal authorities. Yet by concentrating on regional or local issues, the provincial press runs the risk of clashing with *caciques* (local bosses) or gangsters (nowadays engaged mainly in drug trafficking) who tend to behave in a more violent and aggressive manner than politicians. The violent death of the Director and a reporter of the Matamoros-based newspaper *El Popular* in 1986 is a case in point: they had accused a local boss of drug trafficking and as a result were gunned down outside the newspaper offices.

Foreign colleagues have criticized Mexican journalists for writing articles which would almost certainly be ruled libellous by courts in many other countries (i.e. 'he has ten Rolls-Royces in his garage', no source quoted, no facts checked); but as the Manuel Buendía case suggests, even when (or perhaps because) detailed investigative journalism is conducted, a journalist's life is no less at risk. And as has been said more than once in Mexico, if they killed Buendía, they can kill almost anybody.

Nevertheless, unlike television which over the last thirty years has increasingly presented a more monolithic view of the world, press in Mexico, despite signs to the contrary, is now more open and more diverse in its content than twenty years ago. But as Alan Riding comments in 'Distant Neighbours': 'Considering that a combative and independent press would be incompatible with the system as it functions, recent governments have adjusted the limits of freedom of the press to their own needs.'

### Current detainees

Included among those writers, journalists and media workers against whom action has been taken during the course of 1987 or who are still in prison: Jorge Enrique Hernández Aguilar, journalist, held in detention since May 1986; Israel Gutiérrez Hernández, poet, sentenced to ten years' imprisonment; Juan Valdez, writer and poet, imprisoned.

# NICARAGUA

According to the new Nicaraguan Constitution which went into effect in January 1987, 'Nicaraguans have the right to express freely their beliefs in public or private, individually or collectively, in oral, written or any other form' (Art. 30).

The provision of the new Constitution protecting freedom of expression was suspended as soon as it went into effect, however, by the promulgation of a state of emergency. Nicaragua has been governed under emergency decrees since Mar. 15, 1982, and while the decrees in effect at particular times have varied in some respects, all have suspended freedom of the press.

On Aug. 7, 1987, President Daniel Ortega of Nicaragua and four other Central American presidents signed the Esquipulas II peace plan which provides that, as part of the process of establishing peace in the region, 'it will be understood that there shall exist complete freedom of press, television and radio. This complete freedom will include the opening and maintaining in operation of communications media for all ideological groups and the operation of these media without prior censorship'.

|  |  | Year |
|---|---|---|
| Population | 3,000,000 | 1981 |
| GNP ($ per capita) | 870 | 1984 |
| Illiteracy % | 12.0 | 1981 |
| Daily newspapers | 8 | est |
| Non Daily newspapers | } 6 | est |
| Periodicals | | |
| Published books | 26 | 1984 |
| Radio stations | 12 | est |
| Radio receivers | 200,000 | 1985 |
| TV stations | 1 | est |
| TV sets | 160,000 | 1985 |

Press Agencies: Agencia Nicaraguense de Noticias (ANN)

Covenant on Civil & Political Rights _____ 1980

Complete political pluralism should be manifest. In this regard, political groupings should have broad access to communications media, full exercise of the right of association and the right to manifest publicly the exercise of their right to free speech, be it oral, written or televised, as well as freedom of movement by members of political parties in order to proselytize.

In addition, the peace plan provided that the governments in the region would end states of emergency.

Pursuant to the plan, the Nicaraguan government announced in September 1987 that the opposition newspaper *La Prensa*, which it closed fifteen months earlier, would be permitted to re-open and would not be subjected to prior censorship. It also announced that *Radio Católica*, the church radio station shut down twenty-one months earlier, would be permitted to resume broadcasting. *La Prensa* began to publish at the

104

beginning of October 1987 and *Radio Católica* resumed broadcasting three weeks later.

The Nicaraguan government did not end the state of emergency but announced on Nov. 5, 1987 that it would do so when the United States stopped aid to forces seeking to overthrow it (the contras) and when Honduras stopped providing them with bases. Those steps are also required by the peace plan.

From shortly after the time that the Sandinista government took power in July 1979 until the imposition of the first state of emergency in March 1982, the relationship between the country's oldest and largest circulation newspaper, *La Prensa*, and the government had been antagonistic. On several occasions, the government had ordered the newspaper to be closed for one- or two-day periods as a reprisal for articles that were deemed offensive.

After March 15, 1982, prior censorship was imposed on all printed media in Nicaragua. Censorship was justified by the government because of the emergency created by the war in which the contras, based in Honduras and to a lesser extent in Costa Rica, with extensive overt and covert support from the United States, have conducted military operations against the Sandinista government. In theory, censorship was supposed to be limited to matters related to the emergency; that is, information that could endanger national security or engender panic— such as accounts of food shortages that could lead to hoarding.

In practice, however, the items excised by the censor were not confined in this manner. Almost anything that could be considered embarrassing to the Sandinista government was prohibited.

Since March 1982, Nicaragua has had three daily newspapers: *La Prensa; El Nuevo Diario,* a privately-owned newspaper that has been pro-Sandinista; and *Barricada,* the official newspaper of the Sandinista Party (FSLN). All three were edited and managed by members of the same family, the Chamorros.

All three newspapers were submitted to the official censor for prior review. Items from *Barricada* and *El Nuevo Diario* were occasionally removed by the censors; the editors of *La Prensa* claimed that they were regularly required to delete at least 40 per cent of their material. On occasion, *La Prensa* refused to publish, saying that so much had been censored that it did not have enough material to produce an issue. The newspapers were forbidden to follow practices such as *La Prensa* had adopted in response to censorship by the Somozas. In those days, *La Prensa* had adopted the practice of running photographs of actress Ava Gardner to fill spaces that would have been left blank by the deletion of material removed by the censors. Newsboys would call attention to the censorship by hawking their wares to the cry of 'Ava Gardner! Ava Gardner!'. The Sandinistas forbade the use of any practices that would call attention to censorship.

Censorship was relaxed considerably in 1984 during a four-month period leading up to national elections during November. After the elections in which Daniel Ortega was elected President and a National Assembly was chosen in which the FSLN won about two thirds of the seats, censorship again became somewhat more free-wheeling. Another period of relative relaxation in censorship took place in mid-1985, but that came to an end on Oct. 15, 1985, with the renewal of a state of emergency.

About the time that the state of emergency was renewed, the Roman Catholic Church of Nicaragua launched a new magazine, *Iglesia*. The first issue was confiscated on Oct. 12, 1985, apparently because it contained material that was harshly critical of compulsory military service. *Iglesia* has not appeared subsequently; the official reason was that the Church had not sought permission to start up a new publication. In January 1986, the government closed down *Radio Católica*, ostensibly because it had failed to broadcast Ortega's year-end speech to the nation (all Nicaraguan radio stations were expected to broadcast it live).

Some thirty or more radio news programmes are currently broadcast in Nicaragua, only one of them state-run. These news broadcasts are not subject to prior censorship, but the producers are subject to sanctions for what they broadcast and, in practice, prior to the signing of the peace plan, did not engage in harsh criticism of the government or venture far into fields that are considered off-limits. Approximately another twenty news broadcasts were shut down, some at government direction, others because the broadcasters left the country. It is widely believed that many of those will begin broadcasting again in the post-Esquipulas II era. A *Radio Católica* news programme was not permitted to resume immediately when the station reopened in October 1987 because the station had not sought the required permission.

Television is state-run. During the 1984 electoral campaign, opposition candidates were provided with free access to radio and television. Aside from that period, opponents of the government have largely been excluded from these media. Following the adoption of the peace plan, an opposition group announced it would try to establish a television station. This has not proceeded and there has been no indication so far whether the government would license it.

In June 1986, in immediate reaction to its coverage of a vote by the US House of Representatives appropriating $100 million in aid to the contras, the government closed *La Prensa*. At the time, the government cited the paper's acceptance of $100,000 from the US National Fund for Democracy as a justification for closing the newspaper. Since reopening at the beginning of October 1987, *La Prensa* has published without difficulty though it acknowledged when it reopened that it had obtained a total of some $254,000 from US government sources.

The government has also closed down various newsletters. On Jan. 15, 1986, for example, the editors of the *Solidaridad* newsletter, a publication of the CUS labour union, were summoned to appear at state security headquarters in Managua. The same persons, and some others, had also been publishing another newsletter, *Prisma*. The two publications were shut down because they had not been registered with the government and the editors were jailed for several days.

In November 1985, the Permanent Committee for Human Rights (CPDH) was notified that its bulletins must be submitted to the Ministry of the Interior for prior censorship. After protests by international human rights groups, the Minister of the Interior, Tomás Borge, backed down and said that copies of CPDH's bulletins need only be sent to the Ministry at the time they are circulated generally. At the time of writing CPDH's bulletins continue to be circulated without difficulty.

Other forms of expression have also been curbed in Nicaragua. Under the states of emergency in effect since March 1982, outdoor assemblies without explicit advance authorization have been prohibited, except during the four-month electoral period in 1984. Following the signing of the Esquipulas plan, however, outdoor assemblies were again permitted and several opposition political rallies were held in Managua and other cities without interference. Previously, exceptions were made for some religious parades. Indoor meetings have been permitted without prior notification of the authorities.

Considerable controversy prevails over the number of arrests that have been made for the peaceful expression of political views. No law authorizes such arrests. Critics of the government, however, claim that the Law for the Maintenance of Public Order (Decree 1074) has been used extensively to punish peaceful dissent. The government asserts that arrests under this law have been aimed at those active in contra support networks, and that dissent *per se* is not punished.

In fact, it appears that the majority of those arrested under this law since 1982 have been peasants residing in areas in which the contras have been active and who are suspected of aiding the contras by providing them with intelligence, food or medical attention, or by shielding their movements from the armed forces. It is virtually impossible to determine without a case-by-case analysis (which has not been undertaken) whether suspicion of providing such assistance to the contras is based on peaceful dissent or something more substantial. On Nov. 5, 1987, the government announced that it would be releasing 981 prisoners as part of its compliance with the peace plan. Most of these were expected to be peasants accused of aiding the contras.

Between November 1985 and January 1986 the government arrested several known political opponents, many of them residents of the capital and other urban areas. Few of these persons were brought to trial under the Law for the Maintenance of Public Order. Most were freed after detention from one to thirty days; some were held longer. These seem to be the clearest instances of arrest for peaceful political dissent in the last several years. There have been a number of subsequent arrests which appear to fall into this category, but there has not been a repetition of such a sweeping round-up.

It is not yet clear whether the peace plan will succeed. If it does, it will put the government to the test of demonstrating its contention that the restrictions on civil liberties will disappear when the military threat to its survival comes to an end. Though peace has not yet been established, substantial headway has been made in ending the restrictions on expression that have prevailed for five and a half years, and that were most sweeping in the year or so immediately preceding the signing of the plan.

# PARAGUAY

Gen. Alfredo Stroessner came to power in 1954 through a coup which put an end to a period of political instability following the civil war of 1947. Since then he has forged a system of military rule which has managed until recently to insulate itself from the processes of political democratization which cleared neighbouring countries of dictatorships during the first half of the 1980s. Stroessner is still the official candidate of the ruling Colorado Party for the presidential elections scheduled for February 1988.

| | | Year |
|---|---:|---|
| Population | 3,000,000 | 1984 |
| GNP ($ per capita) | 1,250 | 1984 |
| Illiteracy % | 12.5 | 1982 |
| Daily newspapers | 5 | 1982 |
| Non Daily newspapers } | 18 | est |
| Periodicals } | | |
| Radio stations | 12 | est |
| Radio receivers | 624,000 | 1986 |
| TV stations | 4 | est |
| TV sets | 231,000 | 1986 |
| Covenant on Civil & Political Rights _____ | | NO |

**The state of siege**: The republican Constitution of Paraguay, drawn up in 1967, in which 'sovereignty' is formally deemed to lie exclusively in the people, declares that dictatorship is unlawful. However it also contains provisions in its Articles 79 and 181 giving the President powers to proclaim a state of siege in the case of 'international conflict or war, external invasion, internal commotion, or in the case of a grave threat of any of these'. According to the Constitution, exceptional powers can be invoked for a limited period only. In fact, most of Stroessner's rule—from 1954 to April 1987—has been carried out under a state of siege which was justified by the supposed threat of 'communist subversion' and thus renewed every ninety days. In this way exceptional government became the norm, and a constitutional provision became the excuse for thirty-three years of unconstitutional rule.

A state of siege enables the government to arrest any persons suspected of subversion, and to prohibit public meetings and demonstrations. It has allowed the Stroessner regime to silence all opposition and criticism as it pleases, including the sending into exile, arrest, torture and imprisonment without trial of countless journalists, writers and cultural producers of all kinds.

**Constitutional guarantees**: Freedom of thought and opinion are formally guaranteed, as are freedom of expression and information and freedom of the press. Each constitutional article, however, contains a series of caveats, ranging from the quite specific to the very vague, which seriously undermine its significance. For example, Article 71 guaranteeing freedom of thought qualifies this by maintaining: 'It will not be permitted to preach hatred among Paraguayans, nor class struggle, nor make apologies for crime or violence. Criticism of the law is permitted, but no one is allowed to preach disobedience....' Article 72 guaranteeing freedom of expression and information is also subject to some qualifications, and is circumscribed by the proviso that in time of war information relating to national defence may be censored. A periodical may not operate without a 'responsible director' and 'the publication of immoral material' is not permitted.

These constitutional provisions, combined with the state of siege, gave Stroessner the ability to silence opposition at will. There also exist further controls in criminal law which, although similar in their effects, differ in form, since the responsibility for their observance lies with the judiciary and not the government. Nevertheless, the end result is the same because of the de facto violation of the constitutional guarantee of the independence of the judiciary and its subordination to the government and the Colorado Party.

**Law 294**: Passed in 1955, in the international context of the Cold War, this restricts freedom of opinion, belief and expression, and imposes limits on the political and ideological pluralism of the country by making membership of the Communist Party, and belief in or adhesion to communist ideology, a criminal offence. No public institution, nor any private enterprise which has any dealings with the public sector, may employ those who are 'ostensibly or secretly' members of the Communist Party. The government is empowered to close down any teaching institution that employs such people. This law encourages employees to inform on colleagues who they know to be communist. The penalties for not doing so include dismissal or even imprisonment.

**Law 209**: Passed in 1970, this law is directed at the expression of certain beliefs and opinions and the right to disseminate them. It has become the main legal instrument of the state's repressive apparatus. Any person who through any means 'publicly preaches hatred among Paraguayans or the destruction of social classes' is liable to one to six years' imprisonment. The law is of such vagueness that any form of critical thought is liable to be subject to its all-inclusive provisions. In practice it encourages and promotes self-censorship within all media.

## The Media

According to a list drawn up by local journalists, between 1968 and March 1984 there were approximately seventy-five instances of government interference with the media. These include the harassment, arrest and deportation of journalists and editors, and the temporary or permanent closure of newspapers and magazines.

There are two television channels and approximately fifty radio stations in Paraguay. Both television channels are controlled by the government, and neither allows critical news to be aired. During election campaigns opposition candidates are not allowed to broadcast their views. Almost all the newspapers take an openly pro-government line. One (*El Diario Nacional*) is owned by a personal friend of Stroessner, and another two (*Hoy* and *La Tarde*) by his ex-son-in-law. *Última Hora* is perhaps the most independent newspaper, although it too has been attacked by the government's propaganda machinery on many occasions, once for publishing reports on conditions in a state hospital.

*Sendero* is a weekly newspaper published by the Catholic Church. *El Pueblo* was the weekly newspaper of the social democratic Febrerista Party; it gave extensive coverage to the opposition movements, and alongside *Sendero* it was the only voice critical of Stroessner. The paper was closed down towards the end of 1987 for allegedly 'preaching hatred among Paraguayans'. *Patria* is the newspaper of the Colorado Party.

**ABC Color**: None of the above, however, could match the reputation for investigative journalism enjoyed by *ABC Color*, which had a daily circulation of approximately 80,000, or double that of its nearest competitor, *Última Hora*. *ABC Color*'s first issue appeared in August 1967, and while at first it was cautious in its criticisms, it became bolder in its coverage of government policy and official corruption. It also provided a space for the views of opposition politicians and peasant movement leaders. The newspaper was closed down by the government on March 22, 1984, the final step in a campaign which had lasted for several months, and which had included the arrest and detention of several of its journalists, police harassment and interference with the paper's distribution, and violent attacks against it by the official radio network, especially in its national broadcast 'The Voice of Coloradismo'. Finally, Aldo Zucolillo, the Editor, was briefly detained and told that *ABC Color* would be closed for 'an indefinite period'. *ABC Color* has not appeared since.

**Radio Ñandutí**: The few radio stations which have taken an independent line have had a history of almost uninterrupted harassment. *Radio Primero de Marzo* has had one of its journalists banned from broadcasting, and in June 1986 the Catholic *Radio Cáritas* lost its Director, Father Arancon, when he was refused re-entry into the country after a brief visit to Argentina. In the words of its owner, Humberto Rubín, *Radio Ñandutí* 'was a committed radio station, broadcasting the views of the people ... it instituted a national dialogue'. Since it came off the air its headquarters have been the venue for symposia and other meetings in which the most pressing political questions of the day are debated. This has made it one of the most important cultural institutions in Paraguay.

Government harassment of the station began in July 1983 when it was forced to close for a month. The government claimed: 'Its broadcasts systematically disrupt public order and create alarm.... It has become the means by which unscrupulous persons confuse public opinion and put the peace of the nation at risk.' Indeed, Rubín had already been asked by officials of *Antelco*, the national telecommunications agency, to change his

111

journalistic line. What concerned them most were the station's 'open microphone' (*superonda*) programmes. Live telephone interviews with opposition politicians, labour leaders, and even people in the streets, which were critical of the government, were transmitted. The station re-opened in August 1983. Soon afterwards one of its phone-in programmes was banned. In January 1984 Rubín was briefly detained. In November he was prohibited from personally going on the air. In August 1985 the station was closed down for another ten days.

In 1986 the radio station covered the upsurge of popular protest in the streets of Asunción and in rural areas. *Radio Ñandutí* was very popular in both Asunción and the surrounding country—it was one of the only independent stations to broadcast beyond the capital. In response, government supporters attacked its headquarters twice. During the first attack, on April 29, shots were fired and the assailants were accompanied by a group of musicians playing the Colorado Party's anthem.

Since then Rubín has tried to resume broadcasting. The Supreme Court, however, issued a decree stating that since *Radio Ñandutí* had 'stopped' broadcasting it would have to apply for a licence to go on the air again. This has not as yet been granted. In challenging this decision, Rubín maintains that he did not 'stop', but merely 'suspended' broadcasting given that the station was subject to constant harassment and intimidation.

**Banco Paraguayo de Datos**: The BPD, an independent socio-economic research centre, was raided by police in May 1983, and around thirty users of the centre, including several journalists, were arrested under Law 209. The publishing activities of the BPD were halted, although a hunger strike and pressure from human rights groups led eventually to the release of the detainees, several of whom had been tortured and accused of terrorist activities.

## New laws

In April 1987 the state of siege provisions were not renewed by the government. It might have been hoped that this signalled some kind of 'opening' for improvements with regard to freedom of expression. Law 294, and especially Law 209, however, still remain on the statute book, and the closure of *El Pueblo* in August 1987, together with the arrest of the Febrerista leader Fernando Vera after his protest at the closure of his party's paper, reveals that this was not to be the case. In addition, the projected introduction of new laws seems likely to make matters worse. The first of these projected new laws guarantees the 'right to reply'; the second involves the drafting of a new Penal Code, which incorporates into ordinary law those powers made available by the state of siege and Law 209.

The 'Right of Reply' law appears to be modelled on a similar law introduced in Spain, where it was well received. Reading its provisions in the context of a Stroessner state in which the judiciary is completely subordinated to the executive powers of the state, however, this law has given rise to concern. In order to 'safeguard human rights, especially those of the weak', it offers all citizens the right to reply to any mention of themselves in any means of communciation which they deem to be inaccurate or damaging. However, it extends this right to the 'public powers' in the case of 'the diffusion of facts that allude to them'. According to many commentators this will mean that if any newspaper mentions a government department in its news it would have to publish hundreds of letters responding to its 'allusion'. Aldo Zucolillo has pointed out that this would reinforce self-censorship in the media or even force newspapers to close down since they would not be able to afford the expense of filling their publication with letters from all the employees of a government department!

The second legal provision, included within the projected new Penal Code, contains even more serious limitations for the press. Article 158 states that 'a person commits an attempt against the authorities when, without there being a public rising, they attack their representatives or agents, or employ force against them, at the time of exercising their functions or for having exercised them'. The next Article adds: 'If the attempt is committed with any type of weapon or slanderous imputations by the press, the guilty party will be punished with two to four years' imprisonment. When this transgression is perpetrated against a member of the armed forces or the police, the punishment applied will be doubled.' As with the first law, this will merely limit further the space available for freedom of expression in general, and the freedom of the press in particular.

It may only be when the new Penal Code is introduced that both *ABC Color* and *Radio Ñanduti* will be allowed to open again. Then, the limits placed upon them will be as rigorous as they were under the state of siege and Law 209.

# PERU

Peru has lived under a constitutional democracy since 1980, making a successful transition to its second consecutive elected government in 1985. In the last seven years, Peruvians have enjoyed extensive freedom of the press and of other forms of expression guaranteed by the Constitution enacted in 1979. During this period, legislation has been introduced at various stages which indirectly affects freedom of expression, although there is no formal or overt censorship mechanism in operation. Despite the recent growth of the threat posed by the *Sendero Luminoso* insurgency, there has been no attempt to limit the scope of permissible political opinion. At

|  |  | Year |
|---|---|---|
| Population | 20,000,000 | 1986 |
| GNP ($ per capita) | 980 | 1984 |
| Illiteracy % | 15.2 | 1985 |
| Daily newspapers | 30 | est |
| Non Daily newspapers | 13 | est |
| Periodicals | 18 | est |
| Published books | 546 | 1984 |
| Radio stations | 293 | est |
| Radio receivers | 3,969,000 | 1985 |
| TV stations | 8 | est |
| TV sets | 1,701,000 | 1985 |

Press Agencies: Asociacion
Nacional de Periodistas del Peru

Covenant on Civil &
Political Rights _____ 1978

least one daily in Lima has become the unofficial mouthpiece for *Sendero*, and other publications with similar views are also tolerated.

One of the consequences of the atmosphere of free expression which has prevailed in recent years has been an extraordinary proliferation of daily newspapers in the capital, Lima. There are now at least sixteen of them, ranging from the serious to the sensational and semi-pornographic. This is a remarkable figure for a city of about six million people, many of them illiterate. The explanation is low production costs, which enable papers to survive on daily sales of less than 50,000. In addition, three newspapers are owned and subsidized by the government, and the ruling party has its own daily.

The military régime that governed Peru between 1968 and 1980 enacted two Press Statutes and several decrees which gave the government great authority to control publications. Exercising those powers, the military regime appropriated newspapers, suspended the publication of magazines and newspapers, confiscated whole editions of other publications, deported journalists and closed down several press enterprises.

Largely in response to this experience, the 1979 Constitution established freedom of expression as an essential right (Art. 2, Section 4). The relevant clause defines the right broadly, including the right to information, opinion, expression and dissemination of thought, by word, image or print, and without previous authorization, censorship or any

114

impediment, subject only to legal liabilities. The clause specifically states that it is a criminal offence to shut down communications media, and that the right to free expression includes the right to establish means of communication. Article 134 states that the press, radio, television, and the ownership thereof cannot be the object of any monopoly, either by the State or by private enterprise.

**Emergency zones**: Article 231 of the Constitution allows suspension of certain rights when the government declares either a state of emergency or a state of siege. During a state of emergency, only four rights may be suspended, and freedom of expression is not one of them. A state of siege may be declared under more extreme circumstances (invasion, external war, civil war or imminent danger thereof). The decree establishing the state of siege must specify which rights continue to be in effect. Since December 1982, several provinces in Peru have been governed under a state of emergency, but no portion of the territory is or has been under a state of siege. Lima became one of the jurisdictions governed under a state of emergency in 1985.

Although a state of emergency has no legal effect on freedom of expression, some troubling developments have nonetheless taken place. A law regulating the exceptional measures allows for the creation of a 'politico-military command' in the zones of emergency. In effect, this structure, of dubious constitutionality, replaces those authorities that represent the Presidency in the area (though not the locally elected municipal bodies), and establishes a chain of command to the President through the high commands of the armed forces. Applying counter-insurgency doctrine, the 'politico-military command' of certain zones of emergency has exercised its power through orders that are clearly not within its purview. Those orders have affected freedom of expression and information. For example, journalists are regularly excluded from the emergency zone in Ayacucho; both national and foreign journalists have been expelled from rural areas. In the last year, no journalist has been allowed to travel in the rural areas of the Southern Andes. In January 1987, this practice was formalized in a rule published by the politico-military command of Ayacucho.

**Military communiqués**: At the same time, information about the war against *Sendero* is restricted to 'military communiqués' issued by the politico-military command. Even on the basis of the scarce independent information available, those communiqués have frequently been found untruthful.

In 1986, the politico-military command in Lima prohibited performances by two popular music groups in a festival in support of the struggle in El Salvador, on the grounds that the groups were 'obscene' or 'subversive'.

**Attacks on the media**: In June 1986, in the immediate aftermath of the prison massacres at El Frontón and Lurigancho, when almost 300 *Sendero Luminoso* inmates were killed by security forces, the government seized an

115

edition of *El Nuevo Diario*, a newspaper widely considered to be the unofficial spokesman for *Sendero*. The paper resumed publication with the next issue, and has not been harassed further, though it complains from time to time of delays in distribution caused by local authorities.

In early October 1987, *El Nuevo Diario* reported that its situation had taken a turn for the worse. A car bomb exploded outside the paper's offices in Lima, killing two people and injuring one, and a special edition of the newspaper a few days later complained that its offices had been occupied by the security forces, its staff harassed and its operations hampered. Some congressmen expressed the fear that state terrorism was on the increase again.

On Jan. 26, 1987, three members of *Sendero Luminoso* stormed the *Reuters* office in Lima and forced an employee at gunpoint to file an anti-government message on the wire.

**The Anti-Terrorist Statute and Slander**: In 1981, under the government of President Fernando Belaúnde, two very controversial statutes were enacted: one was Decree 046, the Anti-Terrorist Statute, in which Articles 6 and 7 penalized the use of the media for the instigation of terrorist acts or the praise (*apologia*) of specific acts or those convicted of committing them. Most of Decree 046 was incorporated into the Penal Code by a law passed on March 20, 1985, but Articles 6 and 7 were repealed. The other statute was called *Ley de Desacato* (contempt), and created an aggravated form of slander when the aggrieved party was a public authority. This statute was repealed in 1985 at the initiative of the Alan García administration.

In early 1986, two successful television political commentary programmes were scrapped by management. Their directors complained of pressures from the military high command, transmitted to the managers of the station through private calls by government authorities. The journalists affected have continued to work in their profession, though in other media.

By far the most tragic attacks on the media have taken place in Ayacucho. In January 1983, eight journalists who were trying to cover atrocities in the war against *Sendero* died at the hands of the community of Uchuraccay. After protracted judicial proceedings, three members of the community have been convicted (other defendants are still at large), and the trial court has initiated a formal accusation against Gen. Noel, the head of the politico-military command at the time, on the suspicion that he instigated and then covered up the crime.

In 1984, journalist Jaime Ayala Sulca, a correspondent for Lima newspapers in Huanta, Ayacucho, was apprehended by the Marines and has since disappeared. His case is one of the few involving a disappearance that has remained under the jurisdiction of the civilian courts. In early 1986, a warrant of arrest was issued against two navy officers in charge of the Huanta garrison, but they have both absconded, with, it is believed, the protection of the naval high command. At time of writing, twelve Peruvian journalists have died or disappeared as a result of their professional activity. the most recent being José Hernán Tenicela Fierro, shot dead on Sep. 2, 1987, outside his home in Huancayo.

The recent history of freedom of expression in Peru reflects a marked departure from the dark days of the 1970s. However, measures constituting censorship continue to exist. Despite constitutional guarantees which establish freedom of expression as an essential right, it is clear that these provisions have still not been fully implemented.

## Current detainees

Included among those writers, journalists and media workers against whom action has been taken during the course of 1987 or who are still in prison: Jaime Ayala Sulca, journalist, disappeared after being taken into police custody, Aug. 2, 1984

# UNITED STATES OF AMERICA

'If there is any fixed star in our constitutional constellation, it is that no official, high or petty, can prescribe what shall be orthodox in politics, nationalism, religion or other matters of opinion or force citizens to confess by word or act their faith therein.'

The history of freedom of expression in the United States is a complex mixture of a profound commitment to individual liberty, as suggested in this quotation from a Supreme Court ruling, and an intolerance of dissent and unorthodox views.

The extent to which the constitutional ideals have been realized has been determined by continual tug-of-war between government tendencies to suppress those

|  |  | Year |
|---|---|---|
| Population | 238,000,000 | 1985 |
| GNP ($ per capita) | 15,490 | 1984 |

| Daily newspapers | 1,676 | 1985 |
|---|---|---|
| Non Daily newspapers | 7,711 | 1985 |
| Periodicals | 11,969 | 1984 |
| Published books | 51,058 | 1984 |
| Radio stations | 8,462 | 1984 |
| Radio receivers | 478,000,000 | 1983 |
| TV stations | 1,194 | 1986 |
| TV sets | 185,000,000 | 1983 |

Press Agencies: AP, UPI

Covenant on Civil &
Political Rights _____ NO

deemed subversive, and citizen initiatives aimed at expanding the sphere of freedom. The pursuit of liberty has been further strained by recurrent social movements seeking to impose their preferred values on the rest of the population.

In the 1980s freedom of expression has not fared well. During Ronald Reagan's presidential terms unprecedented steps have been taken to narrow the range of public discourse, while moral campaigners have mounted anti-obscenity and book-banning drives to reverse the trend towards greater openness and tolerance that began in the 1960s.

## The Constitution

The cornerstone of political freedom in the USA is the Constitution's First Amendment, which states: 'Congress shall make no law respecting an establishment of religion, or prohibiting the free exercise thereof; or abridging the freedom of speech, or of the press; or the right of the people peaceably to assemble, and to petition the government for a redress of grievances.'

The ideal implicit in the First Amendment is that of a citizenry that can participate fully in political and social affairs without fear of government interference. Yet freedom of speech is not an absolute: laws exist regarding libel, obscenity, and the regulation of electronic mass communications.

The Constitution as a whole makes access to information an important measure of a democracy. An electorate that is well-informed about the activities of government is an essential part of the country's democratic vision. The President is required to make an annual address on the state of the nation; a decennial census must be taken; information should flow from the Executive to the Congress to ensure effective oversight; and, to spur culture and creativity, Congress is given authority to promote writings and inventions through the enactment of copyright and patent laws.

Along with openness in government there is a body of procedural guarantees to prevent the arbitrary suppression of dissident views. The existence of legal requirements in large measure distinguishes the right of free speech from a mere privilege.

The courts play a crucial function in preserving First Amendment principles. In one of the most famous instances, in the early 1960s, as the civil rights movement spread throughout the South, state authorities tried to keep out the national press through the use of libel laws that exacted stiff penalties for damage to a person's reputation. The Supreme Court required public officials suing the press to prove reckless disregard of the truth on the part of a journalist. This landmark ruling (*New York Times* v. Sullivan) was both a product of the social climate of the times and a catalyst for further activism.

Current free-speech controversies revolve around issues such as religion and morality. The Supreme Court has recently considered and rejected demands by parents that government schools eliminate textbooks that fail to teach the Biblical story of creation. In the midst of this debate, the rights of students are being reconsidered. In January 1988, the Court upheld by a five-to-three majority the right of a high school principal in Hazlewood, Missouri, to delete from the school newspaper two pages that contained articles on divorce and student pregnancy. Justice Byron R. White, for the majority, said that 'no violation of First Amendment rights had occurred'.

## Laws affecting freedom of expression

Numerous laws, presidential orders and regulations exist that serve either to advance or limit the flow of information in the society. The most important of these include:

**The Freedom of Information Act:** Prior to 1966, when the Freedom of Information Act (FOIA) was adopted, federal officials arbitrarily decided whether or not to release information. The FOIA, strengthened in 1974 in the midst of almost daily revelations about serious government misconduct, established a policy which was in favour of disclosure, except where withholding can be justified according to designated exemptions. The ever-expanding list of exemptions includes classified documents, confidential business information, and the operational records of the Central Intelligence Agency.

The FOIA has enabled writers, historians and others to uncover a wide range of information. Documents released have revealed FBI harassment of Dr Martin Luther King Jr, illegal CIA and FBI surveillance of domestic political groups, safety problems at nuclear power plants, and lax federal enforcement of environmental and civil rights laws. Recently, FOIA documents showed that the FBI had conducted surveillance of dozens of writers, including Pearl Buck, Carl Sandburg, and John Dos Passos, over a period of thirty years.

The value of the FOIA has risen and declined in accordance with the attitude of successive administrations. In keeping with the notion of procedural guarantees, agencies are supposed to respond to written requests within ten working days, appeals within twenty, and final agency denials may be taken to the federal courts for appeal. However, certain agencies are notorious for long delays and for denying the very existence of information known to exist.

Such devices have been common in the 1980s and have been encouraged by government efforts to weaken the FOIA. An Executive Order issued in 1982 gave agencies authority to classify information retroactively and eliminated an earlier requirement to balance the government's interest in secrecy against the public interest in disclosure of the requested documents. The standard now imposed is—'when in doubt, classify'.

State laws providing access to information are at least as important as federal laws to citizens who are more likely to seek information concerning the policies of a local social welfare agency, school board or housing authority than to go up against a federal agency. All fifty states have freedom of information laws, many modelled on the federal statute.

**The 'Sunshine Act':** A law passed in 1976 declared that 'the public is entitled to the fullest practicable information regarding the decision-making processes of the federal government' and required that the public be given access to the meetings of some sixty federal agencies. The 'Sunshine Act', as it is commonly referred to, makes the deliberations of agencies, as well as their final actions, open to public scrutiny. But certain agencies, especially the Nuclear Regulatory Commission, have sought ways around this law —by redefining the word 'meeting', having commissioners vote over the telephone, or through liberal application of exemptions contained in the law.

**The Federal Depository Library Programme:** Another important access law is the one that created the Federal Depository Library Programme in 1902. Administered by the Government Printing Office, the programme provides government publications free of charge to approximately 1,400 academic, public and private libraries on the condition that they provide access to the public.

**'Whistleblower' Laws:** For most Americans, one of the most significant kinds of censorship occurs at the workplace.

To overcome the doctrine of absolute employer control, laws have been adopted that protect employees who disclose information about improper action on the part of their employers and thereby serve broader social policy objectives. Today there are a number of federal laws which protect private and government employees who 'blow the whistle'.

In 1983, Connecticut became the first of many states to give general recognition to the speech rights of private sector employees with a law that enables workers to sue their employers for discharge or disciplinary action based on the exercise of free speech that does not interfere with on-the-job performance.

**The Paperwork Reduction Act of 1980:** This law was intended to reduce the amount of paperwork companies were required to submit to government agencies as part of regulatory activity and to provide direction for automation of government record-keeping. However, it has turned out to be a potent tool in the Federal Administration's deregulatory campaigns, causing a drastic reduction in the amount of information collected and distributed by federal agencies, including a quarter of all government publications, as well as many corporate reports useful to groups monitoring environmental and other trends.

**The Immigration and Nationality Act of 1952:** More commonly known as the McCarran-Walter Act, this law restricts freedom of expression by giving government officials discretion to selectively deny entry to foreigners. The Act defines thirty-three categories of foreigners who may be deported or barred from the country, including people with dangerous communicable diseases and drug traffickers. More controversial are ideological criteria such as advocacy of communism or anarchism, or a determination by the Attorney-General that the visitor's activities would be 'prejudicial to the public interest'.

Successive administrations have made extensive use of the law to exclude a varied list of those deemed political opponents. Among the 'undesirables' who have been denied visas in recent years are: Nobel laureate Gabriel García Márquez, Colombian journalist Patricia Lara, Italian playwrights Dario Fo and Franca Rama, and Hortensia Bussi de Allende, widow of the assassinated Chilean leader. In December 1987 the US Congress voted to suspend for twelve months the political grounds for exclusion under the Act.

**Foreign Agents Registration Act 1938:** This Act requires any film, produced under the auspices of a foreign country, that is adjudged to be foreign propaganda to be labelled as such, unless the film is 'not serving predominantly a foreign interest'.

In 1982 the Department of Justice attempted unsuccessfully to require three Canadian films to be labelled as propaganda; the anti-nuclear theme of one of the films, 'If You Love This Planet', was claimed to be a propaganda message. The judge who refused the appeal commented that how the film served a foreign interest was difficult to determine.

## National security

The greatest dangers to freedom of expression in the USA today stem from the federal government's preoccupation with national security and terrorism. Under these banners, the executive branch has widened government secrecy while resuming surveillance of dissidents and placing unprecedented restrictions on the media.

In addition to a more stringent use of classification rules, the Administration has created new categories of 'sensitive' information to restrict access to unclassified materials. Military officials have even pressed private information companies to restrict the use of their commercial databases. Stricter controls have been placed on the presentation of certain kinds of scientific and technical information at professional conferences and in scholarly journals. One of the consequences of these policies has been to limit the availability of technical data that could be used to challenge the Administration's Strategic Defense Initiative ('Star Wars') plans.

Two Acts, the International Traffic in Arms Regulations and the Export Administration Regulations, have been revived by the government and used to control the flow of scientific information in universities. While some universities have refused to handle classified information to avoid government interference, restrictions have been placed on visits by foreign academics and students.

In 1981, the President issued an order expanding the authority of the CIA and FBI to conduct domestic surveillance. The intelligence agencies have allegedly returned to activities vilified during congressional hearings of the 1970s, including infiltration, 'phone-tapping and raids on the offices of dissident groups such as the Sanctuary movement aiding Central American refugees. In 1987 it was reported that the FBI was trying to recruit librarians to supply them with information on the reading habits of users from foreign 'enemy' countries.

Efforts to control the media include the requirement that coverage of overseas manoeuvres be limited to Pentagon-supervised press pools —a rule adopted after the total press ban imposed during the Grenada invasion in 1983. The Administration has been obsessed with stopping leaks even though top officials regularly engage in the practice. The late CIA Director William Casey regularly threatened to bring espionage charges against major news organizations, and succeeded in having *The Washington Post* cut details from a planned story on Ronald Pelton, convicted of espionage in May 1986. The threats were taken more seriously after charges were successfully brought against Samuel Loring Morison, a civilian analyst working for the Navy for leaking classified photographs to a London publication. This was the first time in the country's history that an unauthorized disclosure of government information to the press was put on the same level as selling secrets to the enemy.

Another 'chilling' effect was accomplished by requiring government employees to sign non-disclosure contracts of lifetime duration, under penalties ranging from loss of employment to prison sentences. By 1987, when two unions challenged the scheme as an unconstitutional abridgement of speech, some 300,000 people had signed such agreements.

The Intelligence Identities Protection Act, drafted by the Carter Administration, bans disclosure of the names of individuals involved with the CIA, even if they have committed criminal acts. CIA agents are required to submit publications for prior review.

The US Information Agency has established *Worldnet*, a satellite network used for briefings with foreign journalists aimed at influencing their coverage of US affairs. Another foreign propaganda effort is Project Democracy, a private foundation created in 1982 and largely funded by the federal government, which seeks to promote 'Western' values around the world.

National security has been invoked to justify disinformation. In 1986 Defense Department officials admitted that incomplete and misleading information had been given out to the media on more than fifteen military programmes—supposedly to impede the transfer of technical data to the Soviet Union. The government also admitted releasing erroneous reports to the press aimed at convincing Libyan leader Col. Moamer al-Gadaffi that the USA planned another attack on his country.

## The Media

The United States may well be the most media-conscious nation in the world. Television, in particular, is perhaps the most important influence on the way Americans view themselves, their country and the rest of the world. Political advertisements on television can make or break electoral candidates—or even Supreme Court nominees.

Today there are some 10,000 radio and 1,200 television stations, only 15 per cent of which are non-commercial. In addition, more than half of the 85,000,000 television households are wired for cable; 36,000,000 have video recorders; and 2,000,000 have dishes for receiving satellite signals.

Unlike most other countries, the vast majority of radio and television stations in the United States have always been privately-owned (though the airwaves remained a public resource), with advertising providing the bulk of station revenue. The Communications Act of 1934, still the primary law for electronic communications, made broadcasters public trustees through a licensing system that made the granting and renewal of licences by the Federal Communications Commission (FCC) dependent on a broadcaster's ability to serve 'the public interest, convenience and necessity'.

The meaning of these terms, defined through FCC regulations over many decades, was until recently assumed to include emphasis on meeting local needs for information, news, entertainment, and other types of programming, and on providing diversity of ideas.

However, from the late 1970s the media have been progressively 'deregulated'. That is, regulations limiting the number of commercial minutes per hour and requiring broadcasters to cover controversial issues in a balanced fashion, and even guidelines for children's programming, have been withdrawn in favour of 'market forces'.

The one exception to the FCC's drive to deregulate is a policy announced in 1987 that expands FCC enforcement of regulations prohibiting the broadcast of sexually explicit material. Because of this, a significant amount of literature, poetry and music may now be taken off the air. In a letter to poet Allen Ginsberg notifying him that his poems would no longer be aired, the head of non-commercial *Pacifica Radio* explained: 'In this climate, Pacifica cannot risk losing its licence or even the cost of defending ourselves.'

**Concentration of ownership and diversity:** Of enormous significance has been the FCC's easing of ownership limitations for broadcast stations. The rule changes set off a gold rush that has changed the contours of American broadcasting. All three of the major television networks are under new management: *NBC* has been acquired by General Electric; *ABC* by Capital Cities, and *CBS* is now largely controlled by Laurence A. Tisch, a financier with diversified holdings in hotels, theatres and insurance. These new owners have cut back broadcast staffs, particularly in the news and public affairs departments.

But this is only a small part of the growing concentration of ownership in the media. Time Inc., in addition to owning *Time, People, Sports Illustrated* and numerous other national magazines, also owns the *Home Box Office* and *Cinemax* pay-TV services, the second largest cable company in the country, book publishing companies and part of Tri-Star Pictures. Gulf & Western owns Paramount Pictures and Simon & Schuster, the country's largest book publisher.

Gannett controls a chain of nearly ninety newspapers, including the only national paper *USA Today*, whose bite-sized articles have been widely imitated among the nation's dailies. International media magnate Rupert Murdoch purchased a group of independent TV stations and Harper & Row Publishers, adding to his other magazine, newspaper and broadcast properties in the USA, Britain and Australia.

The media are now subjected to strong corporate pressures to treat publications and broadcasts like any other product. The problem has got progressively worse as ownership of media outlets has become concentrated in the hands of a dwindling number of companies. More than ever before, management consultants and financial executives make the decisions, resulting in a narrowing of the diversity of content. There are fewer documentaries carried by the networks. The major cable channels, imitating the networks, serve up conventional fare, with a heavy emphasis on violence. The major book publishers increasingly limit their titles to 'safe' genres such as celebrity biographies, diet books and pop psychology.

The public's response to such changes has proceeded along two lines. First, they are seeking out the available commercial options which allow a greater degree of diversity. These include the burgeoning videocassette business, satellite dishes providing access to dozens of channels, and the thousands of smaller book and magazine publishers.

Some people are also developing alternative media outside the commercial marketplace. Many cable television systems include access channels that carry without charge independently produced programmes by community groups and individuals. Computer users have set up hundreds of non-commercial 'electronic bulletin boards' and networks, such as *PeaceNet* which links disarmament and human rights activists.

Despite the emergence of these new channels of communication, there still remains a serious gulf between the information haves and have-nots. The new technologies involve costs and skills that remain outside the reach of much of the population.

## Freedom of opinion and expression

Book-banning has become a troubling nationwide phenomenon, with many communities dividing over demands for censorship of literary classics, dictionaries, and contemporary works. Organizations such as Parents' Music Resource Center have targeted what they consider obscenity in rock music by pressuring record companies to tone down lyrics. One rock group, the Dead Kennedys, was tried on obscenity charges in California, and although they were acquitted, the case caused the group to disband.

The anti-pornography movement was bolstered by the work of a federal commission on pornography directed by the Attorney-General. Although the Meese Commission was unable to establish a direct link between media images and anti-social behaviour, it nonetheless recommended a crackdown on the production, distribution and consumption of sexually explicit material.

**Censorship in schools:** The banning of books, magazines and films selected as educational materials (and almost invariably chosen by educators according to policies and procedures established by school boards) is widespread today. Censorship controversies have erupted in schools and communities across the country. While a decade ago almost no case law existed, numerous law suits have been filed in recent years.

Two current court cases have received much publicity. In a Tennessee case, a reading series was attacked by Christian fundamentalists who claimed that the requirement that their children read the books, which included excerpts from a very wide variety of works, violated their religious rights. In an Alabama case, forty-four textbooks were banned from the schools for teaching 'the religion of secular humanism'.

In both the Tennessee and Alabama cases, federal appeals courts overturned federal district court decisions banning the books, but further appeals to the US Supreme Court are expected.

Other targets are teaching about religion (often resulting in compromised science teaching), open-ended discussion of moral questions, family life, divorce, sex education, emotional effects of death, women's rights and much literature, both contemporary and classic, including Shakespeare and Mark Twain.

School boards do not always resist demands for censorship. In 1982 the US Supreme Court ruled in the Pico case that students' First Amendment rights to receive information were violated when school boards banned books from school libraries simply because they disliked the ideas contained in them.

# COUNTRY REPORTS—ASIA

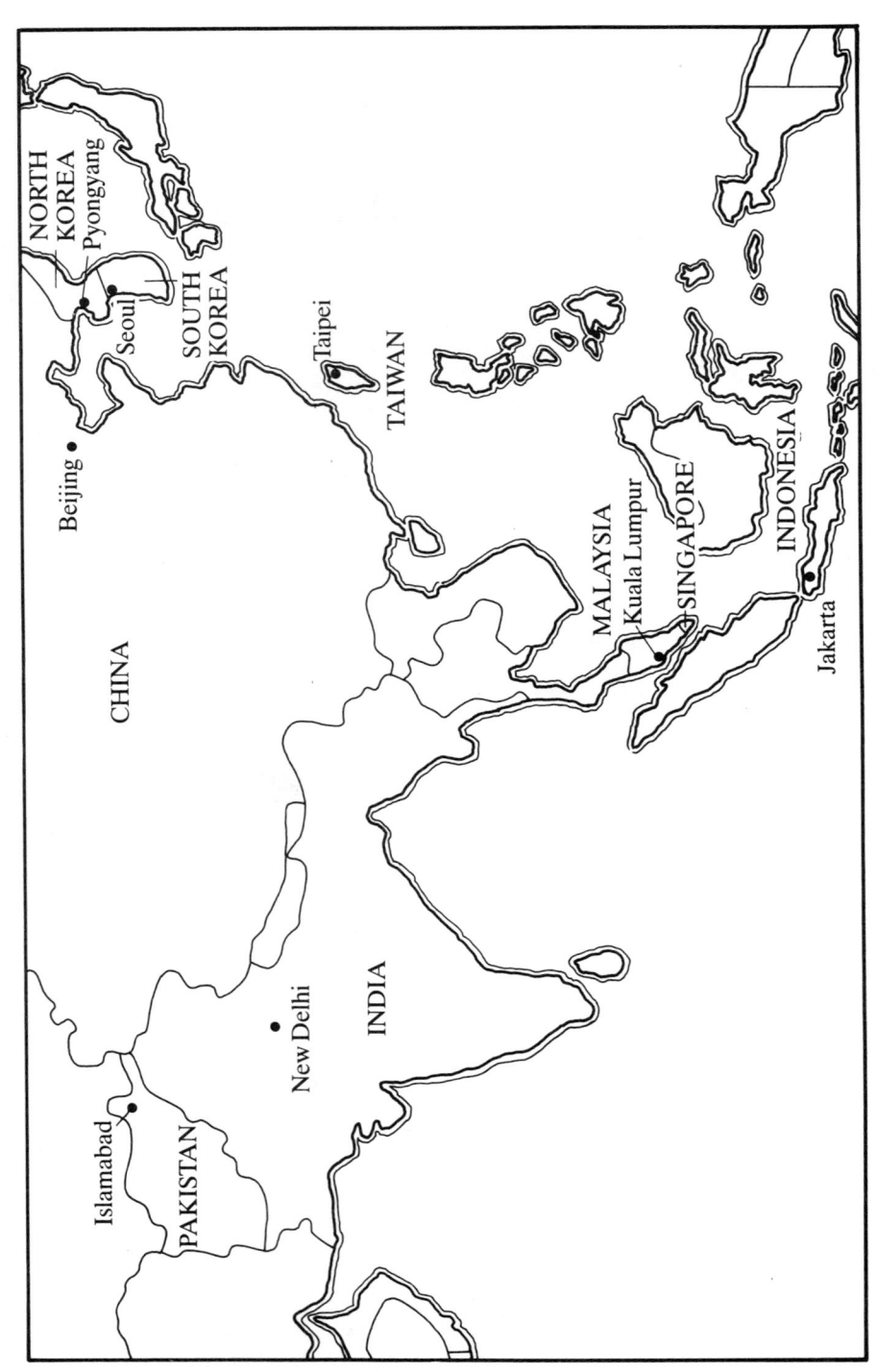

# CHINA

Freedom of expression, assembly, association and demonstration are enshrined in the 1982 Constitution of the People's Republic of China. But there are other provisions which can be read as contradicting these rights. According to Article 51, 'the exercise of citizens of the People's Republic of China of their freedoms and rights... may not infringe upon the interests of the state, of society, and of the collective, or upon the lawful freedoms and rights of other citizens'. Furthermore, 'it is the duty of citizens to safeguard the security, honour, and interests of the motherland; they must not commit acts detrimental to... the motherland' (Art. 54). Other constitutional provisions limiting

|  |  | Year |
|---|---|---|
| Population | 1,059,000,000 | 1985 |
| GNP ($ per capita) | 310 | 1984 |
| Illiteracy % | 23 | 1983 |

| Daily newspapers | 2,191 | 1983 |
|---|---|---|
| Non Daily newspapers | 144 | 1982 |
| Periodicals | 80 | 1982 |
| Published books | 34,920 | 1984 |
| Radio stations | 167 | 1986 |
| Radio receivers | 70,000,000 | 1983 |
| TV stations | 104 | 1984 |
| TV sets | 9,900,000 | 1984 |

Press Agencies:
Xinhua (New China) News Agency

Covenant on Civil & Political Rights _____ NO

rights and freedoms include protection of the citizens from libel, insult and false charge (Art. 38). Moreover, citizens 'must... keep state secrets, protect public property, observe labour discipline and public order, and respect social ethics' (Art. 53).

China's concept of freedom of expression and of other human rights are to be understood within the ideological framework of the CCP's concept of 'socialist democracy' and the principle of 'democratic centralism' (Art. 3). In addition, there are the Four Basic Principles of the party enunciated by Deng Xiaoping in 1979; 'upholding party leadership, Marxism-Leninism-Mao Zedong thought, the people's democratic dictatorship, and socialism'.

## Freedom of expression—overview

Since 1949 CCP policy on cultural expression and the press has oscillated from periods of liberalization to periods of repression which in the period of Mao were violent. In 1957, there was the officially sanctioned 'Hundred Flowers' movement—'Let a hundred flowers bloom, let a hundred schools of thought contend'—which was abruptly halted by the 'Anti-Rightist Drive'. After a period of relative relaxation in the early 1960s, the 'Great Proletarian Cultural Revolution' started in 1966 and lasted ten years. After Mao's death in 1976, the new leader, Deng Xiaoping, launched a policy of modernization (including cultural liberalization) but he too periodically repressed the intellectuals, although without the violence and mass mobilization of the Mao era.

During the 1950s and '60s Chinese writers, artists, scientists and intellectuals bore the brunt of the zig-zag course of the party's cultural policy. During Mao's chairmanship, there were hundreds of thousands of victims, a large number of whom were executed, driven to suicide, or disgraced and sent to labour camps. The Cultural Revolution is now officially regarded as the most tragic episode of modern Chinese history with the country plunged into chaos and warfare, and virtually all artistic and intellectual activity was suppressed.

In early 1987 another government drive started—the 'Anti-Bourgeois Liberalization' policy. Although the eventual outcome of this campaign is far from clear, a number of its consequences are known. They include expulsion from the party of a number of writers, journalists and scientists and the banning of books and films. Some newspapers and scientific and literary journals have closed down. In May 1987, thirty-nine journals were shut in Guangxi province. A radio broadcast cited the reason for the closures as 'straightening out re-registration'. The 13th CCP Congress in October 1987, which approved the election of Zhao Ziyang as party leader and reaffirmed the commitment to modernize China's economy, left future cultural policy unclear. When the campaign against 'bourgeois liberalization' was launched, the CCP announced its Four Basic Principles as the guiding force, but what is intended by 'bourgeois liberalism' has still to emerge clearly. It appears that dissident voices are not now jailed; they are silenced, however, and Wei Jingsheng and other victims of previous campaigns remain in prison.

## The Media

Virtually all press and broadcasting media in China are owned by the State and controlled by the Communist Party. Editors and reporters are, almost without exception, party members and are referred to as 'Party cadres'. Their recruitment and training reflect their ideological and political reliability. The basic function of the press is to propagandize on behalf of the party. *Renmin Ribao* (*People's Daily*), the party's chief official newspaper, has described the press as the party's 'loyal eyes, ears and tongue', and as an 'important bridge for daily contact between the party and the people'. Mao Zedong's concept of a 'proletarian journalist', still used in the Deng Xiaoping era, is that he or she should take part in mass movements in order to enrich practical knowledge and experience.

Newspapers: National newspapers are edited and published in the capital city, Beijing; local newspapers are published in provincial capitals, cities, districts or counties.

National newspapers have their specific functions and readership. The *Renmin Ribao*, for instance, is under the direct supervision of the Politburo. Its editorial content is reprinted by the local party newspapers throughout the country. The *Renmin Ribao*, like *Hong Qi* (*Red Flag*), the party's theoretical fortnightly, is required reading for party officials. *Jiefangjun Bao (Liberation Army Daily)* is published by the General Political Department of the Ministry of Defence. Its circulation is strictly limited to military units and state institutions. *Guangming Ribao (Enlightenment Daily)* is published by the Department of Propaganda of the CCP's Central Committee. Its coverage focuses mainly on cultural, educational and scientific matters. *Gongren Ribao (Worker's Daily)* is the organ of the National Workers Union; *Wen Hui Bao (Literary Gazette)* is for intellectuals, writers and artists. For the young there are *Zhongguo Qingmian Bao (China Youth Daily)* and *China Pioneers Daily*, published by the Central Committee of the Chinese Communist Youth League. Local newspapers are similarly controlled by local party committees and also serve special readerships.

Since 1981 the CCP's Central Committee has published an English language newspaper (*China Daily*) to serve foreign residents in China. A selected few foreign publications are now available in China but their distribution is restricted to international hotels and bookstores.

**News agencies:** There are two Chinese news agencies which serve both national and local newspapers, radio and television stations. *Xinhua (New China News Agency)*, the biggest, is the organ of the CCP. Its director is usually a member of the party's Central Committee. *Xinhua* has correspondents throughout China and in most foreign countries where there are Chinese diplomatic or trade missions. It is the sole distributor of foreign news in China. The other news agency, *China News Service*, supplies mostly local feature stories. Although *Xinhua* has access to news around the world, thanks to exchange agreements with the leading news agencies such as *Reuters, AFP, AP, UPI, TASS* and *Kyodo*, it releases only a few carefully selected items to national and local media.

**Restricted publications:** Much of this semi-secret material is published but available only to a limited circle of party and government officials, policy analysts and policy consultants. These publications include *Can Kao Xiao Si (Reference News)*, *Can Kao Zilino (Reference Materials)* and *Neibu Can Kao (Internal Reference)*. *Neibu Cankao* is the most important of these bulletins. Put out by *Xinhua* twice daily, it contains uncensored news, information and analysis intended for China's political élite. Very little is known about this special bulletin, and its readership is believed not to exceed several thousand. *Xinhua* news and information for its mass readership are invariably mixed with political and ideological propaganda.

## Censorship

Unlike the Soviet Union, where official censors (from *Glavlit*) are assigned to different newspapers, Chinese newspapers practise self-censorship in conjunction with party committees at different levels, except during political campaigns when the party's Propaganda Department intervenes directly. The *Beijing Ribao (Beijing Daily)*, for example, is monitored by the municipal party committee and the national Central Committee of the party. Routine material normally does not require approval, but important news stories, features and editorials must be referred to higher authorities. In the case of the *Renmin Ribao,* sensitive material is referred to the top leadership or the official in the CCP's Standing Committee in charge of the media.

**Purges of journalists:** A reporter or an editor faces difficult decisions during periods of great debate on important ideological issues or following sudden changes of the CCP's policies or leadership. During the Cultural Revolution in the 1960s, virtually all the top journalists of the national and local newspapers were purged, accused of being 'capitalist roaders' because of their loyalty to Liu Shaoqi, the then Head of State. Liu was toppled during the Cultural Revolution. After the 'Gang of Four' was purged in 1976, their followers in the media were also purged and replaced by the followers of the 'reformist' leader Deng Xiaoping.

During the campaigns against 'spiritual pollution' in 1973 and against 'bourgeois liberalism' in the early months of 1987, a number of leading journalists and editors were dismissed. The most distinguished was Liu Binyan, an investigative reporter on the *Renmin Ribao* and best known for his exposé of mismanagement and corruption in the party ranks. He was accused of aping western journalism and was expelled from the party. Liu, the vice-chairman of the Chinese Writers' Association, had also been purged during the 'Anti-Rightist Drive' and again during the Cultural Revolution. After periods in labour camps he had returned to his paper when Deng came to power.

**Banned publications:** Local newspapers such as *Shenzen Youth Daily* (published in Shenzen, a Special Economic Zone near Hong Kong), the *Special Zone Worker's Daily,* Anhui province's *Journal of Scientific Information,* Hubei province's *Youth Forum,* Shanghai's *Society* and Guangzhou's *Modern Man* were reported to have been banned in early 1987. They were accused of being the vehicles of 'bourgeois liberalism' because of their dissenting views. In 1986 the authorities seized 7,000,000 books and magazines specializing mostly in 'yellow' literature, such as the martial arts, and romantic and erotic themes. In March 1987 the *Beijing Wan Bao (Beijing Evening News)* reported that half a million books were impounded in Beijing alone and that ten people were arrested in connection with illegally printing and publishing the material.

## The democracy movement

Although editors and reporters of the recently banned publications are less likely to be arrested or sent to prison or labour camps, this was not the case with those responsible for the unofficial publications in the late 1970s. In 1978, Deng Xiaoping encouraged a liberalization policy in arts and culture. As a result, a 'free speech' or 'democracy movement' started in Beijing and rapidly spread to other major provincial cities. Most of the participants were former Red Guards, who began to put up *dazibao* (wall-posters) and printed unofficial pamphlets calling for democratic

CHINA

reforms and respect for human rights. The best known of their publications were *Exploration, Beijing Spring, April 5 Forum* and *Today* (a literary magazine).

The democracy movement, however, proved shortlived when the authorities saw it as a threat. When *Exploration* magazine began to publish a series of articles and essays charging the Communist Party with lack of democracy, the magazine's editor, Wei Jingsheng, was arrested. Writing wall-posters, which Chairman Mao had put into the constitutional guarantee of freedom of expression, was officially banned. By April 1981, according to Amnesty International, at least twenty editors of these unofficial publications had been arrested. Some were reported to have been charged and tried; Wei Jingsheng was given a fifteen-year sentence. Others were held under the 'administrative detention law' without charge or trial and sent to labour camps. In December 1987 a biologist, Yang Wei, was imprisoned for two years. He was connected with the New York-based magazine *China Spring*. A second person, Quian Da, was arrested when trying to attend the trial. Foreign diplomats and journalists were denied access to the trial. In the same month there were renewed student demonstrations against government authorities.

## Foreign correspondents

Foreign correspondents normally work in China under official governmental exchange agreements. Because of the housing shortage, correspondents live and work in international hotels or in apartments reserved for aliens. Contact between them and the ordinary Chinese can be difficult. Chinese citizens are forbidden to enter these premises without first being screened and registered. Their major sources of information are Chinese newspapers or official statements and reports for the Foreign Ministry. Those who do not know the language must rely heavily on interpreters assigned by the government. Cables sent by foreign correspondents are not censored, but when a story offends the government the journalists may find that they are summoned to the Information Department of the Foreign Ministry to be given a lecture or a 'serious warning'.

During the riots in Tibet in October 1987, fifteen foreign correspondents and some tourists were asked to leave the area and return to the capital city. Since 1984 four foreign correspondents are known to have been expelled from China, accused of 'gathering secret information' or 'entering an area forbidden to foreigners'. Those expelled included Titano Terzani of *Der Speigel* (1984), John Burns of the *New York Times* (1986), Lawrence MacDonald of *AFP* and Suitso Henno of the Japanese *Kyodo* news agency (1987). In China, 'state secrets' include non-official sources and information in the three main restricted publications.

## Current detainees

Included among those writers, journalists and media workers against whom action has been taken during the course of 1987 or who are still in prison: Chen Erjin, teacher and writer of unofficial literature, sentenced to 10 years' imprisonment and 5 years' deprivation of political rights; Liu Jian-Wei, co-founder and deputy editor of *April 5th Forum*, an underground magazine closed down in 1980, arrested November 1979 and sentenced to 3 years' re-education, and in August 1982 sentenced in a secret trial to a further 7 years' imprisonment for 'counter-revolutionary' offences; Xu Wenli, editor, sentenced in June 1982 to 15 years' imprisonment.

# INDIA

The colonial administration's precedent of subsidizing some publications directly, as well as maintaining its own propaganda facilities, left a climate of considerable unease over the future freedom of the press in independent India. This unease has found expression in periods of mutual distrust between the press and the government which became particularly evident during Indira Gandhi's rule.

However, apart from the one major interruption when Indira Gandhi declared a state of emergency in June 1975, imposing censorship and arresting scores of journalists, the press in India has enjoyed freedom since independence, though subject to political, social and economic pressures.

| | | Year |
|---|---|---|
| Population | 751,000,000 | 1985 |
| GNP ($ per capita) | 346 | 1985 |
| Illiteracy % | 63.9 | 1981 |
| Daily newspapers | 1,423 | 1983 |
| Non Daily newspapers | 21 | est |
| Periodicals | 19,335 | 1983 |
| Published books | 9,954 | 1984 |
| Films produced | 741 | 1983 |
| Radio stations | 88 | est |
| Radio receivers | 45,000,000 | 1983 |
| TV stations | 186 | 1986 |
| TV sets | 2,096,000 | 1983 |

Press Agencies:
Press Trust of India, UNI

Covenant on Civil &
Political Rights _____ 1979

During the 1975 Emergency, the government argued that the press was a threat to law and order. The same arguments are heard today. The government controls both radio and television and the large majority of the newspapers in the country are sympathetic to the ruling party. It is the independent section of the press, which gives vent to popular opposition, that is the object of government criticism.

In May 1987, following extensive exposures, particularly in the *Indian Express*, of government corruption in arms deals with Swedish and German companies, the government, led by Prime Minister Rajiv Gandhi, launched a sharp attack on the press.

The Indian Constitution of 1950, which guarantees freedom of speech and expression to all citizens, has been held to guarantee press freedom as well. However, press freedom in India is not absolute; the Constitution allows for 'reasonable restriction... in the interest of the security of the State, friendly relations with foreign states, public order, decency or morality or in relation to contempt of court, defamation or incitement to an offence'. The Supreme Court in many important cases has ensured that such restrictions have not negated freedom of expression.

**Contempt of parliament:** Certain state legislatures have enacted legislation which penalizes newspapers deemed guilty of breach of their privileges. On a number of occasions, such measures have been used to order the imprisonment of journalists whose writings have been critical. A notable instance occurred in 1964 when the state legislature of Uttar Pradesh not only ordered the arrest of a journalist, but issued warrants for the arrest of his lawyer who moved in the State High Court for a writ of *habeas corpus* and of the judge who granted the writ.

In March 1987 the Legislative Assembly of Tamil Nadu arrested and committed to prison the editor of a Tamil weekly, *Ananda Vikatan*, for publishing a cartoon depicting elected representatives in a poor light. This was followed by a law making it an offence for any person in the state to exhibit films containing matter 'derogatory to the conduct of members of the Legislative Assembly' or likely to incite the public against the members. The same legislature has made a law against 'scurrilous journalism'.

**Public health and morals:** The Indian Penal Code makes it an offence to sell or distribute publications or material which are obscene or have a tendency to deprave or corrupt the morals of those reading or viewing them. Likewise any publication which tends to inflame communal or religious passions and thereby lead to public disorder is prohibited. The Indecent Representation of Women (Prohibition) Act prohibits the exhibition of any material derogatory to women.

**Official secrets:** Though there are no administrative rules to restrict public officials from giving information to the press, the Indian Official Secrets Act (1962) makes it an offence to communicate to any person any information that might be useful to an enemy. There is no freedom of information act that could be used by journalists or other citizens to gain access to information a public official might choose to withhold.

In an amendment, passed in May 1986, to the 1952 Commissions of Enquiry Act, the central government took power to withhold from the public reports of commissions set up under the Act. According to the original Act, reports of enquiries had to be laid before parliament within six months of their completion. The immediate reason for the amendment was the government's wish to suppress the report of the Thakkar Commission that enquired into the assassination of Indira Gandhi. The government argued that the publication of the report could endanger national security. The government also withheld for a time the report of the Mishra Commission into the communal riots following Indira Gandhi's assassination.

## The Media

**The press:** The Indian press, while not subject to prior censorship, is subject to pressures that can lead to self-censorship and the distortion of news. A majority of the newspapers are owned privately and concern has been frequently expressed about the relationship between the press and the business world. Newspapers depend on private advertisements for their revenue as well as on government and news and opinions detrimental to big business, however important they may be for public welfare, are rarely published in Indian newspapers.

The views of minorities, the tribal and the scheduled caste population are also inadequately represented in the Indian press.

Government, particularly at state level, exerts influence on newspapers and journals through advertising and the allocation of newsprint. Although government maintains that it is impartial in the placement of official advertisements (which represent 24 per cent of the total advertising revenue), its patronage of small and medium-sized publications cannot be denied.

**The Press Council:** The Press Council was dissolved during the Emergency and reconstituted in 1979. It consists of a chairman and twenty-eight members, thirteen from among journalists, six representing newspaper managements, five members of parliament, one representative of news agencies and three persons from public life.

The Press Council which is established by statute has no power to impose legal penalties and may only give an opinion. Its functions are to develop a code of conduct for journalists and to hear complaints both against newspapers and news agencies on the one side and the government on the other. There is no law conferring a right of reply in India.

**Attacks on the press:** Since the Emergency such threats as exist to freedom of the press have arisen from special laws, passed by state and central governments to deal with violence and terrorism in some parts of the country.

Under the Punjab Special Powers (Press) Act, the state government has taken powers to control the press. In November 1986, the government arrested Shahid Siddiqui, editor of the Urdu weekly *Naj Duniya*, under the Anti-Terrorist Act for publishing an interview with Sikh militant leader, Jagjit Singh Chauhann, in his weekly in 1984. In September 1985 a civil rights activist, N. D. Pancholi, author of a report on human rights violations by the Indian Army during the operation in June 1984 to remove armed Sikhs from the Golden Temple in Amritsar, was arrested on a charge of sedition. In December 1984, a reporter of the *Associated Press*, Brahma Chellany, was arrested on a charge of sedition for his reporting of the same army operation. In all these cases courts ordered the release of the arrested.

On May 1, 1987, attending the centenary celebrations of a Malayalam daily *Deepika*, published from the southern state of Kerala, Rajiv Gandhi accused the press of trying 'to stage a coup against the elected representatives of the country'. The press, he suggested, was attempting to undermine the defence of the nation. Similar sentiments have been expressed by other ministers on various occasions since and the Ministry of Information and Broadcasting is reported to have contemplated introducing legislation to curb what it described as 'scurrilous writing'.

On Sept. 1, hundreds of officials of the Revenue and Tax Departments of the central government raided the offices of the *Indian Express* in eleven centres in the country. Though the government maintained that the raids were solely intended to unearth tax and customs evasion by the newspaper on machinery imported by it in 1984, it was widely accused of seeking to intimidate the newspaper. In November 1987 the government announced that it was to take over the paper's New Delhi offices, by cancelling its rental of the building to the newspaper. The *Indian Express* had been a major target for harassment under the Censorship Regulation of 1975.

**News agencies:** There are two major national news agencies in India, the *Press Trust of India* (*PTI*) and *United News of India* (*UNI*). Both have bilingual services in English and Hindi as well as a wide network of correspondents both inside and outside the country, the *PTI* being much bigger than *UNI*. The *PTI* though theoretically constituted to function as an independent news agency is regarded as controlled by the government. On controversial issues, the *PTI* either remains silent or adopts the government view.

More than ten foreign news agencies maintain offices in India. Since 1948, all foreign news agencies have been required to route all traffic through one domestic agency. Individual newspapers are as a result spared the expense of subscribing to different news agencies.

**Journalists:** There is no licensing of journalists in India. Neither reporters nor publishers need to sign compulsory bonds or security deposits—a notorious weapon against journalists under the British Raj.

**Radio and television:** The most serious media limitation in India concerns the State's control of radio and television. *All India Radio* and *Doordanshan India,* the television network, are state monopolies. News and views put out by both are often managed by the government. The management of news on radio and television reached its peak during the 1975 Emergency. The *Janata* government appointed a broadcasting study group in 1977. In 1978 it recommended that the country's radio and television should be granted autonomy. The proposal was rejected by the government.

There have been instances when films scheduled to be televised were withdrawn reportedly at the intervention of government ministers. Two examples were 'Rajiv's India', a documentary made by American columnist Jack Anderson, and 'New Delhi Times', a film produced by Romesh Sharma.

The state's control of broadcasting continues to be justified in the name of development policy, national interest and security. In 1987 Minoo Masani, a former MP and diplomat, and P. C. Chatterjee, a former Director-General of *All India Radio*, filed a writ in the Bombay High Court in which they challenged the government's monopoly over the electronic media. The petitioners, who wished to set up a private broadcasting company, had duly applied for permission from the government but were turned down, with no reasons being given save that of 'policy'. The High Court admitted the case in September 1987.

**Film:** All films are certified before screening by the Central Board of Film Certification which may refuse to grant a certificate, or censor portions before a certificate is issued. Most cuts are made on the grounds of 'obscenity' and morality. Every cinema is required by law to show official newsreel film at the beginning of every show.

The film industry is taxed at a rate substantially higher than that applicable to the other mass media. Most state governments levy an entertainment duty which often exceeds 100 per cent, apart from several other taxes and cesses. Film-making, despite its reputation and organized nature, is not recognized as an 'industry' by the government, as a result of which institutional finance is hard to come by. In response to repeated pleas by the industry over piracy, the government amended the Copyright Act in 1984, imposing substantial fines. However, the problem persists.

**Interception of mail:** Like freedom of the press, the right to communicate is not guaranteed by the Indian Constitution. This is important because of a 1986 amendment to the Indian Postal Act 1898 which gives unlimited powers to both central and state governments to 'intercept, detain or dispose of' postal articles of any class or description. The amendment was refused assent by former President Zail Singh. The measure contradicts recent recommendations of the Indian Law Commission and the constitutional guarantee of freedom of expression.

# INDONESIA

President Suharto has now ruled Indonesia for twenty-two years. Under his 'New Order' government, the presidency is the strongest political institution in the country and power is concentrated in the hands of a small number of serving or retired military officers close to the Executive. In accordance with the concept of *dwi fungsi* (dual function), the military combines national security and socio-political roles, with armed forces personnel serving as administrators, politicians and businessmen.

|  |  | Year |
|---|---|---|
| Population | 165,000,000 | 1985 |
| GNP ($ per capita) | 540 | 1984 |
| Illiteracy % | 25.9 | 1985 |

| | | |
|---|---|---|
| Daily newspapers | 94 | 1982 |
| Non Daily newspapers } Periodicals | 44 | est |
| Published books | 5,254 | 1984 |
| Radio receivers | 22,000,000 | 1983 |
| TV sets | 5,700,000 | 1984 |

Press Agencies: ANTARA

Covenant on Civil & Political Rights _____ NO

## The Media

**The press:** According to the Indonesian Press Council the Indonesian press is a '*Pancasila* press'. *Pancasila* is a broad set of social and political principles that includes monotheism, humanitarianism, nationalism, democracy and social justice, elevated by President Suharto to a state ideology. Although some elements of *Pancasila* appear to be consistent with political tolerance and pluralism, the government has used the ideology to justify restrictions on freedom of expression. Thus defamation of public officials carries a penalty of up to six years' imprisonment and insulting such officials is also punishable.

The 1966 Press Act as amended in 1982 requires that each 'press enterprise' has a publication permit (SIUPP); establishes a Press Council to assist the government in drafting regulations and reaching decisions regarding the press, and defines the functions and duties of the national press. These duties include obligations to 'fan the spirit of dedication to the nation's struggle', to 'strengthen national unity and integrity', and to 'exercise social control which is constructive'. The Act provides severe sanctions including imprisonment for those who violate its provisions.

The SIUPP licence is a powerful tool of press control. Through threats of licence revocation, the government can decide who may or may not publish, influence personnel decisions and editorial content, and shut down publications which refuse to co-operate.

**The 'telephone tradition':** This is the name given by journalists to a common form of press censorship—governmental warnings not to print certain facts, views or events. These instructions are given over the telephone by representatives of the Ministry of Information, the Presidential Palace or the security forces.

**Blackouts:** In exceptional circumstances, the Ministry of Information or the military will call a confidential meeting with the press to seek a blackout of particular news items, or to present the official version of certain events. A government campaign against crime resulted in the summary execution of several thousand suspected criminals in 1983 and 1984; after international concern over the executions increased, the government called a meeting to curb press reports.

In September 1986 the press was barred from covering a student demonstration in Jakarta. The demonstration, a peaceful protest criticizing, among other things, the Sept. 12 devaluation of the rupiah, went unreported in both the Jakarta and Bandung papers due to a government 'appeal'. At about the same time, a ban was placed on reports of anti-Chinese demonstrations taking place in the city of Surabaya. On July 21 1987 police officers entered the premises of *Akaya*, a daily newspaper published in Pontianak, and seized the layout of the next day's issue. The editor was ordered to withdraw one article entitled 'Persecuting the accused during investigation is unlawful'.

**Licences:** The government's power to revoke newspaper licences was exercised to dramatic effect in 1986 when it permanently closed Indonesia's second largest daily, *Sinar Harapan* (*Ray of Hope*). Following an Oct. 8 article entitled 'government will withdraw forty-four import trade regulations', the Minister of Information issued a revocation notice, stating that *Sinar* would be closed due to 'speculative' reporting that could 'spread confusion, unrest, anxiety and pessimism' among its readers.

In July 1987 the government revoked the publication licence of *Prioritas* and charged the daily with violating the terms of its publication permit, which required it to concentrate on economic rather than political news. It also claimed that the paper carried 'incorrect and tendentious reports and violated the principles of a free and responsible press'.

The government carefully monitors the small but influential ethnic Chinese population. Only one Chinese newspaper is permitted, and less than half its contents are printed in Chinese-language characters. The paper, *Harian Indonesia* or *Indonesia Rze Pao*, is edited by an Indonesian military officer, and relies extensively on the official government news service.

**Attacks on journalists:** In the South Tapanuli District of Sumatra, three journalists from the city of Medan, North Sumatra, were arrested and detained in late 1984 for depicting a pre-trial hearing as packed with intimidating local police. Three other journalists, anticipating similar reprisals, fled to Medan and reported the incident. Eventually the journalists were released from jail and placed under house arrest until a fact-finding team could exonerate them.

Journalists have been subjected to threats and intimidation, in circumstances that raise concerns about official complicity. At the end of 1983, for example, a reporter for the weekly *Inti Jaya* 'disappeared' outside police headquarters in Kendal Semarang. In early 1986, the body of a journalist who had been active in uncovering corruption in the local Public Works Department was found in a sack on an oil palm plantation outside Medan.

**The foreign press:** Under the 1966 Press Act, no foreign press corporation may be established in Indonesia, although foreign correspondents can apply for one-year work permits which may or may not be granted (and once granted may or may not be extended). A 1972 Information Ministry Decision regulates the circulation of foreign publications within Indonesia. Circulation permits may be granted by the Ministry of Information to foreign publications which do not contain concepts 'contrary to *Pancasila* principles'. Measures may thereafter be taken by the authorities should the publications go astray. Foreign publications entering Indonesia are scanned for 'unpleasant' items. Most foreign coverage of Indonesia, as well as any material deemed offensive, is covered over with black ink. At times, entire issues are banned.

The chill in Indonesia's attitude toward the foreign press may be traced in part to an article in *The Sydney Morning Herald* in April 1986. This article, which drew direct parallels between deposed President Ferdinand Marcos of the Philippines and President Suharto, estimated the Suharto family assets at some two to three billion dollars. The article provoked a crisis in bilateral relations which prompted a blanket ban on Australian journalists by the Indonesian government.

While the Suharto government holds the Australian media in special disfavour, reporters from many other countries have been banned. A foreign correspondent who writes critical stories risks being required to leave, usually through the refusal of an application for visa extension. In March 1987 the government announced restrictions on access to rural areas where 80 per cent of the population live. Forty journalists were required to report their presence to the Ministry of Information when visiting any of the twenty-seven provinces.

Foreign journalists have been permitted almost no access to the former Portuguese territory of East Timor, which Indonesia invaded in 1975 and formally annexed in 1976. The few who have been permitted to visit the territory, in which Indonesian forces have confronted the Fretilin independence movement, have been subjected to tight restrictions.

**Television:** While the print media reaches only a small percentage of the population, Indonesian television reaches over 100 million viewers daily, or an estimated 67 per cent of the population. There is only one station in Indonesia, the government-owned and operated *Yayasan Televisi Republik Indonesia* (*TVRI*). The stated goals of *TVRI* are to 'stimulate the process of nation and character building... support and promote development programmes, [and] play an educational role'. Indonesian television has indeed done much to foster a sense of national unity and to spread the use of the national language. On the other hand, the government recognizes television as a tool for disseminating official views and promoting a positive government image, and takes full advantage of this capability.

**Radio:** Indonesian radio is government-dominated, although not to the same extent as television. The government-owned station, *Radio Republik Indonesia* (*RRI*), is the largest and most powerful. It broadcasts throughout the nation, offering national, provincial and district programming. Like the *TVRI*, *RRI* is under the supervision of the Ministries of Information and Tourism, Ports and Telecommunications and its employees are civil servants.

About 140 local government and 420 private stations also operate around the country. All 'independent' stations are closely monitored, and are subject to limitations: they can devote only 25 per cent of airtime to advertisements and they are not allowed to produce their own news programmes. They must instead broadcast fifteen-minute news programmes prepared by *RRI* six times daily. In August 1987 the government announced plans to close down twenty-one private radio stations on the grounds that they had failed to comply with government broadcasting regulations.

**Books:** Censorship of books is an accepted practice in Indonesia, falling under the responsibility of the Attorney-General. Book bans are imposed after publication. Although once the ban is announced the owners of the banned books are instructed to surrender them to the authorities, post-publication banning enables some proscribed books (and photocopies) to circulate.

One repeated target of censorship has been the celebrated novelist, Pramoedya Ananta Toer. Imprisoned since 1965, and still barred from leaving the country, Pramoedya continues to write and to attempt to publish his books within Indonesia. In 1985, the *Hasta Mitra* publishing house produced and distributed two of Pramoedya's books, '*Jejak Langkah*' ('Steps Forward') and '*Sang Pemula*' ('The Forerunner'), which were promptly banned. A number of other books were banned in 1986, several by foreign academics and journalists. In 1987 Australian academic Susan Abeyasekere had a general history book banned because of its criticism of successive Indonesian governments.

**Public performances:** The government requires that all public performances be cleared in advance. Thus, anyone planning to stage a play, poetry reading, short-story reading, or the like, must first obtain permits from local police. In Yogyakarta, a thriving cultural and student centre, several plays have been banned in recent years. Although none contained direct political criticisms, some took the form of allegories that were too thinly veiled for the comfort of the authorities. The banned play 'Shoe Number One' is the story of an absolute monarch who views coughing as subversive and passes a law requiring that all his subjects be muzzled. This play was successfully staged under a different name in Solo in late 1985. Similar difficulties have been experienced by those attempting to stage poetry and short-story readings.

143

**Film:** All films must be examined by the Film Censorship Board, a government office under the Director-General for Radio, Television and Film. The Board also censors video cassettes, although it is considered a lesser priority.

## Freedom of opinion and expression

A number of human rights organizations have expressed fears that among the many Moslems in Indonesia tried for subversion, a great number have been imprisoned for the peaceful expression of political opinion. Opposition has often been expressed by Moslem groups to the policies reflected in the Social Organizations Law, adopted by the legislature in mid-1985. The law requires all organizations to accept *Pancasila* as their sole principle and gives the Executive powers to guide and ultimately suspend and dissolve organizations for 'disturbing security and public order'. Many members of the Islamic community have viewed the 'sole principle' requirement of the law as contrary to their religious principles.

# NORTH KOREA

The Democratic People's Republic of Korea (DPRK) was officially proclaimed in the North in 1948. It has been ruled throughout its existence by Kim Il Sung. Now one of the world's longest-serving political leaders, he has asserted North Korea's independence and devised a state philosophy, *Juche* (self-reliance), to support it. Since the early 1960s, the country has been systematically refashioned into what has been described as a monumental body of worship to him and to his son Kim Jong Il, his designated successor.

North Korea is not a member of the United Nations. It has, however, ratified the International Covenant on Economic, Social and Cultural Rights and the International Covenant on Civil and Political Rights.

|  |  | Year |
|---|---|---|
| Population | 20,300,000 | est |
| GNP ($ per capita) | 1,000 | est |
| Daily newspapers | 2 | est |
| Non Daily newspapers | 2 | est |
| Periodicals | 9 | est |
| Published books | 35,446 | 1984 |
| Radio stations | 1 | est |
| Radio receivers | 4,100,000 | 1984 |
| TV stations | 1 | est |
| TV sets | 1,005,000 | 1984 |

Press Agencies: Korean Central News Agency (KCNA)

Covenant on Civil & Political Rights _____ 1981

Under the 1972 Constitution the citizens of North Korea are guaranteed 'freedom of speech, the press, assembly, association and demonstration' (Art. 53) and of 'scientific, literary and artistic pursuits' (Art. 60). These guarantees have no meaning in practice. The rights formally extended under Articles 53 and 60 are cancelled by the implications of other articles, notably Article 2 which states that North Korea relies on the 'politico-ideological unity of the entire people', and Article 21 which declares that 'citizens must heighten their revolutionary vigilance against... all hostile elements who are opposed to our country's socialist system'.

State power is exercised through the Korean Workers' Party (KWP), headed by Kim Il Sung since its formation in 1949. It bases its policies on the speeches and writings of the party leader, in particular his philosophy of *Juche*. The whole population is expected to show loyalty to party policies and to Kim Il Sung. The KWP places extreme emphasis on secrecy and the maintenance of national security, due to its hostile relationship with South Korea and the United States in particular.

## The Media

All forms of media in North Korea are state owned and in practice controlled by the KWP. The Party defines what subjects are to be treated and the manner of their presentation. Party officials lay down policies for different groups of media workers who are obliged to produce according to planned quotas. Quotas apply to novelists as much as to radio script writers, and as writers and other media personnel are state employed, it results in an approved output limited in quantity as well as quality.

The media are strictly monitored. The press, literary production, broadcasting services, films, and drama must all be passed as ideologically acceptable. This means, in practice, that the media must devote the majority of its time and content to praise of both Kim Il Sung and his son Kim Jong Il, as well as advancing proletarian struggle and uncritically upholding current party policies. Conversely, South Korea must always be shown to be a US-dominated state where starvation is rife. Such propaganda arises from the fact that North Korea is still officially in a state of war with the South; only an armistice was signed in 1953. For the past twenty years all arts and media have been so tightly in the KWP's embrace that independent expression has disappeared.

**Newspapers:** All news is filtered through the *Korean Central News Agency* (*KCNA*). International news is virtually absent, apart from reports of foreign admiration of Kim Il Sung, who is the main subject of most articles. A recent study of newspapers showed that in one six-page issue of the party paper *Rodong Sinmun* in 1981 there were over 200 references to Kim Il Sung and Kim Jong Il. Many reports are elaborate instances of state propaganda. The North Korean authorities often place advertisements in papers like *The Times* and the *New York Times*, and then describe them in the North Korean media as if they were straightforward news or feature items. The North Korean press has also been known to fabricate or embroider writings by well-known journalists and visitors to the country.

Disinformation is also practised. One example of this relates to the AIDS virus which affects some 11,000 people in South Korea. According to the Pyongyang newspapers, the United States has intentionally exported infected blood to South Korea as part of 'living body tests for AIDS biological weapons'.

No foreign newspapers are publicly available in North Korea. An élite has access to a restricted digest of world press reports, as well as to foreign broadcasts. No underground press appears to exist or come to light, nor any literature that can be construed as having a double meaning or that conveys covert criticism of the regime or society.

**Books and publications:** The estimated 350 writers in the Union of Writers and Artists produce, amongst other things, twenty novels and 450-500 short stories each year. Artistic quality and insight find little place in works whose chief demand is to promote the personality cult of the party leader. Censorship of publications is carried out on a number of levels, beginning with numerous criticism sessions at the workplace and continuing through the appropriate higher authority: Kim Il Sung University or the Academy of Science for research publications, the Union of Writers and Artists for literary works. The Education

Commission and the Ministry of Culture and Art (as appropriate) then make their criticisms. The highest level is the General Publications Bureau. Other censorship bodies exist for artistic productions both regionally and nationally, but the most crucial stage is that of political censorship by party officials.

**Radio and television:** South Korea broadcasts to North Korea (and vice versa), but it is doubtful whether North Koreans are able to listen. Most North Korean households and workplaces are equipped not with radios but with installed speakers, which are tuned to the national and local networks. Radios brought in by relatives from Japan have their dials fixed to prevent reception of external broadcasting; those on sale in North Korea already have fixed dials. All radios are reported to be inspected annually.

The North Korean regime broadcasts a flood of propaganda material in eight major languages through its broadcasting body, the Korean Central Broadcasting Committee (*KCBC*). *KCBC*'s total foreign language broadcasting hours rival those of the *BBC World Service*. The vast expenditure incurred to produce very little return seems not to deter the North Korean authorities. Two foreign translators in Pyongyang in the 1960s who were unwise enough to point this out received savage sentences. One died in prison, while the reminiscences of the other (Ali Lameda, a Venezuelan Communist poet) form the basis for what little is known of the North Korean penal system. Television allocates an estimated 50 per cent of its broadcasting time to films about Kim Il Sung.

**Telephones and letters:** The postal services are unreliable, although some citizens are able to correspond with relatives in Japan. Such letters are censored and requests for material assistance, for example, have to be expressed in code. Telephone services, both inland and international, are poor. A separate switchboard exists for diplomatic use. Resident embassies cannot routinely obtain phone numbers of government ministries. There is only one telephone link shared by North and South Korea, between Red Cross offices.

**Travel:** A virtual ban on travel is another factor hindering access to information. Private transport systems do not exist, and even visits to relatives in other parts of the country are carefully controlled. The authorities need to be given guarantees that host and guest will spend much of their time praising Kim Il Sung before they will grant a pass. The movement of goods vehicles in and out of Pyongyang and around the country is carefully planned. These and railway journeys take place chiefly under cover of darkness. This practice is allegedly dictated by the fear of invasion by South Korea, but at the same time it makes it very difficult for North Korean citizens to learn of life in their own country. If they should chance to witness any extraordinary event, for instance a rail crash, it is known that they are sworn to strict secrecy by the authorities.

**Contact with foreigners:** Contact between North Koreans and foreigners is very limited. Only officially approved persons are sent abroad, and very few students study overseas. Tourism until recently has been minimal, and visitors are not permitted to meet with North Koreans.

## Political parties and religious groups

Political parties are permitted under the Constitution (Art. 53) and freedom of religion is guaranteed (Art. 54). However, such political parties and religious organizations that do exist seem to be little more than committees set up by the ruling party, and the existence of a truly voluntary membership has not been adequately demonstrated. The purpose of these bodies appears to be to act as politically useful links with international organizations not open to the KWP itself.

The other political parties, the Korean Social Democratic Party and the Chondoist Chongu Party, do not constitute any kind of active political opposition. Religious bodies may not oppose party or state policies, or act on behalf of the people. Although the regime may and does spread anti-religious propaganda, it does not permit religious organizations to proselytize.

During its period of rule the KWP has made use of an all-embracing control apparatus: periodic purges of its membership and leadership; extensive investigation and detailed classification of the ideological beliefs of every individual citizen; torture and secret trials and convictions; the death penalty; concentration camps which are said to contain some 105,000 inmates; an education system heavily weighted towards ideological indoctrination (down to its choice of examples in maths textbooks); and a neighbourhood surveillance system of groups of five families with twice weekly study sessions. Even trivial remarks construed as disrespectful to Kim Il Sung or critical of the regime can lead to long prison sentences and ideological retraining. Requests for information on human rights from international human rights organizations such as Amnesty International are routinely ignored.

# SOUTH KOREA

On Thursday Nov. 12, 1987, the opposition leader Kim Dae-Jung, whose picture had been banned from the newspapers and who for many years was under house arrest, launched his candidacy for the presidency of the Republic of Korea at a large gathering in Seoul's Cultural Centre. The rally was not interfered with by riot police as countless opposition demonstrations had been before the watershed date of June 29, 1987, when in response to widespread protests, Mr Roh Tae-Woo, of the ruling Democratic Justice Party, announced direct elections for the presidency. A commitment to introduce press freedom was among eight reforms also promised, a key demand made during the wave of protests in May 1987.

|  |  | Year |
|---|---|---|
| Population | 40,000,000 | 1987 |
| Illiteracy % | 5.7 | 1980 |

| | | |
|---|---|---|
| Daily newspapers | 29 | 1982 |
| Non Daily newspapers | 2 | est |
| Periodicals | 9 | est |
| Published books | 35,512 | 1983 |
| Films produced | 91 | 1983 |
| Radio receivers | 18,000,000 | 1983 |
| TV sets | 7,700,000 | 1984 |

Press Agencies: Naewoe Press,
Yonhap (United) News Agency

Covenant on Civil &
Political Rights _____ NO

The initial focus of the protests was the cover-up over the torture and death of a student, Park Jong-Chol, at the hands of the police in January 1987. It was the decision of some newspapers to break censorship regulations and report on the student's death which is now believed to have been the turning point.

Events have moved rapidly since June. In July, an amnesty led to the release of over 500 prisoners and the restoration of civil rights to more than 2,300, including Kim Dae-Jung. A new Constitution, which declares that 'licensing or censorship of speech and of the press shall not be recognized', was approved by referendum on Oct. 27, 1987. It is due to come into effect and replace the October 1980 Constitution on Feb. 25, 1988. Presidential elections were held on Dec. 16, 1987, and were won by Roh after the opposition failed to agree on a single candidature.

Censorship, and 'guidelines' for the media, were relaxed before the elections, although there remained uncertainty about the new limits of freedom of expression; some of the tight legal controls of the past were abolished in press laws enacted in November, but also in that month, five publishers who had allegedly sold books on communist ideology were arrested for 'draconian interrogation' under the National Security Act which remains unaffected by the reforms. It remains to be seen whether the Roh regime will enact further reforms.

## Background

The Republic of Korea—which separates the USSR and the People's Republic of China from Japan, and is host to over 40,000 United States troops—is still technically at war with North Korea (no peace agreement was signed at the end of the Korean War in 1953). It has a large standing army, highly developed and powerful intelligence services which appear to be outside public or legislative control, and a political leadership which has traditionally been intolerant of all forms of dissent from official policy on the ground that these might weaken the state's capacity to defend itself.

Many South Koreans believe that North Korea poses a significant military threat, especially given the turbulent history of the two countries and North Korea's opposing ideology. The two generals who took power through military coups and governed the country in 1961-87 used this threat as their justification for the suppression of free expression and other human rights. Almost every aspect of state policy was subordinated to the needs of national defence as understood by the country's military and political authorities.

Park Chung-Hee, who came to power in 1961, took extensive action to bring the press under his control and to prevent his opposition from having any meaningful access to public debate. The situation did not improve when Chun Doo-Hwan took over power in 1979-80. The Chun government 'purified' public communication by banning 172 publications, closing 617 publishing companies, and arranging for 683 reporters to be dismissed. Only one newspaper in each province was allowed to remain in operation, a single official news agency— *Yonhap*—was permitted to operate, and only two television-radio stations were licensed to transmit news. Others including the *Christian Broadcasting System* (*CBS*), representing the Protestant churches, were obliged to close or restrict the range of their programming.

**The Kwangju uprising:** Suppression was not limited to the media. In May 1980, when police raided the homes of democratic movement leaders and students in Kwangju, students and other citizens reacted through demonstrations. The demonstrators were subdued by an estimated 33,000 riot police and paratroopers who resorted to beating, stabbing, and shooting protesters and non-protesters alike. By the time the incident ended, an unknown number of people had died (191 according to government claims, but the city of Kwangju's statistics suggest that closer to 2,300 were killed).

The Chun government maintained strict control over its opposition until December 1983, when it announced a new liberalization policy. An increased number of books and magazines were published by dissident religious, political, and cultural figures, and some independent reporting appeared in the daily newspapers. In the campaign for the National Assembly elections held in February 1985, opposition politicians were allowed to speak out on such traditionally taboo subjects as the 1980 Kwangju massacre, the South/North Korean dialogue policy and possible revision of the Constitution. This open campaign led to the election of the largest-ever opposition bloc to the National Assembly, led by the New Korea Democratic Party (which has since split).

In May 1985, Chun reversed his policy in response to increased dissension. The majority of the South Korean population, however, continued to demand greater political involvement and more freedom to express political views. The resulting conflict between government and people culminated in the *volte-face* by the government in June 1987.

**The National Security Law:** This law, which punishes activity deemed by the government to be 'aiding the cause of anti-state elements', especially North Korea, has been one of the statutes most widely used to suppress opposition, including publications. Fear of this statute has been cited as one of the major reasons for pervasive self-censorship in Korean media. On Nov. 14, 1987, the Seoul Metropolitan Police announced that they had identified eighty-one publishers who dealt in books on communist ideology. Thousands of copies of over 100 titles were seized, including 'Das Kapital' and Bertrand Russell's 'History of Western Philosophy'. According to Amnesty International, there were over 700 political prisoners still detained under the National Security Law (NSL)in August 1987, including forty adopted as prisoners of conscience. In October 1985 a leading Protestant intellectual journal, *Christian Thought*, was closed for six months. The producers of the journal were arrested and charged for publishing details of a slum-dwellers' meeting. The offending article concerned the eviction of Mak-dong area residents to facilitate construction for the 1988 Olympics.

Two students, Kim Sung-Yong and Song Ki-Yong, were arrested under the NSL on Oct. 29, 1987 on charges of producing pro-North Korean publications. An edition of one of these, *Plaza for Democracy*, was said by the authorities to have carried articles supporting the *Juche* ideology, and another an article which referred to the US army presence in South Korea after World War II as an 'occupation', and the entry of the USSR into North Korea as a liberation from Japanese colonial rule.

The same law had been used in April against three students for listening to and transcribing radio broadcasts from North Korea, and in March against a publisher, Chung Sung-Hyun, under a clause which provides for imprisonment of up to seven years for 'praising, encouraging or siding with' North Korea: he was associated with the publication of a book entitled 'What is Philosophy?'.

## The Media

**Newspapers:** The Basic Press Act 1980 (now repealed) required all publishers to obtain a licence. Licences were not easy to obtain since the law required applicants to own expensive equipment for large-scale printing. Those licensed had to submit advance copies of newspapers, books, and pamphlets to the Department of Public Information Control (DPIC). All broadcast records had also to be delivered to the Department each month. A 'broadcasting committee', appointed by the President, watched over press activities and issued regulations designating what was and was not acceptable for dissemination. Another committee—the Korean Ethics Committee for Public Performance—vetted books, songs, films and theatre.

The government monitored the newspapers daily, and specified the placement of stories and the photographs which should accompany them. Newspaper advertisements had to be submitted to an advertising council which rewarded and punished different papers by deciding where the advertisements would be placed.

**Mal:** The most striking insight into government manipulation of the press was provided at the end of 1986, when the magazine *Mal,* published by a group of banned journalists, reported in great detail the secret daily instructions supplied by the government to the media about what they should and should not report. The details of messages for each day were reported, from Oct. 19, 1985 to Aug. 8, 1986, regarding coverage of the trial of a dissident who had been sexually abused during her interrogation: 'Possibly the article may be carried on the national pages; however, the report made by individual journalists cannot be carried, only the report of the prosecution; the headline must be "sexual insult" not "sexual assault"; the sub-heads should be taken from the analysed data distributed by the public security authority (that is, "Utilization of Sex: For the Sake of Revolution"); the whole text of the report of the prosecution must be carried; but the details of accusations made by barristers for the anti-government side or by the NCC (National Council of Churches), and the communiqué concerning the incident published by other women's associations, must not be reported.'

In August 1987 the government ceased to issue daily guidelines, but was said to be relying on self-censorship by editors especially on coverage of North Korea. Censorship rules on magazines and books were also ended. A committee was appointed to review bans on 1,000 pop songs previously banned as critical of the government.

**Broadcasting:** The *Korean Broadcasting System (KBS),* which is under the control of a Board appointed by the President, holds 65 per cent of the shares of *Munhwa Broadcasting Corporation (MBC),* the other major television and radio station. (The two private networks which existed before the Chun government were forced to merge with *KBS.*) *KBS* is the most powerful shareholder of *Yonhap,* a nominally private news agency whose president is a former government official. *Yonhap* has control over the transmission of all domestic news, and distributes all the news and features for foreign news agencies. *KBS* also controls two newspapers. The *Christian Broadcasting System (CBS),* a primary source of independent news in Korea before 1980, was ordered to broadcast only religious services. It operated on contributions made by churches around the world since it was not allowed to accept commercial advertisements.

After June 29, 1987, when the ruling Democratic Justice Party offered to meet the demands of the opposition, the *CBS* unilaterally began broadcasting news again. This followed a long petition campaign for normal broadcasting. In September, the government relented on the station which may now run news programmes and advertisements. On July 16, television reporters from *MBC* stopped work for twelve hours to demand the resignation of the government-appointed director of the station and the reinstatement of dismissed journalists. During the December presidential election campaign thirty reporters from *KBS* held a sit-in to protest against what they termed biased news coverage of the election.

**The new press laws:** In November 1987 the Basic Press Law of 1980 was repealed and replaced by two laws on periodicals and broadcasting. The Registration of Publications law abolished the power of the Minister of Culture and Information to revoke the registration of newspapers and magazines. Only a court may now close a newspaper. However, strict criteria of scale are laid down for newspaper proprietors. Korean language newspapers must be equipped with presses capable of printing at least 20,000 copies of a minimum four-page tabloid per hour.

Foreign-language dailies and Korean monthlies are required to have one or more rotary presses for their sole use. News agencies and broadcasting stations are prohibited from owning newspaper companies. The Act, therefore, still requires licensing of newspapers and appears to exclude the smaller publications from registering.

The Broadcasting Law guarantees that broadcasting stations may serve the public interest without government interference. However, it bans 'private enterprises' from running broadcasting businesses. The implications for the *CBS*, the only non-state service apart from the US forces network, are unclear. A further Bill, on the registration of publishing and printing companies, disputed between the government and opposition, is pending.

## Current detainees

Included among those writers, journalists and media workers against whom action has been taken during the course of 1987 or who are still in prison: Lee Tae-Bok, publisher, sentenced January 1982 to life imprisonment, commuted to twenty years in August 1983; Kim Hyon-Jang, freelance journalist, sentenced to death but sentence commuted to life imprisonment in March 1983; Kim Sang-Bok, publisher, sentenced to four years' imprisonment, due to be released March 24, 1990; Koy Kyong-Dae, publisher, sentenced to three years' imprisonment, due to be released March 24, 1989.

# MALAYSIA

Malaysia is a multi-racial, multi-lingual and multi-religious society. About 53 per cent of the population are Malays, 35 per cent Chinese, 10 per cent Indians and 2 per cent others. Most of the Chinese and Indian population are descendants of immigrants who came to Peninsular Malaya during British colonial rule in the last century. Bahasa Malaysia, based on Malay, is the national language. In addition, there are Chinese (Mandarin and other local dialects), Tamil, Punjabi, Hindi, Urdu and a number of aboriginal and East Malaysian tongues. Islam is the dominant and national religion and is practised mostly by the Malays. Other religions include Buddhism, Taoism, Hinduism and Christianity. The different races live side by side but inter-racial and inter-religious marriages are rare.

|  |  | Year |
|---|---|---|
| Population | 15,000,000 | est |
| GNP ($ per capita) | 1,990 | 1984 |
| Daily newspapers | 39 | est |
| Non Daily newspapers | 7 | est |
| Periodicals | 26 | est |
| Published books | 3,975 | 1984 |
| Radio stations | 3 | est |
| Radio receivers | 6,500,000 | 1983 |
| TV stations | 3 | est |
| TV sets | 1,502,000 | 1984 |

Press Agencies: BERNAMA

Covenant on Civil & Political Rights ———— NO

The existence of these different communities has been a constant source of tension, sometimes resulting in open conflict. In 1969, for instance, there were violent race riots in which many lives were lost. At that time 117 people were arrested in the biggest crack-down since the passage of the 1960 Internal Security Act (ISA). This Act was again invoked by the government in October 1987 when over 100 leaders and activists from a broad spectrum of political parties and other organizations were detained, including ten members of parliament and the opposition leader Lim Kit Siang. Three newspapers, *The Star*, *Sin Chew Jit Poh* and *Watan*, had their publishing licences withdrawn.

**'Rukunegara':** A blueprint for the Malaysian government concept of 'development journalism' is the *Rukunegara* (national ideology), adopted shortly after the 1969 race riots. The *Rukunegara* includes five beliefs (a united nation, and a democratic, just, liberal and progressive society) and five principles (belief in God, loyalty to King and country, upholding of the Constitution, rule of law, good behaviour and morality).

## The Media

The government regards the mass media as a tool for nation building, development and national unity. To that end, the broadcasting media which are government owned and controlled have been instructed since the early 1970s to help oppose 'anti-national elements'. Radio and television producers were instructed to explain clearly the country's domestic and foreign policy and to use the broadcasting media to attract foreign investment. Government guidelines remind broadcasters to avoid the 'mindless aping of bourgeois values and styles of the West'. In the 1970s, radio and television were forbidden to broadcast bad news before noon in order not to upset people on their way to work. Stories about air crashes were banned altogether so as not to upset pilgrims who hoped to fly to Saudi Arabia during the *Hajj*.

A new law was passed on Dec. 7, 1987, allowing the Information Minister to monitor all programmes to ensure that they are consistent with government policy. The Minister has the power to revoke the licence of any station judged to be in violation of the law.

**Bernama:** The government also controls the national news agency, *Bernama*, which was set up by an act of parliament in 1967. *Bernama* provides all local news and information to the media. Since May 1984 it has also become the sole distributor of news and features from foreign news agencies. Its stated aims are to strengthen the national news service and to combat the problem of news flow imbalance between developed nations and the developing nations such as Malaysia, and to correct the 'inaccurate and biased' reporting of events in the Third World. Malaysia was, in fact, one of the most vigourous proponents of the 'New International Information and Communication Order' during the debates on the media at UNESCO in the 1970s.

**Newspapers:** The privately-owned press in Malaysia is expected to co-operate with the government in promoting official policy and campaigns rather than act as critics or adversaries. With a few exceptions, most of the large circulation press is, in fact, owned and controlled by individuals or groups close to the political parties which form the ruling coalition government, the *Barisan Nasional* (National Front). The English language daily, the *New Straits Times*, for instance, is the organ of the United Malays National Organisation (UMNO), the dominant Malay party in the Front, whereas the English language *The Star* is controlled by the Malaysian Chinese Association (MCA), a Chinese political party in the ruling coalition. The largest Malay language daily newspapers *Utusan Malaysia* and *Berita Harian* are owned by supporters of UMNO. Party politics tend to dictate the news values and editorial policy of these major newspapers.

The government-guided press policy, controls through ownership of major newspapers, and legal controls and restrictions, make it difficult for the small private press to remain independent.

**Licensing:** On Dec. 2, 1987, the Printing Presses and Publications Act (1948) was amended as follows: (1) Malicious publishing of false news is an offence. 'Malicious' is defined as including 'not taking reasonable measures to verify the truth'. To prove their innocence, journalists may be forced to expose their sources. On conviction the writers, editors, printers and publishers can receive heavy fines and up to three years' prison sentences. (2) If the Home Affairs Minister deems that a manuscript or publication could prejudice bilateral relations, public morality, security, public order, national interests, or alarm public opinion, he can ban its publication, import and circulation. The Act ends the possibility of appeal to a court from a ministerial refusal, suspension or revocation of a licence.

**Prohibited publications:** Prohibited publications include not only offending articles, but any 'extract, precis [or] paraphrase thereof'. Offending publications include counselling 'disobedience to the law', or promotion of feelings of 'ill-will, hostility, hatred, disharmony or disunity'. The word 'publication', either local or foreign, now encompasses 'anything which by its form, shape or in any manner is capable of suggesting words or ideas'. It includes 'audio recording', whether voice or music.

'Oppressors and apologists', a book written by Fan Yew Teng who is the secretary-general of the opposition Socialist Democratic Party, is banned because it contains a prohibited article written in 1983. Fan was fined M$2,000 (US$900) and imprisoned for one day in July 1987. His publisher was also fined M$1,500. Earlier, in March 1985, Haji Suhaimi Said, legal adviser of the fundamentalist Moslem opposition Pan-Malayan Islamic Party (PAS), was arrested in Pahang state for publishing pamphlets giving an account of clashes between supporters of PAS and UMNO in Lubku Merbau. Haji Said was detained for trying to 'split the country's Malay and Moslem community' and 'threaten public order and national security'. His office was raided by the police and a number of documents were confiscated.

Moslem preachers who are critical of some aspects of Islam can also be banned. In July 1986, Kassin Ahmad was banned from giving sermons or lectures on Islam because of his book '*Hadis*—a Re-evaluation', in which he argued that there was no proof that Islamic traditions outlined in the '*Hadis*' came from the Prophet, a common argument among some Islamic scholars. The book was banned and those found in possession of it could be fined up to M$500.

**Foreign publications:** The Control of Imported Publications Act deals specifically with foreign publications circulating in the country (the Official Secrets Act is also used). The Minister of Information has absolute discretion to ban any foreign publications which are deemed prejudicial to public order, morality and security of Malaysia. Magazines such as *Playboy* and *Penthouse* are banned under this law. Political and financial publications such as the Hong Kong-based *Far Eastern Economic Review* and the *Asian Wall Street Journal* are occasionally banned, especially when their coverage on Malaysia touches on sensitive subjects such as race problems or financial scandals among members of the government.

In September 1986 the *Asian Wall Street Journal* was banned for three months and its correspondents, John Berthelsen and Raphael Pura, were expelled. The Malaysian authorities did not give specific reasons for their action. The Deputy Home Affairs Minister, Datuk Megat Junid, said simply that the paper had created 'feelings of uncertainty among the people... in a way there is a sabotage of the economic development of this country'. According to the *Far Eastern Economic Review*, the move against the *Asian Wall Street Journal* came after an escalating campaign against the foreign press in Malaysia, a campaign identified closely with Prime Minister Mahathir Mohamad. One of the Prime Minister's favourite themes about major American newspapers such as the *New York Times* and the *Asian Wall Street Journal* is that they are controlled by 'Zionist forces'. He is believed to view criticism of Malaysia from these newspapers as an attempt to sabotage his country because of his government's support for the PLO.

A US-made television series about the life of Golda Meir called 'Against the Odds' was banned in 1986. In August 1984, the New York Philharmonic had to cancel its two concerts in Kuala Lumpur because the Malaysian government insisted that Ernest Bloch's 'Schelomo', (a Hebrew rhapsody for cello and orchestra), be dropped.

## The Internal Security Act

A law which is seen as the most repressive of press freedom and freedom of expression, association and assembly is the Internal Security Act (ISA) of 1960, a relic of British colonial emergency legislation which allowed detention without trial for long periods.

The ISA has often been used to suppress opposition views and political opponents, most recently in October 1987. The ISA, which gives the government unlimited powers in the name of 'state security', is used by the Malaysian Special Branch, whose activities include monitoring, surveillance, telephone tapping and harassment of suspected 'subversives'.

Under Section 73 of the Act, the Home Affairs Minister can order the detention for sixty days for interrogation by the Special Branch of any person, on the suspicion that 'he or she acted or is about to act or is likely to act in any manner prejudicial to the security of Malaysia or any part thereof'.

The Official Secrets Act, passed in 1972 and considerably strengthened in 1983, has also been used against foreign correspondents. In October 1985 James Clad, Kuala Lumpur bureau chief of the *Far Eastern Economic Review* was fined a total of M$10,000 and expelled from the country for offending against this Act. He insisted that the article for which he was penalized was accurate, and his editor stood by the story. He later told other journalists in Hong Kong that he considered the charges against him 'a technical violation of a widely drafted statue that would—if applied vigorously—make the practice of journalism as understood in Malaysia and abroad impossible'.

On Dec. 5, 1986, the Act was amended to provide for a mandatory one-year minimum prison sentence, despite strong representations from the National Union of Journalists and the newly-formed Freedom of Information Group.

# PAKISTAN

Censorship and denials of freedom of association have long been a feature of Pakistan, particularly during periods of martial law. Since 1953 martial law has been invoked four times, including the period from 1977, when Gen. Zia-ul Haq came to power in a military coup, to 1985.

Since the ending of martial law in 1985, the position has gradually improved. But the authorities still exercise considerable control and the tenets of an Islamic state have had a pervasive influence on the circulation of information and ideas.

| | | Year |
|---|---|---|
| Population | 97,000,000 | 1986 |
| GNP ($ per capita) | 300 | 1984 |
| Illiteracy % | 70.4 | 1985 |
| Daily newspapers | } 118 | est |
| Non Daily newspapers | | est |
| Periodicals | 1,300 | est |
| Published books | 8,260 | 1984 |
| Radio stations | 8 | est |
| Radio receivers | 2,165,000 | 1986 |
| TV stations | 5 | est |
| TV sets | 1,530,000 | 1986 |

Press Agencies:
AEI, JA, ALI, Unipress

Covenant on Civil & Political Rights _____ NO

## The Media

The National Press Trust has been government-run since 1964. The Trust publishes four of the most important daily newspapers, the English language *Pakistan Times* and *Morning News* and the Urdu language *Mashriq Daily* and *Imroze*. The state also owns the *Associated Press of Pakistan (APP)*, one of the two national press agencies, and the only other agency, *Pakistan Press International (PPI)*, is heavily dependent on government support. All broadcasting media are also government-owned.

The Press and Publications Ordinance of 1963 requires licensing and security deposits for newspaper publishing. Although technically the declaration to publish a newspaper is authenticated by a district magistrate, all cases are as a rule referred to the federal government which issues licences at its discretion. The Ordinance also gives the government powers to close down publications deemed objectionable. Publishers and printers who offend the authorities have in the past found their licences revoked or their security deposits forfeited. These powers cannot be challenged or questioned in a court of law. The present Junejo government is committed to repeal of the Ordinance.

Other legal controls and sanctions are used against publishers, printers, editors and reporters. These include provisions in the Security Act (1952), the Maintenance of Pakistan Public Order Ordinance (1960), the Defence of Pakistan Ordinance (1965), and the Official Secrets Act. A positive development for press freedom came in 1986 when the National Assembly passed a bill repealing a section of the penal code (inserted in 1979) on defamation, which had banned publishers from printing any information that might harm the reputation of any person, even if that information were true.

**Economic pressure:** The authorities can and do apply economic pressure on the independent press over newsprint quotas and government-sponsored advertisements. It has been estimated that about 70 per cent of advertising is from state-controlled undertakings. The supply of newsprint is in the hands of the government, and those publications which oppose government policy often find their supplies cut off or erratically available. Government pressure frequently takes the form of 'press advice', such as telephone calls to newspaper editors by officials of the Ministry of Information and Broadcasting advising them not to publish news items or features. Those who ignore the 'advice' often find government advertisements stopped or greatly reduced. Since January 1986, press freedom has improved, but the press is still cautious about a number of topics, such as questioning the actions of President Zia, some prominent religious leaders, matters relating to national security issues, secessionist movements, the budget and actions of the military.

The press has been able to cover the activities of opposition politicians, including their criticism of government policy. Foreign correspondents have been allowed into the country without restraints. In April 1986, for instance, when Benazir Bhutto, the leader of the opposition Pakistan People's Party (PPP), returned to Pakistan from her exile in London, foreign journalists were allowed to accompany her and report her activities freely, including her tour around the country. The jamming of foreign radio and television broadcasts has also stopped.

## Martial law 1977-85

When martial law was declared in 1977, freedom of speech, assembly and association, as well as basic safeguards against arbitrary arrest, detention and maltreatment were abrogated. Martial Law Regulation No. 4 stated that 'no person shall publish, print, circulate, or... otherwise [be] in possession of any... publication... calculated to promote or attempt to promote feeling or enmity or hatred between different provinces, classes, sects or religious order' (maximum punishment: ten years' imprisonment and thirty lashes). Under Martial Law Regulation No. 49, the government required prior censorship of printed matter which the Chief Martial Law Administrator considered prejudicial to Islamic thought or morality.

Between 1977 and 1985, thousands of people were arrested and detained, including publishers, printers, editors, reporters and writers. They were tried by the military courts without either the right to a defence by a lawyer or a right of appeal. In 1978, 150 journalists and press workers were arrested for protesting against infringements of press freedom, and three of them were flogged in Lahore jail. In October 1979, six daily newspapers were banned permanently. In November 1979, Salamat Ali, a correspondent of the Hong Kong based *Far Eastern Economic Review*, was arrested for writing an article on Baluchistan, one of Pakistan's four provinces. He was tried by a military court under Martial Law Regulations, found guilty and sentenced to one year's imprisonment with hard labour. He was, however, released four months later on 'compassionate grounds', following international protests.

In September 1981, Irshad Rao, former editor of the banned *Musawat* newspaper and publisher of the Urdu and Pushtu language weekly *Al Falah*, a pro-PPP publication, was sentenced by a summary military court in Karachi to one year's imprisonment and ten lashes of the whip for 'printing objectionable literature and creating unrest among the masses and disaffection against the armed forces of Pakistan'. Zamin Shah and Abdus Salim, two calligraphers on *Al Falah*, were also sentenced to one year's imprisonment and five lashes.

In 1983, ten journalists working for the National Press Trust in Lahore were dismissed from their posts for protesting against the government's harsh treatment of opponents in Sind province. Five of the journalists were later reinstated by court orders and others are still fighting their cases in court.

Book publishers and writers were also subjected to harassment. In 1984, Abdur Malik of the *People's Publishing House* and Najam Sethi of *Vanguard Press* were detained for a month for publishing material offensive to the government. Ahmad Faraz, one of the leading poets writing in Urdu and director-general of the Academy of Letters, was arrested and held in solitary confinement for over a month without charge for writing a poem called 'Pesha War Qatilo' ('The Mercenaries'), in protest against the shooting of students in Lahore by the Army. He was later dismissed from his post at the Academy. He and other prominent writers and poets, together with a number of academics and intellectuals, were forced to leave the country.

**Nuclear secrecy:** The most recent case of government action against a journalist was the dismissal of Mushahid Hussain Sayed, editor of *The Muslim*, an influential English language daily newspaper published in Islamabad. He was forced to resign in April 1987 following the publication of an article abroad revealing that Pakistan had developed an atom bomb, at the Khan laboratories at Kahuta. The article was written by the Indian journalist Kuldip Nayeer after an interview with Pakistan's leading nuclear scientist Abdel Qader Khan. Mushahid Hussain had allegedly arranged the interview. Khan later denied the interview had taken place but this in turn was denied by Hussain in a leading article in his newspaper. According to press reports in Pakistan, the government put pressure on *The Muslim*'s owners to dismiss Hussain or face the withdrawal of all government-sponsored advertisements. He was later banned from leaving the country and had his telephone disconnected.

## Islam

Pakistan's status as an Islamic state has implications for freedom of expression. For instance, television, films, publications and art works may

160

not show nudity or persons attired in what is considered immodest clothing. Scenes of nudity or kissing in imported television programmes and films are severely cut. Women's hockey is only allowed when the players are fully covered from head to ankles, and no men are allowed as spectators. Women athletes have protested against a ban on their participation in international tournaments. Authors and publishers avoid controversial political and religious subjects.

In January 1987, the editor, printer and publisher of the *Frontier Post*, Peshawar's English language daily newspaper, were persecuted by the provincial government of the North West Frontier Province for publishing a photograph of a painting of Adam and Eve by the Renaissance artist Lucas Cranach. According to the charges, the painting was sacrilegious and the naked human forms injured the sentiments of Moslems. The photograph appeared beside an article entitled 'The Tree of Knowledge', and was reprinted from the London newspaper *The Guardian*. Earlier, an angry mob of about 2,000 people had attacked the offices and printing works of the newspaper. Part of the building was set on fire.

Despite official proscription, however, banned publications (including sexually explicit literature and video cassettes) can be bought under the counter. A typical example is Salman Rushdie's book 'Shame', which caused a government outcry and is still banned. A pirated edition can be obtained in most major bookshops, as can other banned books. Political writings that continue to be suppressed, such as magazines and leaflets, promoting cultural and linguistic interests of minority ethnic groups (mostly Sindi) can be obtained during political rallies or through an underground network. Security police often know who are believed to be responsible for these publications but apparently ignore them. Banned political poems are often read during political rallies. There are fringe theatre groups staging controversial political plays, mostly to a restricted audience in private homes.

## Academic freedom

Lack of academic freedom in colleges and universities is a serious issue in Pakistan. During the martial law period, as part of the Islamization policy, school and university syllabuses were revised. By 1980, more than 500 text books were expunged as being 'un-Islamic' or 'anti-Islamic'. They included such works as the love poems of Robert Browning and the novels of D. H. Lawrence in English degree courses and Charles Darwin's works on the theory of evolution in science degree courses. Most of these textbooks are still banned today. University vice-chancellors (mostly military men) and administrators, who were appointed during martial law periods, are still in control of higher education. Violence against 'socialists' and 'secularists' on campuses still occurs periodically. It is reportedly carried out by the *Islami-Jamiat-i-Talaba* (JIT), an armed student wing of the fundamentalist *Jamaat-i-Islami* party, which is close to the government. During the martial law period from 1977-1985,

161

fundamentalist religious leaders from this party were responsible for the imposition of Islamic law—*Sharia*—and they acted as judges in the *Sharia* Courts. The JIT who were known to their critics as the 'B team of Martial Law' had enormous influence in the running of universities and colleges, including the appointment of new teachers and the admission of new students.

## Current detainees

Included among those writers, journalists and media workers against whom action has been taken during the course of 1987 or who are still in prison: Ahmed Kamal Warsi, journalist, sentenced to seven years' imprisonment following eighteen months spent in pre-trial detention.

# SINGAPORE

According to the Singapore government, there are 3,700 foreign publications circulating in the island city state. The country plays host to the main *BBC* short-wave relay station for Asia and Oceania and the *BBC World Service* is available in Singapore on FM 24 hours a day, at the specific request of the government. In addition, there are ninety-six accredited journalists, press photographers and cameramen working for sixty foreign news organizations, including correspondents of *TASS* and *Xinhua* (China) news agencies.

Singapore is proud of this openness to foreign media, but it contrasts with the government's intolerance and sometimes high-handedness towards any

|  |  | Year |
| --- | --- | --- |
| Population | 2,000,000 | 1985 |
| GNP ($ per capita) | 7,260 | 1984 |
| Daily newspapers | 8 | est |
| Non Daily newspapers | 2 | est |
| Periodicals | 16 | est |
| Published books | 1,927 | 1983 |
| Radio stations | 3 | est |
| Radio receivers | 593,000 | 1986 |
| TV stations | 1 | est |
| TV sets | 486,000 | 1986 |
| Covenant on Civil & Political Rights | | NO |

writings critical of itself or the country, published at home or abroad. Recent illustrations of this were the decisions to restrict the circulation of *Time* magazine in 1986 and of the *Asian Wall Street Journal* in 1987, and the detentions in May 1987 of members of Catholic organizations for alleged involvement in a communist network.

Freedom of opinion and expression in Singapore is circumscribed, especially when the subject deals with race, language, religion and culture. In addition, the government is very sensitive to any forms of criticism of its policy, and seems to be particularly preoccupied with 'threats' or 'conspiracies' to challenge or undermine its authority.

## The Media

The *Singapore Broadcasting Corporation* is run by the government. There is a wired radio network for subscribers, owned by the London-based *Rediffusion International* company. The government owns or controls no newspapers other than the *Government Gazette*. The independent press is little more than a shadow of its former self. As one Singapore journalist put it: 'if you antagonize the government and do not toe its line, your newspaper will disappear like the rest. Opposition journalists are liable to be arrested and imprisoned or exiled abroad. Critical foreign correspondents are simply expelled without any explanations, their publications might be banned, and all this in the name of the laws of the country.'

163

**The Internal Security Act:** One such law is the Internal Security Act (ISA). This Act stems from emergency British colonial legislation passed in Malaysia in 1948 during the communist insurgency, codified as Malaysia's ISA of 1960 and extended to Singapore when it became an independent state in 1965. Under Section 20 the Minister of Home Affairs is empowered to prohibit any publications which he deems to be 'prejudicial to the national interest, public order, or security of Singapore'.

It is mainly under the ISA that opponents or critics of the government have been arrested and detained over the last twenty years, including newspaper editors, publishers and journalists. In 1963 the most widely reported case was that of Said Zahari, a poet and editor of the then leading Malay language newspaper *Utusan Melayu*, who was arrested and then detained for nearly sixteen years without trial, followed by nine months in exile on an offshore island before his final release in August 1979.

The most serious purge of the press, however, was in 1971 during the government campaign against 'black operations'—'local and foreign intrigues hostile to Singapore's general interests'. Among those arrested were four senior members of staff on the Chinese language newspaper *Nanyang Siang Pau*, who were detained for two years for 'stirring up racial issues and glamorizing communism'. These were *Nanyang's* editor-in-chief, Shamsuddin Tung Tao Chang, its leader writer Ly Singko, its managing director Lee Mau Seng and its public relations officer, Kerk Loon Sing. All four were later released after they had agreed to make public confessions. In January 1973, *Nanyang's* Managing Editor Lee En Seng was also arrested and detained for five years because the newspaper continued to publish hostile articles against government policy.

In 1971, the government forced the permanent closure of two independent English language newspapers, the *Herald* and the *Eastern Sun*, for 'covert subversion' and receiving funds from abroad. Initial government actions against the two newspapers included the denial of normal press facilities, banning of reporters from official press conferences and briefings, denial of official press releases and withdrawal of all government-sponsored advertising. In the case of the *Herald*, three senior staff, all expatriates, were refused the renewal of their work permits and asked to leave Singapore on 48-hour notice. Finally, the *Herald's* annual printing permit and publishing licence were withdrawn.

Legislation in 1974 provided for the compulsory government 'vetting' of newspaper managements, and for the transfer of all newspapers to public companies.

Further clampdowns on the press occurred in 1976 and 1977 when a number of local journalists and those writing for foreign publications were accused of taking part in 'communist conspiracies'. In June 1976 Hussein Jahidin and Azmi Mahmud, then editor and assistant editor of the Malay language daily *Berita Harian*, were detained under the ISA for carrying out activities 'aimed at influencing a number of people to carry out prejudicial activities'.

In 1977, Arun Senkuttwan, correspondent of the *Economist* and the

*Financial Times* of Britain, and Ho Kwong Ping of the Hong Kong-based *Far Eastern Economic Review*, were charged with 'anti-government activities'. All four were later released after agreeing to make 'confessions' on television, admitting that they had systematically used their articles to discredit the Singapore government. They too were detained without trial under the powers of the Internal Security Act.

**Newspaper and Printing Presses Act:** There are two other laws which are often used to restrict or ban undesirable publications, mostly foreign ones. The Newspaper and Printing Presses Act (NPPA), with its 1986 amendment, empowers the Minister of Communications and Information to restrict the sale or distribution of foreign publications which have been declared as having 'engaged in the domestic politics of Singapore'. The government's definition of 'engaging in domestic politics of Singapore' includes 'publishing material intended to generate political, ethnic and religious unrest; indulging in slanted, distorted or partisan reporting; or persistently refusing to publish government rejections to mis-reporting and baseless allegations'.

Once a foreign publication is found guilty of 'engaging in domestic politics', it is declared a 'gazetted publication' and its circulation restricted to a limited number of copies decided on by the Minister. The circulation of *Time* magazine was cut from 18,000 to 2,000 copies at the beginning of 1987 and the *Asian Wall Street Journal* from 5,000 to 400 copies a day. Copies of the 'gazetted publications' may be sold only by authorized dealers.

In defence of its action against the two publications, the government maintained that censorship was not at issue. It claimed that it was defending its 'right of reply' to articles which it considered contained 'biased, erroneous and baseless allegations' about Singapore. *Time* and the *Asian Wall Street Journal* had agreed to publish parts of lengthy government statements of rebuttal, but stuck by their stories. The authorities then took punitive action against the two publications by invoking the Newspaper and Printing Presses Act.

Apart from body and baggage searches at entry points to Singapore, mail searches for unmarked copies of 'gazetted publications' are sanctioned by the authorities. Postal subscriptions to such publications are prohibited, and their distribution carries maximum penalties of S$10,000 (about US$4,700) in fines or two years' imprisonment. However, in a new twist, a law is proposed for 1988 which will permit restricted publications to be photocopied without penalty.

The government's treatment of foreign correspondents based in Singapore is often harsh. Those who are known to have regularly written critical articles about the country are either expelled or refused extended visas. During the past ten years, for instance, five correspondents of the *Far Eastern Economic Review* have been expelled, the latest victim being Nigel Holloway, expelled in May 1987. Like other previous cases, Nigel Holloway's expulsion was not explained despite persistent requests from the *Review*'s editor in Hong Kong.

**The Undesirable Publications Act:** Under this 1967 Act, the government is also empowered to ban foreign publications 'engaging in domestic politics of Singapore'. According to the review Committee on Censorship of the Ministry of Communications, other material banned under these powers includes publications depicting undesirable themes such as sexual permissiveness (*Playboy* and *Penthouse* magazines, for instance), indecency, drug abuse, excessive violence, books with illustrations of sexual positions (such as 'The Joy of Sex') and song lyrics which make reference to drugs or have obscene connotations. Publications which consist exclusively of printed words are treated more liberally, provided that the substance of the book is not judged obscene, vulgar or exploitative of sex and violence.

**1987 arrests:** In May and June 1987, twenty-two young professionals belonging to the Justice and Peace Commission of the Catholic Church, Catholic welfare organizations, the opposition Workers' Party and an English language theatre group known as the 'Third Stage' were arrested by the Special Branch for what the authorities called 'involvement in a clandestine communist network'. According to the government allegations, they were part of a 'Marxist conspiracy to subvert the existing social and political system in Singapore through communist united front tactics to establish a communist state'. The mastermind was allegedly Tan Wah Piow, a law student at Oxford University. Vincent Cheng, the executive secretary of the Justice and Peace Commission, was accused of being Tan Wah Piow's principal subordinate in Singapore.

The twenty-two were detained under the Internal Security Act, and so were not allowed defence lawyers or the opportunity to challenge the accusations against them. After being held for thirty days, a two-year detention order was imposed on Vincent Cheng, and a one-year detention order on another fourteen, subject to renewal depending on their rehabilitation. The rest were released a month later subject to restriction orders as their 'involvement in the conspiracy was secondary'. Due to its coverage of these events the *Far Eastern Economic Review* had its circulation limited from 9,000 to 500 copies in December 1987. The magazine *Asia Week* was similarly limited. The government refused to extend the work visa of the *Far Eastern Economic Review's* correspondent Nigel Holloway or to issue a visa for his replacement, Hamish McDonald.

## Current detainees

Included among those writers, journalists and media workers against whom action has been taken during the course of 1987 or who are still in prison: Chia Thye Poh, writer, held without trial since 1966.

# TAIWAN

In July 1987, the government of Taiwan announced the lifting of martial law, which was imposed in 1949 by the mainland Chinese government under the *Kuomintang* or Nationalist Party (KMT). For nearly four decades the people of Taiwan had been subject to such vaguely defined (but severely enforced) restrictions on freedom of expression as a law against 'spreading rumours... sufficient to harm the social order or create disturbances in the people's minds'.

|  | | Year |
|---|---|---|
| Population | 18,800,000 | 1984 |
| GNP ($ per capita) | 3,016 | 1984 |
| Daily newspapers | 41 | 1986 |
| Periodicals | 27 | 1986 |
| Radio stations | 33 | 1986 |
| Radio receivers | 6,000,000 | 1986 |
| TV stations | 3 | 1986 |
| TV sets | 5,653,113 | 1986 |

Press Agencies:
Central News Agency

Covenant on Civil &
Political Rights _____ NO

During the long period of martial law, military courts dealt severely with those peacefully expressing political views critical of the government. In November 1975 a military court sentenced an opposition politician, Pai Ya-tsan, to life imprisonment, ostensibly for 'attempting to stir seditious feelings' through circulating views 'contrary to basic national policy'. The prosecution was based on his distributing a campaign brochure containing 'Twenty-nine Questions', including a request that the then Prime Minister Chiang Ching-kuo make his finances public. Pai's Questions also dealt with, among other things, the possibility of engaging in trade with the People's Republic of China (PRC) and opening diplomatic relations with the USSR. In January 1980, a military tribunal sentenced writer and educator Chang Hua-min to ten years' imprisonment for suggesting negotiations with the PRC. Both Pai and Chang are still in prison. Other examples of persons sentenced for peaceful political activity are numerous.

Improvement in the right to free expression in Taiwan, including the lifting of martial law, followed from the emergence, in late 1986, of an opposition party, the Democratic Progress Party. Its successful performance in the December 1986 elections challenged government restrictions against opposition political parties imposed by the Election and Recall Law. In Taiwan today more opposition members speak openly against the government in public.

A new National Security Law contains significant restrictions on peaceful expression of opinion. Article 2 provides that '[no] person may... advocate communism or the division of national territory in the exercise

167

of the people's freedoms of assembly and association'. Nonetheless, the new law—which abolishes military trials of civilians—is generally viewed as an improvement on the martial law it has replaced.

The Constitution of Taiwan guarantees 'freedom of speech, teaching, writing and publication' (Art. 11). However, it also contains provisions which have empowered the government to impose martial law, deny these rights and impose censorship.

## The Media

Under Taiwan's Publications Law a licence is required to publish and the Government Information Office (GIO) may fine publishers and ban, confiscate and suspend publications which instigate offences 'against public order', or are considered 'detrimental to law and order while the nation is in a state of emergency'. Before the lifting of martial law, a second agency, the Taiwan Garrison Command (TGC) shared censorship responsibilities with the GIO, and administered strict 'wartime' regulations for the control of published materials. On July 14, 1987, the GIO announced that it would establish a committee to take on the job of screening books, newspapers, and magazines, previously the responsibility of the TGC.

**Newspapers:** Taiwan has thirty-one daily newspapers which have each been limited to twelve pages each. Since 1951 no new daily newspapers have been permitted. The original justification for these limitations was the high foreign currency cost of imported newsprint during a period of currency shortage. Today, however, Taiwan has among the largest foreign exchange reserves of any country in the world. Some have argued that the main reason for the continued restrictions is to ease the burden of monitoring daily news coverage which is, theoretically, limited to 372 pages per day under existing regulations. From Jan. 1, 1988, the ban on new newspapers was lifted and the limit on the size of each paper increased to twenty-four pages.

**Ownership:** The immediate beneficiaries of the change would be Taiwan's two dominant morning papers—the *China Times* and the *United Daily News* —both owned by KMT Central Committee members. The two papers account for 80 per cent of all newspaper circulation. The next largest paper is the KMT's official organ, the *Central Daily News*. Recently, the *United Daily News* sent a chief assignments editor to work for the *Central Daily News* and continued to pay his salary.

When the government does not have a controlling share in a newspaper, it may acquire one if the newspaper becomes 'uncooperative'. According to a number of sources, the KMT forced the *Taiwan Times* to sell out because it provided too much coverage of the political opposition.

Many reporters and editors also belong to the KMT. The result is that overt censorship is almost never necessary. Numerous journalists have reported that prior to major events the government or the KMT

Department of Cultural Affairs will call with 'suggestions' on how a story should be handled.

When suggestions and self-censorship fail, however, the government may take direct action. When the *Min Chung Daily News* published foreign policy comments by the Premier of the People's Republic in June 1985, the authorities stepped in and suspended the paper for seven days. Lee Tung-teh and Hsu Lu of the *Independent Evening Post* were charged following a visit to China as reporters in September 1987. The ban on such visits has since been lifted.

**Electronic media:** All three television stations and some of the most popular radio stations are wholly or partly owned by either the government or the KMT. According to a report in the *Asian Wall Street Journal Weekly*, thirty-three radio broadcast companies 'are either government-owned or held by interests close to the government'. The largest network, the *Broadcasting Corporation of China*, has as its chairman a former deputy secretary-general of the KMT. Thus, there is little need for the government to exercise direct censorship over the electronic media's news content, as it reflects the KMT position on controversial issues.

**Magazines:** Freedom of the press in Taiwan is something of a paradox. In contrast to newspapers, there are a large number of active and licensed opposition magazines; however, they are subjected to intensive censorship by the government. Several topics are sensitive, including Taiwanese independence, communism, and reunification with the mainland. Other subjects that have spurred the censors to action include news that is potentially embarrassing to the leadership, or political commentary that questions the ideological foundation of the rule of the *Kuomintang*. Censorship of these journals is exercised by banning, suspension or confiscation.

**Banning:** The most common form of censorship is a government decision to ban an entire issue of a publication. The reasons for a banning order are not usually stated, and appear in many cases to have been made without regard to the content of the issue in question. Many publishers operate on the assumption that each and every issue of their magazines will be banned.

**Suspension:** Suspension of a licence to publish is another means of censorship. Suspensions are often issued for one-year periods. A suspension, though technically a more severe punishment than a banning, often has little effect on whether opposition publishers are able to continue their work. This is because most keep several alternative magazine titles registered and ready for use. One magazine was reported to have ten of these so-called 'spare tyres'. Some magazines suspended in 1986 continued to publish under their suspended title in defiance of the government.

**Confiscation** : A third method of censorship employed by the government is confiscation of copies of magazines. This is far more damaging than either bannings or suspensions. With a banning, publications can be sold illegally, and a suspension does not necessarily mean the publisher must go out of business. A bulk confiscation is like a heavy fine: the publisher has incurred costs of production but is deprived of profits from sales. A recent example was the seizure in February 1987 of the first issue of *Min Cha Pao*, the weekly of the opposition DPP, on the grounds that it had not yet received a licence.

According to the figures obtained by the Asia Watch Committee, 411 issues of opposition magazines were published in 1986. Of this total, 255 issues—62 per cent—were banned; 145 issues were subjected to some amount of confiscations; and a total of about 1.1 million copies were seized by the authorities. During the first eight months of 1986, at least five magazines closed due to financial problems; these problems may have been caused or exacerbated by confiscations and other forms of censorship.

# COUNTRY REPORTS—EUROPE

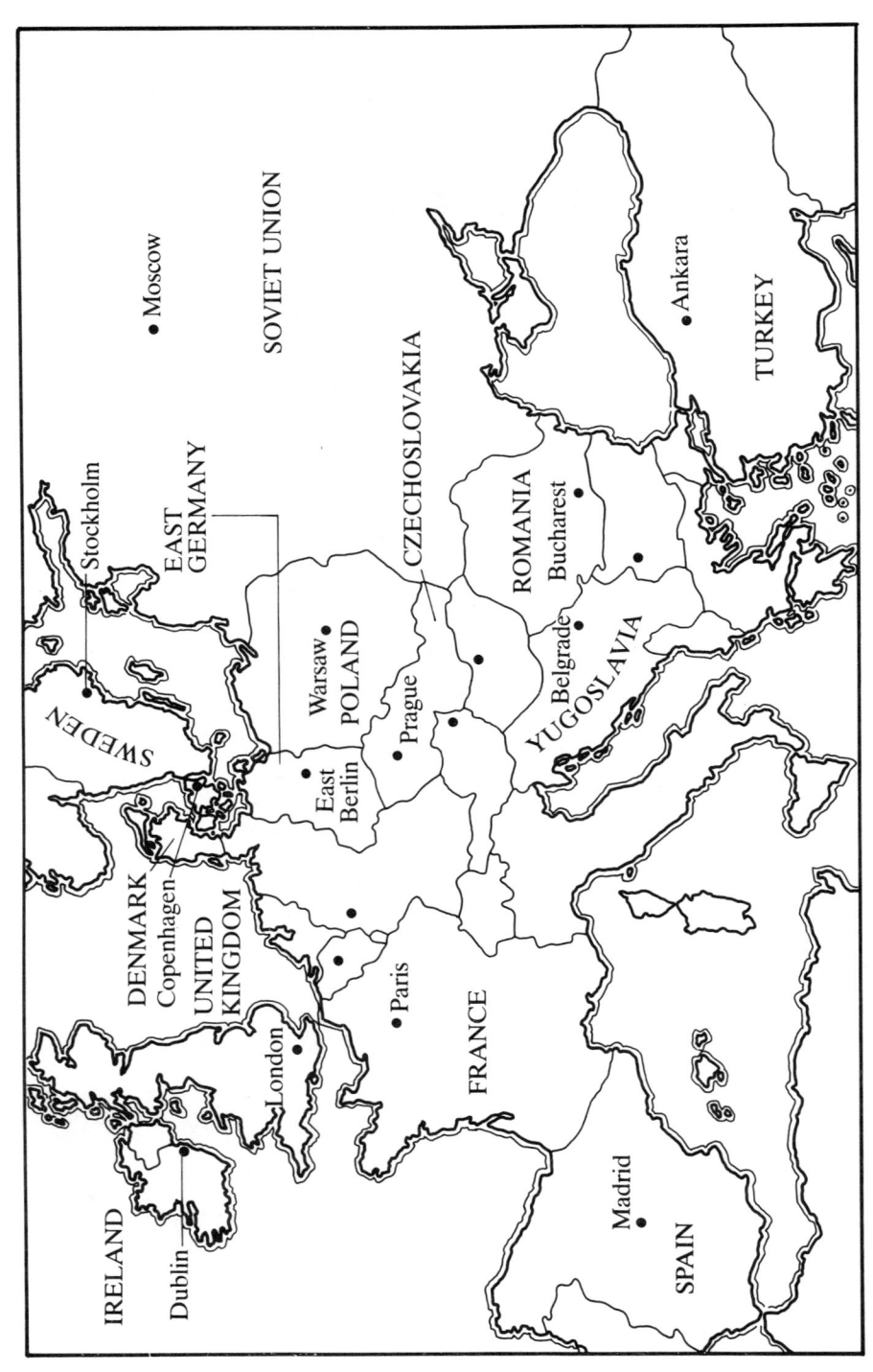

# CZECHOSLOVAKIA

In May 1987 one of the country's most famous actors, Milos Kopecky, speaking from the platform at the congress of the Union of Dramatic Artists, told Czechoslovakia's post-1968 leadership that it was time for them to go. *Rudé právo*, the party newspaper, reported the part of his speech referring to the genuineness of the Soviet 'renaissance of socialism', but omitted the following remarks: 'Just as there is an art to entering on cue, so there is an art to exiting on cue... If you do not do it yourselves, then you will go—admittedly a little later... no longer with dignity but as figures of farce.' The censors went on to add their own material to Kopecky's rostrum speech. 'The artist needs freedom'

|  |  | Year |
|---|---|---|
| Population | 15,000,000 | 1984 |
| GNP ($ per capita) | 5,820 | 1980 |

| | | |
|---|---|---|
| Daily newspapers | 30 | est |
| Non Daily newspapers | 118 | 1984 |
| Periodicals | 1,072 | est |
| Published books | 9,911 | 1984 |
| Radio receivers | 4,209,000 | 1985 |
| TV stations | 5 | est |
| TV sets | 4,600,000 | est |

Press Agencies: CTK

Covenant on Civil &
Political Rights _____ 1975

Kopecky announced. In *Rudé právo* this became: 'The artist needs creative freedom.' By 'freedom' Kopecky had intended the freedoms listed in the Helsinki Final Act, the Universal Declaration of Human Rights, and the other international human rights commitments undertaken by the government: among them freedom to travel, freedom of expression, and the free exchange of ideas.

Since February 1948, all published expression in Czechoslovakia has been controlled by the member-organizations of the National Front, an association of political and non-political organizations approved by the state and the Communist Party.

In theory, the most important sections of the media (radio, television, party newspapers and magazines, official state publications, books) are controlled directly by the state and the rest indirectly through their publishers' membership of the National Front, but in practice there is not a great difference between the two. The entire structure is designed to support the state and the party, which according to the Czechoslovak Constitution has the 'leading role' in the country. Czechoslovakia schools of journalism teach that the true journalist must be 'a collective organizer, a collective propagandist and a collective agitator'. The resulting system is reported to be characterized by deletion, selective information, and biased presentation of facts. So far, this state of affairs has not been significantly affected by Soviet *glasnost*: it seems rather that the situation has worsened in some respects. For example, the principle of selective information is now often applied in the reporting of certain events in the USSR as well.

## Press laws and censorship

Censorship has had a colourful history in Czechoslovakia. After World War II, the press legislation of the pre-war republic remained valid up to 1950. In the first period (1945-48) the theory and practice of press regulations were based on the so-called December Constitution of 1867 under which censorship had been abolished altogether. After the assumption of full political power by the Communist Party in February 1948, censorship and other interference (closure of newspapers, discontinuation of newsprint supply, arrests of journalists) were for a time without any legal basis.

To legalize the new situation, the first press law was passed on Dec. 20, 1950, entitled 'On Publication of Periodicals and the Union of Czechoslovak Journalists'. The law proclaimed it a mission of the media to 'assist the constructive efforts of the Czechoslovak people and its struggle for peace, as well as to help educate the people for socialism'. While containing no mention of censorship, the 1950 law assigned 'responsibility for the content of the periodical' to the editor-in-chief. This censor-editor, installed by the party, had the duty of supervising all that was published and ensuring that it was in keeping with party instructions.

## HSTD

A major change occurred in 1953: an unpublished Government Decree No. 17 of April 22 provided for the establishment of an Office of State Press Supervision as a non-public government body, which was incorporated in 1954 into the Ministry of the Interior (Main Administration of Press Supervision).

The Main Administration of Press Supervision (HSTD in the Czech and Slovak abbreviations) was given extensive powers to ensure the political and ideological directives of the party. Besides the mass media, prior censorship was applied to all public performances as well as cultural and artistic activities, and to all publications and printed material, from posters to matchbox labels. In addition, the HSTD checked all publications arriving in Czechoslovakia from abroad.

## Central Publication Authority

The HSTD operated without parliamentary legislation or official admission for the next 13 years. In 1966 a new Press Law formally provided for censorship. This law described the task of the mass media as 'unfolding the socialist consciousness of the citizenry in the spirit of the Constitution and of the ideas of the Communist Party of Czechoslovakia as the leading force'. The main agency was once again renamed, this time as the Central Publication Authority. It remained within the Ministry of the Interior but survived only until the short-lived abolition of censorship during the 'Prague Spring' period in June 1968.

# CZECHOSLOVAKIA
# ÚTISK

After the Soviet invasion in August 1968, legislation was rushed through to restore central control over the media. The Office for Press and Information *Úrad Pro Tisk a Informace* was set up; it became commonly known as *Útisk*—not only an abbreviation of its long official title but a Czech word meaning 'oppression'. Since January 1969 there have been two such offices, the Czech and the Slovak. This dual machinery was somewhat belatedly made federal by the Czechoslovak Federal Assembly at its meeting on Dec. 15-16, 1980 at the government's suggestion, apparently without debate and by unanimous vote.

**The Federal Office for Press and Information**: This Office accounts for its work to the federal government. No special body of censors is mentioned; the blue pencil is again wielded by editors and journalists themselves, a return to the 1948-53 state of affairs. Federal Deputy Prime Minister Karol Laco, the chairman of the government's Legislative Council, presenting the 1980 bill to the cultural committees of the Assembly, defined the mission of the Office as follows: 'It will contribute to the implementation of information and press policy of the Communist Party of Czechoslovakia and ensure uniform implementation and co-ordination of the policy of the state in the mass media... Many daily papers and periodicals have a state-wide and society-wide impact, and their demanding tasks... require united and co-ordinated control.'

The December 1980 law gave the Office six duties: (i) to propose to the government principles of the state's policy in matters regarding press and information and to ensure their uniform implementation; (ii) to effect registration of the periodical press which is of importance to the whole of society; (iii) to ensure protection of important state interests; (iv) to make decisions on the importation and distribution of foreign publications as well as distribution of publications printed in Czechoslovakia by foreign publishers, and on the distribution of releases by foreign press agencies; (v) to decide on authorization permits for editors-in-chief who are not Czechoslovak citizens; (vi) to grant authorization to organizations which are entitled to receive or distribute periodical publications.

While the first of these duties can be categorized as information guidance, the remaining five deal with information curtailment. Censorship by deletion is best expressed in the terse statement, under heading (iii), on the 'protection of state interests'. The elastic formula, the 'interests of the state', has been employed in legal stipulations in the post-1968 period with increasing frequency. It has been used at dissidents' trials and to justify rejection of foreign travel permits. The reference to foreign nationals in editorial posts relates to the number of journals and bulletins published by international organizations with headquarters in Czechoslovakia. Most, if not all, of them are communist-dominated organizations, such as the World Federation of Trade Unions and the International Student Union, or party undertakings, such as the journal *Problems of Peace and Socialism*.

Among the first public duties of the chairman of what otherwise is the publicity-shy office was the signing of a tripartite co-operation agreement with the Czechoslovak Union of Journalists and the Soviet *Novosti* press agency on Feb. 11, 1981. No details have been released but one result has been an increased supply of Soviet articles to the Czechoslovak press.

## Samizdat

Alongside the official (censored) information structure, there also exists in Czechoslovakia an important and impressive unofficial structure in the form of *samizdat*. The *samizdat* movement started immediately after 1948 with the *ad hoc* production of underground leaflets which were circulated within the country. However, over the years, the movement changed. The original function of arousing popular feelings against oppression and in the defence of democracy diminished. Instead the movement took on the role of alternative uncensored publishing, and this in turn later developed into what is now a vast system of independent culture. Since private ownership of copying machines is illegal, individual *samizdats* are produced mostly on typewriters. These uncensored periodicals, essays, collections of short stories, poems and even novels and plays are passed from hand to hand, and are typed out again and again for and by interested people.

It is impossible to estimate the number of readers who have been reached by *samizdat* periodicals and literature. An open letter sent by a group of banned writers to the Premier of the Czech Socialist Republic, Ladislav Adamec, on March 28, 1987, states that 'since 1970 approximately 1,000 prose and poetic works, essays, memoirs and plays have been written and although some of these have found fame in the outside world, none of them has been published (officially) within Czechoslovakia'. According to the latest (summer 1987) estimate from the Documentation Centre for the Promotion of Independent Czechoslovak Literature, based in West Germany, twenty-five *samizdat* journals on various subjects have been periodically published; some of these are monthlies (for example, *Informace o Charte 77*—Information on Charter 77, published since 1978), others appear ten times a year or less. Specialized *samizdat* journals are devoted to problems of history, philosophy, economics, literature, religion etc. and consist usually of several hundred typewritten pages. (The spring 1987 issue of the magazine *O Davadle*—(*One Theatre*)—consisted of 450 pages.)

As well as these periodicals, hundreds of manuscripts circulate throughout the country, dealing with topical events or problems, notably the reports of the Committee for the Defence of Persons Unjustly Persecuted (VONS) which provide detailed information on concrete cases of human rights violations. Since the creation of VONS in 1977, roughly 668 such reports have been issued.

Among the most outspoken critics of the lack of freedom of expression in Czechoslavakia is the Charter 77 human rights movement, which has experienced sustained and systematic repression. Members of the 'jazz section', an independent cultural group, were put on trial in March 1987. Several have since been released from prison and there are now attemps to achieve legalization for the group. On Dec. 10, 1987, more than 1,000 people publicly commemorated International Human Rights Day in Prague. It was the first time that Charter 77 had appealed for such a public demonstration. The leaders of the organization were prevented from participating.

## Current detainees

Included among those writers, journalists and media workers against whom action has been taken during the course of 1987 or who are still in prison: Jiri Wolf, writer, six years' imprisonment; Helmut Chromy, poet, two years' imprisonment; Edward Vacek, writer, one year's imprisonment.

# DENMARK

The 1953 Danish Constitution at Law states that 'any person shall be entitled to publish their thoughts in printing, in writing, and in speech, provided that they may be held answerable in a court of justice. Censorship and other preventive measures shall never again be reintroduced' (Art. 77). Traditionally, this provision has been seen as guaranteeing only freedom from prior restraint ('formal protection') and not freedom from subsequent civil or criminal sanctions ('substantive protection' of free speech). It has been argued, however, that the Constitution at Law does uphold substantive protection in matters concerning the public interest.

|  |  | Year |
| --- | --- | --- |
| Population | 5,000,000 | 1986 |
| GNP ($ per capita) | 11,290 | 1984 |

| Daily newspapers | 47 | 1984 |
| --- | --- | --- |
| Non Daily newspapers | 11 | 1984 |
| Periodicals | 39 | 1985 |
| Published books | 9,554 | 1985 |
| Films produced | 11 | 1985 |
| Radio receivers | 174,000 | 1985 |
| TV sets | 545,000 | 1985 |

Press Agencies:
Ritzhaus Bureau I/S

Covenant on Civil &
Political Rights _____ 1972

In a 1980 test case concerning the publication of a poster representing a pig with the caption 'Danish pigs are healthy—they are bursting with penicillin', the Agricultural Products Association tried to obtain a court ban on publication of the poster on the ground that it would damage Danish exports and pig breeders. The Supreme Court refused an injunction: although the text of the poster was not correct, the issue it raised was of importance and in the public interest to debate.

**Defamation**: Restrictions on information are contained in defamation law. Section 267 of the Danish Penal Code makes it an offence for 'any person who violates the personal honour of another by offensive words or acts or by making or spreading accusations of [a kind] likely to disparage them in the esteem of their fellow countrymen'. The maker of a defamatory statement may, however, invoke Section 269 which, among other circumstances, allows 'justified protection of obvious public interest' as a legitimate defence. In practice, criminal cases are rare: reputation is normally defended through a civil action claiming damages or through asking the courts for a declaratory judgement that the defamatory statements are null and void.

The Code also explicitly rejects any distinction in defamation proceedings between a public figure and a private citizen. In a 1930s case a libel action brought by a politician failed on the ground that statements about politicians should be more liberally judged. The Penal Code was amended to remove any difference in protection. The amendment has, however, never been invoked and in the present day climate in Denmark, politicians are expected in the interest of free debate to tolerate criticism and comment that might be actionable in the case of the private citizen.

**Freedom of information**: There is no constitutional recognition of freedom of information—that is the right of access to official information—although consolidation laws of 1987 define this right. Laws concerning professional secrecy of employees in the public sector are contained in *Offentlighedsloven* (the Law on Public Administration) and *Forvaltningsloven* (the Law on Government Services) which came into force on Oct. 1, 1987. The principal rule of the former confirms that everyone has the right to demand to be informed of documents received or produced by an administrative authority.

Exceptions are set out in the Law on Government Services. These relate to working documents for internal use; letters circulated within an agency; documents concerning affairs of state; letters between ministers; documents concerning European Community legislation, and data for statistical use. Access to documents can also be limited to the extent necessary for the protection of the state, foreign policy, the investigation of crime, public order or the protection of private and public economic interests.

## The Media

**Newspapers**: In Denmark there is no censorship of the press, which is in private ownership. Press freedom was first written into the law in 1849. There are no registration or licensing requirements but according to the Press Act, all published material—be it articles, advertisements, books or posters—must be published by a named author. An article can be published anonymously as long as it is evident from the periodical who can be held responsible for its contents according to the Press Act. This restriction on anonymity can encourage self-censorship among journalists and authors. Absence of controls on publication extend to matter that would be suppressed in most countries as pornography. There are no restrictions of any kind on foreign journalists. Most major daily newspapers are published from Copenhagen with the exception of *Jyllands-Posten*. The other main papers are the tabloids, *Ekstra Bladet* and *B.T.*, and the quality dailies, *Berlingske Tidende*, *Politiken* and *Information*. *Aktuelt*, owned by the trade unions, is currently seeking to attract a more general readership.

**Protection of sources**: Article 172 of the Court Procedure Act ensures the right of editors and journalists of periodicals and newspapers to protect their sources. This right can be overruled by a court if the case has to do with an offence which can lead to a defendant's imprisonment, or if the case concerns leaks by civil servants who are obliged to maintain confidentiality. However, the enforced revealing of sources must also be considered absolutely necessary to the investigation by the court.

In 1986 the Supreme Court ruled that Article 172 does not protect journalists who work in radio or television. Kurt Madsen of *Radio Aarhus* was taken to court following an interview on air in January 1985 in which an unnamed spokesperson explained why a group had destroyed a Macdonald Burger Bar two days earlier. Madsen refused to comply with police requests to name the perpetrators. A ruling by the High Court— confirmed by the Supreme Court—held that Madsen must go to jail for a maximum period of six months unless he supplied the information. The law protecting sources of journalists was held not to apply to the electronic media. The Danish Journalists' Union, representing more than 5,000 active journalists, protested and stated that it was prepared to call for international support. On Dec. 4, 1986 the Chief Constable of Aarhus decided not to take Madsen into custody, apparently considering it was futile to try to make him reveal his sources.

In September 1987 the Supreme Court ruled that the editor of the newspaper *Information*, Peter Wivel, had to reveal information which could help identify the person responsible for writing an article (published May 20, 1987), in which responsibility for a fire at a Shell petrol station was claimed on behalf of an anti-apartheid group. The court ruled that it was in the interest of justice to require Wivel to give information about the case in order to investigate the crime. In this case it was said that the reasons for granting the press a right to protect its sources could not outweigh the interest of justice.

The Wivel case has provoked debate primarily among lawyers and journalists. The journalists claim that the law permits an unacceptable limitation on the right to protect sources; even in cases involving a serious criminal offence, the rights of a free and investigative press should prevail. On the other hand it is argued that in the interest of justice and to prevent crime there must be the possibility to require journalists to reveal their sources. Wivel refused to reveal the identity of the writer following the court decision and was ordered to pay a daily fine of Dkr 500 (US$60) until he did so. After a month, this was doubled by the court to Dkr 1,000. By the end of 1987, he was still refusing to name the source. A government commission on media responsibility, chaired by a Supreme Court judge, was established in 1986.

**Television**: *Danmarks Radio (DR)* has sole rights over radio and television under the 1973 Radio and Television Service Act. In 1987, the Danish parliament passed a bill establishing a second channel and at the same time changing the structure of the management of the existing channel. The current board has been controlled by the political parties and there were complaints over political in-fighting and inefficiency. The new board to be nominated by the Minister for Cultural Affairs and confirmed by parliament will act independently and include media personnel. There is free access to Swedish and German TV channels, but the state has a monopoly on the use of satellite dishes and can determine what channels are received and distributed. This fact has been the subject of discussion over the past few years, and a new bill is expected, giving the public free access to all satellite transmissions.

# DENMARK

**Advertising**: The Danish 'Consumer Ombudsman' ensures that advertisements are in accordance with *Markedforingsloven* (law on marketing). The Ombudsman can prohibit the intended publication from printing 'misleading' or 'improper' advertisements. This form of prior restraint is considered to be in accordance with Article 77 of the Constitution. On the other hand, there are many examples where a publisher has been fined after an advertisement has been published.

**Films**: Film and video distributors must submit films and videos that are to be viewed by children under sixteen for approval by state advisors on film. Films of all kinds may not receive state subsidies if they are not approved by the state advisors on films. The state is, therefore, able to exercise a form of censorship by refusing to approve a film for subsidy.

**Public records**: Computers have made it possible to gather large amounts of information in private or public databases, information that is often of a sensitive nature such as personal IQ-ratings, personal solvency, political affiliation, etc. A new bill on public and private registers has been passed to ensure protection of such data. A Board supervises the management of the registers (*Registertilsynet*). It ensures that information stored is not abused, for example, that it is not accessed for advertising. However, the Act has been criticized because it fails to control the storage on computers of personal information on individuals, or the transfer of such information.

## Freedom of opinion and expression

**Racism and free speech**: In Article 265b of the Penal Code, it is a criminal offence to make derogatory remarks directed at a person's ethnic background. A radio programme broadcast by the state-owned *Danmarks Radio* (*DR*) produced by an extreme right-wing group, caused widespread discussion. Since the Radio network is a monopoly, Article 7 of the Press Act provides that due to the danger inherent in a media monopoly, the programmes should be as comprehensive as possible, covering all aspects of public opinion. *Danish Radio* allowed the broadcast, having overruled protests by the Jewish community, former members of the World War II resistance movement and politicians. Statements denying the killing and deportation of Jews during World War II were however deleted prior to broadcasting.

In the summer of 1985, an interview was played in a news broadcast on *DR* with a racist group, *Groenjakkerne* (Green Jackets). There was a public outcry over the remarks made against immigrants and the reporter, Hans Olaf Jersild, was prosecuted, convicted and fined over the interview. The racist group was also prosecuted.

# FRANCE

The Declaration of the Rights of Man and of Citizens of Aug. 24, 1789 proclaimed: 'The free communication of thoughts and opinions is one of the most precious rights of mankind. Each citizen may therefore speak, write, print in liberty, except in abusing this freedom in cases set forth by the law.' This historic affirmation of the freedoms of opinion and expression is subject to the qualification concerning abuse. Despite reaffirmation of the importance of freedom of information in the Constitutions of 1946 and 1958, much of the French experience can perhaps better be recounted in terms of this clause permitting restrictions than the better-known positive language of

|  |  | Year |
| --- | --- | --- |
| Population | 55,000,000 | est |
| GNP ($ per capita) | 9,860 | 1984 |
| Daily newspapers | 84 | 1983 |
| Non Daily newspapers | 246 | est |
| Periodicals | 804 | est |
| Published books | 37,189 | 1984 |
| Radio stations | 849 | est |
| Radio receivers | 47,000,000 | 1983 |
| TV stations | 135 | est |
| TV sets | 20,500,000 | 1983 |

Press Agencies:
Agence France – Presse (AFP)

Covenant on Civil & Political Rights _____ 1980

the Declaration praising freedom of speech. However press freedom has been guaranteed since the Law on the Freedom of the Press of July 29, 1881. This law abolished the requirement of official authorization for the setting up of a newspaper or periodical, abolished the requirement for financial pledges from proprietors and ended censorship and *délit d'opinion*.

## The Media

**Media concentration:** In contrast to the expansion of radio and television into private networks, the written press has contracted since the war from 193 daily papers to eighty-four in 1983 accompanied by a concentration of papers under a handful of proprietors. Hersant controls forty different papers, Hachette thirty and Filipacchi twenty. This has led to an increasing uniformity of information in French newspapers followed by powerful conglomerations of multi-media ownership. Sofirad, Havas, CLT, Hachette and Hersant control, to varying degrees, interests in the written press, radio, TV, recording, cinema, electronic publishing, computers, book publishing, posters and advertising.

**Hersant:** The most dramatic example of concentrated control is the Hersant group. Robert Hersant has recently acquired joint ownership of the fifth TV channel along with the Italian media magnate Silvio

Berlusconi. Legal action was taken against Hersant in 1978 for having violated the legal limits of ownership of the press (around 20 per cent of French daily newspapers employing some 8,000 persons and 1,000 journalists) stipulated by the Ordinance of 1944. Similar proceedings commenced following his takeover of *Le Progrès,* a regional Lyon newspaper. Neither action proved successful. In the second case Hersant enjoyed parliamentary immunity as a member of the European Parliament. The Hersant press had been the centre of controversy when, between July 1975 and January 1978, 120 journalists left *Le Figaro,* one of his dailies, in the name of *'esprit de maison'.*

In reaction to owners such as Hersant, the Constitutional Council has pushed for greater resistance to media concentration, invoking the Law of October 1984 on the Limitation of Concentration in the Press, the Law on the Press of July 1986, and most recently the Law of Nov. 27, 1986 designating the degree to which groups can have shares in national TV channels. Although the constitutional recognition of pluralism contained in the Nov. 27 law is positive, there is still a great deal of room for manoeuvre as far as proprietary groups are concerned. Thus a group cannot have more than a 25 per cent interest in a national channel but can have interests in another channel of up to 15 per cent. The government in June 1987 sold off TF1 to property magnate François Bouygues and other private interests.

Those in favour of concentration of the press in France argue that it is necessary if French multi-media groups are to compete with other international networks, especially those from the English-speaking media.

**Television and radio:** With over fifty million radios, over eighteen million TV sets and the introduction of satellite TV and cable technology, France's broadcasting industry exerts a powerful influence over its citizens. The state monopoly has given way since 1984 to the existence of five private TV stations and a host of private radio stations. In comparison, the written press now accounts for only a third of popular information sources in the country.

The first major change in the control exerted by the government came in the 1982 Law on Broadcasting, which stipulated the 'legal existence of a pluralistic radio network'. This has led to the liberalization of radio and an explosion of private radio stations, many of which had existed previously as a network of illegal or 'pirate' radio broadcasters.

For all its promise, however, the 1982 law has failed to improve significantly relations between government and broadcasting management. Every change of government brings with it the fear of job losses and changes in appointments. Control is also exerted through the government's complaints over programmes. Repeated criticisms of the quality of a news feature or the quality of research have led to alterations in news stories and journalists' resignations. Such attacks have tended to produce in time 'auto-censure' or self-censorship among journalists.

**The National Commission of Communications and Liberty:** An independent authority, the *Haute Autorité*, was created in 1982 with the twin goals of monitoring the broadcasting industry and of defending its independence. This organization lasted for only three years until the election of a new government in 1986. The *Haute Autorité* was then replaced by the National Commission of Communications and Liberty (CNCL), which had a similar but broader mandate.

The CNCL is now under public scrutiny. Its decision to replace those heads of the broadcasting media selected by the *Haute Autorité* has caused alarm. Of the first five heads named, three belonged to the Information Commission of the ruling coalition's major party.

Other pressures also bear on the broadcasting media. Under Giscard d'Estaing, for example, the heads of TV channels were asked to reduce coverage of one of his rising political opponents and pressure was exerted to limit information being given to the public over the 'diamond affair' in which Giscard d'Estaing was alleged to have accepted diamonds from Emperor Jean-Bédel Bokassa. Following press coverage of the event, criminal charges were brought against the editor of *Le Monde* in 1980. The government under Fabius not only sought to impose an 'official' version of information on the sinking of the Rainbow Warrior in 1985 but also tried to impose a upon the *Haute Autorité* a selected candidate to manage one of the TV channels. Under the present government, Bernard Langlois, a journalist and presenter of a human rights programme on TV called '*Résistances*', was forced by the head of his channel to resign from the programme following his criticism of the government's new law and order policy which he considered constituted a threat to civil liberties. His contract has not been renewed.

**Photographic agencies:** Several photographic agencies were subject to police visits designed to obtain evidence relating to violent student demonstrations in November and December 1986. Fears that such visits might lead to an identification of photographers with the police led to a collective statement by *Agence France-Presse (AFP)*, *Collectif-Presse*, *Cosmos, Kestone, Kopa, Magnum, Ralpho, Vu* and *L'Association Nationale des Journalistes, Reporters, Photographes* (ANJRPC) condemning the visits. Similarly, a detailed questionnaire issued by the Senate Committee of Inquiry relating to information connected with the same demonstrations was distributed to heads of TV channels. The questionnaire met with indignation from broadcasters.

**Right of reply:** Under the press law of 1881 public officials have a right to insist on rectification of published information concerning them. Individuals equally have a right of reply. Any member of the public can insist on being given space to answer coverage which refers to him or her. Publishers must print the reply in three days or face a fine or imprisonment, and a court order to print the reply. The right of reply is absolute: it is not necessary that the person should have been defamed or that the statement be untrue. Most French journalists accept the right of reply as a necessary counterbalance to the power wielded by the press. According to M. Devieux, president of the *Syndicat National des Journalistes* and a journalist with *Le Monde*, abuses of the right of reply are less frequent than might be supposed and emanate usually from eccentrics rather than people seeking additional publicity. His only criticism is that the maximum permitted length of the reply, 200 lines, is excessive.

**Books and book burning:** The Law of July 16, 1949 sets out the limits within which there can be free circulation of books and publications to children and young people. Under this law a commission is charged with the supervision of publications for children and adolescents. Until recently the law was used to control the import of foreign material deemed pornographic, but it was extended under Interior Minister Charles Pasqua and culminated on March 17, 1987 with a series of banning orders against journals published by the *Société Française, Fortune*, the Filipacchi group and *Gai Pied*. This coincided with a bizarre initiative by Pasqua who opened a '*Salon du Livre'*, an illustrative chamber of horrors containing his selection of publications thought likely to damage the morals of French children.

In October 1986 the Paris Council established a working group to draw up a monthly booklist from which libraries must base their acquisitions of children's literature. In response, librarians, authors and publishers formed a collective in 1987 called *Renvoyons la Censure* (Reject Censorship).

On March 4, 1987 60,000 copies of a book by Laurent Gally, '*L'Agent Noir* ('The Black Agent'), were seized on orders from the Interior and Defence Ministries and orders were given to cut twenty-five pages from the text. 17,191 copies were subsequently burned by the bailiff of Pithiviers. The publishers *Editions Robert Laffont* had complied with the court order to cut pages from the work allegedly containing information relating to the French intelligence services.

**Foreign publications:** By 'foreign publications' is meant publications 'that are materially and intellectually of foreign origin' (Council of State, June 4, 1954), and these have always been subject to stricter control. Article 14 of the Law of July 29, 1881 gives the Ministry of the Interior powers to decide whether or not journals, periodicals and books of foreign origin are a threat to public order and to prohibit their circulation, distribution and sale. The Minister's decisions may not be reviewed, even by an administrative judge. These powers have been abused to protect political interests; in the most recent case a book on Bokassa (published by *Editions Maspero*) which mentioned the 'diamond affair' was banned. Legal actions under this law have led to the financial collapse of publishing companies.

In December 1986 the journal *El Badil*, produced in France by the Movement for Democracy in Algeria (MDA), was banned by the Minister of the Interior. The movement is led by the former Algerian president Ben Bella. The MDA brought out a new publication, *L'Alternative*

*Démocratique,* which was also banned on March 20, 1986 on the grounds that it 'could damage French dipomatic interests'.

The same official reason was given by the Ministry to justify its banning of the book '*Yahdouss si Tunis*' ('This is Happening in Tunis'). The book, written by the Syrian journalist Kussai Saleh El Darwish, had caused a sensation when it was published in Tunisia in Arabic, prompting the Tunisian authorities to take legal action to have the book banned in France.

**Minitel:** On May 14, 1987 the Minister of Posts and Telecommunications set up a new telecommunications commission composed of members of parliament, government representatives, the press, and clients of services to examine the problems arising from the rapid expansion of *Minitel,* the electronic public information service, criticized for promoting 'pornography and prostitution'. Fearing that the new service would render ineffective the 1949 law governing information available to young persons, the commission is involved in elaborating a code of ethics applicable to the whole range of telecommunications services.

**Film:** A Board of Film Censors exists which vets films for sexual or violent content. Concern has been expressed over the arbitrary prohibition of films by municipal authorities even when they have been cleared by the censoring commission, as occurred with the 1986 film, '*Je Vous Salue Marie*'.

## Freedom of information (Transparence)

The slow development of French law related to the right to information has been the product of a belief in the functional efficacy of secrecy as an administrative tool allied to a centralized and bulky bureaucracy.

In 1978 and 1979 legislation was introduced which finally addressed the issue of public access to official information. The laws are: the Law of Jan. 6,1978 on Informatics and Liberty, dealing principally with the protection of computerized data banks; the Law of July 17, 1978, relating to Access to Administrative Documents; the Law of Jan. 3,1979 ensuring the right of access to documents in French public archives; and the Law of July 11, 1979, which obliged the administration to give reasons for refusing an individual's demand for information.

Such reforms have had a liberating effect. Although there are clauses in the law of July 1978 for instance, relating to national security, the private life of individuals and public order (Art. 6), the right to have access to information is considered the rule and censorship the exception.

**CADA:** The Law of 1978 established an independent commission (CADA) to oversee the implementation of its provisions and to arbitrate between the public and the administration. Difficulties remain in the implementation of the law however, which undermine its potential. The major problem concerns the excessive delay over individual applications for administrative documents. If an individual is refused access to the information required he or she may have to wait up to two months for notification of that refusal. The citizen may then take it to the CADA who will write to the agency concerned. The agency in turn can then take another two months in replying, making a possible total of four to five months before the application is granted (if successful). By this time the information required may have become obsolete or irrelevant. In addition, the CADA has no legal means of obliging an agency to supply the documents. A final possibility is to put the case before an administrative judge which can result in a legal battle that may last six months. Of the 2,000 applications for documents referred to the CADA (the worst offenders against the spirit of the law being the Ministry of Defence and the Customs) 70 per cent were considered by it to be lawfully communicable to the applicant.

The CADA is little used and little known, and the length of time involved in securing access to information through it defeats many of the objects involved in its creation.

**Data protection:** The need for data protection became a public issue in 1974, when the press revealed a government project named 'Safari' involving the use of the social security number of each citizen for all other individual dossiers and public files. This project was designed to link a variety of data banks and index files on individuals. The public outcry which followed led to the formation of the CNIL (National Commission on Informatics and Liberties). The work of this commission in turn led to the Law of January 1978 on computers, indexes and individual liberties. Article 1 of the law states: 'Computer science has to be at the service of each citizen; its development has to operate within the framework of international co-operation; it should not damage human identity, nor human rights, private life or individual and public liberties.'

Special attention is paid to the control of personal records. The law stipulates that such information must be pertinent and exact and not contain unwarranted information (information on the political opinions, religious beliefs or health of an individual) outside the declared goal of the data bank requirements. The commission also sees that individuals are informed that they are registered on a computerised file. Individuals should have access to their files and be able to add or to correct information registered. Authorization from the CNIL is a condition for setting up a data bank and involves rigorous checks.

Exceptions to the individual's right to inspect personal files exist for national security interests. Here the individual (someone suspected of an offence for example) may verify the information on his dossier only through the intermediary of a magistrate. This control on access has been criticized by human rights groups.

**Nuclear secrecy:** It was only two weeks after the Chernobyl disaster that the French public was given full details by the SCPRI (the Central Service for Protection against Ionising Radiation) about the effects of radiation clouds passing over France. This revealed that the government had given

187

false information about abnormal levels of radioactivity in the first days of May. Monique Sène, president of the Scientific Group for Information on Nuclear Energy, referred to a 'blockade' of information.

Following Chernobyl a nuclear information service was instituted on *Minitel,* the French public information service. The aim is to supply 'timely up-to-date information' on levels of radiation and other questions of nuclear safety. There is as yet no commission similar to the CNIL and the CADA charged with securing the free flow of information about the nuclear industry. The Atomic Energy Commissariat (CEA) is criticized for its hesitancy in publicizing emergency stoppages in nuclear centres due to radiation leakages. The organization *'Combat Nature'*, an ecologist movement, campaigns for the establishment of an independent commission to monitor the release of information on nuclear issues.

# GERMAN DEMOCRATIC REPUBLIC

In April 1987, responding to questions on the relevance of *glasnost* and *perestroika* to the German Democratic Republic (GDR), Kurt Hager, a member of the Politburo of the ruling Socialist Unity Party (SED) with responsibility for cultural affairs, commented: 'Would you, if your neighbour had his apartment repapered, feel obliged to have your apartment redecorated?'

In contrast, the GDR human rights group Initiative for Peace and Human Rights addressed an open letter to Mikhail Gorbachev calling for more democracy and openness in the GDR. In September 1987 East Berlin members of the group issued a statement demanding greater openness in the GDR

|  |  | Year |
| --- | --- | --- |
| Population | 17,000,000 | 1985 |
| GNP ($ per capita) | 7,180 | 1980 |

| Daily newspapers | 39 | 1986 |
| --- | --- | --- |
| Non Daily newspapers | 32 | 1986 |
| Periodicals | 522 | 1986 |
| Published books | 6,175 | 1984 |
| Radio stations | 5 | est |
| Radio receivers | 6,415,000 | 1983 |
| TV stations | 1 | est |
| TV sets | 5,970,000 | 1983 |

Press Agencies:
Allgemeiner Deutscher
Nachrichtendienst (ADN)

Covenant on Civil &
Political Rights _____ 1973

media. The statement described an independent press as 'an essential prerequisite for the development of a country's democracy' and expressed the need for 'journalistic cleanliness, media work which is faithful to the truth and the development of a creative struggle of opinions in society'.

The Constitution of the German Democratic Republic guarantees (Art. 27.1) the right to free expression and free press, radio and television, but the official commentary to the Constitution (published in 1969) stipulates the 'constitutional duty to oppose ... the spreading of anti-socialist ideology which is practised in the name of "freedom", "democracy", or "humanity"'.

**The Criminal Code**: Freedom of expression can be directly restricted by application of in particular six articles in the Criminal Code. They relate to 'crimes against the GDR' (Arts. 99, 110, 106) and to 'crimes against the state and social order' (Arts. 214, 219, 220). The Code prescribes imprisonment for persons who collect and send information to foreign organizations which, although not 'classified', is detrimental to the interests of the GDR. Equally, persons who 'discredit the GDR's social conditions' or its 'ties of friendship and alliance', or who distribute 'writings, objects or symbols' which are liable 'to disturb the socialist way

189

of life' may face imprisonment. Under Article 209 anyone who, for example, seeks help from foreign organizations to emigrate may be subject to arrest. A number of such people were arrested after their names were publicly released abroad.

The broad wording of these Articles means that it is easy to obtain convictions. Such offences are incompatible with international human rights standards on freedom of expression, including the International Covenant on Civil and Political Rights ratified by the GDR in 1973. In an open letter to SED general secretary Erich Honecker in August 1987, members of the Initiative for Peace and Human Rights called for greater legal security for GDR citizens. They criticized the formulation of some paragraphs of the Criminal Code, for example on 'subversive agitation' and 'treasonable passing on of information' as having an imprecise definition, and called for the repeal of these 'arbitrary regulations'.

**Contacts with foreigners**: The authorities discourage contact between GDR citizens and individuals from outside Eastern Europe by declaring a large number of citizens 'carriers of state secrets'. Any person categorized in this way may not contact any foreigner; they include members of the military, police, and other government workers and employees in cultural and scientific areas. The regulations do not however fully reflect the reality of contacts with foreigners, especially West Germans. There are still many citizens with family ties in the Federal Republic of Germany (FRG); people maintain contacts and travel, including those who are 'carriers of state secrets'.

In 1987 the East German government eased travel restrictions to allow over 1,000,000 GDR citizens under retirement age to visit the FRG for a week to 10 days. Pensioners from the GDR travel much more freely. According to Honecker, in an interview with a Dutch newspaper on June 2, 1987, approximately 2,000,000 East Germans were to visit the FRG in 1987 for the first time.

## The Media

All newspapers in the GDR are owned and managed by political or other organizations, such as party committees, and organizations approved by the authorities. Almost all dailies are affiliated to the various political parties which make up the National Front government. The most influential is *Neues Deutschland*, controlled by the SED and generally considered to be the official newspaper. There are also local papers affiliated to the SED in the major cities. All radio organizations in the GDR are co-ordinated by the *State Committee for Radio Broadcasting at the Council of Ministers*; state television is overseen by the *State Committee for Television Broadcasting*, and the national news agency, *ADN*, has been a state monopoly since 1946.

East Germans are widely regarded as avid newspaper readers. They are used to reading between the lines; regular readers of *Neues Deutschland* have stated that it is important to read the paper for what is not there.

# GERMAN DEMOCRATIC REPUBLIC

Reporting on the development of *glasnost* and the visits and speeches of Mikhail Gorbachev and other Soviet leaders in the main newspapers and on radio and television provides a recent example. When Mikhail Gorbachev met Honecker, in early March 1987, state television showed the Soviet leader touring a local exhibition, but restricted his on-the-air comments to a minimal 20-second spot. *Neues Deutschland* limited its report of the talks to a bland four-sentence despatch. The official media have been criticized for routinely censoring Gorbachev's speeches, in particular by deleting references to *glasnost* and *perestroika*. These tactics led to issues of *Pravda*, the Soviet newspaper, being sold out in East Berlin on various occasions.

In early June 1987, Western media reported clashes between rock fans and the police in East Berlin. The clashes occurred as police tried three nights running to prevent fans (about 4,000 on the third night) from listening to a pop concert on the other side of the Berlin Wall. The clashes were the first serious disturbance of its kind in ten years. More than 50 people were arrested, and three West German journalists were reportedly beaten up. Protest notes were exchanged between the two Germanies. However, the GDR authorities denied that the events occured. They said that reports were based on the imagination of zealous Western correspondents. No mention of the clashes nor of the denials were made on GDR television. GDR citizens were able to watch live coverage of the incidents on West German television.

The Synod of the Federation of Evangelical Churches in the GDR criticized GDR media attitudes following its meeting on Sept. 18, 1987. The conference criticized in particular the way information was generally presented in the GDR, which according to the Synod often means one-sided positive reports that do not coincide with personal impressions of events.

**Access to Western media**: About 80 per cent of the population live in areas where they can receive radio and television programmes from the FRG. This fact has an important influence on popular awareness of the reality in and around their own country. As Stefan Heym of the Writers Union said in a recent interview on BBC television, strict censorship does not work any longer in the GDR, as people know the other side of the information.

Following the visit of Honecker to the FRG in September 1987, GDR television broadcast for the first time a political programme from the FRG in its entirety, including a live studio discussion between GDR and FRG experts.

On the other hand, Western newspapers, with the exception of the West German Communist Party newspaper *Unsere Zeit*, are unavailable to most East Germans, although small quantities are for sale for hard currency in international hotels. Some libraries and official institutions receive Western journals, but circulation is restricted.

Publications from abroad that do not appear on the GDR's 'approved' list, the Postal Publication Register, are regularly confiscated at the border. This happened to Mikhail Gorbachev's book '*Perestroika*' in late

1987. Only after lengthy consultation was a copy—under plain covers—allowed into East Berlin.

**Artistic freedom**: The SED conceives of art and literature as a means of promoting political goals. Publishing houses practise self-censorship, and works must receive official clearance before they are published, performed or exhibited. A state-run literary agency approves all publishing, including publishing abroad.

Professional associations of writers and artists are headed by party members and are strongly influenced by the state. Writers can be imprisoned under the currency law for having income from unregistered works published abroad. Music groups must have lyrics approved by the state. These restrictions also apply to Western groups wishing to perform in the GDR. There is, however, no known recent case of a writer having been imprisoned under the currency law. Some writers publish only in the West and without permission. According to Stefan Heym, a well-known writer, fines for such offences have not been imposed in recent years.

**Emigration of artists**: Most of an older group of dissenting writers have either been expelled or have emigrated. The new generation is a product of the general stalemate in official cultural policy. Rolf Schneider, a well-known GDR writer living in East Berlin and the FRG, recently concluded that these policies have given authors in 1987 less intellectual freedom than there was in the USSR under Brezhnev. Frustrated with the lack of change and the pressures they are under, the younger generation of authors and artists either begin to develop their own subculture or move temporarily to the Federal Republic. Most of those who leave legally want to maintain their GDR citizenship and hope to return.

The cultural 'brain drain' over the last decade has affected all aspects of artistic expression in the GDR. Actors and theatre directors and producers are among those to move. Alexander Lang, internationally acclaimed director at East Berlin's *Deutsches Theater* and a member of the prestigious Academy of Arts is one of the most recent examples. He left for Hamburg in late 1987.

**Die Distel**: One unique institution that has maintained a level of critical comment on day-to-day reality in the GDR is the political cabaret. The best-known cabaret is *Die Distel* (Thistle), which has been operating for almost 35 years and attracts a packed house every weekend. Although it specializes in political jokes and satirical comment, *Die Distel* is state-funded and its scripts are censored by the Culture Ministry. The cabaret, which avoids attacks on personalities and the political system, is regarded as an important outlet for critical opinion.

**Der Grenzfall**: A *samizdat* publication, *Der Grenzfall*, first surfaced in June 1986. Eight issues have appeared, the eighth in September 1987. It is a monthly bulletin on peace, ecology and human rights, and reports on police repression and the development of independent initiatives in the GDR. It is independent both of the state and the Church.

# GERMAN DEMOCRATIC REPUBLIC

**The Church**: The Protestant Church is the main independent institution in which East Germans can assemble, discuss social questions and publish material. The Church owes its relative independence to agreements between the President of the federation of Churches and the government, under which it is declared to exist 'within socialism'. The Church's importance as an umbrella for various alternative groups is recognized throughout GDR society, but the limits within which it operates have led to increased tension with human rights activists. In 1986 certain issues of Church newspapers, which are usually subject to less censorship than most publications, were withdrawn from publication over coverage of the independent peace movement and state environmental policies. The cancellation of a Church peace workshop in June 1987 led to protests at the *Kirchentag* (Church Day). The group of young people who organized the protest called themselves '*Kirchentag von Unten*' ('*Kirchentag from Below*'). On June 27, about 600 protestors met with church leaders to voice their criticism of the Church for compromising with the state on 'fundamental questions' and for not recognizing the work of protestant youth as 'a natural component' of the Church's work. The 'fundamental questions' ranged from issues of peace, environment, human rights, democracy, women's issues and militarism to the discriminatory treatment of Christians and minority groups. Church leaders subsequently spoke of the need to build constructive relationships with youth groups. At the concluding church service, the protesting youths held up a banner calling for '*glasnost* in the Church; *glasnost* in the state'. In November 1987 the police raided the 'Zion' church centre in East Berlin, confiscated printing equipment and arrested five people working in the 'environmental library' housed in the centre. It appeared that the main target was the magazine *Grenzfall*. Although the detainees were relased after a few days, twenty people faced charges in connection with 'anti-government propaganda', and 'belonging to an illegal organization' arising from the raid. Church leaders protested strongly and vigils were held throughout December 1987 protesting at the interference.

# IRELAND

While the Irish Constitution of 1937 guarantees freedom of expression, with a specific reference to the freedom of the press to criticize government policy, it is qualified by the duty cast on the state to ensure that 'organs of public opinion', i.e. radio, television, the press and cinema, are not used to undermine 'public order or morality or the authority of the State' (Art. 40.6.1). While such constitutional language is by no means unique to Ireland, when taken in conjunction with the teachings of the Catholic Church its effects on determining censorship become apparent, particularly in relation to the protection of morality.

|  |  | Year |
|---|---|---|
| Population | 3,000,000 | 1985 |
| GNP ($ per capita) | 4,950 | 1984 |

| Daily newspapers | 7 | 1985 |
|---|---|---|
| Non Daily newspapers | 68 | est |
| Periodicals | 251 | est |
| Published books | 799 | 1984 |
| Radio stations | 3 | est |
| Radio receivers | 1,600,000 | 1983 |
| TV stations | 2 | est |
| TV sets | 918,000 | 1986 |

| Covenant on Civil & Political Rights _____ | NO |
|---|---|

If the British, Ireland's neighbours, have been obsessed with state secrecy, the Irish have been preoccupied equally with sexual morality. State censorship machinery, customs and excise officers and Catholic lay militants have pursued the 'indecent and obscene' down the years with a verve that contradicted Ireland's general reputation as a relaxed and mature society.

Censorship extended not only to the original target of the Church, the 'unclean' English Sunday newspapers, and magazines, but at one time or another, to the classics of modern English literature and the work of many Irish writers including Bernard Shaw, Frank O'Connor, Samuel Beckett, Brian Moore, Edna O'Brien and John McGahern. Catholic teaching on contraception and abortion was rigidly enforced. Until the 1970s it was an offence to import contraceptives and a crime to publish advocacy of 'unnatural prevention of conception'. It remains an offence to advocate, publish, or, following a recent court decision, to provide information on the subject of abortion. While much has changed—Ireland has the youngest population in Europe and they have a choice of no less than sixteen channels including ten via satellite—prurience and insularity at bureaucratic levels on matters of sex remain. The government campaign against AIDS advised a visit to the doctor to find out about condoms and in May 1987 Alex Comfort's book 'The Joy of Sex' was banned.

One problem has been that censorship of literature and film operates through administrative agencies and the functioning of these bodies has never been scrutinized by the courts. Although an Irish court has held that there is a guaranteed right to communicate, the implication of the constitutional protection of free speech has had little airing. In December 1986 however the High Court refused an injunction to the British legal authorities who sought to restrain the publication of an Irish publishers' book, 'One Girl's War', written by a former and deceased member of the British intelligence services, Joan Miller. Miss Justice Carroll said that 'what is at stake is the very important constitutional right to communicate now and not in a year's time or more when the case has worked its way through the courts'. (The distribution of the book in Britain was subsequently stopped by a British temporary injunction on grounds of national security which had not been discharged by the end of 1987.)

The courts have taken a different line on Irish national security: in 1982 the Supreme Court upheld a ministerial ban which prevented *Sinn Fein*, the IRA's political counterpart, from making a party political broadcast during a national election for which its members were lawfully standing. The court invoked the duty of the government under the Constitution to uphold the authority of the State.

**Emergency laws**: Ireland's Offences Against the State Act 1939 contains wide powers to proscribe unlawful organizations considered subversive and to prohibit or seize publications. While organizations such as the IRA remain banned, there is no attempt to prohibit its publications which are sold openly in both the Republic and Northern Ireland.

## The Media

**Newspapers:** Ireland has a strong independent newspaper tradition. There are no formalities in starting up a newspaper and there is no censorship at national and local community level. The Irish have among the highest readership of newspapers in Europe; every week 95 per cent of the adult population read at least one of the national dailies. Over 80 per cent read one of the four Sunday papers—*The Sunday Tribune, The Sunday Press, The Sunday Independent, Sunday World*. The principal dailies are *The Cork Examiner, The Irish Press, The Irish Independent,* and *The Irish Times*. The latter paper is controlled by a trust which requires it to serve the public interest by the impartial reporting of the news. *The Sunday Tribune,* an investigative paper, offers a voluntary 'right of reply' scheme for its readers. Unlike the British popular press, Irish papers do not specialize in scandals affecting public figures and media stars. But the local press is now concerned about the inroads made by the cheaper British tabloids which sell approximately 150,000 copies daily in the Republic. Newspapers' circulation has been declining and market share of advertising revenue is low by international standards. The papers blame competition from RTE (*Radio Telefis Eireann*), the broadcasting authority. The industry also complains about the libel laws which in practice weigh heavily against the press. Politicians regularly achieve high damages in libel suits that would not succeed in other countries such as the

USA or Denmark. The government has admitted that it underwrites the legal costs of civil servants who sue newspapers for defamation.

**Radio and Television:** These media are run by a broadcasting authority established by statute, RTE. Broadcasting operates at 'arm's length' from government on the model of the BBC. There are two television channels and three radio channels, but most of the country also receives all of the British television channels via cable. Ireland has an extensive advanced cable network originally designed to catch British television but now also capable of receiving satellite channels, giving the country per capita one of the largest cable television audiences in Europe. There is currently no fee or licence charged for a personal satellite dish as part of a government experiment to assess demand. Irish viewers can receive satellite channels such as *Sky* (the major shareholder is Rupert Murdoch); *Super* (British *Independent Television* and Richard Branson's Virgin Records); the *Children's Channel* (Thompsons, the Scottish comic publishers, owners of the Beano and the Dandy); *Worldnet* (the US Government's Information Service); and *TV5* (the French international cultural service).

*Radio Tara*, a new long-wave station, is planned as a joint venture between RTE and *Radio Luxembourg*. In November 1987 a government Bill proposed a new independent commercial radio structure involving one national station, twenty-four local stations, and up to 100 'town-size' and a further 100 'neighbourhood' stations. The existing 70 'pirate' stations will be entitled to apply for licences and local newspapers will be permitted to invest in the stations.

The major censorship issue affecting both radio and television is the prohibition on broadcasting interviews with a number of organizations including *Sinn Fein* (see below).

**Books:** Following a rather inactive phase when many had frankly forgotten of its existence, the Censorship of Publications Board established in the 1920s again hit the headlines with decisions in early 1987 to ban Alex Comfort's 'The Joy Of Sex', and Thames and Hudson's art book, 'The Erotic Art of India'.

The ban on Thames and Hudson's book, apart from the question of principle, had at least no practical effect—the publishers say the book has been out of print for a number of years. Comfort's book was different. There was considerable protest from doctors and clinics who have used the book widely in counselling. Over 1,000 copies had been sold by the Irish Family Planning Association.

The censor's decision focused attention on the subject of censorship and the hitherto obscure procedures of the Board. Information on who the members of the Board are proved difficult to come by. The press was told that it was not the practice of the Board to disclose the occupations, qualifications or addresses of members. Members were not free to discuss decisions; the Board's deliberations were confidential. The chairman, Judge Diarmaid Sheridan, did, however, venture a comment on 'The Joy of Sex' decision which gave an insight into the Board's thinking: 'What we have in mind is this. You put this book on an ordinary bookshelf. Imagine the effect it would have on a thirteen-year-old. There is all the difference in the world between adults and juveniles.'

The news that the Board decides what to ban on the basis of what is suitable for adolescents was greeted with calls for its abolition from the Writers' Union and other groups. There is an Appeal Board and Quartet Books, the publishers of 'The Joy of Sex', may appeal.

**Film and video:** A Video Recordings Bill was circulated in October 1987 in response to the increasingly widespread use of video cassettes, and concern over the content of the more lurid varieties. The Bill, following the UK Act, brings them under the same legislation applying to cinema film censorship and provides for the banning of any film which would be likely to incite crime, racial or religious hatred, or to deprave or corrupt. The legislation has been objected to as unnecessary and a fresh invasion of freedom of expression, but this is a minority view and the legislation is likely to become law in 1988. Censorship of films has become more liberal in recent years.

**Access to information:** The question of public morality arose in the Dublin High Court's decision of 19 December 1986 to ban two Dublin clinics, Open Line Counselling and Well Woman Centre, from offering non-directive counselling and referral information on abortion to pregnant women. Abortion is unlawful in Ireland and approximately 4,000 Irish women travel to the UK for terminations each year.

The clinics claimed to be impartial on abortion but in favour of women's mental and physical health. In the judgment, however, the Court ruled that the procurement of an abortion was in breach of Article 40.3.3. of the Constitution, and that the right to life of the unborn took precedence over all other constitutional rights such as the right to privacy or the right to receive or disseminate information. The decision is under appeal to the Irish Supreme Court.

Following the High Court decision women's groups launched a 'right to know' campaign. Copies of British women's magazines such as *Cosmopolitan* were auctioned at a public meeting to draw attention to the possible next target—magazines that carry advertisements about abortion clinics in Britain. Ireland has no legislation entitling access to government-held information and public files. The Official Secrets Act 1963 is as wide and loose as the much criticized British Act although it is rarely invoked.

## Freedom of opinion and expression

Much controversy has been generated over the ban on the IRA's political counterpart, *Sinn Fein,* from appearing on television and radio. A recent report—'Censoring the Troubles'—by the International Federation of Journalists (IFJ) called the ban on *Sinn Fein* and various paramilitary groups an 'indefensible political censorship'.

Since 1971, successive Irish governments have directed the broadcasting authority (RTE) not to record or transmit interviews with spokespersons for any such group on any subject whatsoever. This was made part of the law in 1976 in an amendment to Section 31 of the Broadcasting Act. The main target, *Sinn Fein,* is nevertheless a lawful political party in both parts of Ireland. It has a large number of local elected councillors. Its president, Gerry Adams, is MP for West Belfast in the UK Parliament. He is interviewed by the British channels and most of the Republic receives British TV. There is no prohibition on newspaper interviews with *Sinn Fein,* nor any ban on *Sinn Fein* publications.

The government position was put recently by one minister: 'The Constitution provides for censorship: the ban is intended to prevent access to the national airways of members of organizations which include murder as part of their published policy; access would lend validity and respectability to these people.'

The opposing point of view has been put by *The Irish Times:* 'There is no more effective way of countering IRA propaganda than by letting it stand on its merits in the market-place.'

While earlier in 1987 the government stated that the ban was under review, it announced in December that it would be renewed through 1988, in toto. The IFJ report drew attention to the extensive self-censorship that the prohibition provoked among journalists in covering the conflict in Northern Ireland, including the print media to whom the order does not formally apply.

# POLAND

Freedom of expression in Poland presents a persistent contrast between the legal controls available to the state which are, in principle, total, and their application. The mass media can be made subject to unwieldy state control mechanisms. Despite the scope of official powers to censor and stifle unofficial publications, continued pressures exerted both by the underground and the licensed Catholic press have had a major impact on the delicate relationship between state, officially independent and unofficial media bodies. Increased possibilities have therefore emerged for independent publication and for access to information. One result has been that the official media, having encountered and been influenced by strong competition from its diversified, pluralised and unofficial counterpart, now concentrates on producing more accurate information on such topics as the economic crisis, economic management and environmental issues. In addition, the number of officially banned topics has decreased.

| | | Year |
|---|---|---|
| Population | 37,000,000 | 1985 |
| GNP ($ per capita) app | 3,900 | 1980 |
| Daily newspapers | 45 | 1985 |
| Non Daily newspapers | 52 | 1985 |
| Periodicals | 2,614 | 1985 |
| Published books | 9,649 | 1985 |
| Radio stations | 2 | est |
| Radio receivers | 1,020,000 | 1986 |
| TV stations | 1 | est |
| TV sets | 9,500,000 | 1986 |
| Press Agencies: PAP | | |
| Covenant on Civil & Political Rights | | 1977 |

The position of unofficial publications remains precarious, however, and the threat of a future government crackdown persists. A licence to publish can be withdrawn, for instance, should there be repeated reference to 'unfavoured' subjects, particularly relations with the Soviet Union. Although martial law was lifted on July 22, 1983, changes in the law ensured that many of the martial law restrictions affecting freedom of information became a permanent feature of the legal system. Martial law also brought with it the suspension of hundreds of associations, societies and professional organizations, many of which have since been 'dissolved'. This was the fate, for instance, of the Union of Journalists and the Union of Writers. The Board of Polish PEN was prevented from holding independent elections which resulted in Polish PEN being 'frozen' by International PEN. According to Stefan Bratkowski, the last president of the now banned Union of Journalists, journalists have been the hardest-hit (apart from Solidarity activists) by official 'normalization'. Over 1,000 journalists lost their jobs and about the same number were demoted. Many resigned rather than appear before the special

199

commission to declare support for Gen. Jaruzelski.

Seen in this light, the effects on freedom of expression of the current reform initiatives of Gen. Jaruzelski remain uncertain. A national referendum which sought consent for tough economic measures and 'profound democratization ... aimed at strengthening self-government, expansion of citizens' rights and their enlarged participation in ruling the country' was held in November 1987 but failed to win majority support.

## The Media

The Polish Constitution guarantees freedom of expression and of the press (Art. 83). In a recent report to the United Nations Human Rights Committee the Polish government declared that 'every citizen has the right freely to express his or her opinions under the constitutional principle of freedom of speech and print'. Such formal guarantees came closest to having real impact for a brief period in 1981. But in December of the same year, the Polish government declared martial law and civil and political rights were suspended.

Censorship in post-war Poland was introduced by the Decree on the Establishment of the Central Office for the Press, Publications and Public Performances of July 5, 1946. This legislation has gone through many changes, but its main features remain; there is institutionalized control of a preventive character of all forms of public expression and of dissemination of information and ideas.

**The 1981 Press Law**: The reduction of censorship was one of the principal demands of the striking Polish workers in the summer of 1980. An unprecendented public and legal debate between Solidarity and government representatives concerning future censorship legislation culminated in the passing of the Act on the Control of Publications and Performances which became law on Oct. 1, 1981. In the event, the 1981 Act functioned until the end of the year in its original form only. Following the lifting of martial law, the Act went through several revisions.

Although the new law retained the principle of preventive censorship and listed instances when the exercise of freedom to write or publish was prohibited, it placed a greater emphasis on safeguards and formal restrictions on the censor's activities. The Central Office for the Control of Press, Publications and Public Performances is, however, answerable not to parliament but to the Council of State.

There was a novel clause giving the author or the publication the right to appeal to a court against the censor's decision. The author or editor could ask to have the deletions in a text marked by dashes, with the number of the article of the law which the censored text violated, or the author could choose to appeal against the censor's decision to a court. The editor or author was thus given a choice between challenging the decision in court, or making the existence of censorship interference plain to readers. The option of appeal to a court was unprecedented and has been used to some effect. But the need to choose between remedies has been criticized.

# POLAND

The 1981 Act introduced another improvement, according to which the Censor's Office had to cease the earlier practice of 'blacklists' of names and the circulation of guidelines on factual descriptions of events and phenomena.

Amendments in 1983 and 1984 have meant that the state's formal censorship powers of pre-Solidarity days were largely restored, although not necessarily applied in practice, and some of the 1981 gains survive. The amendments did include a clause under which reprints of publications that had already passed by the censors, which were previously exempt from censorship, had to be resubmitted.

One casualty was a history textbook (with 650,000 copies printed for distribution) which was ordered to be shredded. The book, 'Modern History' by Andrzej Leszek Szczesniak, touched upon 'sensitive' facts which had been passed over in previous school books.

Traditional attitudes came to be expressed once more in official speeches. Kazimierz Molek, the deputy head of the Cultural Department of the ruling Polish United Workers' Party (PZPR), addressing a meeting of Poland's officially recognized publishers in February 1984, stressed that publishing was the 'chief sector of the front of ideological struggle' and that books published in Poland had to reflect 'socialist values' and be 'socialist in literary form'. Kazimierz Molek read a list of Polish writers of whom the party did not approve. It was decided at the meeting that authors known to be critical of the regime would be excluded from the publishing plans for 1984 and that literary editors would be given regular ideological and political training.

**The 1984 Press Law**: The Press Law of Jan. 28, 1984, deprives journalists of autonomy and subordinates them to the will of editors-in-chief. According to this law the 'function of the journalist is to serve society and the state' and 'a journalist has the duty to implement the general programmatic policy of his editors and publishers'. 'Activities contrary to this principle constitute a violation of his duties as an employee' (Art. 10).

A licence to publish a newspaper or periodical is issued by the Central Office for Control of Press, Publications and Public Performances. The applicant has, among other things, to provide 'the evidence concerning the sources of newsprint and availability of printing facilities'. Newsprint however, is distributed solely by the government, and the PZPR owns the *RSW Prasa* publishing concern which provides 90 per cent of printing facilities. It is not difficult for the authorities to block publications simply by making use of this monopoly.

**The Catholic press**: The Catholic press accounts for little more than 1 per cent of all newsprint in the country and is the only legal press not directly controlled by the government. The government has in the past done its utmost to constrain and harrass it. Thus, the popular Warsaw weekly *Przeglad Katolicki* (Catholic Review) cannot buy sufficient newsprint and publishes only four pages a week.

In 1984, an entire issue of the Catholic monthly *Znak* was confiscated because it dealt with a Polish-Ukrainian subject. *Znak* was the first periodical in Poland to receive a warning based on the new press law. The editors were informed that the next time they dealt with such a sensitive issue, the Central Office might suspend the journal's licence to publish. However, the tendency now is for a further decrease in the number of subjects 'banned' as a result of the pressure of alternative publications and new policies of the government.

In July 1985, another Catholic weekly, *Tygodnik Powszechne* published in Kraków, challenged in court the decision of the censorship office to ban an entire article critical of changes in the Penal Code. The Central Office claimed that the article could stir public unrest. The Court ruled that the role of the press was to 'disseminate information and express opinions serving the development of socialist social relations' and upheld the decision of the Office. The same journal was heavily censored during the November 1987 referendum.

**'Second circulation'**: In spite of the fact that publishing without a licence is punishable under the law, the so-called 'second circulation' (independent, underground publishing) has thrived in Poland. The authorities at least in the past tried hard to fight this kind of activity and publishers, printers and distributors of independent publications constituted the majority of political cases dealt with by the courts. In recent years, however, there have been no trials of authors for publishing articles in either the Polish émigré or underground press.

One of the independent journals, *Res Publica*, which was published clandestinely between 1979 and 1981, was finally granted a licence in March 1987 after its third attempt. It is the first time that an underground publication has been allowed to appear 'overground'. This monthly cultural affairs journal is privately-owned and is allowed a circulation of 25,000 copies. But already the first issue, in July 1987, bore marks of censorship. The most notable were in the book review section (clearly marked in accordance with the law) where the censors did not allow the magazine to print reviews of two books published abroad by Polish émigrés.

Official statements by Poland's Catholic Church are often subject to censorship. Even statements by the Pope do not escape. In June 1987, Catholic bishops, assessing the Pope's pilgrimage to Poland, issued a communiqué supporting calls by Pope John Paul II for more political freedom and respect for human rights. References to the themes he raised in his homilies were censored from a version of the statement reported by the official *PAP* press agency and published by government and party newspapers.

**Films**: Polish cinema has long been accustomed to rigorous censorship. Films already made, their scripts approved before the start of production, sit on the shelves. Many documentaries, but also quite a few full-length feature films, have not been shown, among them 'The Faithful River' by Tadeusz Chmielewski, an adaptation of a classic Polish historical novel by

POLAND

Stefan Zeromski which is on the compulsory reading list of secondary schools, and 'Interrogation' by Ryszard Bugajski.

At the same time, Poland has a flourishing market of underground films and videos with wide distribution and there are some 250,000 video recorders. Many previously banned films were released in 1987, and 'The Lonely Woman' by Agnieska Holland, which was withheld from cinema distribution, was shown on television in November.

**Radio and television**: These media reflect the least change or difference between the theory and practice of censorship. They are subject to very strict control and are directly bound by the regulations of the Press and Propaganda Department of the PZPR Central Committee. Polish viewers note, however, that there have been improvements in the presentation of news programmes, which are more interesting and professional than in the past. Western radio broadcasts to Poland are still jammed on occasions. Jamming of BBC Polish Service broadcasts stopped at the end of 1987.

## Access to information

Other amendments to the Act on the Control of Publications and Performances have stringently restricted the inflow of information from abroad and give the authorities the power to decide who is entitled to access. Customs regulations prohibit the import or export of any materials which may serve purposes contrary to the interests of the Polish People's Republic. A 1981 law on the Protection of State Secrets includes in the category of official secrets information on public health and foreign debt. But the ready availability of such information and its public discussion contradicts the formal terms of the law.

In its report to the Human Rights Committee in 1987, the government explained that, for the first time, the law required state authorities and enterprises to provide information to the press on their activities. This requirement extended also to the business activities of co-operatives and private entrepreneurs. Information could be refused only on grounds of protecting state and professional secrecy, guaranteed by law.

However, given that the new State Secrets Law of 1987 also stipulates that any state official may decide what is secret in their area of responsibility, in practice the press may be unable to gain information from the state sector.

The law does not require organizations such as political parties to provide information to the press about their activities; this has the important implication that the PZPR and the other parties are not accountable to the media to the extent envisaged by the law for other public bodies. In November 1987 the government suppressed the revival of the Polish Socialist Party. Police broke up the party's founding meeting.

# ROMANIA

Gaspar Miklos Tamas, an ethnic Hungarian writer from Romania now living in Hungary, has said that 'in Romania any criticism of the Party-State is unthinkable. But praise is obligatory. This everlasting praise has to be organized and that is the primary goal of censorship.'

In June 1977 a series of legal acts and decrees was published which modified the entire structure of the country's information and cultural policy. Since then Romanian officials have stressed that censorship has been abolished and that there is no external control of the media.

The censorship office—the Press and Printing Committee—was abolished by Decree 472/77, but the responsibility for 'directing, guiding and providing unified control over all cultural-educational activity' is, according to this decree, now vested in the Council for Socialist Culture and Education. In reality, it has far greater powers than its predecessor. It is, for example, entitled to guide publishing houses and to exert control over their output; it also 'approves' all scheduling of professional and amateur performances, and is directly responsible politically and ideologically for the import of all books, films and records.

The Council for Socialist Culture and Education provides the editors of all media, as well as publishing houses, with lists, prepared by ministries and other national agencies, of the type of data and information which according to the law may not be published. It also has 'the right to suspend the dissemination of books, publications, other printed matter, graphic, audio and visual material'. The Council controls the distribution of newsprint. A licence to publish is also granted by and registered with this body.

| | | Year |
|---|---|---|
| Population | 29,000,000 | 1986 |
| GNP ($ per capita) | 2,540 | 1981 |
| Daily newspapers | 36 | 1985 |
| Non Daily newspapers }Periodicals | 422 | 1985 |
| Published books | 5,276 | 1985 |
| Radio receivers | 3,208,000 | 1985 |
| TV sets | 3,879,000 | 1985 |

Press Agencies: Agerpres
(Romanian News Agency)

Covenant on Civil &
Political Rights _____ 1974

## The Media

**The press**: The Amended Press Law 1978 (which applies to all media; the press, for purposes of this law, encompasses all 'the activity of public information achieved by any form of printing, recording, broadcasting or communication'—Art. 5) declares that freedom of the press is a fundamental right of citizens.

Each 'press organ' has a 'leading council' and an editorial board made up from the council. At least one third of this council are members of the Romanian Communist Party (PCR), the General Union of Trade Unions and other 'mass and public organizations'; there are also journalist representatives. The editorial board is similarly composed and includes the secretary of the local party organization.

The function of the leading council is to 'guide and control the entire activity of the press organ and bear full responsibility for its orientation, in accordance with the programme of the PCR... [and] for the political, ideological content and quality of the materials published' (Art. 19).

Article 69 provides a list of materials which are prohibited 'in protecting the interests of society and persons against the misuse of the right to publish'. Some of these limitations are exceptionally general and their interpretation is at the discretion of officials or bodies such as the Council for Socialist Culture and Education.

**The duties of the press**: Apart from the educational aim to develop 'the citizens' social awareness', the press has to 'foster love for the PCR and the socialist fatherland, respect for the glorious traditions of the workers' class struggle and the struggle of the Romanian people for social justice, national freedom and progress.

Among the duties of a journalist, according to the law, is 'devotedly to serve the cause of socialism, and to struggle for implementing the party and state domestic and international policy'.

Violations of these duties 'will incur the temporary or final withdrawal of the journalist's credentials and his transfer to another activity in keeping with the law' (Art. 59).

Foreign journalists are regularly denied access to Romania. In May 1987, seven were refused visas to cover the visit of Mikhail Gorbachev. The reasons given were that previous articles written by them were perceived in Romania as unfair or unfriendly.

**Radio and television**: Radio and television are government-owned and the terms of the Press Law of 1978 apply. Radio broadcasts from outside Romania are received within the country without interference. It is understood that due to energy difficulties, television has been reduced to one channel operating for 22 hours per week. During the autumn of 1987 it was reported that police were responding to the growth of satellite television by removing rooftop aerials.

**Typewriters and copiers**: The control that exists for newsprint and paper exists equally for typewriters and copying machines. A decree of 1983 which empowers the Romanian authorities to decide who may or may not possess a typewriter is the most restrictive of its kind known. The Ministry of Internal Affairs, through the local militia, maintains records on the production, use, and maintenance of duplicators, typewriters, ink, typewriter ribbons and other materials for the reproduction of printed matter.

Ownership of copying machines and materials is restricted to socialist units and organizations which are required to register them with the local police. A private person wishing to copy any document can do so only in a specially authorized place.

Individuals may, once they have permission, own a typewriter, but to buy one he or she must apply to the local militia. The right to own a typewriter can be refused on the grounds that the individual has a police record, or that his or her behaviour poses a threat to public order or state security. It is prohibited for a private person to manufacture a typewriter.

A person duly authorized is required, having bought the typewriter, to report with it to the local militia to obtain a licence to use it, and to enable detailed impressions of the typeface to be made for the records. A similar sample has to be provided annually, as well as after every repair to the typewriter, which can be done only in authorised servicing depots. Failure to do so could mean withdrawal of the licence, as well as a heavy fine, which can be as high as two months' average salary.

The same regulations apply to typewriters which have been inherited or given as a gift. Their new owner has to obtain permission to use them without delay. If the owner of a typewriter moves, the new address of the typewriter has to be reported within five days to the local militia. Owners are strictly forbidden to rent or lend out their typewriters.

## Freedom of opinion and expression

**The Hungarian minority**: Allegations continue to be made, in particular by the Hungarian minority in Transylvania, that the government is pursuing a policy which is systematically eliminating Hungarian schools, churches, traditions and language from Romanian society. These reports talk, among other things, of Romanian-speaking teachers being assigned to Hungarian-speaking areas and vice-versa, both groups teaching in Romanian; but also that high schools for the Hungarian minority are being replaced by Hungarian language sections within schools. Teachers of history and geography in Transylvania must, according to government decree, be Romanian. This is deemed a provocative move in view of the conflicting interpretation given by the Romanians and Hungarians to the region's history.

Further allegations are that books in Hungarian have an especially low print-run, are not available in libraries and are often sent for sale to Romanian-only speaking regions where there is no demand for them. Visitors from Hungary are searched thoroughly at the borders and frequently Hungarian books in their possession are confiscated.

**Artistic expression**: Numerous cases exist of writers, film makers and theatre directors who have found themselves in conflict with the authorities because of criticisms made regarding some aspects of Romanian life. This has resulted in published works being withdrawn from bookshops, films confiscated, plays banned and the loss of jobs for those involved. When writers and artists emigrate, their works are removed from bookshops and libraries.

Attempts by editors to defend artistic freedom have also brought them into conflict with the law. Such was the fate of Octavian Paler, editor-in-chief of *România Libera* (the daily organ of the PCR-dominated Socialist Democracy and Unity Front), who was dismissed from his post in 1983; Dorin Tudorin, editor of the literary magazine *Luceafărul* was dismissed from his post in 1981; Georgeta Naidin lost her job as an editor at the publishing house *Cartea Românească*, and her husband Bagriel Disimianu was removed from the editorial board of the magazine *România Literară*.

In the summer of 1984, two prominent Romanian intellectuals resigned from the Communist Party in protest against the party's domination of the country's literary and cultural life. Mircea Sandulescu, a writer, and Mircea Daeliuc, a film maker, took this decision because of what they called 'totalitarianism' in Romania. They said it was impossible to write or to make films without constant state interference. (Sandulescu's novel 'Placebo' was banned from the bookshops and Daeliuc's film 'Glissando', completed in 1982, never reached the cinema screens because of censorship.) Prof. Nicolae Stoia, whose book '*Adevarul*' was critical of the goverment, was arrested in 1984 and his whereabouts are unknown.

**Contact with foreigners**: Entry into Romania does not guarantee free access to its citizens. There exists an unpublished law, Decree No. 408, reinforcing a 1971 law restricting contact with foreigners. The decree is understood to require Romanians to report all contacts with foreigners within 24 hours. It is a criminal offence for a Romanian citizen to offer overnight lodging to a foreign visitor or to have discussions with colleagues from abroad, including East European countries, without approval from the appropriate authorities. Although there appears to be no published text of the decree, a press campaign has called for strict observance of its terms.

# SOVIET UNION

The past two years in the Soviet Union have been a period of extraordinary cultural change, with the emergence of investigative journalism and a considerable extension of the limits of public debate. Continuing calls for *glasnost*, *perestroika* and *demokratizatsia* point to new directions in government policy and indicate the perceived relationship between economic reform and greater freedom of information. There has been an increasing flow of information, both from above and from below. Restrictions have been eased or lifted from a whole variety of formerly taboo subjects. The dramatic evolution of the last two years is, however, still without institutional foundation and could easily be reversed and there are formidable remaining constraints on the right to freedom of expression.

|  |  | Year |
|---|---|---|
| Population | 278,000,000 | 1986 |
| GNP ($ per capita) | 4,450 | 1980 |

| | | |
|---|---|---|
| Daily newspapers | } 8,327 | 1984 |
| Non Daily newspapers | | |
| Periodicals | 5,231 | 1984 |
| Published books | 82,790 | 1984 |
| Radio receivers | 81,200,000 | 1984 |
| TV sets | 80,300,000 | 1984 |

Press Agencies: TASS, APN

Covenant on Civil & Political Rights _____ 1973

## Constitutional provisions

The present Constitution of the USSR, which came into force in 1977, guarantees to Soviet citizens freedom of speech and of the press, free association and public demonstration.

Despite such constitutional guarantees, the right to free expression has consistently been violated in practice. The Constitution makes it clear that the rights of the individual in the Soviet Union are fundamentally conditional on the interests of the state as defined by the Communist Party—'the leading and guiding force of Soviet society' (Art. 6).

There is a new recognition, however, that the legitimate interests of the individual may need to be defended, if not against the party, then at least against the arbitrary actions of a bureaucratic state. This development has provided the impetus for the current reviews of legislation on human rights and the press. But the legislators face a formidable task: how to reconcile the need to 'restructure' legal institutions so as to promote adherence to procedural norms in dealings with individuals while preserving the 'leading role' of the party? Unless the party is subordinate to the law, as required by the international human rights treaties by which the state is bound, freedom of expression will remain at risk.

Article 50 of the Constitution states that: 'freedom of speech, of the press, of assembly, of meetings, and of street marches and demonstrations' may be exercised 'in accordance with the interests of the working people and in order to strengthen and develop the socialist system'.

Similarly, 'freedom of scientific, technical and artistic creation' (Art. 47) and the 'right to unite in social organizations' (Art. 51) are acknowledged 'in accordance with the goals of Communist construction'.

The section of the Constitution concerning the duties of the Soviet citizen—regarded as inseparable from his rights—requires that the citizen must not only refrain from injuring the State, but must 'exercise his rights' to the positive benefit of the system.

Such provisions have provided a background for severe restrictions on freedom of expression as exemplified by Articles 70 and 190-1 of the Russian (RSFSR) Criminal Code ('anti-Soviet agitation, slander and propaganda'). Enthusiasm for *glasnost* must be tempered by the knowledge that Articles 70 and 190-1, and their equivalents in the Criminal Codes of the other union republics, remain on the statute books and that there are still prisoners of conscience in the camps and psychiatric hospitals.

**Anti-Soviet activities**: Article 70 of the RSFSR Criminal Code prohibits 'agitation or propaganda carried out with the purpose of subverting or weakening Soviet power or of committing particularly dangerous crimes against the state, disseminating for the said purposes slanderous fabrications which defame the Soviet state and social system, as well as circulating, preparing or harbouring, for the said purposes, literature of similar content'.

The maximum penalty for this offence is 12 years' imprisonment and internal exile, or 15 years in the case of a prior conviction for the same offence. Article 190-1 similarly prohibits the 'systematic dissemination of fabrications known to be false, discrediting the Soviet state and social system'.

This offence carries a lesser penalty (a maximum of three years' imprisonment). Persons convicted under this Article are not deemed guilty of seeking to undermine the state.

The careful wording of these provisions has allowed Soviet jurists to argue that current Soviet laws do not allow anyone to be convicted merely for the expression of their beliefs or opinions, and that there are, in this sense, no political prisoners in the Soviet Union. Whereas the notorious Article 58 of the previous 1926 Code gave *carte blanche* for the arrest of anyone remotely suspected of holding 'counter-revolutionary' views, current legislation, introduced during the post-Stalin 'thaw' in 1960, was designed in part to prevent a repetition of the abuses which took place under Stalin.

But both of these Articles have been used arbitrarily to arrest and imprison thousands of citizens who have, for example, written appeals to the government or to the press, who have circulated their work in unofficial journals or published it abroad, or who possessed literary works by such authors as Solzhenitsyn or Orwell deemed to be 'anti-Soviet' by the government.

Statements, whether oral or written, concerning human rights violations in the USSR have consistently been regarded as 'slanderous', as, very often, have the reasons cited by would-be emigrants for their desire to leave the USSR. Proof that such statements are untrue or 'malicious' has rarely, in the past, been required for conviction under either Article. Freedom of expression has also been curtailed by means of the internment of dissidents in psychiatric hospitals.

**Review of sentences**: In January 1987 Yury Kashlev, the head of the Humanitarian and Cultural Affairs Departments at the Ministry of the Interior, announced that the government had begun an intensive review of the sentences of persons arrested for 'anti-Soviet activities'. In February the government issued decrees sanctioning the release, subject to certain conditions, of a large number of prisoners convicted under Article 70 of the Criminal Code. Between February and July 1987, as a result of these decrees or of individual pardons, over 160 prisoners were released from camps and prisons, exile or compulsory confinement in psychiatric hospitals. Release was conditional in many cases on their requesting a pardon or promising to refrain from 'anti-Soviet' activities in the future.

In the course of 1987 there has been only one known arrest under Article 70, and pending cases have been dropped. In February 1987, the Director of the Institute of State and Law at the USSR Academy of Sciences said that the entire Criminal Code was under review, including Articles 70 and 190-1.

But, as of late 1987, there are still over 400 known cases of persons in some form of detention or exile as a result of their dissenting beliefs or political activities. The real figure is certainly higher than this. Of those still detained, over 100 were convicted under Articles 70 or 190-1. There have been no recorded arrests of religious believers in 1987 under laws specifically restricting religious activities. However, there have been continued incidents of harassment of unregistered religious sects, including Baptists, Jehovah's Witnesses and followers of Hare Krishna. Many of those still in detention are religious believers, some arrested as late as December 1986.

Approximately one half of those prisoners of conscience still in detention are expected to benefit or have already benefited—either by a reduction in their sentences or by unconditional release—from an amnesty in honour of the 70th anniversary of the October Revolution.

## The Media

All Soviet media are owned by the state. One of the first steps taken by the Bolshevik government was to issue a decree (Nov. 9, 1917) banning press organs hostile to the Revolution. All printing offices and stocks of paper were immediately nationalized, and special permission required for personal ownership of any form of reproduction machine. A new law permitting limited private enterprise (in force since May 1, 1987) appears now to sanction the private use of such technology for commercial purposes, but its application on this point has so far not been tested.

The media in the USSR, operating under the overall supervision of the Communist Party of the Department of Propaganda Central Committee (CPSU) are seen to serve three main purposes. First, they are used as a vehicle for ideological teaching to inculcate in Soviet citizens a Marxist-Leninist outlook and communist morals. Second, they provide a means for mobilizing the people for the social and economic goals set by the party. Third, as stated by a CPSU Resolution on the functions of the press, the media are 'to unfold sharp and principled criticism and self-criticism directed against indolence, bureaucratism, waste, idleness and other anti-social phenomena, and to popularize good examples'.

## Glasnost

The statement quoted above was issued in 1963, and serves as a reminder that 'self-criticism' in the media did not begin with the glasnost or 'openness' of the Gorbachev era. The Soviet government has consistently used the media to criticize recognized shortcomings within the system and to wage carefully-orchestrated campaigns against those held responsible.

The scale of self-criticism unleashed by glasnost is, however, unprecedented. Various stages within the 'openness' campaign can be identified. Initially its impact was evident chiefly in media discussion of the economic and social ills which Mikhail Gorbachev has sought to tackle in his 'restructuring'. Official corruption and economic waste, alcoholism, drug abuse and low morale among young people became the everyday subject matter of the official press and television. In addition, the media began to give more detailed information on disasters and accidents of a kind that in the past had been ignored or rated only a passing mention in the press (on the grounds that the Soviet media were not concerned with 'sensationalism'). More detailed coverage was designed both to dispel rumour and to expose—as in the case of the Chernobyl disaster—the role of slack management and poor judgment .

Gradually, however, glasnost has acquired a momentum of its own and its scope has significantly widened. Exposés have spread to topics such as police brutality in dealing with 'unofficial' gatherings of hippies and punks, corruption in the courts, and the maltreatment of offenders. In January 1987, in an unparalleled move, a top KGB official was disgraced on the pages of Pravda for arresting on trumped-up charges a journalist who had been investigating inadequate safety measures in Ukrainian mines. The journalist, Victor Verkhin, has since died as a result of beatings in prison. Corruption in law enforcement agencies in Voroshilovgrad was also thoroughly exposed. In April 1987, the weekly Literaturnaya Gazeta published a letter from an inmate of a labour camp, charging that the prison system created repeated offenders; and in August the newspaper Sovietskaya Rossiya took up the argument, giving a detailed account of life in a labour camp in the Leningrad region and criticizing the administration's treatment of its prisoners. *Izvestia* related the cases of two Moscow women who had been improperly diagnosed as insane and incarcerated in psychiatric hospitals. In the past, labour camps and mental hospitals were never mentioned in the press.

Discussion of present problems has in turn given rise to questions about their roots in the past and led to a public re-examination of some aspects of Soviet history. The official highpoint of this to date was the speech by Gorbachev at a Kremlin rally in October 1987 to mark the 70th anniversary of the Revolution. Criticism of the Stalin era, both in the press and in artistic works such as the film 'Repentance' by Georgian director, Tengiz Abuladze, has become more and more outspoken. Once-proscribed names, such as Trotsky and Bukharin, are now being mentioned again. Historians have spoken out about the need to tell the truth about the past and to uncover distortions: in August, for example, *Literaturnaya Gazeta* published an interview with leading historian Yury Poliakov, who castigated colleagues for their 'obviously exaggerated assessments' and glorification of Brezhnev's and Chernenko's war records.

This questioning of the Soviet experience to date has in turn led to more open debate about the future, and to a limited competition of ideas within the official press. Space has been given to economists in *NovyMir*, *Kommunist* and *Ogonyok* arguing for such unorthodox strategies as the abolition of central planning and the creation of a stock market. There has been heated debate in the press and on television about the possible abolition of the death penalty, the value of secret ballots, and other topics.

One result of *glasnost* is that the Soviet press has begun to look less monolithic: newspapers and journals have acquired more distinct voices as editors (many of them newly-appointed) have felt free to give expression to their own views or those of their readers (by no means all of whom are in favour of Gorbachev's 'restructuring' or indeed of *glasnost* itself). Meanwhile, criticism of 'boring' news presentation, particularly on television, has forced editors and journalists to respond more swiftly to events and to modernize their style. The Soviet media as a result have become more informative and, simply, more interesting, as increased circulation and viewing figures show.

**The arts:** *Glasnost* has had a considerable impact on the arts as well as the media. A major 'restructuring' has taken place within the film and theatre unions which has led to the showing of films that have been banned for years and to greater independence for theatre directors in choosing more adventurous repertoires. Once-proscribed authors, such as Vladimir Nabokov and the poet Nikolai Gumilev, are now being published, and works by living authors concerning 'touchy' historical subjects—such as Anatoly Rybakov's novel on the effects of Stalinism, 'Children of the Arbat'—have begun to surface from desk drawers.

This campaign for openness has not gone unopposed. Both Yegor Ligachev, Gorbachev's second-in-command, and Viktor Chebrikov, the head of the KGB, have made strong speeches criticizing the media and the artistic intelligentsia for 'washing up scum and debris' rather than using *glasnost* 'constructively', and for providing an opportunity for Western secret services to exploit the new openness.

**Radio jamming**: The government has now stopped jamming the *BBC*'s Russian Service and *Voice of America*. *Radio Liberty*, German-based, American-funded and staffed by a number of émigrés, is still regarded as too 'hostile' to be permitted to broadcast freely. Expensive jamming has, in the past, failed to prevent millions of listeners from tuning in to foreign radio broadcasts (many of which were then taped and circulated clandestinely).

The government's decision and its willingness to embrace other changes appears to reflect an awareness that it is, in the new technological age, in any case fighting a losing battle to defend its monopoly over information. It is perceived that in the long run it is more feasible to provide a credible 'competitive' news service at home, thereby increasing the population's trust, rather than to attempt to silence alternative sources of information from abroad.

The new approach was signalled in a television address to the Soviet people by Mikhail Gorbachev following the Reykjavik summit of October 1986. He said that he had made an offer to President Reagan to cease jamming the *Voice of America* if the Americans allowed the Soviet Union to set up medium wave band radio broadcasts beamed at the United States.

Meanwhile, a growing number of video owners are now able to re-record television programmes from Finland which are easily picked up by Estonian viewers, and the advent of satellite television potentially offers an even greater range to enterprising viewers prepared to place home-made satellite dishes on the roofs of their houses. Clearly, too, the government cannot forever forestall the consequences of necessary computerization at home, which offers vast possibilities for disseminating information through 'unofficial' channels.

**The new press law**: A new press law was expected in 1986, but at the beginning of 1987 it was anounced that 'the widening of *glasnost*' and 'substantial changes in the media' had held up work on the project. From the discussions to date, it is clear that the aim of the new law is to provide a firm legislative base for Gorbachev's 'open' policy, giving greater protection to journalists in their new watchdog role and permitting them greater access to information from state organizations, while at the same time assuaging critics of *glasnost* by defining its limits more clearly. M. A. Fedotov, a prominent jurist involved in drafting the new law, has said that the Constitution gives no precise definition of freedom of the press and allows scope for 'arbitrary interpretation of this democratic institution'.

**The future of censorship**: The law will also, according to Prof. Fedotov, 'define the functions of control over the press', or, in other words, censorship. Censorship as such has existed in the USSR since 1922, when *Glavlit* (the Main Administration for Literature and Publishing) was introduced under Bolshevik rule. In the late 1950s and '60s *Glavlit* underwent major reorganization to cope with the increasing complexity of the information structure. An 'Administration for the Protection of State Secrets in the Press' was set up with offices at all administrative levels of government, while separate departments were established to deal with theatre, film, televison and radio, and military, atomic and space affairs. All printed matter, however trivial, and all 'cultural products' are subject to checking by officials of *Glavlit*, who use a handbook nicknamed the 'Talmud' to guard against the mentioning of secrets or of proscribed names and events.

The role of ideological guardians has been taken over by a vast editorial apparatus which extends from the staff of newspapers, publishing houses and broadcasting stations (almost all of whom, at the higher levels, are party members) through regional levels of the party apparatus, right up to top officials of the government and party—including officials of the KGB—who act as guides and consultants on matters of policy and ideology.

It is likely that the new law on the press will confirm the *de facto* status of *Glavlit* as an institution responsible primarily for the technical safeguarding of government secrets, while leaving relatively undefined the overall mechanism by which a form of self-censorship effectively operates throughout the media.

## Freedom of opinion and expression

There are still many taboo subjects not covered by the official press and it is being argued in the Soviet Union that it will not be possible to speak of full freedom of expression until some form of independent press and freedom of association are allowed. However, those who have argued against or are testing the government's view of the value of an independent press (or of independent informal associations, such as the Socialist *Perestroika* Club), would not necessarily identify themselves as dissidents. This is a new development.

Members of the Moscow Writers' Union have recently been permitted to set up a co-operative, financed by shareholders, to publish their own books.

In June 1987 a new journal, appropriately entitled *Glasnost*, was launched with the express purpose of providing information and discussion on topics not yet fully covered by the offical media. Its editors are Sergei Grigoryants, until recently imprisoned for his involvement in an unoffical human rights publication, *Bulletin V*, and Lev Timofeev, an economist likewise imprisoned for publishing abroad critical remarks on the Soviet economy, many of which are echoed in the official press today. They have emphasized from the outset that they aim to work in a spirit of co-operation rather then combat the government, and that they saw no reason—in view of the government's more open policies—to operate underground.

The Deputy Chairman of the State Committee for Printing, Publishing and Bookselling, Dmitry Mamleev, told Grigoryants that, owing to a 'shortage of paper', the right to publish was reserved for 'state and public organizations'. He added that *Glasnost* was, in any case, unnecessary, since all its materials 'could now be published in the official press'. At the same time, however, he did not expressly forbid the editors to continue their work.

**Public demonstrations**: The authorities have responded with similar ambiguity to recent attempts by other unoffical groups—e.g. would-be emigrants, peace activists, and activists of various national movements — to express their view through demonstrations. In pre-*glasnost* days, such demonstrations were routinely broken up as soon as they began and the participants arrested. But on several recent occasions the authorities have allowed them to take place unimpeded, and have even acknowledged that they represent a legitimate means of exercising the rights to free expression—while reminding the participants that their rights should not be abused.

## Current detainees

Included among those writers, journalists and media workers against whom action has been taken during the course of 1987 or who are still in prison: Nikolai Horbal, poet and teacher, sentenced April 1985 to eight years' special regime (the severest category of labour camp) and three years' internal exile; Viktoras Petkus, specialist in Lithuanian literature, sentenced July 1978 to ten years' special regime and five years' internal exile; Vladimir Lvovich Gershuny, writer and poet, arrested June 1982 and sentenced indefinitely to psychiatric care in Alma-Ata.

# SPAIN

The rights to freedom of expression and information in Spain have been determined by the course of a recent history of intense political conflict and by the legacy of a forty-year dictatorship. New values and practices have had relatively little opportunity to flourish in the face of a long established tradition of exercising significant degrees of control over information. Since Gen. Franco's death successive governments have inherited institutions and customs of a pre-democratic vintage and the transition from dictatorship to democracy has seen military pressure and the challenge of political violence. Governments have consequently deemed it expedient to retain some of their inherited prerogatives.

|  |  | Year |
|---|---|---|
| Population | 39,000,000 | 1985 |
| GNP ($ per capita) | 2,260 | 1984 |

| | | |
|---|---|---|
| Daily newspapers | 143 | 1977 |
| Non Daily newspapers | 4 | est |
| Periodicals | 140 | est |
| Published books | 30,764 | 1984 |
| Radio stations | 21 | est |
| Radio receivers | 10,450,000 | 1984 |
| TV stations | 6 | est |
| TV sets | 9,912,000 | 1984 |

Press Agencies: EFE

Covenant on Civil & Political Rights _____ 1977

Article 20 of the Spanish Constitution, approved by parliament in October 1978 and ratified by referendum in December 1978, guarantees 'the right to communicate freely or receive any accurate information by any means of dissemination whatsoever'. In addition, 'the exercise of these rights cannot be restricted by any form of prior censorship'. The same article points out, however, that these rights are limited by 'the right to honour, privacy, personal reputation, and the protection of youth and children'. Further limits are contained in Organic Law 8/1984 (the 'Anti-Terrorist Law') and by Organic Law 1/82 concerning the Right to Honour, Personal and Family Intimacy and Personal Reputation (*proprio imágen*). Article 55 of the Constitution further states that the right of free expression may be suspended by the proclamation of a state of emergency or a state of siege.

Some ambiguity remains over the term 'accurate information' in the Constitution which is included again in Organic Law 2/84 regulating the right of redress. This law makes it possible for individuals to request the media publicly to correct inaccurate information published about them and to appeal to the courts if the media refuse such a request. A similar protection is afforded by Organic Law 1/82.

216

# SPAIN

## The Media

**Television:** There are two government-run channels based in Madrid, *TV1* and *TV2*, which are broadcast by *Radiotelevisión Española* (RTVE). There are also three local channels backed by regional authorities, *TV3* in Catalonia, *Euskal Telebista* in the Basque region and another channel in Galicia. In a country where newspaper readership is low, television has assumed considerable influence over the ideas and opinions of the population. Recent opinion polls show that at least two-thirds of the population turn to television as a primary source of information.

Following three years of delay, proposals for the privatization of television were finally launched by the government on March 3, 1987. The proposed *Proyecto de ley de Televisión Privada* is to come into effect by 1989/90. Under the new law, television is to remain a public service as stated in the existing Law for the Regulation of Telecommunications, but in addition to the country's two major government channels three new channels are to be created. The channels will be open to public tender for ten years (renewable). At the moment, the new owners will have to accept a level of national coverage of at least thirty-two hours per week in addition to coverage of regional issues.

The government's promise to break its own monopoly was made in the face of repeated criticism which alleged biased coverage of political and ideological issues. Indignation was particularly voiced over coverage of the political debate prior to the referendum on Spanish membership of NATO, held on March 12, 1986. Article 24 of the 1980 Radio and Television Statute stipulates that access to television is guaranteed to the country's 'main' social and political groups and the government has promised that its choice of concessional companies will be conditioned by 'the need to guarantee free and pluralistic expression of ideas and currents of opinion'.

The projected law would not allow currently operating newspaper or communications businesses to participate in more than 15 per cent of the future channels' capital. Other interested parties however, including foreign investors, may buy up to 25 per cent of shares.

**Satellite:** The continued debate on the possible ramifications of these provisions in terms of the balance of ownership of the airwaves has been complicated by the development of plans to introduce cable television into the country. In January 1988 a new company, *Channel 10*, based in London, is to begin transmitting 24-hour television programmes in Spanish by satellite to Spain. The company, established by *RTVE's* former director general José María Calviño Iglesias and other Spanish businessmen, has booked space on the Intelsat satellite system.

**Radio:** The Projected *Ley de Ordenación de Telecomunicaciones* (LOT)— Statute on Telecommunications—is meeting opposition during its progress through parliament (las Cortes). Radio broadcasters in particular have cause for concern if the bill goes through. For over fifty years a mixed system of public and private radio broadcasting has operated in Spain, which would be jeopardized by this bill. The bill would enable the state to grant concessions to certain broadcasters, and the potential political abuse of these powers is feared. Under the bill the government proposes to integrate private or regional broadcasting centres to form 'the most convenient public network'. Private broadcasters reject this proposal, arguing that it is the equivalent of forcing newspapers in a given city to be printed in specified printworks. The bill would also exclude the foreign ownership of radio stations (while not affecting television broadcasting) and would impose a five-year time limit on radio frequency concessions. Furthermore, radio companies would be required under the law to set aside airtime to broadcast government messages. All of these restrictions amount to an erosion of the right to free expression which is not addressed or acknowledged by the 'technical' status of the bill.

**Newspapers:** Spain's reputation as having the lowest circulation and readership of newspapers of all industrialized western European countries (only eighty out of every 1,000 people buy a newspaper each day) is a matter of concern to the government. *El País*, the country's most popular paper, reaches a daily circulation figure of only 340,000 and 600,000 on Sundays. Development is very slow; since 1982 newspaper circulation has gone up by only one-fifth. In reaction to these figures, Law 29 of Aug. 2, 1984 which granted 'Assistance to Journalistic Undertakings and Information Agencies' provided that the press should receive annually a number of subsidies to be used for disseminating publications, meeting the cost of newsprint and updating and replacing printing machinery. These subsidies have encouraged greater modernization of an industry that had been ailing under Franco.

Existing legislation, however, inhibits the degree to which the press may act in an investigative capacity. Close adherence to the 'right to honour and personal reputation' frequently leaves newspapers in a compromising position. In July 1987 the IPI (International Press Institute) announced that it would lobby the Spanish parliament to bring about reform of this law. However, in October 1987 a magazine published in Madrid lost a civil case in which a matter of 'honour' was involved. A journalist from *Diario 16* had accused in print a court official of falsifying a judge's signature; the official chose to defend his honour in court. *Diario 16* lost the case and was fined approximately £70,000 for having presumed guilt before trial. No more was said of the court official's alleged offence.

The government appears particularly sensitive over press representations of the monarchy and leading political figures. In December 1987 for instance, the political cartoonist Jesús Francisco Zulet was brought to court accused of contempt. He had drawn an unflattering cartoon of the Prime Minister, Felipe González. In November 1987 a journalist, Juan José Fernández Perez, was sentenced to an extraordinary six years' imprisonment for insulting King Juan Carlos in *Punto y Hora* magazine. Satire aimed at the Pope or the Catholic Church can also be out of bounds.

**Magazines:** Magazine sales are on the increase in Spain. The most popular magazines are news weeklies such as *Cambio 16, Tiempo, Panorama* and *Interviú* and the recently formed *El Globo*. The so-called 'heart-throb press' specializing in photo layouts of royalty and media personalities is also highly popular. An interesting feature of the magazine market is the existence of glossy, popular magazines such as *Interviú*, which contain articles on fashion, social gossip and nude photography directly alongside investigative reporting. In 1983 for instance, Xavier Vinader was prosecuted for 'professional irresponsibility' after publishing an article in *Interviú* which exposed links between the police and right-wing terrorist groups. Named individuals in the article were later killed by rival gunmen.

**Licensing of journalists:** On Nov. 8, 1985 the autonomous parliament of Catalonia approved a law (Law 22/85) reserving access to the media to members of the Professional College of Journalists. This organization will award a certificate recognized by the Catalonian parliament after 'a transitional period' of five years. In order to qualify for the certificate an applicant must have studied at university for a degree in information sciences, or else must either possess a degree from another university and have two years' professional experience, or have five years' professional experience as a journalist. The Spanish parliament and other autonomous governments are considering similar legislation.

Concern over the possible adverse effects of this legislation led to a request from the Spanish National Committee of the IPI to the Ombudsman that Law 22/85 be declared unconstitutional. The Ombudsman, Joaquín Ruiz Jimenéz, decided in favour of the IPI's request, stating that 'now that the crime of expressing an opinion has disappeared from our Constitution, the creation of a *Colegio* for journalists brings back the possibility of judicially punishing a person exercising the activity of [receiving and imparting] information while not being a member of a *Colegio*'.

## Freedom of opinion and expression

Spain's Organic Law 8/1984 was designed to deal with 'the activities of armed bands and terrorist groups'. It was directed however not only at the activities of such groups but at anyone justifiying their activities. It was made an offence to support or praise 'insurrection or the activities typical of a terrorist organization... or the deeds or commemorative dates of their members by publishing or broadcasting via the mass media, articles expressing opinions, news reports, graphical illustrations, communiqués and, in general, by any other form of dissemination'. Demonstrations expressing solidarity were also prohibited.

Under Article 21 of the law judges and courts were until recently able to close newspapers or radio stations accused of disseminating such information as an 'exceptional precautionary measure'. In December 1986 the Constitutional Tribunal overruled the Madrid Supreme Court and cleared a Basque newpaper of condoning terrorism. Mr José Félix Azurmendi, former editor of the newspaper *Egin*, had been sentenced to two years' imprisonment for printing two ETA communiqués. In its judgment, the Tribunal made reference to the fact that the right to receive and impart information was enshrined in the 1978 Constitution. In January 1987 the government permitted six articles of the Anti-Terrorist Law, including Article 21, to lapse. This followed pressure from three Basque parties in the lead-up to the formation of a regional coalition government.

Although court action was rare when the Act's terms were operative, journalists and newspapers had been charged, for example, for reporting the slogans chanted or written on banners during a demonstration. Allegations of police brutality or explanations and statements from terrorists could also be ruled as an offence if printed in the newspapers. Many observers, including Juan Luis Cebrián Echarrí, editor of *El País*, have commented on the dangerous effect this law has for freedom of the press. Moral responsibility for violence was transferred from the perpetrators onto those who report on them, a fact which was bound to encourage high levels of self-censorship and did little to discourage terrorism.

# SWEDEN

In 1766 the Swedish parliament adopted a Freedom of the Press Act as part of the Constitution, the earliest legislation of its kind. The emerging press was given the right to act as a watch-dog. The present Freedom of the Press Act dates from 1949, and is also specially protected by being part of the Constitution. Any amendment or abrogation of the Act must be confirmed by two successive parliaments with general elections taking place between first and second readings. Today the Swedish press, radio and television operate in a rare climate of freedom, but paradoxically by the standards of countries less fortunate the media are considered less forceful and enterprising in reporting on public affairs.

|  |  | Year |
|---|---|---|
| Population | 8,300,000 | 1985 |
| GNP ($ per capita) | 1,180 | 1985 |
| Daily newspapers | 188 | 1985 |
| Non Daily newspapers | 28 | est |
| Periodicals | 398 | est |
| Published books | 9,657 | 1985 |
| Radio stations | 27 | 1985 |
| Radio receivers | 3,300,000 | 1985 |
| TV stations | 2 | est |
| TV sets | 3,257,000 | 1985 |

Press Agencies: Svensk International Pressbyran (SIP)

Covenant on Civil & Political Rights _____ 1971

Most Swedes are proud of their open society and accordingly shocked when it is violated, as it was when the unprotected Prime Minister Olof Palme was shot dead in central Stockholm late one Friday evening after leaving a cinema. But few voices have been heard proposing a new direction in the wake of the assassination. The failure of the Swedish police investigations to solve the Palme murder has been much criticized in the Swedish press. But the point has also been made that the press had done little by way of independent investigative reporting into the assassination, including suggestions of a link with illegal Swedish arms sales to Iran.

## Freedom of information

The principle of free access to public documents goes back to the Act of 1766, and is regarded as a vital part of Swedish democracy. The principle which gives access to public documents reads as follows: 'Everyone shall have the right to request that he may examine the documents in matters which are or have been under consideration by the public administration.'

This principle gives anyone, including aliens, the right to go to a state or municipal agency and ask to be shown any documents in their files, regardless of whether the document concerns them personally or not. Officials are legally required to comply and even to supply copies of the document if requested. In most cases the officials may not ask the applicant for identification or the reason for the request. If, for instance, anyone is interested in reading the letters to the Prime Minister or any official document sent to the authorities, he or she has the right to do so according to the law. As soon as any letter or document arrives at a public authority's office, anyone has the right to read the content regardless of whether the addressee has read it or not. Not only is post to the authorities public, but equally most of the documents written by the authorities themselves.

The computer storage of information by the authorities caused initial problems. But in 1974, the law also recognized computerized material as public documents, although citizens themselves were not entitled to search for information. After debates on this issue, an amendment was adopted in 1982 which permits anyone who so requests to use a computer terminal provided by the authorities in order to inform himself of what is stored. Concern has been expressed however over the failure to address personal privacy values alongside open access to computer data.

**Exempted documents:** Documents that may be withheld from public scrutiny are those dealing with national security, foreign policy and foreign affairs. Other documents relating to criminal investigations and information concerning the personal integrity or the financial circumstances of individuals are also restricted to prevent criminal misuse. Exceptions to the general rule of accessibility are spelled out in great detail in the Official Secrets Act. Any type of document not explicitly listed in this Act is by definition available to the public.

If someone is refused a public document he or she is immediately entitled to a written statement quoting the legal authority for withholding the document. Information must also be given about a right to appeal, ultimately to the Supreme Administrative Court. The only cases in which there can be no appeal against the refusal to honour requests for public documents are those in which secret decisions are made by cabinet, parliament, the supreme court and the *justitieombudsman* (parliamentary ombudsman). The latter, however, considers it one of his major duties to supervise the implementation and the enforcement of the right of access to public documents.

## The Media

**Censorship:** In Sweden, censorship of the press is explicitly forbidden. Anyone has the right to establish a newspaper or magazine. No concession is needed and the Press Act prevents the authorities from raising obstacles to printing, publication and distribution.

**Journalist liability:** By protecting those who communicate information to the media, the Freedom of the Press Act also encourages the supply of information. The responsibility for the content of newspapers, magazines and other periodicals is, for instance, vested in one single person, known as the 'responsible publisher', who is usually the editor-in-chief. The Act protects all other persons, both those who are members of the editorial staff and third parties from prosecution or from liability to pay damages on account of their contribution to the publication.

**Protection of sources:** In legal proceedings reporters' names may not be mentioned nor may they be summoned to appear before a court. In fact, the law explicitly prohibits the investigation or disclosure of a journalist's sources. A reporter is thus not only allowed to keep sources secret, but is compelled by law to do so. He may be sentenced for breaking the obligation to secrecy. This protection is extended even to state and municipal employees, who are thus free to give information to newspapers and other media without fear of legal repercussions or extra-legal pressures and intimidation. Similar 'whistleblower' laws are being adopted at state and federal level in the United States.

In 1981, a Swedish newspaper published an article indicating that a well-known lawyer was the legal adviser of a crime syndicate. It was obvious that a police officer had disclosed the information. But there was no way to find out which one it was as he had the right to anonymity. The officer had committed no dereliction of duty in giving the secret information to a journalist, and the journalist could not be questioned about his source. The lawyer won his libel suit against the newspaper's editor, who could not prove the truth of the information.

It is not regarded as a problem in Sweden that immunity of informants might induce some of them to leak irresponsible, harmful or even untruthful statements to the media. The law may protect the informant, but does not exonerate the crime. The 'responsible publisher' has reasons of his own for not risking publication of matters actionable by law.

There are some exceptions to the general rule of immunity and anonymity of sources. If state employees, including military personnel, inform the media of matters that could jeopardize state security, this could warrant legal action against informants. The same applies when a doctor, for example, violates professional secrecy, by disclosing information given in confidence by a patient. Similarly, the protection of anonymity may be overruled in a criminal case which does not involve the freedom of the press, and where the court finds that the disclosure of a source is called for by an overriding public or private interest.

**Legal safeguards:** The media are further protected from legal harassment, by special rules and institutions for prosecutions under the Freedom of the Press Act. A decision to prosecute must be made by the Chancellor of Justice; a prosecution cannot be initiated by the ordinary local prosecutor. The Chancellor is furthermore obliged to obtain the consent of the Cabinet before acting in cases with political ramifications.

The regular courts of law are also modified in a special way when trying press cases. Cases are tried by a jury, an institution otherwise alien to the Swedish judicial system. At least six of the nine jurors must be in agreement for a conviction. The judges may acquit a person under the Press Law despite a jury verdict of proven, but may not overrule a finding of not proven.

**Investigative journalism:** The Freedom of the Press Act does not give the Swedish media access to everything. The private sector is protected and has no obligation to give journalists the information they ask for. Many journalists tend to pick up information from the easiest sources, i.e. where the law automatically gives them access to documents and other information. Hence the state and local authorities are scrutinized, while private companies and other privately-run bodies often have a comparatively easy ride. Two of the country's most infamous international scandals, the alleged Bofors bribes over illegal sales of arms, and the bizarre Fermenta affair, were first exposed by non-journalists, who having sought to interest local newspapers contacted the foreign press who reported abroad on the scandals. Only then was it picked up by the Swedish media. The Fermenta scandal involved the sudden collapse of what was regarded as one of Sweden's leading enterprises, managed by a man who had impressed the international business community with academic qualifications which proved to be false.

**Code of ethics:** As distinctive as Sweden's formal guarantees of extensive press freedom is the discipline achieved by its journalists' own ethical code and procedure. It has been criticized as tending to induce unnecessary self-censorship, given the clear legal freedoms offered to the journalist. The first step was taken in 1916 when the Swedish Press Council was founded by the National Press Council to function as a tribunal, for reviewing and assessing the practices of the press. A Code of Ethics was adopted for the guidance of the press and also to serve as a basis for the Council's work. In the 1960s, in response to increasing criticism of press behaviour and to avoid a threat that the Freedom of the Press Act might be changed, the press organizations (the National Press Club, the Newspaper Publishers' Association and the Union of Journalists) volunteered a number of reforms.

The most important of these were lay representation on the Press Council and the creation of the office of Press Ombudsman. The system is voluntary, and is financed entirely by the press, including the journalists' union. There are no state subsidies and the system is not regulated by any legislation.

**Press Ombudsman:** The task of the Press Ombudsman is to be mediator between the general public and the newspapers and to help individuals in asserting their rights against newspapers (by ordering the publication of corrections and rejoinders, for example). Public complaints are directed to him. If the complaint concerns a minor breach of the Code of Ethics, the Press Ombudsman can issue a censuring opinion. This can be either accepted and printed by the newspaper concerned or an appeal can be made to the Press Council for judgment. Other valid complaints, after investigation by the Press Ombudsman, are transferred to the Press Council for judgment.

If the Press Council censures a newspaper, the paper has to print the decision and also to pay administrative fines to the Council. Fines equivalent to US$2,000 can be imposed and help to finance the Council's operations. But neither the Press Ombudsman nor the Press Council are competent to enforce payment of damages by a newspaper to the complainant, who is, however, free to sue the newspaper for damages in court in accordance with rules of the special court system for press cases. Damages are low, rarely more than the equivalent of a few thousand US dollars.

The annual number of complaints is approximately 400. Only one quarter of these are transferred to the Press Council. About 20 per cent of the complaints result in a censuring opinion, either by the Press Ombudsman or by the Press Council.

**Open justice:** It is considered unethical in Sweden to mention the names of defendants in court cases although justice is otherwise public and open to the media. Considerations of the defendant's personal integrity and family's embarrassment are taken to override those of the public right to know. However some foreign journalists have wondered if an effect of this convention from the journalists' code of ethics is to disincline the media from close reporting of legal cases that ought to have public attention. It has been said that Swedish papers readily re-publish stories of political intrigue, scandals and corruption abroad, but are loath to do so at home.

In 1986, Lars Engqvist, the editor of *Arbetet*, was censured by a defamation court for publishing the name and photograph of Lennart Gunnarsson, arrested in connection with the Palme assassination. Engqvist's defence was that his readers had a right to know the same news as readers of foreign papers which had used the name and picture on the same day.

**Film:** Films intended for public showing in Sweden are previewed by the National Board of Film Censorship which can delete certain sequences or ban the film altogether. There have been attempts through the years to have film censorship abolished, but they have all been defeated.

# TURKEY

Martial law was finally lifted in all parts of Turkey in July 1987, but a state of emergency is still in effect in nine out of sixty-seven provinces. Martial law was imposed throughout the country after the 1980 military coup which brought Gen. Evren to power. The new Constitution was adopted in 1982 and the influence of martial law is evident in its provisions, including numerous restrictions on political parties, trades unions and freedom of expression. Military courts continue to operate. On Nov. 29, 1987, Prime Minister Turgut Ozal, first elected in November 1983 in the context of the Evren regime's transition from military to civilian status, was returned to power in the first election without military supervision since the 1980 coup.

|  |  | Year |
|---|---|---|
| Population | 50,000,000 | 1985 |
| GNP ($ per capita) | 1,200 | 1984 |
| Illiteracy % | 25.8 | 1984 |

| Daily newspapers | } 1,115 | 1979 |
|---|---|---|
| Non Daily newspapers | | |
| Periodicals | 65 | est |
| Published books | 6,869 | 1983 |
| Radio receivers | 6,023,000 | 1984 |
| TV sets | 6,933,000 | 1984 |

Press Agencies:
  Akajans, Anatolian News Agency

Covenant on Civil &
  Political Rights _____ NO

Article 2 of the Constitution provides for respect for human rights 'within the concepts of public peace, national security and justice'. Article 13 lays the groundwork for restricting those rights: 'Exercise of fundamental rights and liberties may be restricted by law in conformity with the letter and spirit of the Constitution, with the aim of safeguarding of the state comprising its territory and the nation, national sovereignty, the Republic, national security, public order, general tranquillity, public wealth, public morals and public health and also for special reasons designated in the relevant articles of the Constitution.'

There are provisions in the Constitution against 'anyone who writes or prints any news or articles which threaten the internal or external security of the state ... or which tend to incite offence, riot or insurrection'. Under other Articles, those who overstep the state's boundaries on free expression may as punishment be deprived of the freedom to express their opinion; opposition and minority opinions may be silenced, foreign publications may be prohibited, and any publication may be confiscated or suspended temporarily.

## The Media

**Newspapers:** There is no prior censorship of the printed press, which is privately-owned. Istanbul is the home of most major Turkish newspaper offices. The two most important daily newspapers are *Milliyet* and *Cumhuriyet* which, like most Istanbul newspapers, are also printed in Ankara and Izmir. After martial law was lifted in November 1985 the press experienced an extraordinary surge in freedom to cover political debate and to publish accounts of human rights abuses including torture. Newspapers now quite openly criticize Prime Minister Ozal and members of his government, but not President Evren or the military. Articles are printed that journalists would have gone to prison for three to four years ago. Nevertheless, many journalists convicted under martial law are still imprisoned. The restrictive Press Law, which can be invoked at any time, includes requirements that reporters be licensed, but refuses certification to journalists with convictions. Journalists are still frequently charged with crimes for what they publish, and sometimes sentenced and imprisoned. Some recent examples illustrate the problems faced by journalists: in November 1986 two reporters on the daily *Hergün*, Veyis Sozuer and Mustafa Karapinar, were sentenced to ten-month prison terms for having insulted the government in an article published in 1978.

In February 1987, *Cumhuriyet* reported that criminal proceedings had been brought against writers, translators and publishers of 240 publications within the previous three-and-a-half years.

In March 1987 Ilhan Selehuk and Okyay Gonensin, reporter and editor of *Cumhuriyet*, were tried for a December 1986 column which purportedly insulted members of the National Security Council. In April 1987 two cases were brought against the weekly *2000'e Dogru* (*Toward 2000*) for articles insulting President Evren and insulting 'the revered memory of Kemal Ataturk'. In September 1987 a whole issue of the magazine was confiscated by court order.

**Banning of books:** Recently, the government has confiscated magazines in large numbers and the banning of books appears to be systematic and thorough. In October 1986, the Ministry of Justice published a detailed list of titles banned to that time and publications whose entry into Turkey is prohibited by government decrees. The list was sent to the political sections of local prefectures and to directors of educational institutions. On Dec. 18, 1986, thirty-nine tons of books, periodicals and newspapers were sent to be pulped. Among the pulped publications were 'The Penguin Map of the World', 'National Geographic Atlas of the World', the Turkish edition of the 'Encyclopaedia Britannica' and the '*Nouveau Petit Larousse illustré*'. All of them have been declared 'means of separatist propaganda' by the Turkish authorities for containing articles or maps related to the history of the Armenians or the Kurds.

**Radio and television:** *Turkish Radio and Television* (*TRT*) is government-owned and censors artists and topics that are deemed too controversial. Although *TRT* has traditionally devoted most of its news coverage to the activities of the President and other government officials, in 1986 it significantly increased coverage of opposition politicians, occasionally making them the lead story.

227

**Film censorship:** A new film law moved the film censorship committee from the Ministry of the Interior to the Ministry of Culture and Tourism, which raised hopes for greater freedom of expression in film. These hopes have not been realized, however; representatives from the military and the Interior Ministry still exert a great deal of influence on the committee.

The Ministry of Foreign Affairs must clear any invitations to foreign artists, scholars, or musicians to participate in local events.

## Freedom of expression

The Penal Code in force as well as the proposed new one includes articles specifically used to punish non-violent opposition in Turkey. Many court decisions show that the application of the legislation violates freedom of expression and religion.

For example, under the current constitution and laws, the establishment of a communist party by legal means is not possible. Haydar Kutlu, secretary-general of the Turkish Commmunist Party in exile and Nihat Sargin of the Turkish Labour Party were detained upon their return to Turkey on Nov. 16, 1987, from seven-year self-exile. The State Security Court has decided that they will stand trial. The charges are expected to include membership of a banned organization (Article 141) and dishonouring Turkey abroad. Article 140 allows for imprisoning citizens who make statements that are damaging to Turkey's reputation abroad. This Article has also been used both before and after the coup to close newspapers and imprison journalists critical of the government or its policies.

Article 163 prohibits membership of 'a society for the purpose of adapting the state to religious principles and beliefs or propaganda for this purpose'. It is used to suppress advocacy of religious sects, particularly Islamic fundamentalism. On several occasions during 1987 members of religious groups were detained, some of them arrested for holding 'anti-secular meetings'. Amnesty International has reported that the number of people persecuted in Turkey for religious activities had increased substantially during 1987, including some who have not used or advocated violence.

**Minorities:** The Constitution states that the official language of the country is Turkish. One article prohibits discrimination on the basis of language, while others ban the public use of 'language prohibited by law'. No specific language is banned, although Kurdish—the language of some 20 per cent of the population—may not be used for any official purpose or in such private situations as receiving visitors in prison. All Kurdish publications are banned, as are Turkish language publications that discuss Kurdish ethnic identity in a positive light.

The government has stated that the intention of its ban on publishing in Kurdish is to encourage Turkish as the language of all citizens. About a quarter of the Kurds speak Turkish. Kurds see the ban as an important tool in Turkey's efforts to destroy their ethnic identity and to silence Kurdish demands for autonomy.

Punishment for disobeying the Kurdish ban is severe. In September 1986 the weekly *Karacdag* was closed down indefinitely for publishing an article about torture of villagers in the East (the Kurdish area) by the commander of a gendarmerie unit. The publisher, Recep Marasli, is serving sentences totalling thirty-six years in Diyarbakir Prison for publishing books about the Kurdish minority.

Ismail Besikci, a non-Kurdish sociologist, was sentenced in 1982 to ten years in prison to be followed by five years internal exile in connection with his writings, which had recognized the Kurds as a separate ethnic group.

Until recently, the word 'Kurd' itself was never used in print. In February or March 1987, however, a *Milliyet* reporter wrote about 'the Kurdish problem'. Since then, newspapers and magazines have begun using the word Kurd, though in order to appear in print the word must be used in a negative context, such as 'terrorist Kurd'.

**Law to Protect Minors:** Turkey has recently introduced two new measures that threaten freedom of expression. The first is the 'Law to Protect Minors', which was enacted on March 12, 1986. It is ostensibly a measure against pornography, but may also be used to restrict 'items of a political nature which may influence minors adversely'. Since its enactment, the law has not often been used against newspapers, but it has been frequently invoked against magazines, writers and publishers of books.

The law provides for a board of eleven, with one journalist member, to hold meetings eight or nine times a month to examine all publications. Publishers and editors who do not comply with the law are subjected to heavy fines. If three editions of the same periodical are judged harmful, the entire publication will not be sold on open shelves.

Items falling under this proscription include David Hume's 'On Religion' (in translation), the film 'Gandhi', and the TV programme 'Dallas'. Authorities removed paintings by a Polish artist, Jan Dubkowski, after President Evren called the painting obscene. Medical activities are censored as well; slides and films were prohibited at a panel discussion on sexual dysfunction at a military medical academy. Video cassette club owners have been fined for possession of obscene materials.

Recently the government has used the new law as a pretext for confiscating magazines in large numbers. A new weekly, *Akis*, published a story about Ayatollah Khomeini's sex life; all unsold copies were confiscated. Pinar Kur, a popular novelist, has had two of her books banned by the Council to Protect Minors. The Council thought her book, 'Unending Love', contained obscene descriptions of love-making and said that the novel has no literary value and 'would corrupt minors by causing them to misunderstand the contemporary era, rendering them daydreamers'. The Council also said that 'a literary novel should not contradict the value systems of the society; it should not have slang or obscene language'.

Many criminal investigations have begun as a result of this law. The daily newspaper *Cumhuriyet* was charged for a series of articles in April

1986 for referring to the law as 'harmful' and criticizing the board that supervises compliance. *Cumhuriyet* reported in February 1987 that fifty-seven legal proceedings had been brought against five daily newspapers and twelve weekly or monthly magazines for 'harmful articles' since the Law to Protect Minors went into effect.

Protests against the law have come from virtually every quarter, including members of the Prime Minister's own Motherland Party and the Istanbul Journalists' Association. The Social Democratic People's Party (SHP) has argued that the law deprives the judiciary of its right to judge pornography and determine censorship and that it deprives the population of the right to privacy. The law has been legally challenged, and the Constitutional Court has agreed to review it.

**Press council:** A disturbing development related to the enactment of the Law to Protect Minors is the creation of a self-regulating press council which began to operate in July 1986. The council describes itself as a defender of free expression and of the public's right to know, but also as the protector of integrity and dignity of the press. Members, who include television officials, newspaper owners and a few journalists, are bound 'voluntarily' by a press moral code. The council has the right to penalize journalists who report 'false' information.

The Ankara branch of the Turkish Journalists Union has challenged the establishment of this Council, linking it to a threatened government crack-down on the press and expressing concern that it will function in a quasi-governmental capacity.

## Current detainees

Included among those writers, journalists and media workers against whom action has been taken during the course of 1987 or who are still in prison: Irfan Asik, editor, arrested December 1980, tried thirteen times for different publications, sentenced to 111 years' imprisonment, later reduced to thirty-six years, and due to be released in 1995 under new remission laws; Recep Marashi, publisher, after six separate trials, sentenced to a total of thirty-six years' imprisonment and one year's internal exile; Feyzullah Ozer, journalist and former editor, sentenced in March 1982 to eighteen years and six months' imprisonment.

# UNITED KINGDOM

The United Kingdom has no written constitution, only a series of constitutional principles and conventions, the most fundamental of which is the sovereignty of Parliament. There is no constitutionally significant protection of freedom of expression or freedom of information. Any protection there is depends upon the restraint of the law-making and law-enforcement authorities. Restraint does exist but has become increasingly superficial. This has been amply demonstrated in recent years as Margaret Thatcher, the UK Prime Minister, has sought to re-assert secrecy as a central principle of government, and the courts have set novel and far-reaching precedents of prior restraint on the press, radio and television.

|  |  | Year |
| --- | --- | --- |
| Population | 56,000,000 | 1980 |
| GNP ($ per capita) | 8,530 | 1984 |

| | | |
| --- | --- | --- |
| Daily newspapers | 108 | 1984 |
| Non Daily newspapers | 882 | 1984 |
| Periodicals | 6,408 | 1984 |
| Published books | 51,411 | 1984 |
| Radio receivers | 63,500,000 | est |
| TV stations | 21 | 1987 |
| TV sets | 18,996,000 | 1986 |

Press Agencies: Ass. Press Ltd., Exchange Telegraph Co Ltd., PA Ltd., Reuters, UPI

Covenant on Civil & Political Rights _____ 1976

At the end of 1987, virtually every newspaper in the world was free to probe the allegations of sedition and other wrongdoing by members of the British secret service contained in Peter Wright's book 'Spycatcher' except the press in Britain where it all allegedly happened. Through the use of the courts, the government had succeeded in preventing the British media from reporting on the book. Parliament was also silent. The Speaker of the House of Commons ruled that because the matter was before the courts, no discussion of the book or of the government's legal battles to block media coverage could be debated. The legal proceedings are set to continue and it may be well into 1988 before the press finally knows when, if ever, it can discuss 'Spycatcher'. (See 'Spycatcher' below.)

Although without its own written constitution, the United Kingdom has acquired two external constitutional laws; the treaties establishing the European Community, and the European Convention on Human Rights. The Community treaties do not contain any principles relating to freedom of expression. Community law is, however, beginning to move into areas where that becomes relevant, such as television broadcasting, telecommunications and copyright. Other areas of Community activity which are indirectly but significantly relevant include taxation, especially value added tax, state subsidies and free movement of goods and services.

The Council of Europe's European Convention on Human Rights, Article 8, protects privacy, and Article 10 protects freedom of expression and information. Both Articles, however, contain limitation provisions which are expressed in quite wide terms. The UK is a full member of the Convention system (it has accepted the right of individual petition and compulsory jurisdiction of the European Court of Human Rights) and has defended several Article 10 cases before the Court, winning some (e.g. Handyside) and losing others (e.g. the Sunday Times case). Unlike most other contracting states, the UK has not adopted the Convention into its domestic law. Several initiatives to adopt it as a Bill of Rights have failed. Article 10 therefore cannot be applied by the courts, although legislation has been changed as a result of the Convention; the Sunday Times case led to the Contempt of Court Act 1981 and Malone led to the Interception of Communications Act 1985, regulating phone tapping.

## Laws restraining expression

Several of the laws restraining expression in the UK involve censorship as a central element of their enforcement. Thus the obscenity laws are enforced by criminal process before juries or magistrates. But in neither case is it permitted for evidence to be called on whether the objectionable work falls within an appropriate legally defined category, for instance on whether it could be said 'to deprave and corrupt'. That is regarded as a matter of fact, to be decided by the jurors as their own personal reaction to a mere reading or viewing of the offending object. Although there is the form of a normal trial, what happens in fact is no different from the deliberations of a twelve-member censorship board following a slightly more elaborate procedure.

Contempt of court, as applied to publications which might hinder the course of justice, is similarly decided by the judge in his own discretion with no legal rules to identify the offence and few principles to guide him.

An extreme illustration of the application of contempt of court was the ban issued by the Court of Appeal on Dec. 3, 1987, preventing *Channel 4* television from broadcasting a re-enactment using professional actors of highlights of the 'Birmingham Six' appeal, an ongoing appeal (dismissed in late January 1988) by six Irishmen concerning an alleged miscarriage of justice arising from their conviction for IRA bombings in Birmingham in 1974. The case had been referred to the Court by the Home Secretary after much public disquiet. The Lord Chief Justice held that the broadcast 'was likely to undermine public confidence in the administration of justice' and would therefore amount to a contempt of court.

A new concern in Britain is secret justice—the ability of courts, especially it seems magistrates' courts, to go into secret session, with the public and the press excluded, for a wide variety of reasons. One published estimate stated that in one week of 1987 approximately 350 cases had been held wholly or partially in secret in the High Court. Such procedures have already been criticized by the European Court of Human Rights and other cases are pending.

# UNITED KINGDOM

**Libel:** Although procedural reforms have removed the 'gagging writ', the fear of libel actions against even innocently produced material is a felt restraint on proper reporting of events (leading to the famous euphemism: 'Mr X is helping the police with their inquiries', meaning that he is detained at the police station and is being interrogated); it is also a serious hindrance to proper debate on public issues since public figures and institutions may, and often do, sue against attacks on their public conduct. British law draws no distinction between a public figure and a private plaintiff. But there is no offence of lèse-majesté or insulting the State or the armed forces. A private members' bill on 'Unfair Reporting and the Right of Reply' was to be debated early in 1988. Its supporters argued that sueing for defamation was beyond the means of most of the population and was in any event an inadequate remedy against falling journalistic standards which were particularly evident in the tabloid newspapers.

**Privacy:** There is no privacy law as such in the UK, except for the Data Protection Act 1984 which applies privacy principles to computerized databases. The Act's broad reach has been criticized. Even a computerized address book or a bibliography containing authors' names would be covered, as are journalists' notes. The Act has three effects on freedom of expression: first, databases must be registered (if they contain personal information), a process which evokes for some the ancient licensing of the new-fangled printing presses; second, the contents may only be used for purposes which have been declared on the register; third, a number of positive data principles must be applied to use of the data. The first prosecution under the Act occurred in December 1987 when a company was fined £500 for failing to register personal computer records.

**Journalist's Sources:** Newspaper privacy, which has traditionally been jealously guarded, particularly as regards journalists' sources, was gravely weakened by the Police and Criminal Evidence Act 1984 which gave extensive powers to the police to seize press material, including unpublished notes and photographs to be used in preparing a criminal prosecution. *The Independent* newspaper has appealed an order requiring it to hand over photographs taken at demonstrations outside the premises of News International, publishers of *The Times*. Under different legislation, in January 1988 the financial correspondent of *The Independent,* Jeremy Warner, was fined £20,000 for refusing to disclose confidential sources to Department of Trade investigators following articles he wrote on insider dealings and City takeover bids.

**'Spycatcher':** Prior to the publication of Peter Wright's memoirs in the now notorious book 'Spycatcher', his allegations, including those of Soviet penetration of MI5 and that certain MI5 members plotted to destabilize the administration of former Prime Minister Harold Wilson, had been widely known and discussed. A considerable number of books had been published and television programmes made with no effort to suppress them. The government's moves against Peter Wright were said to be because he was an 'insider' and therefore owed an absolute duty of confidentiality to the British Crown. However, the government had not acted to prevent an earlier television programme in which Wright had made his allegations or a television interview in March 1985 with an MI5 officer, Cathy Massiter, who spoke of widespread telephone tapping against organizations such as the Campaign for Nuclear Disarmament, trade unions and the National Council for Civil Liberties.

This and other inconsistencies were among the reasons why the British government's case in Sydney to prevent publication of the book by Heinemann Australia ultimately failed after a five-week trial and an appeal in mid-1987. The government did not attempt to prevent publication of a US edition by Viking or its publication by Heinemann in Ireland. By October 1987, over 700,000 copies had been printed in the USA alone, and by the end of the year, the rights had been sold for publication in twelve other languages. No attempt was made to prevent the importation of the book into Britain by individuals, although copies may not be sold in British bookshops, advertised in the press or lent out by British public libraries.

**'Spycatcher' and the media:** In June 1986, the government obtained an injunction against the *Observer* and *Guardian* newspapers (and later the *Sunday Times*), which had run stories outlining some of the allegations to be made in the then forthcoming book. In April 1987, *The Independent,* Britain's newest quality paper, and several others, carried reports based on the book. The newspapers argued that they were not affected by the injunction against the other papers. However, the government obtained a ruling from the House of Lords in July that banned all media in Britain from reporting on the book's allegations on pain of being in contempt of court. Subsequently, a court granted a further injunction against the *British Broadcasting Corporation (BBC)* which meant that it could not name the author of the book, but only its title. This was modified subsequently to place the Corporation in the same position as newspapers—it might not discuss the contents of the book pending the final outcome of the legal proceedings against the *Observer* and *Guardian.* The government's campaign in foreign courts to prevent dissemination of the book by newspaper coverage was successful in Hong Kong but failed in New Zealand.

British newspapers won one significant verdict upholding their right to publish in the ongoing legal battle with the government. In December 1987, Mr Justice Scott set aside the injunction against *The Guardian* and *The Observer,* giving a powerfully reasoned defence of freedom of the press in a democracy and an equally powerful rejection of the government claim that national security must always have priority over that freedom.

The judge dismissed the claim made by Sir Robert Armstrong, then Cabinet Secretary and the government's chief witness in the Australian and other proceedings, that the duty of confidentiality owed by former agents such as Wright was absolute and that they must go silent to the grave. A duty of confidentiality could not be imposed to protect useless information or information already in the public domain, the judge said.

Of equal importance, he upheld a public interest argument for disclosure. 'The press has a legitimate role in disclosing scandals in government. An open democratic society requires that to be so.' The judge held that whatever damage to national security the book represented, had already happened, given its world-wide dissemination.

However, since the government has appealed the decision, the restraint on the press remains until the case is finally determined. It is expected that whatever the outcome in the courts in 1988, the government will introduce new and more restrictive legislation governing publications by former secret service employees.

On New Year's Day 1988, the High Court granted a temporary injunction against *The Observer* and *The Sunday Times* preventing them from reporting or quoting from a book of memoirs by an ex-MI6 officer, Anthony Cavendish. Having failed to get his memoirs cleared (he worked for the secret service in 1948-1953), he decided to publish the book himself and circulated 500 copies as Christmas presents. The editors of both papers were first asked for an undertaking that they would not use the material '... I resent such attempts by the government as prior restraint on the press and regard it as a threat to our freedom of speech', said the *Observer* editor, Donald Trelford. The opposition leader Neil Kinnock commented that 'when a government is seeking and getting from the courts prior restraint injunctions, the courts are being used as an arm of government and the separation of powers which is essential to British democracy is being destroyed'.

**D-Notice Committee:** The Defence and Broadcasting Committee, better known as the D-Notice Committee, in the traditional and voluntary British system involving self-censorship by the media on national security matters. The committee, which has a secretary from the Ministry of Defence, distributes a list of eight subjects or D-Notices which might potentially lead to security breaches. Editors are expected but not compelled to clear stories touching on these subjects with the secretary, Rear-Adml. William Higgins.

In December 1987, newspaper editors and broadcasters threatened to abandon co-operation with the D-Notice system after the government successfully stopped the broadcast by the *BBC* of a radio programme on the security services, 'My Country Right or Wrong'. The programme had been discussed at length with the Secretary of the D-Notice Committee who had raised no objections. The government, however, ignored the Committee and prevented the broadcast through the courts in a hearing of which the *BBC* had no notice and at which it was not represented.

## The Media

**Newspapers:** The press and all forms of printed publication are free from special regulation. No registration or authorization is required to publish a newspaper or periodical. Registration as a newspaper is a procedure solely aimed at obtaining concessionary postal rates: it is automatic for publications appearing weekly or more frequently, if they ask for it. All printed publications are fiscally privileged by being zero-rated for value added tax, although EC proposals for fiscal harmonization by 1992 include the abolition of zero-rating.

The British newspaper industry has gone through historic changes at national and local level. A combination of greater concentration of ownership and new technology has resulted in the abandonment of Fleet Street in the City of London, the traditional centre of the industry, for other and dispersed locations, including Wapping, the new home of *The Times* and *The Sun* and the scene of bitter clashes in 1986 between the police and former employees of News International.

The character of papers has also been changing with much complaint voiced over the standards of reporting in the popular daily tabloids, which emphasize entertainment values and focus on royalty and the lives of television stars and other celebrities. In a parliamentary debate on press freedom in November 1987, concern was expressed over journalistic standards and, while speakers were divided over whether concentration of ownership of the press was desirable at all, cross-party objections were raised over the possibility that Rupert Murdoch, who already owns five titles—*The Times,* the *Sunday Times, The Sun,* the *News of the World* and *Today*—might successfully acquire a further title, the *Financial Times.* Members of Parliament pressed for a reference of any bid to the Monopolies and Mergers Commission.

**Broadcasting:** Broadcasting is a state monopoly under the Wireless Telegraphy Acts and so requires a special licence from the Home Secretary. Such a licence is granted to the *BBC* and the *Independent Broadcasting Authority* (*IBA*) and, together with ancillary documents, sets out the structural rules under which those two branches of British broadcasting are organized. Powers are included for the Home Secretary to order the *BBC* or *IBA* to include specified material in their broadcasts or to refrain from broadcasting specified programmes or matter; but this power is rarely used. Cable television is similarly controlled under separate legislation, but is not yet a significant part of the broadcasting pattern in Britain.

There is not yet any domestic satellite broadcasting in Britain, although provision is made for it in the cable TV legislation. The government has taken the view that private reception of foreign satellite broadcasts is not at present covered by the ordinary domestic receiver licence since the broadcasts, being from low power satellite, are 'point to point' (closed-circuit) rather than DBS (broadcast to the world at large). However, it has, unlike many other European countries, encouraged the domestic reception of such signals by making available (for a small fee) a special domestic satellite-receiving licence. Major reforms are expected soon including a significant expansion of commercial radio and two further national television channels.

Broadcasting content is controlled internally by the *BBC.* The *IBA* is responsible ultimately for the content of broadcasts made by independent programme contractors under its jurisdiction (*ITV* and *Channel 4*). It does not operate a systematic pre-censorship scheme; but it is required to keep a close supervision over the programmes and to call in for prior scrutiny any which might cause offence. Cable television programmes are subject to similar supervision by the *Cable Authority*. Because of the inability to control the content of satellite signals broadcast from outside the country, a European Community draft directive which provides for free movement of television signals throughout the EC also requires member states, including Britain, to ensure that the content of broadcasts is checked prior to transmission and that programmes be prohibited if they might seriously harm the physical, mental or moral development of children and young persons. The Home Secretary proposed in autumn 1987 that a Broadcasting Standards Council be set up to monitor sex and violence on television. There is also a Broadcasting Complaints Commission which adjudicates on complaints from members of the public, usually regarding their misrepresentation in a programme.

**Government interference:** There is now more direct interference by government ministers in the *BBC's* decision-making, which is widely seen as having compromised the Corporation's traditional independence and its much-admired philosophy of public broadcasting which required government to be kept at arm's length. Broadcasting has been seen as the victim of a wider phenomenon in contemporary Britain: the government's unwillingness to tolerate any rival centres of power in the State, whether political, institutional, economic or moral. Thus the *BBC* has faced sustained government criticism over alleged bias, particularly over its coverage of the US bombing raid on Libya. The Corporation has been served with a number of court orders including, most recently, an order banning 'My Country Right or Wrong', a radio documentary on the security services.

The most dramatic occurrence, in February 1987, was the seizure by security police of tapes for a television series, 'The Secret Society', in a raid on *BBC* offices in Scotland. The series, planned for transmission in March, included a programme on Zircon, a secret electronic monitoring satellite, which allegedly involved illegal concealment of expenditure from Parliament. A further programme, on the workings of the Cabinet, was not shown when the seized tapes were finally broadcast. The producer of the programme, Duncan Campbell, won the 1987 Freedom of Information Media Award.

A long campaign to apply the Obscene Publications Act to broadcasting is a symptom of the government's desire to interfere with the broadcasting media's self-regulating approach. This is matched by a powerful groundswell of objection to the portrayal of violence on television programmes. All this, together with basic uncertainty about the future of the existing broadcasting structure in the face of new technology such as cable television and satellites, has created a deep insecurity and timidity and consequently an unwillingness to transmit programmes which probe and question existing accepted social, political and other values and issues.

**Film:** Since the abolition of theatre censorship, formal censorship has been restricted to the audiovisual media. Film censorship has long been exercised by a combination of public and private bodies: the actual censoring is done by a private, industry-appointed but independent body, the British Board of Film Censors; but its rulings are given effect by local government bodies through their general powers to license cinemas (compliance with the BBFC's classifications being one of the licence conditions).

The rapid development of a new type of film distribution in the form of video cassettes which are rented out or sold by specialist video shops, record shops and some chain stationers has led to a campaign against 'video nasties', or horror films, many having overtones of sexual violence. Revulsion against these induced Parliament to pass the Video Recordings Act (1985) which subjects all sale or hire of videograms, whether commercially or not and whether they are video nasties or not, to a systematic pre-censorship system. The BBFC, with its name changed to the British Board of Film Classification, was deputed to administer the scheme as the first statutory censorship board to be introduced in Britain since theatre censorship was initiated in 1737.

**Access to information:** Secrecy has been described as being as British as the sweet tooth. The country has no general freedom of information legislation, and a secrecy code—The Official Secrets Act—which is widely regarded as unenforceable and far too extensive. Government papers are made accessible after a thirty-year period, which can be extended up to 100 years for materials considered sensitive.

For over a decade the Freedom of Information Campaign, a broad alliance of groups and individuals, has sought new legislation to open up central and local government and to reform the Official Secrets Act, Section 2. Three of the four main political parties, the Labour, Liberal and Social Democratic parties, support such legislation. However, the Conservative party government is committed only to reviewing the Official Secrets Act, and it is not believed that such a review will lead to greater openness. Some limited advances have been made however. The Local Government (Access to Information) Act 1985 provides for greater access to local council meetings (including sub-committees), agendas, reports and documents. The Access to Personal Files Act 1987 gives an individual the right of access to files on themselves, but at present only those relating to housing and social services records. The Bill initially covered a wide range of records but was eviscerated in its passage through Parliament. The government has promised to extend the principle to educational records under separate legislation.

The campaign for reduction of secrecy was given a boost when, under the thirty-year rule, records released for 1957 disclosed that the then Prime Minister, Harold Macmillan, had ordered the suppression of information on an accident at the Windscale nuclear plant. The release of radioactivity reached levels 600 times those of the Three Mile Island accident in the United States, making it the worst known nuclear accident before

Chernobyl. However, these facts had been suppressed until the release of the government papers in January 1988.

The British record on freedom of expression has always charted a zigzag course and never more so than today. None of the old principles are safe against adventitious dilution or breach. Philosophical principles cut no ice and short-term considerations are dominant. As far as freedom of expression and information is concerned, Britain is going through a very stormy period.

# YUGOSLAVIA

The operation of censorship is no secret in Yugoslavia. It has recently been described in a popular Belgrade magazine: '1,200 to 1,400 books or periodicals are delivered monthly to the Office of the Public Prosecutor in Belgrade alone... How prosecutors manage to determine whether a publication includes "hostile" or other "unacceptable" contents among such large numbers of books we could not find out.' (*Intervju*, March 1987, pp. 8-9).

Yugoslavia's six federal republics and two autonomous provinces enjoy a high degree of self-governance and virtual power of veto can be exercised by each unit over major federal decisions. There are additional internal, regional divisions related to language (there are seven main languages, Serbo-Croat, Macedonian, Albanian, Hungarian, Czech, Slovak and Romanian), levels of economic development and illiteracy rates. This is reflected in the quality and quantity of information available to sectors of the national community and in the application of laws governing its flow in the different republics.

|  |  | Year |
|---|---|---|
| Population | 23,000,000 | 1985 |
| GNP ($ per capita) | 2,120 | 1984 |
| Illiteracy % | 8.0 | 1985 |
| Daily newspapers | 27 | 1984 |
| Non Daily newspapers | 6 | est |
| Periodicals | 1,474 | 1984 |
| Published books | 10,918 | 1984 |
| Radio receivers | 4,706,000 | est |
| TV sets | 4,062,000 | est |

Press Agencies:
Novinska Agencija Tanjug

Covenant on Civil &
Political Rights ———— 1971

The fundamentals of freedom of opinion, expression and information are set by the 1974 Constitution and basic federal legislation. Article 166 states that 'freedom of the press and of other information media, of public expression, of gatherings and public assembly is guaranteed'.

Article 203 however, specifies that 'nobody may use freedoms and rights determined by this Constitution in order to destroy the foundations of the socialist, self-management, democratic system established by the Constitution, to endanger peace and equality, to jeopardize the realization of freedoms and civil and human rights guaranteed by the Constitution, to endanger peace and equality in international co-operation, to stir up national, racial and religious hatred or intolerance, or to instigate the commission of penal offences, nor may freedoms be used in a manner offensive to public morals'.

# YUGOSLAVIA

## The Media

**Newspapers**: The Federal Law on the Fundamentals of the System of Public Information states that 'publication and dissemination of information is free'. However, the right to publish a newspaper is subject to a range of conditions. At least 10 citizens must initiate the procedure for the publication of the paper, none of whom can have been charged at any time for an offence against the foundations of the socialist system of self-management. A further condition requires that publishers submit their proposals to the Socialist Alliance, the country's official communist-dominated political organization.

The Socialist Alliance's view of the 'social justification' (*drustvena opravdanost*) of a prospective paper is forwarded to the government registry of periodicals and also to the applicants. A negative response by the Alliance amounts to a ban on the proposed publication. Similar provisions exist in the laws of republics and autonomous provinces (for example Article 61 of the Law on Public Information of Serbia).

**Ownership and control**: Newspapers are founded by the relevant socio-political organizations (usually the Socialist Alliance), and managed by editorial councils and editorial boards. In theory the public at large owns all means of production for a newspaper. In practice however, control is exercised through editorial boards, a third of whose members are from the newspaper itself. The tasks of the editorial board include analysis of editorial policy and content, structure and layout of the newspaper, along with discussion of the role of the newspaper in the community.

Editorial staff must exhibit 'ideological-political commitment' to the system of socialist self-management, as well as 'moral and and political eligibility', *moralno-politcka podobnost*; in practice this means membership of the League of Communists of Yugoslavia (LCY) and acceptability to the political leadership. The editor-in-chief is responsible for the day-to-day running of the newspaper while the editorial council determines overall policy. There has been an increasing trend to appoint temporary, 'acting' editors-in-chief, accompanied by frequent dismissals and resignation for 'editorial failures' from that position.

The editor of the weekly magazine *Intervju*, Peter Ilic, was dismissed in 1987 for printing a front-cover photograph of Milovan Djilas, an outspoken critic of the state system. Miran Lesjak, the editor of the student magazine *Katendra*, resigned in April 1987 after being criticized by authorities for publishing an interview with Djilas and other controversial articles. Similarly, the editors-in chief of the student magazines *Tribuna* and *Intervju* have felt constrained to resign. One of the more outspoken organs of the student press, *Tribuna*, which has frequently been threatened with prohibition, published an article in May 1987 denouncing such semi-official pressure. The article called for clear rules on what should and should not be published: 'We demand the introduction of normal censorship. Let the repression be public.' In

November 1987 the editor-in-chief of *Belgrade Television News*, Michailo Eric, was dismissed for 'one-sided and untrue reports which constituted crude disinformation'. He was the third senior editor to lose his job in that month.

**Books and periodicals**: Despite the economic crisis and shortages of paper, the number of periodicals and magazines in circulation has increased enormously. There are hundreds of general interest magazines, the most noted being *NIN* (*Nedeljne Informativne Novine*) and *Intervju* from Belgrade and *Danas* from Zagreb. A vast number of special interest magazines also exist covering anything from home computers to maritime affairs, with entertainment and fashion among the bestsellers. Sexually explicit journals are also popular. It is interesting to note that the treatment of sexual themes does not attract the law or the censor. Although prohibitions on pornography exist, there have been no prosecutions in recent years; this contrasts with the regular traffic through the criminal courts of those who offend because of political speech or publication. Recent public controversy failed to halt the legalization of a self-styled 'porno-movie theatre' in Belgrade. News magazines outsell most daily newspapers. There are 28,000 officially registered authors (writers and translators) and 100 publishing houses in the country. Such scales of production are associated with the diversity of languages and the frequent need for translated editions . A large proportion of publishing caters for the education system.

The rich variety of publications in Yugoslavia is matched, however, by an equally rich array of restrictive laws and controls. Penalties for contravening these laws are severe. Under the Law on the Fundamentals of the System of Public Information, and the Law on the Prevention of the Abuse of Freedom of the Press and the Media, a broad range of restrictions are stipulated from military secrets and criticism of the socialist system of self-management to offences 'against the honour and reputation' of Yugoslavia, its president or parliament or of foreign states and international organizations. Printers and publishers are required to deliver the first two issues of any printed text (before the text is bound and ready for distribution) to the Office of the Public Prosecutor.

**Prohibited books**: In 1986 and 1987 these included: 'Hunting the Heretic' by Vojislav Seselj, banned for making 'untruthful allegations' against the leadership of the Republic of Bosnia-Herzegovina; 'State's Worries' by Rastko Zakic, a collection of aphorisms banned because 'it could disturb the public'; The 'Trial of High Treason' by Vojislav Seselj, a book of documents related to the author's 1984 trial, banned because it 'contains assertions undoubtedly showing the subjectiveness and arbitrariness of the author', and 'The Allies and the Yugoslav War Drama', a historical treatise on World War II by Veselin Djuretic which had sold out in its first edition and was subsequently banned because of 'contents which impart falsehoods and which could disturb the public'. In July 1987 the Supreme Court rejected Djuretic's appeal against the ban and insisted that all copies of it should be destroyed.

**Broadcasting and film**: A temporary injunction can be issued under the Law on the Prevention of the Abuse of Freedom of the Press and the Media through the Office of the Public Prosecutor, and a permanent prohibition through the District Court on any publication, radio and television broadcast, film or audio-tape.

**Verbal crimes**: There are a number of penal provisions associated with the 'crime of thought' (*delikt misljenja*) or *délit d'opinion*, a term borrowed from French. Article 133 of the Federal Penal Code states that 'whoever by means of an article, leaflet, drawing, speech or in some other way advocates or incites the overthrow of the rule of the working class and working people, an unconstitutional alteration of the socialist system of self-management, the disruption of the brotherhood, unity and equality of the nations and nationalities, an overthrow of the organs of socialist self-management or their executive bodies, resistance to decisions of competent government or self-management bodies which are significant for the protection or the defence of the country; or whoever maliciously and untruthfully portrays socio-political conditions in the country, shall be punished by imprisonment from one to ten years'.

The catch-all nature of this law and the ambiguity of its wording ('malicious', 'untruthful') make all expression through any media vulnerable to severe official reprisal. No distinctions are made between violent and non-violent advocacy or opinion. In March 1987 a mining engineer in Tuzla was sentenced to three and a half years' imprisonment for having expressed the opinion that 'state and party officials are responsible for the country's economic crisis'.

There are similar penalties under this article for the duplication of 'hostile' propaganda, in peace or wartime. The penal codes of republics and provinces include as verbal crimes the dissemination of 'untruthful news' with the intention 'to cause dissatisfaction or disturbance of a large number of citizens' which can lead to a maximum of five years' imprisonment. A theology student, Dobroslav Paraga, was recently imprisoned for allegedly spreading 'false information' and 'alarming the public'. He had written articles in the youth magazine *Mladina* and the monthly journal *Nova Revija*.

Since overt or violent acts of political opposition are rare in Yugoslavia, verbal crimes are proclaimed by officialdom to represent the political crime in the country. There are from 400 to 700 cases annually. All books, periodicals or newspapers may be subject to provisions ruling verbal offences. On average, a dozen books are prohibited each year under this provision. It is difficult, however, to determine the many 'silent sanctions' (non-dissemination of published books, dismissals, resignations or last-minute cancellations of exhibitions or theatre performances) brought about through this law.

**Independent freedom of information bodies**: Four independent bodies were established in the period 1981 to 1986 for the defence of freedom of information. In 1987, three were operative. The original four were the

Committee for the Protection of Creative Freedom, the Committee for the Protection of Man and the Environment, the Committee for the Defence of Freedom of Opinion and Expression and the Solidarity Fund. In February 1987 the Solidarity Fund, a group of 225 journalists who, with the aid of writers and academics, work to support colleagues who have been dismissed for criticizing LCY policies, reported that they had suffered from a purge by LCY officials. Several journalists associated with the Fund have been expelled and the Fund's bank account has been frozen as part of the crack-down on its activities.

## Current detainees

Included among those writers, journalists and media workers against whom action has been taken during the course of 1987 or who are still in prison: Rrahim Sadiku, journalist, sentenced December 1983 to ten years' imprisonment and a further five-year ban on practising his profession, reduced by two years in 1985; Vjenceslav Cizek, poet, sentenced August 1978 to fifteen years' imprisonment, later reduced to thirteen years; Adem Demaci, writer, sentenced February 1976 to fifteen years' imprisonment; Alija Ali Izetbegovic, writer, sentenced August 1983 to fourteen years' imprisonment, reduced on appeal to nine years.

# COUNTRY REPORTS—MIDDLE EAST AND NORTH AFRICA

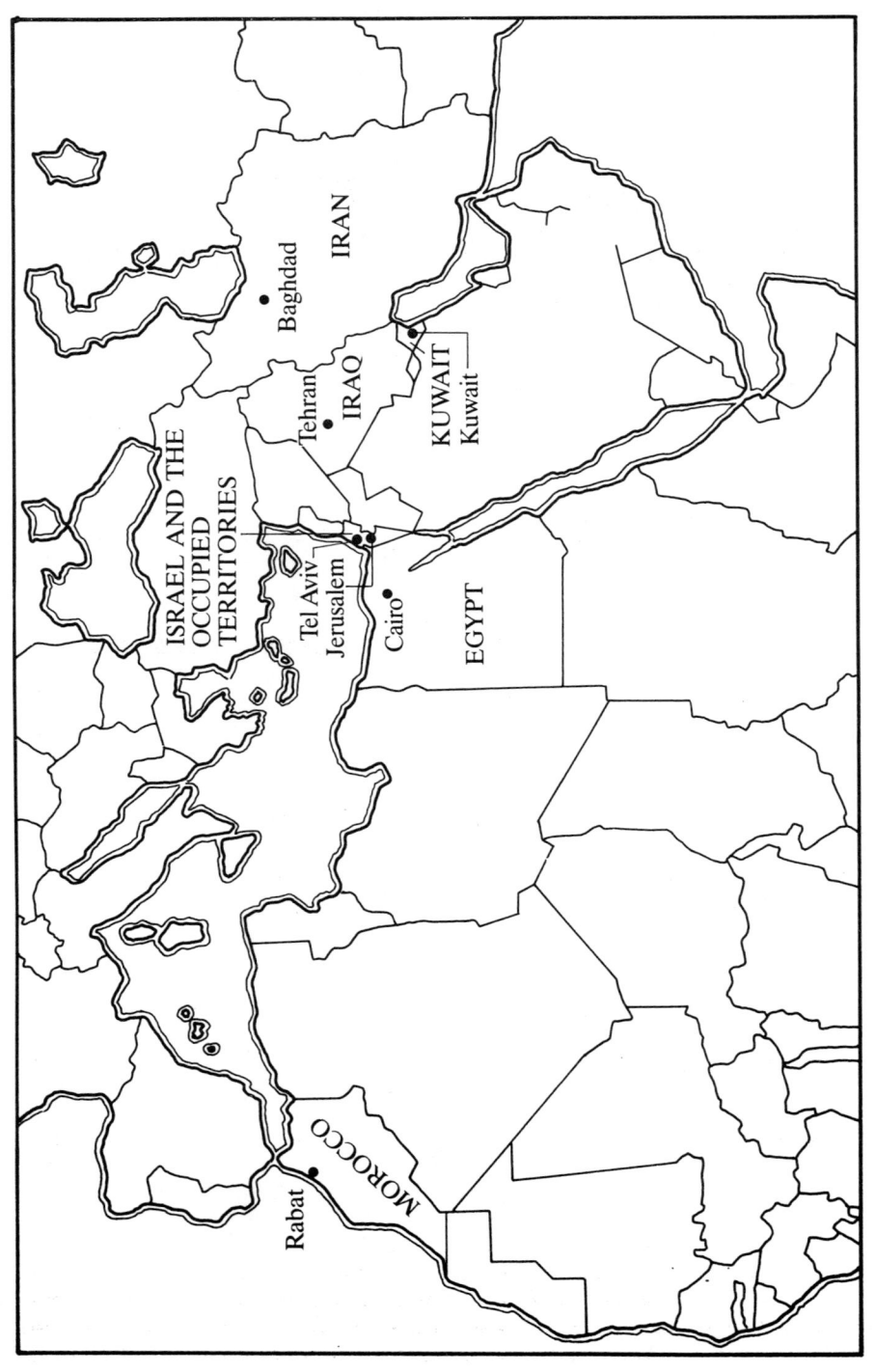

# EGYPT

On Oct. 5, 1987, Hosni Mubarak was elected to a second six-year term as President in a single-candidate referendum. He had been nominated earlier in the year by the People's Assembly, in which the ruling National Democratic Party (NDP) holds a commanding majority.

Egypt's Constitution states that 'Freedom of opinion is guaranteed... within the limits of the law. Self-criticism and constructive criticism is the guarantee for the safety of the national structure' (Art. 47). Article 48 declares that 'censorship of newspapers is forbidden'. A variety of laws and measures, however, restrict these freedoms. The state of emergency permits extensive restrictions on freedom of the press and other forms of communication.

|  |  | Year |
|---|---:|---|
| Population | 48,000,000 | 1985 |
| GNP ($ per capita) | 1,220 | 1984 |
| Illiteracy % | 61.8 | 1976 |
| Daily newspapers | 9 | 1979 |
| Non Daily newspapers | 25 | 1982 |
| Periodicals | 204 | 1982 |
| Films produced | 52 | 1983 |
| Radio stations | 2 | est |
| Radio receivers | 12,000,000 | 1985 |
| TV stations | 3 | est |
| TV sets | 3,860,000 | 1985 |

Press Agencies:
Middle East News Agency

Covenant on Civil &
Political Rights _____ 1982

All periodicals must be licensed, and licences are issued only to organizations or parties, not individuals. Applicants must prove considerable financial assets in order to qualify. A constitutional amendment approved by referendum in May 1980 established a Supreme Press Council to safeguard press freedom, check government censorship and protect the rights of journalists.

Under the 1980 Press Law which followed the 1979 'Law of Shame', it is an offence to challenge the truth of divine teachings, to advocate opposition to or hatred of state institutions, or to publish abroad false or misleading news or information which could damage the interests of Egypt.

## The Media

**State of emergency:** President Mubarak has maintained the state of emergency that has been in effect since the assassination of President Sadat in 1981. His extensive emergency powers include the censorship of letters, publications, printed materials and drawings, together with all forms of expression, information and advertising before publication, as well as their confiscation or banning, and the closure of printing facilities. Mass meetings, rallies and demonstrations are tightly restricted by authorities, and there have been many arrests for 'sectarian sedition' or the spreading of 'tendentious rumours'.

Mubarak's use of emergency laws against the press has been limited and selective. In June 1987 Mohammed Moro, an Islamic writer who is the editorial secretary of *al-Mokhtar al Islami* magazine and correspondent for the London-based *al-Alam* magazine, was detained without charge. To date no reasons for the arrest have been given. Journalists from *al-Wafd*, the organ of the opposition New *Wafd* Party, have also suffered harassment including arrest and detention. In October 1987 copies of the opposition weekly *al-Ahali* were seized by the authorities. There had been no previous closures or confiscations of newspapers, although in 1984 an attempt was made to seize an issue of *al-Wafd*, a move that Egypt's judiciary quickly overturned. Distributors of Islamic fundamentalist leaflets have occasionally been arrested, as on Aug. 31, 1986. Ten alleged communist propagandists were arrested in April 1987.

**Magazines and periodicals:** In early 1987, the law was invoked to shut down a flourishing cottage industry of unlicensed bulletins and journals. There had been a marked increase in the number of publications from every political tendency or affiliation as well as cultural, labour, religious and women's publications. The authorities decided that too great a freedom had been allowed. All printing shops were ordered to print only periodicals that possessed licences.

**Newspapers:** The government's main method of press control remains its power to appoint editors-in-chief at the three main Cairo dailies, *al-Ahram, al-Akhbar,* and *al-Gomhouriya,* and at several other important publications. There are no signs that this system is about to change. No censors are needed at these publications, because the editors-in-chief are granted complete authority and they are chosen on the basis of their loyalty to the NDP. They can be relied upon to know precisely the boundaries between criticism that is deemed constructive and that which is unwelcome. Writers who cross that line simply do not get published, although they continue to draw salaries, since by law they cannot be dismissed.

The increasingly powerful and popular Islamic movement has forced a greater degree of freedom for opposition political parties and their newspapers. As of 1987, there were five legal opposition parties, each with its own newspaper. Although not legal, the Moslem Brotherhood and the Nasserites had their own publications. Competition from these has led to greater openness in the government-controlled press.

While Egypt's problems and official policies are discussed a little more openly than before, the overall tone remains that of a 'mobilizational press', urging readers to support the government in the tasks that lie ahead. If there is an unwelcome development, a clash between fundamentalist students and police in Upper Egypt for example, the pro-government press will minimize the event and adhere closely to the version of the Interior Ministry. Egyptians who want a fuller account must sift through the various foreign Arabic language radio broadcasts and the opposition newspapers.

EGYPT

Coverage of the Amnesty International report on human rights abuses around the world, released in late September 1987, showed the contradictions of the Egyptian press. The opposition weekly *al-Wafd* described Amnesty's account of torture in Egyptian prisons. On the same day, the government-controlled daily *al-Ahram* ran a three-inch story on the Amnesty report saying that Syria, Iran and Libya were among the worst violators.

State television and radio are still highly controlled. During the 1987 parliamentary election campaigns, opposition party leaders were allowed only forty minutes each to present their platforms, while the NDP was given saturation coverage.

**Books and periodicals:** The Ministry of Information has broad powers to censor imported material for political, sexual and religious content. Although Egypt is a permissive country with regard to imported publications, the Ministry readily acknowledges that it will censor an article for saying certain things that the domestic opposition press can publish with impunity. For example, an issue of the Athens-based *Middle East Times* was kept out of the country in August 1987 because it was suggested that some Egyptians favoured Iran in its war with Iraq, a view that is sometimes expressed in the opposition press but is anathema to the government.

**Film and theatre:** At the Ministry of Culture, sex, politics and religion are the targets for the censors, who must approve every film or play and be present during production to monitor their content. Completed films are screened by a three-person panel. Appeals against censorship are heard by a twelve-member board under the Ministry of Culture. Political criticism will not pass if it is too pointed.

Stage actors who depart from the approved script are technically in violation of the law, although one of Cairo's longest-running plays, 'On the Sidewalk', is an improvised work full of barbs directed at Egyptian officials past and present.

Authorities read works as they come off the press or arrive at customs, and occasionally ban them. Although few books are banned for their politics, works that treat sex or religion in a bold fashion are often sent to the Grand Sheikh of Al Azhar, the foremost government-recognized religious authority, for an opinion. As a result, novelists and others censor themselves to ensure that their works will reach the bookshops.

**Foreign journalists:** Visas are easily obtained, and no foreign correspondent has been expelled since the Sadat period. Dispatches and footage are transmitted without interference.

Local authorities, however, have sometimes hindered reporters, both Egyptian and foreign. In several incidents over the last two years, reporters who were conducting street interviews or who were present at demonstrations or scenes of unrest have been detained briefly. These occurrences cannot be taken to represent any official policy, but the government has not gone out of its way to urge local authorities to permit accredited journalists to go about their news-gathering without interference.

# IRAN

In January 1984 Iraj Jannatie-Ataie, a prominent playwright who fled Iran, spoke of those writers still 'writing for the oppressed' in Iran: 'the horrible and indiscriminate language of censorship has turned the language of our literature into a symbolic language. A writer is forced to write in such a way that some of his or her message will escape the censor and reach his or her readers.' Immediately after the 1979 revolution, he said, newspaper circulation and print-runs of books increased massively: writing was 'taken out of its intellectual zones and was now closer to the masses than ever before'.

The revolutionary euphoria was, however, short-lived. There was

| | | Year |
|---|---|---|
| Population | 48,000,000 | 1986 |
| GNP ($ per capita) | 2,060 | 1976 |
| Illiteracy % | 38.0 | 1986 |

| | | |
|---|---|---|
| Daily newspapers | 5 | 1984 |
| Non Daily newspapers } Periodicals | 43 | est |
| Published books | 2,349 | 1984 |
| Radio stations | 53 | est |
| Radio receivers | 10,000,000 | 1985 |
| TV stations | 30 | est |
| TV sets | 2,100,000 | 1985 |

Press Agencies: Islamic Republic News Agency (IRNA)

Covenant on Civil & Political Rights_____ 1975

little agreement among different political groupings on what sort of political system or society they wanted to replace the Shah. The forces which had been active in toppling the Shah's regime ranged from the religious parties (such as the recently-disbanded Islamic Republican Party, the Islamic People's Republican Party and the *Mujaheddin*), to the secular parties (such as the National Front, the Kurdish Democratic Party, and the National Democratic Front), and left-wing parties (such as the *Fedayeen* and the pro-Moscow *Tudeh* Party).

By mid-1979, it became increasingly clear that the seventy-six year-old Ayatollah Khomeini, who had returned from exile in 1978, had gained majority support from the religious parties and the population. The Ayatollah's vision of the nature of the revolution and the Islamic society he wanted to build was soon to take precedence over all other visions and interpretations. The ultimate approval of his authority was confirmed by the December 1979 Constitution. This provoked violent opposition from secular and left-wing political forces, who saw themselves as having been duped and betrayed by the religious leaders. Opposition was countered by fierce repression. Thus, a new phase of violence ensued before the religious leaders (then represented by the Islamic Republican Party) were able to consolidate their power, and finally enforce new Islamic political institutions and an Islamic Republic.

The Islamic Constitution granted the religious leadership a central role,

251

not only in government, but in all aspects of Iranian life, through the Shia Moslem religious institution of *Faqih* (the rule of theology). Khomeini, having been proclaimed as the *'Imam* of the *Ummat'* (the Leader of the Islamic Community), was also acclaimed as the *Wali Faqih* and was invested with supreme authority.

**Islamic law:** *Shariat* or Islamic law was proclaimed as the primary source of law in the country. Principle 4 of the Constitution, for example, reads: 'All civil, penal, financial, economic, administrative, cultural, military, political and other laws and regulations must be based on Islamic criteria. This principle governs absolutely and universally all the principles of the Constitution, laws and other regulations, and any determination of this matter is entrusted to the religious jurists of the Council of Guardians.'

Thus, under the new Islamic law, all the pre-1979 legislation, secular common law and the Penal Code were *ipso facto* null and void. Iranian Islamic law is also considered to prevail over international law, such as the various UN Human Rights Covenants and Conventions.

## The Media

**Radio and television:** Following the founding of the Islamic Republic a system of control and censorship of the media was imposed in order to prevent 'counter-revolutionary and non-Islamic influences'. The task to 'cleanse' and 'purify' Iran's state-owned radio and television was first entrusted to Sadegh Ghotbzadeh, Ayatollah Khomeini's close aide and 'spiritual son'.

Ghotbzadeh began with the purge of all secular journalists and employees, whom he accused of being former supporters of the Shah or agents of Savak (the Shah's secret police). Many of those dismissed had in fact known imprisonment under the Shah and had taken part in strikes which helped to bring down his regime. (Ghotbzadeh was later executed for treason, having been accused of plotting to overthrow the new government.)

Under Ghotbzadeh's direction, Iranian radio and television went through fundamental changes, and some peculiar transformations in the programmes. Documentary films about the revolution were, for instance, heavily doctored. According to Gholam Hossein Sa'edi, an Iranian playwright who witnessed the early phase of the revolution before he left the country, 'all indications that intellectuals or any members of the university community took part in the revolution simply disappeared'.

As for other programmes on television, Sa'edi wrote: 'radio and television archives were destroyed at the outset, and invaluable material for future historians was lost. The purpose was clearly for the regime to keep people and to erase their past.' After the beginning of the war with Iraq in 1980, news bulletins focused mostly on 'victories' at the front and praise of 'martyrs', some of whom were as young as twelve or thirteen years old. In addition, there have been constant attacks on internal opposition individuals and groups, and foreign enemies such as the 'Great Satan America'.

Friday prayers and sermons were broadcast live, and there was wide coverage of marches and demonstrations in support of the Ayatollah and the Islamic Republic. Radio was referred to as the 'government's minaret'.

Nine years later, according to newly-arrived Iranian exiles, Iran radio and television have not changed much.

**The press:** Early restrictions applied to the press, including the severe press law promulgated in August 1979, led to a number of protests. One of the main national newspapers, *Ayandegan* (*The Future*), published an edition of four blank sheets, which many people bought to show their support. There were also large demonstrations in protest at the lack of free expression, which were attacked by '*hizbollahis*', or partisans of the Party of God. By the end of 1979, there were few independent or opposition newspapers or magazines to speak of.

In 1980, following Ayatollah Khomeini's famous 'break their pens' speech, *hizbollahis* attacked the editorial offices of several newspapers. Journalists were subjected to arrest and harassment, and labelled as agents of communism, imperialism and fascism. The *hizbollahis* also attacked theatres and beat up actors.

Within weeks, according to some estimates, more than a thousand publications throughout the country were banned—a process which continued into 1981—and thousands of journalists and print workers were arrested. Several dozen were later executed or simply disappeared.

Iran's two most important newspaper groups, Kayhan and Ettelat, were taken over by the 'Foundation of the Disinherited' (set up by Khomeini's son-in-law) without compensation. Other pro-government newspapers were soon published. *Jomhoori Islami* (*Islamic Republic*) was published by the Islamic Republican Party and is still considered to be the official organ of the Ayatollah himself. Other dailies and weeklies were published by other religious leaders.

There is, however, an underground press, its publications sold under the counter as smuggled goods. Some (mostly those from Kurdistan) are locally produced, but most are smuggled in from abroad. Those caught printing or distributing them usually pay a heavy price, such as arrest and sometimes execution.

**Exile publications:** The Iranian diaspora today is estimated at two million people, spread over Western Europe, North America and some Arab states.

Publishers and editors of exile publications say they run the risk of being assassinated by supporters of the Islamic regime abroad. Hadi Khorsandi, publisher and cartoonist of the very successful satirical magazine *Ashghar Agha*, says he receives frequent death threats from supporters of the Islamic Republic because of his lampoons of Ayatollah Khomeini and other religious leaders. Others have been shot in London and Paris. Orders to execute these journalists or political dissidents are reported to have come from Tehran and are alleged to be co-ordinated by the various diplomatic or trade missions abroad.

**Foreign press:** A small number of foreign publications are allowed but they have to be approved by the authorities. Few foreign correspondents, mostly from news agencies, are allowed in Tehran, but face expulsion if they file stories which displease the authorities. *Reuters* correspondent Trevor Wood was expelled in 1985, his successor Hugh Pope in 1986, and *AFP* correspondent Jacques Charmelot in 1986. Like his colleagues from *Reuters*, Charmelot was accused of 'spying'. Roger Cooper, a British businessman and freelance journalist, was arrested on espionage charges in December 1985 and remained in custody in January, 1988. Occasionally, the government will allow in foreign television crews from abroad or correspondents based in the Middle East, but for some specific public relations or propaganda purposes, such as the occasions when chemical weapons used by the Iraqis at the front were displayed. Those specially-invited journalists can also run the risk of being arrested if they venture beyond the limits within which they are supposed to operate. Gerald Sieb, the Cairo-based Middle East correspondent of the *Wall Street Journal*, who was allowed into the country with a number of foreign correspondents in February 1986, was arrested and imprisoned having been accused of 'spying for Israel'. He was later expelled after strong protests from his newspaper and other journalistic organizations.

## Cultural expression

In 1979, the Ministry of Arts and Culture was replaced by the Ministry of Islamic Guidance, whose main task was to supervise and control every aspect of Iranian cultural, artistic, literary, intellectual and scientific life.

The 'Islamic Cultural Revolution' was officially proclaimed in the spring of 1980 after Ayatollah Khomeini's New Year speech on March 21, 1980, when he ordered Iranians to forget the pre-Islamic past and modern 'isms', and to return to 'the correct path' of Islamic culture.

This ignored traditional Persian and national culture and civilization which date back some three thousand years, a policy which has been met with strong resistance from those who regard the present-day 'Islamic' culture as essentially that of Gulf State Arabia, the birthplace of the Prophet.

A systematic campaign was launched against Persian classical heritage, such as books, architecture, songs, music, dances, theatre and the educational system. '*Shahnameh*' ('Book of Kings'), Iran's national epic and the foundation of Iranian nationalism, was immediately banned. Poems of Hafez and Saadi were 'edited' and 'purified'. Omar Khayyam has been banned because of alleged 'hedonism'. Some historical monuments were destroyed as they were 'relics of the age of idolatry'.

Modern school and university textbooks were also purged and replaced by Islamic texts, including books on science and medicine. University staff were also systematically purged and replaced by 'Islamic scholars'.

Some three hundred Iranian writers, poets, playwrights and translators are known to have left the country. Those who have stayed on are mostly in hiding, and little is known about them. By January 1983, the Iranian

Writers' Association in exile, based in Paris, had documented the death of thirty-nine of its members. Some were executed after summary trials, others without trials. Saeed Soltanpour, a renowned poet and theatre director, was arrested on his wedding day in 1980, and shot shortly afterwards. Soraya Momtaze, a twenty-three year-old poet, was executed after having been found guilty of 'advocating sexual freedom'.

**The Bahais:** Tha Bahais are considered to be heretics, and as such *maddur ad-damm,* or 'those whose blood must be shed', instead of being considered members of a different faith. Before 1979, there were an estimated 300,000 Bahais in Iran, but since the revolution, and especially since the faith was banned in 1983, many thousands have fled the country. Those who remain live in constant fear of being discovered. Some three hundred Bahais are reported to have been executed because of their religion. In addition, they were accused of being 'agents of Israel', because the Bahai's holy place is in Jerusalem. The small Jewish community has also suffered, its parliamentary representative being arrested in 1987.

The number of people who have been executed in Iran since 1979 is reported to be over 10,000. but some put the figure much higher. According to Amnesty International's latest report on Iran, political detainees continue to be tortured in prisons and detention centres throughout the country. Political trials are summary, with no rights of defence. Floggings and other physical punishments continue to be normal practice. Iran ratified the International Human Rights Covenants under the Shah's government; the Islamic government has never renounced these international human rights instruments.

255

# IRAQ

After a military coup in Iraq in 1963, all political groups and parties were banned along with their press organs, except for the *Ba'th* Party. A state press was established, with a variety of publications which adhered to strictly prescribed policy positions. In the 1970s, a few publications linked to the Kurdish and Communist Parties, who were then participating in the National Front, were permitted, subject to severe restrictions. In 1978 however, following a crackdown by the *Ba'th* Party, these political parties were supressed, and the staff of their news organs dismissed and replaced. Soon afterwards, the papers were taken over by the military and then closed.

| | | Year |
|---|---|---|
| Population | 14,000,000 | 1982 |
| GNP ($ per capita) | 3,020 | 1980 |
| Daily newspapers | 6 | est |
| Non Daily newspapers | 7 | est |
| Periodicals | 22 | est |
| Films produced | 82 | 1983 |
| Radio stations | 4 | est |
| Radio receivers | 2,200,000 | 1985 |
| TV stations | 5 | est |
| TV sets | 600,000 | 1985 |

Press Agencies:
    Iraqi News Agency (INA)

Covenant on Civil &
    Political Rights _____ 1971

In its Eighth Regional Conference in 1974, the *Ba'th* Party reviewed its programme for the media. A report noted that the party sought to supervise the principal organs of information and use all means to accelerate their transformation in terms of ideas, personnel and technology in order to make information accord with the aims of the party'. The report stated that this objective had not yet been reached because 'most organs of information and culture lack competent and revolutionary executives... many reactionary elements lurk in these organs and are unconcerned about the tasks called for by the party ...'.

The *Ba'th* Party removed all non-Ba'thist personnel from key culture and information posts and set up a new policy which culminated in the Ministry of Culture and Information Act of 1981. The Ministry under this Act, according to the official translation, 'shall patronize culture and arts in all their fields of activities, shall develop them in accordance with the principles of the *Ba'th* Party and the aims of the revolution... In the field of media and information, the Ministry shall propagate and deepen the ideology, principles, and stands of the *Ba'th* party'. This Act also gives the Ministry 'the mission to supervise all media functions and activities and to exercise cultural supervision over all public and private libraries, and to inspect and license the recording on tapes and discs of all music and vocal production used for commercial purposes'.

Article 26 of the Provisional Constitution of 1968 guarantees 'freedom of opinion, publication, meeting and demonstration, and of forming political parties, unions and societies'. However, the Constitution requires that these freedoms be exercised 'in accordance with the aims of the Constitution and within the limits of law'. The state is required 'to provide the means for practising those freedoms which accord with the nationalist and progressive line of the Revolution'.

**Censorship of the laws:** Iraqi law itself may be subject to censorship. Certain laws and decrees are given restricted circulation only and others remain unpublished. According to Law No. 78 (1977), 'the President of the Republic may decide on the publication of laws, resolutions, texts of treaties, agreements, instructions in special numbers of *al-Waqai al-Iraqiya* (the Official Gazette) if the supreme interests of the State require so... the President of the Republic may decide on the non-publication of laws, resolutions and regulations which concern the security of the state or which have nothing of public interest in their provisions'.

## The Media

**The press:** Information is tightly controlled. Nothing appears in the print or broadcast media that is in any way critical of prevailing policy or the leadership. Although there are at least three dailies published, *al-Jumhuriya, Baghdad Observer* and *al-Thawra,* the news content is the same in each because it is taken directly from the state news agency (INA). The authorities view the press, first and foremost, as a means of controlling public opinion. The media are required to promote whatever the regime wants promoted. As an Iraqi writer notes, 'it is pointless to talk about censorship of the press, because the press was created by the state. Nothing that offends the system will appear, so censorship is unnecessary. What is found in the papers was put there by the Ministry of Information'. The entire press is dedicated to extolling President Saddam Hussein (his picture routinely appears on the centre of page one). Beyond that, it is dedicated to uncritical coverage of the war with Iran.

There is nothing in the Iraqi Constitution which specifically affirms the freedom of the press. However, the officially-sponsored Union of Journalists does support, according to its statute, 'the struggle for the freedom of the press and the rights of journalists', including protection of journalists in fulfilling professional duties. One of the Union's aims is 'to resist the fabrication of news [and] misleading [coverage] of events and to support the right of people to be informed'. These objectives cannot be said to have been implemented. The school of journalism is open only to members of the *Ba'th* youth organization.

**The Press Code:** The 1968 Press Code lists a wide range of forbidden subjects that the censor shall not allow to be published. These include: any criticism of the President, of members of the Revolutionary Command Council (RCC, the inner cabinet) or of those who act on their behalf; defamation or criticism of the state and its apparatus, or news which may cause the devaluation of the national currency or government bonds or discredits their value in Iraq and abroad. Other subjects requiring the approval of the censorship officer prior to publication include: any words or statement attributed to the President or members of the RCC; discussions or decisions of the Council of Ministers or other officials; agreements and treaties concluded by the government of Iraq; criminal investigations, or decisions concerning price fixing, importation, custom tariffs or currency exchange.

**Insulting the authorities:** Under the Penal Code severe penalties are imposed on free expression, journalism and publication. It provides for life imprisonment, confiscation of property or the death penalty for insulting the President of the Republic or those who are acting on his behalf, the RCC, the *Ba'th* Party, the National Assembly or the government. This decree has been implemented many times. The most recent punishments occurred on May 28, 1987, when four Iraqis were executed in Baghdad's Abu Ghraib prison for insulting the authorities.

**Foreign correspondents:** From 1970 until 1981, no foreign publications were permitted in the country. In 1984, all foreign publications were banned except those produced abroad that are actually financed by Iraq. News about Iraq has to be circulated clandestinely within the country, although it is an offence to be found with banned publications. News agencies working there are careful not to offend through their coverage of events. The *BBC* was banned in Iraq for a while because it ran a human rights story using information from the US Embassy.

The chief means of controlling foreign correspondents is through the issue of visas. Many news organs no longer even attempt to send journalists to Iraq to report, since they feel their coverage will be compromised. Journalists are escorted from one government official to another. Telephones and telex lines are tapped. Correspondents are not able to use the telex personally, and can only communicate with their home offices through an operator. There are heavy restrictions on the use of communications equipment. For example, a licence is needed for typewriters and photocopiers, and licences are rarely given. When foreign journalists (and diplomats) enter the country, the model number of their typewriters is written in their passports. They must have the typewriter with them on leaving the country. The same rules apply to recording equipment and short-wave radios.

Reports by foreign news organizations are seen as a threat to the information system the regime has erected. Local journalists working with foreign news agencies must exercise extreme caution. One *Reuters* correspondent was held for several months by Iraqi intelligence because one of the articles he filed was somehow confused with an Iranian report filed in Bahrain.

**Radio and television:** In 1983 there were an estimated 2,000,000 radios and 535,000 televisions. The Ministry of Culture and Information controls the stations through the State Organization for Broadcasting and Television.

**The Arab press abroad:** The Iraqi government owns and heavily subsidizes a range of magazines and newspapers published in London, Paris and Cyprus. These publications are produced both for the Arab community abroad, and for circulation in the Arab countries to promote the government's views throughout the region as a whole.

**Film:** A Department of Home Information at the Ministry of Culture and Information includes an Information and Media Censorship Branch whose function is to control everything which is produced in the country or which comes from abroad.

Censorship of films is undertaken by a Committee composed of representatives of the Ministries of Culture and Information, Defence and the Interior. The decisions of the Committee clearly implement the ideological and political objectives of the *Ba'th* Party. The display and sale of imported slides, microfilm records, recording tape, screenplays, cinema films of all kinds, commercial and private videotapes are prohibited, 'if they propagate atheism or affect public order and internal security, have anti-masses objectives, interests and aspirations or are of low intellectual and artistic standards and not dealing with useful subjects' (Law No. 64 of 1973 on Censorship of Classified Material and Cinema).

Independent Iraqi film-makers need a licence from the Ministry of Culture and Information, and in order to ensure that their work is not banned, they produce films which avoid depicting the present situation in the country.

Many film-makers unwilling to film in line with the *Ba'th* Party's aims have been dismissed, transferred to other posts unrelated to their qualifications, or simply forced to retire.

## Freedom of expression

The State has undertaken a complete reorganization of the intellectual and cultural life of the country. Artists must belong to the state-controlled Artists' Union and their work is dictated by the Committee of the Union. No non-Union artist has the right to work. The rules of the Union provide that its activities have to conform to *Ba'th* Party principles.

In 1980, the State dissolved all cultural and literary federations and societies and replaced them with a 'General Federation of the Literate and Writers'. It has been reported that many former members of dissolved organizations have been forced to join the Federation and those who have refused to work under the supervision of the Federation have been persecuted, jailed or assassinated. A decree made on Oct. 5, 1987, requires that artists who opt for retirement rather than work under the direction of the state must pay back all state money spent on their education unless they have worked for at least fifteen years. On Dec. 5, 1986, the Lebanese newspaper *As-Safir* published a petition signed by well-known Arab intellectuals announcing that 'more than 500 creative writers and thinkers have been subjected to questioning and torture in order to extort expressions of support or to oblige them to modify their opinions, 400 others were condemned to exile'.

**Political parties:** Opposition political organizations are banned by law and their members harassed, arrested, jailed or simply executed. Among the many banned movements are the Iraqi Communist Party, the *Dawa* Party (The Call), the Democratic Party of Kurdistan (DPK), and the Patriotic Union of Kurdistan.

The death penalty may be imposed under Article 200 of the Penal Code on members of the *Ba'th* Party who deliberately conceal current or previous political affiliation or who join or persuade another member to join another party. Retired members of the military, police or intelligence services who have had links with any other party since 1968 may also be punished under the Article. Those found in possession of any published political material critical of the *Ba'th* Party may be sentenced to up seven years' imprisonment.

# ISRAEL AND THE OCCUPIED TERRITORIES

Israel has no written Constitution and its laws do not provide any formal guarantee of freedom of expression. Although the country's courts have repeatedly emphasized the importance of such a right they have upheld censorship affecting, to highly differing degrees, the Hebrew and Arab media. Although the Hebrew press enjoys a fair degree of freedom of expression, the Palestinian Arab papers within the country's 1948 borders are more restricted, while those published in East Jerusalem with their readership in the Occupied Territories suffer from censorship that is both harsh and erratic.

Censorship within Israel and in East Jerusalem, annexed after the occupation of the West Bank in June 1967, is based on the 1945 British Mandatory Emergency Regulations. The military censor or the District Commissioner, now the Interior minister, have as a result of these regulations draconian powers of censorship over the press. Article 87(i) of these regulations enables the censor to 'prohibit generally or specially the publishing of matter ... prejudicial to the defence of Palestine or to the public safety or to public order'. Newspapers and publications require a permit from the District Commissioner who, according to Article 94(ii), 'in his discretion and without assigning any reason therefore, may grant or refuse any such permit... and may at any time suspend or revoke any such permit'. Article 97(i) of the regulations further empowers the censor to require editors and publishers to submit to him material intended for publication. According to Article 110(i), 'any printing press or other instrument or apparatus used for the printing of any unlawful publication... may be seized by any police officer', and the censor may prohibit its operation for any length of time.

| | | Year |
|---|---|---|
| Population | 4,000,000 | 1985 |
| GNP ($ per capita) | 5,100 | 1984 |
| Daily newspapers | 21 | 1985 |
| Non Daily newspapers | 149 | est |
| Periodicals | 890 | 1985 |
| Published books | 1,892 | 1982 |
| Radio stations | 5 | est |
| Radio receivers | 3,000,000 | 1983 |
| TV stations | 1 | est |
| TV sets | 582,000 | 1983 |

Press Agencies:
 Jewish Telegraphic Agency (JTA),
 ITIM (Newsagcy. Ass. Israeli Press)

Covenant on Civil &
 Political Rights _____ NO

## The Media

Israel has seven major Hebrew daily newspapers, four of which— *Ha'aretz, Ma'ariv, Yedioth Aharonoth* and *Hadashot*—are independent. The other three are aligned to various political groups: *Al Hamishmar*

(*Mapam*), *Davar* (*Histadrut*) and *Hatzofeh* (National Religious Party). The English-language *Jerusalem Post* is independent but sympathetic to *Histadrut*. There are a number of Arabic dailies and in addition there are many weekly, bi-weekly and monthly journals.

**The Hebrew press:** Censorship of the Hebrew press is limited to military or security issues and operates through the Editors' Committee. Since 1949, the Committee, which includes senior editors of the daily press and officials of the *Israel Broadcasting Authority* (*IBA*), has accepted the obligation to refrain from printing information that could be harmful to national security. Under this agreement editors voluntarily submit to the censor all news relating to security issues. The legal requirement to submit all other copy is rarely insisted upon. Appeals against the censor's decision, or the censor's complaints on press violations, are heard by a three-member committee consisting of a representative of the Editors' Committee, a representative of the General Staff and an independent chairperson. According to an article in the 'Israel Yearbook on Human Rights 1984', only 180 appeals were brought to the committee between 1949 and 1984, half by the Hebrew press and half by the censor. This figure represents a high degree of understanding between the press and military.

One recent exception to the censor's general leniency towards the Hebrew press was the case involving *Hadashot*, a daily that does not belong to the Editors' Commitee. In April 1984, following the hijacking of a bus, two Palestinian prisoners were killed. The Minister of Defence subsequently notified newspaper editors that a commission of inquiry had been appointed to investigate the deaths and asked them not to publish any information concerning the commission. The following day, April 27, *Hadashot* published an article entitled 'Kidnapped Bus Issue—Inquiry Appointed to Investigate Killing of Terrorists'. Using powers granted under Article 100(i) of the Emergency Regulations, the censor ordered the paper to be closed for four days. *Hadashot* took the case to the High Court, arguing that publishing an article on the formation of a commission of inquiry did not threaten any of the three conditions mentioned in the regulations—security of the state, public safety or public order. They asked the court to uphold the principles of freedom of publication and the right of the public to information. The court, however, supported the closure order, ruling that the censor had acted properly and that *Hadashot* had violated the censor's order not to publish.

**The Alternative Information Centre:** The Jerusalem-based *Alternative Information Centre* (*AIC*) which aims to 'cover events which do not receive the attention they deserve' was closed down in February 1987 for six months by an order issued under the Prevention of Terrorism Act. The authorities claimed that the *AIC* was linked to the Popular Front for the Liberation of Palestine (PFLP). The centre's equipment was seized and the director, Michael Warschawsky, was detained for two weeks and subsequently released on bail of US$50,000. He was charged under Article

85(i) of the Regulations with providing typing services to a prohibited organization. He has not, however, been charged with rendering services to the PFLP but to student, women's and trade union organizations, which Israel's security services claim are a front for the PFLP. Although the centre was allowed to re-open in August 1987, its equipment had been confiscated, and the director was prohibited from working within the centre or from taking on any work—paid or unpaid—which involved typesetting, printing, copying or editing.

**The Arab press:** Censorship of the Arab press within Israel is alleged to go beyond military security objectives and to be overtly political. News concerning *Shin Bet* (Israel's internal security service) is controlled, with the Arab press prohibited from publishing anything that deviates from what appears in the Hebrew press. Apart from military matters, articles describing conditions for Palestinian prisoners are also considered sensitive and are censored. On Nov. 5, 1987, for example, an article in the Communist Party daily, *Al-Ittihad,* based in Haifa, describing conditions in al-Fara' prison, was partially censored. Sections of material dealing with torture allegations have been deleted from the Nazareth-based weekly, *as-Sinara.* This weekly was also prevented from publishing an interview with Faisal Husseini, director of the Arab Studies Society in Jerusalem, who was himself put under administrative detention for three months. An interview with him was published in the *Jerusalem Post.* Articles interpreted as inciting Palestinians—such as encouraging Palestinian prisoners to go on hunger strike—are censored. Accounts of demonstrations or the aggressive behaviour of soldiers or police are often deleted. When an Israeli Navy patrol shot at a boat, drowning a number of Palestinians, reports carried by the Arab press were deleted.

On July 12, 1987 a co-operative set up by the Printers' Co-operative Association and the Jerusalem Printers' Union in November 1985, and based in the Shu'fat refugee camp, was closed down by the authorities for a six-month period. No warnings had been received from the authorities that any of its publications (mainly for area unions) were illegal.

**Nuclear secrecy:** Mordechai Vanunu was put on trial in the summer of 1987 following his revelations to the London paper *The Sunday Times,* concerning Israel's nuclear weapons potential. It was alleged that Vanunu was abducted abroad by Israeli agents and brought to Israel to stand trial. These allegations were banned from publication by the military censor. The trial, which is continuing, is being held entirely in camera.

**Foreign press:** Prior censorship of copy with security implications is required of foreign correspondents, but they do not always comply. Once censorable material is published abroad, however, it can be published in Israel. Information is thus often leaked by Israeli journalists to their foreign colleagues, published abroad and then reprinted in the country. West Bank journalists use the same tactic by having items first published in the Israeli press (see below). Foreign journalists can also be subject to other more subtle kinds of censorship. In July 1987, after the American

TV network *NBC* broadcast a film on Israel's twenty years of occupation which displeased the authorities, the bureau chief was told that *NBC* would be boycotted by the Prime Minister, the Foreign Minister and Defence Minister until the situation was 'rectified'. The move was described by *NBC* president Lawrence Grossman as 'an attempt to extend Israeli censorship to the US'.

**Radio and television:** Israel has, at present, one television channel broadcasting in Hebrew and Arabic, with a second undergoing trials. Its four civilian radio stations are controlled by the *Israel Broadcasting Authority (IBA)*, while the army radio station, *Galei Zahal*, is controlled by the Ministry of Defence. Television and radio in Israel enjoy considerable independence, although subject to government censorship under the Emergency Regulations. Israeli television carried graphic coverage of the December 1987 disturbances in Gaza. As with the written press, there is a consensual censorship on military and security matters.

In one case, a ban by the *IBA* Board of Directors on an interview with persons identified with the PLO was overturned by the Supreme Court, which argued that the ban was illegal as it deprived the population of the right to know. The court would not have allowed speech calling for the destruction of the state of Israel, but did not approve of a blanket ban. The court used a similar argument to allow coverage of Rabbi Meir Kahane. The *IBA* said that although it would cover events of journalistic importance involving Kahane, such as the frequent and provocative anti-Arab demonstrations he and his supporters hold, it would not broadcast interviews with the man himself. The Supreme Court again overturned the ban, arguing it interfered with Kahane's freedom of speech and the people's right to information, although statements which were clearly incitements to racial hatred would not be allowed.

There is also a marked difference in content between Israel's Hebrew and Arabic radio and television broadcasts. While the former enjoys liberties similar to that of the Hebrew-language press, the latter is more strictly controlled and its aim is more clearly propagandist in nature. The Arab population within Israel's 1948 borders is, in general, shown to be content with its lot, enjoying supposed improvements in its standard of living, and while interviews with Arab members of Zionist political parties are shown, members of Palestinian nationalist movements are more often excluded.

**Film and theatre:** The Board for Film and Theatre Review, generally known as the Censorship Board, supervises films and plays. Although the Israeli government decided in 1972 that the theatre censorship law should be repealed, the decision has not been implemented and theatre remains subject to the Mandatory regulations. Several plays have been subject to censorship: in December 1986, 'The Last Secular Jew' was banned by the Board on the grounds that it was 'liable to stir up hatred against all religious people'. However, after protests, the play was permitted with certain cuts. Another play, about the aggressive behaviour of soldiers on

264

the West Bank, was not allowed to be performed at the Haifa Municipal Theatre. Before the Supreme Court, the Board argued that the play gave a distorted picture of the military government and would incite an Arab audience. The Board also said that in one passage the playwright, Yizhak Laor, compares the Israeli authorities to the Nazis. The court revoked the ban on the grounds of the 'paramount importance of free speech in a democratic society'.

As with the Arabic-language press, Palestinian theatre groups must submit to the censor the text of any play they wish to perform. The Palestinian theatre, *Al Hakawati*, in East Jerusalem, has been closed at least fourteen times since it opened in January 1986 for various periods to prevent the holding of 'illegal meetings'.

In July 1987, a performance of 'Androcles and the Lion' presented in Arabic by secondary students from the Friends' Girls' School in Ramallah, which was to have been staged in Jerusalem, had to be abandoned. A notice in Hebrew on the theatre door said the theatre was closed because 'illegal meetings' were prohibited. No other explanation was given. Although under Israeli rather than military law, these closures were nevertheless by order of the military.

**Books:** In July 1986, the Israeli authorities raided a Palestinian book exhibition in Galilee, confiscated nearly 1,000 books and arrested three of the organizers. The exhibition was part of a three-day festival commemorating the Palestinian writer, Ghassan Kanafani.

# West Bank and Gaza Strip

A variety of sources of law apply in the West Bank and the Gaza Strip. Occupied by Israel after the 1967 war, the dominant mode of rule in these territories is military, beginning with a June 1967 proclamation which gave military commanders 'any power of government, legislative, appointive or administrative'. Over 1,100 military orders have been issued for the West Bank and over 800 for Gaza. The Israeli authorities claim that there is greater freedom of expression in the territories than under Jordanian rule and that newspapers and other publications are interfered with only for public order and security purposes. The Palestinian view is that control and censorship have wider objectives; the eradication of their culture and their national consciousness.

While the factual details and the justification in each almost daily incident are invariably subject to intense dispute between Palestinians and the Israeli authorities, the pattern seems clear: in the Occupied Territories, it is military policy to maintain as comprehensive a control as possible over the expression of political opinion which is deemed unacceptable, however manifested. This is achieved through censorship, through the banning of organizations, meetings and gatherings, through the closure of universities and theatres or newspapers, and through arrest, detention, prosecution and the deportation of opinion-makers, journalists, writers and others. These practices, which vary in intensity and consistency according to the political environment and the level of violence, have been widely criticized, often within Israel itself.

Newspapers and publications continue to publish and to convey muted Palestinian feelings, though subject to a far-reaching and arbitrary military process of censorship. On April 6, 1987, Saab Erakat, an academic who also writes for *Al Quds,* was convicted of incitement. He was prosecuted essentially on the basis of a single line in an article he wrote in 1986 for the newsletter of Al-Najah University in Nablus. 'Palestinians', he wrote, 'must learn how to endure and reject and resist' all forms of occupation. In a one-day trial, a military judge ruled that the terms 'reject and resist' could be interpreted as incitement to violence, even though the newsletter was written in English and circulated mainly abroad. The words might be translated into Arabic, the judge said, and be circulated in the territories or quoted by a newspaper.

Erakat was convicted under Military Order 101, which provides for prosecution for inciting readers to violate the 'security and public order' of the area. He was fined US$6,000 and given a five-year suspended sentence.

## The Media

**Newspapers:** The daily reality of military rule is demonstrated by the situation of the press. Newspapers servicing the Occupied Territories are published in East Jerusalem, annexed by Israel after the 1967 war. In consequence, they are subject to the full force of censorship regulations of Israeli law, regulations that can be applied to the Hebrew press, but in practice are not. Military authorities in the West Bank and Gaza may independently prohibit the distribution of publications—even those with the required permits to publish and distribute under that law and printing only material approved by the military censor in Jerusalem—may confiscate copies and may punish persons for being in possession of the newspapers. It is prohibited to publish in the West Bank any matter 'with political significance' except after obtaining a licence from a military commander (Military Order 101 (1967) as amended). On the other hand, M.O. 1140 (1985) requires newspapers to print unaltered and without reimbursement all military announcements. These pronouncements, often signed by the administrators of the districts of 'Judea and Samaria'—the biblical names used by Israeli officials for the territories, but offensive to Palestinians—appear frequently in the newspapers. Similar restrictions apply to the importation of other publications such as books, deemed to be a risk to 'public order and security', even if they are permitted in Israel.

All of the major newspapers are based in Jerusalem; the most prominent Arabic publication inside Israel is the Haifa-based daily *Al-Ittihad*, (Unity) the organ of the Israeli Communist Party, which has been refused distribution permits in the Occupied Territories through the invocation of a Jordanian law that prohibits communist publications. In late 1987, a new daily was planned for Gaza, *Al-Hoda* (*The Guidance*). It is to be published by Gaza's former mayor, Rashad Al-Shawa.

As of January 1988, the Palestinian press consisted of four dailies, *Al Quds* (*Jerusalem*), *Al-Fajr* (*The Dawn*), *Al-Sha'ab* (*The People*), and *Al-Nahar* (*The Day*); several major newsweeklies, *Al-Bayadir Al-Siyasi* (*The Political Barn*), *Al-Tali'ah* (*The Vanguard*); and a bi-weekly, *Al-Awdah* (*The Return*). *Al-Mithaq*, another daily, was closed in 1986 by the Israeli authorities, who alleged that it was 'directed and financed' by the Popular Front for the Liberation of Palestine (PFLP).

The *Palestine Press Service* sends news items to foreign news organizations and facilitates coverage of the Occupied Territories, and there are two English-language papers (*Al-Alwdah*, weekly, and *Al-Fajr*, daily). There are also many smaller political publications, including the Hebrew-language weekly, *Ha-Gesher* (*The Bridge*).

A few publications are based in the Occupied Territories, including university newsletters, magazines of professional associations, and various modest general-interest magazines.

The Palestinian newspapers vary in their outlook on Palestinian goals and strategies, but all have consistently opposed Israel's rule over the territories it captured in 1967. All are shaped by the concept of *sumud* (steadfastness) that many Palestinians have adopted in their daily lives in response to occupation.

The frequent temporary closures and ongoing censorship of these newspapers by the Israeli military authorities are formally justified on the grounds that the newspapers overtly or covertly support the PLO and hence are a threat to public order and security. Some of the Palestinian dailies are alleged by the Israeli authorities to receive PLO subsidies, although every editor has denied this.

*Al-Fajr* was closed down for ten days in December 1987 for 'incitement and subversion'; it had reported, as fact rather than conjecture, that an Israeli Army truck which killed four people in Gaza had done so deliberately. The story had not been submitted to the military censor.

All of the dailies run between eight and twelve pages and provide a mix of local and international coverage. Foremost is news of the Occupied Territories (especially the West Bank and Arab Jerusalem), then Palestinian politics outside the territories, followed by news of the Arab world, Israel, and the international scene. The papers all have sections devoted to sports, home life, culture and religion. They run editorials, political cartoons, advertisements and personal announcements.

Approximately 20 per cent is cut: deletions can range from the obvious—a picture or article about the PLO—to the not-so-obvious—a crossword or sports column. Most sales are in the West Bank.

**The functioning of press censorship:** Prior censorship is the most constant point of contact between the Palestinian press and Israeli authorities. The evening before publication, managing editors are required to dispatch messengers carrying galley sheets of the next day's issue to the office of the censor in Beit Agron, the press building in West Jerusalem, and then to await the verdict.

On arrival, the galleys are turned over to the censors on duty, mostly civilian employees of the army, who work under the supervision of career officers. After a brief reading, the censors stamp each article or sheet with one of three stamps: square (approved), triangle (rejected), and round (approved, provided that certain alterations—usually deletions—are made).

Editors said that because of the uncertainty of the process, they must keep 'refrigerators' full of innocuous or approved but unused copy that they can use to plug any gaps they are left with as a result of censorship cuts. Leaving blank spaces in newspapers in order to indicate that censorship has taken place is forbidden under the Emergency Regulations, unless with express permission. The editors are often left with little choice but to translate into Arabic news already published in the Hebrew press.

Appeals against decisions made by the censor's office in Jerusalem can be directed to the country's chief censor in Tel Aviv, currently Brig.-Gen. Yitzhak Sheni. Such appeals are rare. More frequently, editors engage in a more informal appeals process, 'phoning the head of the censor's office in Jerusalem, currently Lt.-Col. Avi Gur-Ari, to contest a decision. In this manner, decisions are sometimes reversed, often in exchange for modifications in a disputed article. The Palestinian press have, however, never received any official statement of censorship policy.

**Journalists:** Officials occasionally shut Palestinians out of press conferences and frequently ignore their 'phone calls and requests for information. Palestinian journalists are often treated differently from Israeli and foreign correspondents. They are more likely to be arrested at demonstrations and scenes of unrest, and are more vulnerable to harassment when their reporting angers military authorities.

Ori Nir, a correspondent with the Israeli daily *Ha'aretz,* described being on the scene of university unrest in Gaza in mid-February, 1987, along with a German television crew and a Palestinian journalist. When soldiers caught up with the journalists, who had defied orders to stay off the campus, the only one arrested was the Palestinian, Baher Ashhab of *Al-Fajr.* Ashhab was held for several hours and charged with incitement for making a 'V'-for-victory sign and encouraging demonstrators to throw stones, accusations that he and Nir say are false. 'It was astonishing to me,' said Nir, 'because there we were, journalists of different nationalities, in the same place, doing the same activities, and immediately the Palestinian is suspected of negative activity.' According to Nir, an officer on the scene had explained that Ashhab's presence as a resident of the Occupied Territories was immediately suspect regardless of his profession.

Apart from arrest and prosecution, journalists are also subject to extra-judicial security measures. By the end of 1987 at least twenty-three Palestinian journalists out of a total press corps of fifty have been deported, detained, or subjected to town arrest or travel restrictions.

Akram Haniyeh, editor of *Al-Shaab* was ordered to be deported on Nov. 3, 1986, on the grounds that he was a senior officer of the PLO. Haniyeh denied the accusation and appealed to the Israel High Court. When the Court ruled that the evidence against him could not be revealed, he withdrew the appeal and after fifty-five days in prison was deported to Zürich.

Hassan Abd Al-Jawad Farrajeh of the *Bethelem News Service* was deported to Jordan on Jan. 31, 1986. It was claimed that he was a leader of the PFLP. He also withdrew an appeal to the Court on the grounds that he would not get a fair hearing. The lack of due process in the deportation procedures has been criticized by human rights groups.

In 1985, after the revival of administrative detention without trial, three Palestinian journalists, Qaddoura Musa, Muhammad Amireh and Kemal Jbail were held for six months. The authorities, while not disclosing reasons, said that none were arrested for their journalist work. A recent example involved Radwan Abu Ayyash, President of the Arab Journalists Association, arrested and detained on Dec. 8, 1987. The day before his arrest, he acted as a guide for a delegation of seven members of parliament visiting refugee camps.

Since 1980, at least fourteen Palestinian journalists have been issued orders confining them to certain towns or restricting their travel. In many cases, this has made it impossible to continue their professional work. In 1984 Amnesty International concluded that the use of town arrest is 'in many cases a punishment for... non-violent political activity'.

No reason is usually given for preventing foreign travel by journalists except that it might endanger state security. A recent case was that of the editor-in-chief of *Al Quds*, Mahmud Abu Zalaf, who was ordered not to leave Israel and the Occupied Territories from July 1987 to June 1988.

**Radio and television:** Radio and television channels are subject to censorship. In terms of content, the propagandist flavour of staple broadcasting has been noted above: pro-Jordanian figures, members of the Israeli-sponsored village leagues, the positive gains of the occupation, etc. are shown, rather than opposition and resistance. Observers have noted that media policy is, however, changing. Arab radio broadcasts are not jammed and so Palestinians are able to listen to a diversity of foreign broadcasts from all over the Middle East.

**Book banning:** Under Military Orders (101 as amended by 718) the military authorities issue lists of titles of books banned in the West Bank. The list published in 1982 contained 1,002 titles and over 600 further books have been banned since that date. A similar though not identical list exists for the Gaza Strip. Booksellers or institutions which wish to import books must submit the requested title. Most titles are approved but according to a 1983 study by the Fund for Free Expression the disapproved titles include works that 'express, instil or foster Palestinian-Arab national feelings and national heritage'.

### Current detainees

Included among those writers, journalists and media workers against whom action has been taken during the course of 1987 or who are still in prison: Sa'eb Erakat, journalist, arrested September 1986, six months' suspended sentence and a fine of 7,000 Israeli shekels, currently appealing; Abdul Sattar Qassem, lecturer and publisher, outcome of charges under Military Order 101 (7) unknown; Salah Zuheikah, journalist, in March 1987 placed under town arrest for 6 months, the order being renewed in September 1987 until March 1988 (with no reasons given by the authorities).

# KUWAIT

Until July 1986, Kuwait prided itself as an oasis of freedom in a region where government control of information was, and remains, virtually absolute. Following independence in 1961 and particularly with the oil boom of the 1970s, Kuwait's press developed a reputation for independence and outspokenness unparalleled in the Gulf, and the country began to inherit some of the mantle of war-torn Lebanon as an Arab media centre. Within fifteen years of the establishment of the first Kuwaiti daily in 1961, seven privately-owned daily newspapers were founded—supported by a modest government subsidy—with a readership and influence far beyond the country's borders.

|  |  | Year |
| --- | --- | --- |
| Population | 2,000,000 | 1985 |
| GNP ($ per capita) | 15,410 | 1984 |
| Illiteracy % | 30.0 | 1985 |
| Daily newspapers | } 81 | est |
| Non Daily newspapers | | |
| Radio stations | 3 | 1987 |
| Radio receivers | 750,000 | 1985 |
| TV stations | 2 | est |
| TV sets | 580,000 | 1985 |

Press Agencies:
Kuwait News Agency (KUNA)

Covenant on Civil &
Political Rights _____ NO

On July 3, 1986, a series of disputes between elected deputies and the government, which was dominated by members of the ruling family, culminated in the Amir dissolving the National Assembly and assuming legislative authority, suspending parts of the 1962 Constitution in the process. The Assembly, which had earlier been suspended in 1976-81, had become more outspoken after the victory of several prominent government critics in the 1985 elections. Simultaneously, the government imposed a regime of prior censorship on all publications and newspapers, some of which had been vocal supporters of the parliamentary opposition.

In theory, the Constitution and laws provide a range of guarantees protecting freedom of information. In practice, the exercise of these rights has depended entirely on the political climate, with the Ministry of Information in ultimate control of all that is published, broadcast or distributed. The Information portfolio is considered one of the key cabinet posts and has been reserved in successive governments for a senior member of the ruling al-Sabah family.

## The Media

Articles 36, 37, 39 and 43 of the Constitution assure freedom of opinion, the press, communication and association, but only within the context of the 'relevant laws'. Until July 3, 1986, this meant above all the Printing and Publishing Law of 1961, which empowers the government to impose

271

fines and prison sentences for prohibited material. This includes material considered an 'incitement to hatred or overthrow of the system of government', reports of secret government agreements or contracts, and news 'designed...to spread disquiet about the economic situation'. The law requires official approval before any periodical can be established, and empowers the authorities to prevent distribution of foreign publications 'to preserve public order or morals'.

With the 1986 clampdown came a series of restrictive amendments decreed by the Amir. The cabinet was empowered to close down any newspaper that 'serves the interests of a foreign state or organization, whose policy conflicts with the national interest, or which receives help, support or benefit in any form and for any reason from any other state or source without permission from the Ministry of Information'. The Ministry's permission was also required before anything, apart from periodicals and commercial publications, could be printed. The Minister could suspend any newspaper for three months 'when necessary'. Prior censorship was imposed on all newspaper articles and prison sentences of up to three years were ordained for anyone defying the censor by publishing 'non-commercial advertisements or statements issued by organizations, groups of people or any foreign state of authority' without prior approval.

At the time of the Assembly's dissolution, the government had been in the process of drafting a new press law which would impose further restrictions, including a ban on anonymous articles or pen-names, and catch-all bans on 'false news' and 'directing blame against government actions'.

**Self-censorship:** Over the years, official tolerance has been conditional on acceptance by the press of strict unwritten rules defining the limits of freedom. A system of self-censorship operated, under which the government allowed the papers a margin of freedom in return for the assurance that sensitive material would be played down or omitted altogether.

This practice had its formal trappings: periodic briefings by top ministers for newspaper editors at which the official line on certain issues would be made clear. But its strength lay in the fact that it was essentially informal, and was understood by every journalist, working on the principle that the further an issue was from home, the more freedom was permitted in discussing it. Accordingly, direct criticism of the Amir, ruling family, or overall state policy was forbidden. Important government decisions would be reported with a minimum of comment, and due deference accorded to ruling circles. Aspects of domestic policy could be criticized within limits, though often only indirectly. Comparable rules applied to regional and international news. Reports reflecting unfavourably on close allies, for example, would be tolerated only if oblique. Further afield more leeway was permitted, and it was indeed in its coverage of wider Middle Eastern issues that the Kuwaiti press excelled.

With 60 to 70 per cent of its population ( and an even higher proportion of its journalists) made up of expatriates, mostly from other Arab countries, the Kuwaiti press began to attract some of the best known writers in the region. This often irritated friendly governments. Over the years, several papers and magazines have been suspended for various periods, but for the most part the system of self-censorship remained intact.

The imposition of prior censorship in 1986 partly reflected a breakdown of this *modus vivendi*. But in some respects it merely constituted a redefinition of what was and what was not acceptable within the well-established system of self-censorship. No closures took place as a result, though Kuwait's most outspoken weekly magazine, the leftist *At-Tali'a* halted regular publication in protest.

**Expulsion of journalists:** In parallel with the formal curbs, the government has in recent years expelled several non-Kuwaiti journalists from the country. In 1985 the Kuwait-based Palestinian political cartoonist Naji al-Ali, one of the Arab world's best known satirists, was ordered to leave, apparently because his drawings had offended several Arab regimes (he was assassinated in London two years later). There followed a wave of expulsions during which the residence permits of some two dozen Arab journalists, including some of the most prominent editors and columnists in the local press, were cancelled. Questioned about the expulsions, Kuwait's Crown Prince and Prime Minister remarked that if resident nationals of other Arab states were so keen on free speech 'let them practise it in their own countries'.

The remark reflects a constant theme of the government's justification for the 1986 clampdown: that the press (and parliament) had been made vehicles of 'alien ideologies'. This argument played on the underlying tension between the privileged native minority and the large expatriate population. The government is clearly determined to limit the already restricted role of expatriates in the press, a move which would have profound consequences. Newspapers have been subjected to stronger pressure than other institutions to increase the proportion of nationals among their employees. The draft press law which the authorities failed to pass through parliament before its suspension included a clause which would make employment of non-Kuwaitis in any editorial capacity conditional on their having been registered for five years with the official journalists' regulatory authority in their own countries (one of the strengths of the Kuwaiti press had been as a forum for Arab writers banned or otherwise frowned upon at home). Other provisions in the draft law stipulate tougher penalties for insults to 'heads of Arab or Islamic states' and an outright ban on anything likely to 'disturb relations with Arab or Islamic states'.

The apparent drive to tame the regional impact of the press is linked by many Kuwaiti intellectuals to the influence of Saudi Arabia, Kuwait's powerful neighbour, renowned for its rigid media control and sensitivity to criticism. Longstanding Saudi irritation at Kuwait's democratic experiment and vociferous press grew more influential in the 1980s as political tension in the Gulf put the region's traditional monarchies on the defensive and pulled both countries closer together under the umbrella of the Gulf Co-operation Council (GCC). Despite pressure, however, Kuwait has not signed the GCC's Security Agreement. The Agreement includes a clause which prevents any member tolerating 'hostile propaganda' against another, while the Council's so-called 'Charter for Honour in Information' effectively commits all six member-states to banning any publication prohibited in any of the others. It remains unclear to what extent Kuwait plans to abide by these measures: strict implementation would severely curtail the range of permitted publications.

**Foreign correspondents:** Control of foreign correspondents in Kuwait has not traditionally involved overt censorship. Instead, the denial of visas or extensions of residence permits in response to 'negative' coverage, has been the main tool employed, particularly since 1984. Kuwait-based correspondents must be licensed by the Ministry of Information and visiting journalists are put through a cumbersome, time-consuming and frequently futile procedure to obtain visas. The Ministry has developed a method of issuing mass invitations, often expenses-paid, to selected foreign media representatives to cover major events, meetings or press conferences. Many foreign journalists, particularly regional specialists, freely admit to 'toning down' their coverage in order to secure continued access to the country. In recent years, subjects such as internal dissent, sectarian tensions connected to the Iraq-Iran war and disputes within the ruling family appear to have aroused the most official sensitivity, in addition to unfavourable reporting of other Gulf regimes.

**Foreign publications:** Coverage of these subjects has in the past often been sufficient cause for the banning or censorship of foreign publications. Distributors of foreign publications must submit copies of each issue to the Ministry of Information. Past experience suggests that if an undesirable article is carried by a normally acceptable publication, the offending page is either removed or blotted out from every copy of the issue concerned before it reaches the news-stands. If material is considered particularly unpalatable, one or more issues of the publication are normally banned. A wide range of foreign newspapers and magazines are banned outright, mostly those whose views or ideology are in direct opposition to government policy. Although official lists are unobtainable, in practice this has been applied mainly to Arabic language political periodicals. Prior to the 1986 clamp-down, many banned periodicals circulated informally, with customs officers often turning a blind eye (with varying proportions of tolerance and mere inefficiency) to anything not considered overtly subversive. Since then, however, a stricter code of practice appears to have been enforced.

**Television and radio:** Broadcasting has always been a government monopoly in Kuwait, with the Ministry of Information directly in control of the two television and three radio channels. Even before the latest press restrictions were introduced, that control was absolute: radio and television news is restricted to the official version and priority of events, and controversial material is kept to a minimum. In a celebrated exception to the rule in 1984, the Ministry felt compelled to permit the screening of an interview with a leading opposition politician after originally banning it. The post-1986 environment has involved still tighter adherence to the official line.

**The Kuwait News Agency:** Similarly, the state-owned *Kuwait News Agency* (KUNA), set up in 1976 as a theoretically independent organization answerable to the Information Ministry, has since 1986 come to function more as an official mouthpiece. Although in contrast to its regional counterparts it had developed a reputation for lively coverage of Arab affairs, it had always been restricted in its reporting of Kuwaiti and Gulf developments. In recent years, the Agency's margin of independence has been steadily eroded by government guidelines.

**Books, films and plays:** The Ministry of Information must approve the publication of all books—an industry of relatively modest size—and a large number of books is banned for political, religious or moral reasons, mainly foreign titles but including a number of political works by Kuwaiti authors. All video tapes brought into the country must be submitted to the Ministry, though in practice this is used mainly to prevent the import of pornography. Similarly, official tolerance of theatre has varied with the political climate: in the 1970s and early '80s, the country's theatre companies produced plays mocking Gulf society and Arab politics, despite prior censorship involving the omission of certain passages. No field of communication is exempt from the tougher line now being followed.

# MOROCCO

The 1972 Moroccan Constitution guarantees to all citizens: 'freedom of opinion, freedom of expression and freedom of association' (Art. 9(2)). However these guarantees are seriously qualified in law and practice. In particular, restrictions on freedom of association have led to the banning and imprisonment of hundreds of critics of the political system.

Three main topics are subject to restriction: the King's person, the monarchy and the Islamic religion. The King's person, according to Article 23 of the Constitution, is 'inviolable and sacred', and as a consequence his actions and words cannot be judged. Article 28 states that 'the content of his messages [to the nation and to parliament] can-

|  |  | Year |
|---|---|---|
| Population | 20,000,000 | est |
| GNP ($ per capita) | 670 | 1984 |
| Illiteracy % | 66.9 | 1985 |
| Daily newspapers | 10 | 1984 |
| Non Daily newspapers ⎫ Periodicals ⎭ | 38 | est |
| Films produced | 12 | 1983 |
| Radio stations | 3 | est |
| Radio receivers | 3,000,000 | 1985 |
| TV sets | 1,099,000 | 1985 |

Press Agencies: Wikalat al-Maghrib al-Arabi (WMA)

Covenant on Civil & Political Rights ———— 1979

not be subject to debate'. Parliamentary immunity can be removed and a member can be detained and put on trial 'when opinions or votes expressed by him whilst exercising his functions, challenge the monarchical system or the Moslem religion or constitute an attack on the respect owed to the King' (Art. 37).

## The Media

**Newspapers:** In January 1987, there were about 178 periodicals of which 101 were Arabic titles, twenty-one are owned by the state and 157 are independent. The Moroccan press is technologically under-developed. Its readership and market are limited compared to other Arab countries such as Egypt and Tunisia. The illiteracy rate is 65 per cent. It is estimated that only one in five of the literate population buy a newspaper. In order to reach new readers, the national press (mainly the press owned by the political parties) is attempting to introduce new production technology. Competition from foreign newspapers and the cost of imported paper have, however, impeded modernization. Four newspapers and magazines have recently been given permission to print in Casablanca; the London-based Arabic newspaper *ash Sharq al-Awsat* (The Middle East) and three French newspapers, *Le Figaro, France-Soir* and *Paris-Turf*.

In 1983 the national dailies ceased publication for one day, as a protest against allegedly unfair competition from *Ash Sharq al-Awsat* which was

276

reported to have reached sales of 10,000 copies a day in Morocco. The *Syndicat de la Presse Nationale* (the National Press Union), which represents the organs of the political parties and trade unions in Morocco, accused the paper of 'dumping' its editions. The cost of each copy (1 dirham) was about the average cost of a national daily, but for the price it offered forty-eight pages of good technical quality and more international news.

A spokesman for the Union said that the strike was necessary to alert the state to the possibility of the national press disappearing. In response to the strike the Prime Minister informed the leaders of the political parties in December 1986 that in 1987 an annual subsidy of 20,000,000 dirhams would be distributed to their newspapers in order to finance modernization.

In November 1987 the Minister of the Interior announced new measures to help resolve the financial crisis of the national press. These included subsidizing 25 per cent of the cost of imported newsprint; reducing the cost of distribution of the newspapers abroad by 70 per cent, and of telephone and telex charges by 50 per cent. Journalists are to have a 50 per cent concessionary fare on foreign travel with Royal Air Maroc; free internal rail travel (provided they hold a press card) and free subscriptions to the service of the national press agency, *Wikalat al-Maghreb al Arabi* (WMA).

According to many observers, the consequence of this decision could be the reduction of opposition criticism due to its financial dependence on the state. There is an additional risk to non-political publications with smaller budgets and no financial support.

**The Press Code:** Under the Press Code of Nov. 15, 1958, the requirement to obtain a licence for the publishing of magazines and newspapers provides the basis for prior restraint of free speech.

While there is no mention of prior censorship in the law on Public Freedoms (1958), it has in the past been used by the state to control and restrict information. Since 1972, the year of the second coup d'état, there has been prior censorship particularly of the independent and the opposition press. Newspapers were sent to the Office of Information, a censorship branch in the Ministry of Information, where they were examined by the Minister's assistants and sometimes by the Minister himself. This practice stopped a few days before the 1976 parliamentary election after demands for its abolition by the political parties.

Prior censorship was re-established by the Ministry of the Interior after the Casablanca riot of June 20, 1981. Newspaper copy had to be forwarded to the local district administrative authorities who in turn sent it to the Secretariat of the Governor of the Prefecture for examination. This restrictive measure cost newspapers time and money and delayed their circulation.

Following the January 1984 riots in Marrakech and towns in the north of the country, prior censorship was extended to cover all Moroccan newspapers and publications, even pro-government papers. Instructions were given by the Interior Minister that every copy of any publication anywhere in the country had to be examined before circulation. While this measure lasted only one week, it succeeded in preventing the press from covering the riots. Limited prior censorship affecting only some opposition newspapers appears still to be in operation.

**Suspension and banning:** The Press Code gives extensive powers to the Interior Minister (Art. 77(i)) to order the 'administrative seizure of any number of newspaper or periodical whose publication is of a nature to disturb public order'. He can also order the suspension for an unlimited period of any publication which 'attacks the political and religious institutional foundations of the Kingdom' (Art. 77(ii)). *Al Bayane*, the organ of the opposition Party of Progress and Socialism, was suspended in 1983, and again from October 1986 to January 1987 following an editorial concerning 'national consensus' in which the newspaper criticized the King's adviser, Ahmed Guedira. On Feb. 18, 1987, the Parisian daily *Le Figaro*, which prints in Casablanca, was stopped from distributing because of a long feature about the Polisario Front. On Aug. 4, 1987 a July issue of the weekly *Al Massar* was seized because of an editorial on the Moroccan-Israeli meeting in Ifrane. On March 28, 1987, 20,000 copies of *Anoual*, the organ of the opposition Organization of Democratic and Popular Action, were seized because of an article about conditions in Moroccan prisons.

The Prime Minister may ban indefinitely any newspaper or other publication which violates Article 77. The organs of the Socialist Union of Popular Forces, *al-Mouharir*, a daily in Arabic, and *Libération*, a French-language weekly, were banned because of the party's alleged provocation of the 1981 Casablanca riots. Two years later the party was allowed to publish one newspaper, *Al-Ittihad al-Ichtiraki* (*The Socialist Union*). After the 1984 riots, five cultural magazines were banned. These magazines were, according to observers, the highest quality local reviews since the magazine *Souffles,* which was closed by the government in 1972.

## Freedom of opinion and expression

The Moroccan Constitution prohibits the 'one party system' and the 1958 Code of Association guarantees freedom to establish associations and parties of a political nature. The same code requires prior declaration and authorization, and bans any political association or party 'established under an illicit cause contrary to law and to accepted standards of behaviour (*bonnes moeurs*), and which constitutes an attack on the territorial integrity or the monarchical form of the state'. No political organization can challenge the government position on the Western Sahara or promote a political system other than the current monarchy, without been banned.

At present five political organizations are banned and their members in hiding, or imprisoned on charges of 'establishing illegal organizations, possessing banned literature, conspiring to overthrow the government and disturbing public order'. Two are Marxist organizations, *Ila al Amam* (Forward) and *23 Mars* (23 March), and the others are Islamic associations: *mojahidine al-Maghrib, Achabibe-al-Islamiyya* (Islamic Youth), and *Jamiyyat ad-Dawa oua Takfir* (Association for Proclaiming and Preaching). In 1984, thirty-one people, most of them students, were accused of being members of *al-Qa'idiyin,* an underground student movement linked to *Ila al Amam.* They were sentenced to prison terms of up to fifteen years on charges which included conspiracy to overthrow the government.

During 1984 and 1985, the Human Rights Association in Morocco monitored the cases of 1,600 people in eighty-four political trials, which resulted in thirteen people being sentenced to death and thirty-seven to life imprisonment. There were twenty-six acquittals and the rest were sentenced to between three and twenty years' imprisonment.

**Prisoners' rights to information:** Political prisoners in Morocco had staged frequent hunger-strikes in protest against, among other things, the denial of their right to receive information. In a letter dated Nov. 12, 1986 to a human rights organization in Europe, Ben Smail Abdellaziz explained the reasons for the hunger-strike he and twenty-five colleagues were staging: 'We have not the right to receive newspapers even of a non-political nature; nor do we have the right to receive radio or television. Books are selected, even if they are educational, which limits our right to education.' The writings of prisoners are sometimes banned. Ali Idriss Kitonni, a poet sentenced in 1982 to fifteen years, has had his collection '*Charara*' ('Spark') denied publication. Abdelkader Chaoui, sentenced in 1974 to twenty years' imprisonment on charges of 'plotting against the internal security of the state', had his recent book about political imprisonment in Morocco banned from circulation. He has been Amnesty International Prisoner of the Month (July 1987) and is an honorary member of the Finnish PEN.

## Current detainees

Included among those writers, journalists and media workers against whom action has been taken during the course of 1987 or who are still in prison: Ali Idrissi Kaitouni, painter and poet, sentenced May 18 1982 to fifteen years' imprisonment; Abraham Serfaty, writer for radical magazine *Souffles*, arrested in 1974 and sentenced to life imprisonment.

# COUNTRY REPORTS—OCEANIA

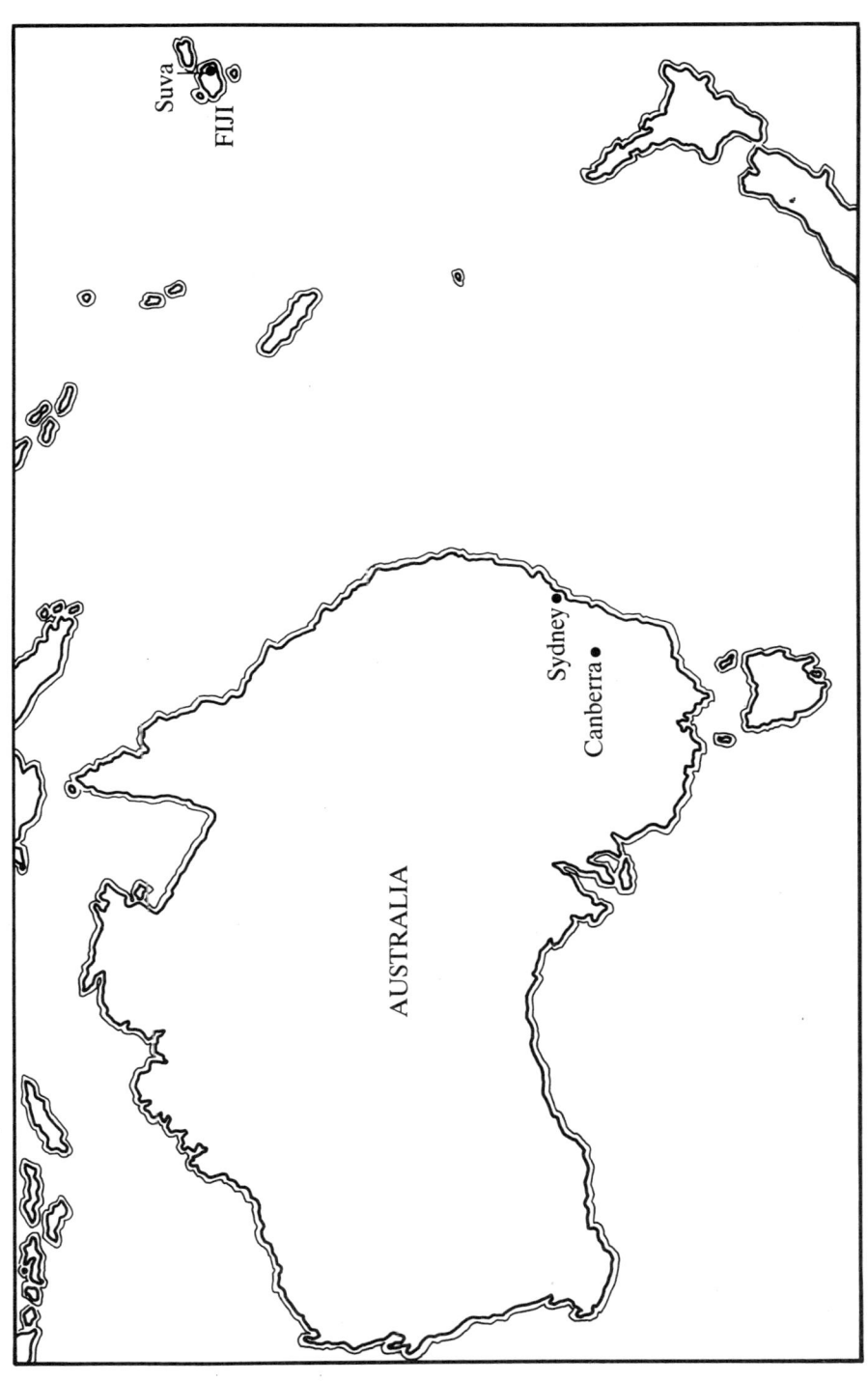

# AUSTRALIA

Australia has been described as a country without a well co-ordinated or ideological approach to anything. While freedom of expression is enjoyed, this freedom does not arise from any formal organized information structure.

One legacy of two hundred years of colonization is that local laws and institutions are a patchwork of items borrowed from a range of northern hemisphere countries, the United Kingdom and the United States in particular.

Law-making and planning are dispersed between the Federal Parliament and the six state parliaments. Most aspects of freedom of expression are governed by the states, which tend to be slow to agree to reform and to be suspicious

|  |  | Year |
|---|---|---|
| Population | 16,000,000 | 1985 |
| GNP ($ per capita) | 11,890 | 1984 |
| Daily newspapers | 56 | 1987 |
| Non Daily newspapers | 470 | 1979 |
| Periodicals | 74 | 1984 |
| Published books | 4,714 | 1987 |
| Films produced | 42 | 1987 |
| Radio stations | 350 | est |
| Radio receivers | 20,000,000 | 1983 |
| TV stations | 154 | est |
| TV sets | 6,500,000 | 1983 |

Press Agencies:
    Australian Associated Press

Covenant on Civil &
    Political Rights _____ 1980

of the Federal Parliament, the only one which has attempted serious reform. In broadcasting, telecommunications and implementation of international obligations, the Federal Parliament is empowered to override the states. Neither the federal Constitution nor any of the state constitutions guarantees freedom of speech or other human rights, although there is a limited federal guarantee of religious freedom. This reflects British influences on the constitutions rather than any positive disregard for human rights.

Australia ratified the International Covenant on Civil and Political Rights in 1980. In 1981, it established the Federal Human Rights Commission, an independent body which reviews legislation, investigates complaints and undertakes research and educational programmes. The commission is a federal body, which leaves many state activities untouched; and it does not have power to vindicate the rights of the citizen. During the 1970s and the 1980s there were several unsuccessful initiatives to enact a federal bill of rights to make the International Covenant directly enforceable.

## Restrictions on freedom of expression

**Defamation:** By far the greatest legal restriction on communication in Australia is private defamation law. Community leaders and others are able to recover many thousands of dollars in damages through cases brought to protect their reputations. In some states it is not a sufficient defence against a defamation action to prove that the material published was true; a publication must also be 'on a matter of public interest' or 'for the public benefit'. There are other defences intended to protect the media when, without any malicious intention, they make a factual mistake or publish a defamatory comment. In one famous case, an architect recovered thousands of dollars in damages from a newspaper which said that he had designed a defective building; several years afterwards millions of dollars had to be spent on repairs.

The procedural complexities and delays of defamation law, and inconsistencies between state and federal jurisdictions, are a threat to anyone seeking to expose corruption or to criticize powerful people. As soon as a controversy breaks in the media, it is normal for one of the personalities involved to commence a defamation action. Among the most frequent plaintiffs are those involved in politics, business, sport and entertainment. The commencement of the action has a chilling effect on further airing of the controversy, even in the frequent case of an action not being pursued after controversy has died down. One effect is to make journalists over-cautious, particularly if they are not employed by one of the major media organizations which has the resources to defend a defamation action that may last for years. The major media can defend a number of cases at one time; but a small publisher can face bankruptcy if one case is lost.

**Contempt of court:** Laws designed to protect trials from prejudicial comment are also a major restriction on free expression, not least because they lack precise definition. In 1986 a newspaper was fined A$200,000 for publishing a statement by Neville Wran, the New South Wales Premier, that Justice Lionel Murphy, a judge facing trial for corruption, was of good character and innocent.

The range of material about pending trials actually restricted by contempt law is narrow. It is mainly material of the kind which would bias the deliberations of a jury in a current trial. A recent report of the Law Reform Commission provides a blueprint for reform at least in matters under federal jurisdiction. It includes a suggested new defence of publication in the 'public interest' and a 'public safety' defence covering warnings of danger, that could override the considerations of preventing prejudicial statements affecting fair trial. The report also proposes a defence of innocent publication; editors would be able to plead that they did not or could not have known that publication would affect a trial.

Prosecutions for contempt by denigrating the courts are rare, although it is dangerous to say that courts have bowed to pressure in reaching their decisions. In 1982, a trade union official was sentenced to three months' jail for making such an allegation.

**Disclosure of sources:** Another form of contempt is refusal to disclose sources of information to a court or commission of inquiry. This particularly affects journalists, whose union code of ethics prevents disclosure of sources ('the newspaper rule'). Some have gone to prison rather than breach the code. An important test case in this area concerned an article which appeared in *The Sidney Morning Herald* in February 1985 under the headline 'Corruption as an Art Form'. The article alleged that former President Marcos of the Philippines, and a close associate, Eduardo Conjuangco squandered US$9 billion of their country's US$42.6 billion debt. Conjuangco won an application in court for the newspaper to disclose its sources. When the case was taken to the New South Wales Court of Appeal the paper's defence was rejected on the grounds that 'the newspaper rule' was not absolute and was overridden by the defamation action.

## Freedom of information

**The Freedom of Information Act:** The Australian Freedom of Information Act, loosely based on the US model, has been successively strengthened through amendments since its enactment in 1982. Nevertheless, the Act has as yet provided only a small improvement in access to information and scarcely reaches into the controversial or decision-making processes of government. Around three-quarters of all requests under the Act have been for access to personal files primarily held by social security and tax departments. Among the many difficulties involved in effective implementation of the Act has been the pressing need to reconcile existing secrecy provisions with the Act and so supply adequate coverage of security organizations. A lack of vigorous public or media campaigns in favour of greater freedom of information, proposals to increase fees and decrease agency compliance for the production of documents, and efforts to undermine the Act by calls for strict 'need to know' standards, have created an ambience in which reform seems unlikely.

**Official secrets:** State and federal laws impose criminal penalties for disclosure of official government information, but prosecutions are rare and detection of sources is difficult. There are heavy penalties for disclosure of material about the Australian Security Intelligence Organization and related agencies, such as disclosure of the identity of agents.

While the criminal offences have been laid down by parliament, the courts have been very reluctant to restrain publication of information held by governments. Thus in the 1975 Defence papers case the High Court allowed the content of diplomatic papers about relations with Indonesia to be disclosed, despite statements that disclosure would disrupt relations with that country. In the 1987 'Spycatcher' case, the courts refused to restrain publication of a book about British intelligence services.

## The media

There are few special laws which apply to print media as such. Since 1970 laws have been repealed that once required registration of printing presses and newspapers.

**Obscenity:** Machinery for censorship of written publications remains. It is largely confined to obscenity under the different federal and state codes, with protection of children being the main aim. The targets of the censorship, sometimes itemized in the legislation, are violence, cruelty, sexual violence, sexual abuse of children and bestiality. Blasphemous and terrorist material is sometimes also restricted.

The print censorship laws generally indicate what is obscene, then prohibit distribution or publication of such material. They leave the onus on the publisher of a potentially obscene work first to submit it to the censorship authorities and obtain an appropriate classification. Films and video cassettes are similarly treated, except that importers and exhibitors are obliged to obtain a classification before displaying their material to the public.

**Broadcasting:** Official pre-classification of television or radio material is actually prohibited, except for some special children's television programmes. There are few controversial restrictions on broadcast material. Examples of those which do exist are: rules to identify speakers and authors of political broadcasts; a largely ineffective requirement for 'reasonable opportunities' to be given to political parties at election times; a requirement that stations provide a limited amount of broadcast time for religious broadcasts; and a ban on cigarette advertising.

The two publicly-funded broadcasters are the *Australian Broadcasting Corporation* (*ABC*) and the *Special Broadcasting Service* (*SBS*). The latter is a multicultural and multilingual service . The law guarantees the *ABC* (and to a lesser extent the *SBS*) freedom from government intervention, although it is impossible to prevent financial, bureaucratic and political influence. The most prosperous broadcasters are the privately-owned commercial television and radio stations. Commercial radio is probably the least regulated in the world. Commercial television is regulated mainly through requirements for production of local, Australian material imposed by the Australian Broadcasting Tribunal, the licensing authority. In essence, the requirements are for the broadcasting of a specified minimum of quality local programmes. There is no maximum limit on imported material. The Tribunal also sets classification 'standards' for commercial television stations to apply when determining the kinds of programmes suitable for different parts of the day, having regard to the size of the child audience.

**The Press Council:** There are no laws offering a right of reply, or correction, or 'fairness' for those defamed. Money damages is almost the only remedy. Nor is a right to privacy guaranteed. Issues like privacy are sometimes considered through the internal disciplinary processes of the Australian Journalists' Association which upholds the ethics of its members. The Press Council is a voluntary body. It provides correction of unfair reporting and censure of privacy invasion on some occasions. Journalists' representatives withdrew from the Council in 1987 after it refused to oppose further acquisitions of newspapers by Rupert

Murdoch's company, News Ltd. However in the same year, almost all of the major publishers acting together subscribed to the Press Council and its statement of priciples concerning a free and responsible press.

**Ownership of the media:** Despite the burden of defamation law, the current legal restrictions are not considered the greatest threat to free communication in Australia. Rather it is the concentration of ownership of mass media in the hands of a small number of large private corporations. There is only minimal suppression of any material advocating any viewpoints. The difficulty is rather that there are not many publishers with a motive to produce it. It has been said that the modern Australian approach to business, government and media is inherited from a penal colony ruled by military governors. All enterprises began with grants of land and labour from the government, and were carried out by friends of government. The early governors in turn became interdependent with those entrepreneurs, and sometimes subservient to them. One of the main roles of government was to regulate competition among the colonial entrepreneurs, who came to share the deliberations of governors. Overseas observers are usually unaware that much of this model still operates behind the facade of institutions borrowed from other countries. The extremely high level of consensus between media controllers and Australian governments of various complexions is not visible to them and not scrutinized in the popular media.

The strategically important parts of television are owned by three groups, and the major print media are owned by four groups. There is more diversity in radio, and among the minor print media and television. The print groups—Fairfax, Consolidated Press, News Ltd and the Herald and Weekly Times Group—are among the largest in Australia. In 1986 and 1987, there were takeover bids between these groups, initiated by News Ltd's successful bid for the Herald and Weekly Times Group. Following an intervention by the Trade Practices Commission the percentage of daily newspaper circulation controlled by the Murdoch conglomerate News Ltd was reduced from 75 to 58 per cent. The other holdings are: Fairfax (23 per cent), Northern Star (8 per cent), and Bell Group and United Media Holdings of West Australia (10 per cent). The main investigative reporting of the last decade was carried out by the Fairfax and the Herald and Weekly Times groups. The Australian Journalists Association opposed News Ltd's takeover of the Herald and Weekly Times Group. During the 1987 general election in Australia, it was noted that Murdoch's ten city dailies did not take a common editorial position. Concern had been expressed about Murdoch, an American newspaper proprietor, telling Australians how to vote in their elections.

The government decides when new television or communications licences will be called for. A long-standing approach has been to exclude competition in these areas so as to protect the 'commercial viability' of existing services. Radio has slightly more diversity of ownership, although several large groups nevertheless dominate. Public radio stations, run by community or educational bodies, provide the one clear exception to this.

There are about seventy of these stations, which present an unlimited range of information and comment. The main limit on them is financial, since they receive virtually no government funds and are not allowed to broadcast advertisements.

# FIJI

Occupying a strategic position in the South Pacific, Fiji was until recently regarded as a model of parliamentary democracy in the region. Two military coups swept aside existing institutions and placed an interim military government in their stead. On Oct. 14, 1987, the military government installed by Col. Sitiveni Rabuka issued Fundamental Freedoms Decree No. 12, which suspended all legal guarantees of freedom of expression.

Fiji achieved independence within the Commonwealth on Oct. 10, 1970. Freedom of expression was protected in Section 12 of its Constitution, with extensive qualifications invoking restrictions recognised in international law.

|  |  | Year |
|---|---|---|
| Population | 700,000 | 1986 |
| GNP ($ per capita) | 1,840 | 1984 |
| Illiteracy % | 14.5 | 1985 |

| Daily newspapers | 3 | 1982 |
|---|---|---|
| Non Daily newspapers | 1 | 1982 |
| Periodicals | 8 | 1982 |
| Published books | 110 | 1980 |
| Radio stations | 2 | est |
| Radio receivers | 400,000 | 1983 |

| Covenant on Civil & Political Rights | NO |
|---|---|

Fiji is a telecommunications centre for the South Pacific region and is linked by the Commonwealth Pacific Telephone Cable (COMPAC) to the international telecommunications network. The Fiji Broadcasting Commission runs the two national radio networks which broadcast programmes in English, Fijian and Hindi. The first commercial radio station, FM 96, opened in 1986. There is no public television service although there were plans to introduce the first television channel in 1987. There are two national daily newspapers, the *Fiji Times* (owned by the Herald and Weekly Times Group of Australia) and the *Fiji Sun*, (part of the Sally AW Asian publishing group), as well as a number of weeklies publishing in English, Fijian and Hindi, business periodicals and tourist magazines.

The Fijian political system came to reflect the combination of political institutions inherited from the British and the continuing strong influence of tribal traditions. Beset by racial problems and friction between the indigenous Melanesian population and descendents of Indians brought to Fiji as indentured labour in the last century (comprising 47 per cent and 50 per cent of the population respectively), the ethnic Fijians were in control of the political institutions while economic power was concentrated in the hands of the Fijian Indian community.

Since independence Fiji was ruled by the predominantly native Fijian Alliance Party until elections on April 12, 1987, brought to power a multiracial, Indian- dominated coalition led by Dr Timoci Bavadra. One month later, on May 14, Parliament was stormed by soldiers led by Lt-Col. Rabuka, and members of the government were arrested. Executive authority passed to the Governor-General, Sir Penaia Ganilau, who was entrusted with the task of resolving the country's political and constitutional crisis, which for some ethnic Fijians required the drafting of a new constitution restricting the rights of Indians to political power. Dissatisfaction with the pace and possible outcome of constitutional reforms precipitated another coup by Rabuka on Sept. 25, 1987.

**News coverage of the coups:** Both coups brought in their wake assaults on the freedom of the press through the imposition of severe restrictions on reporting by the press and broadcasting media of political developments in the country, arrests and harassment of local and foreign journalists together with suppression of internal opposition to the coup.

It was in response to stinging editorials criticizing the first coup that the two national daily newspapers, the *Fiji Times* and the *Fiji Sun*, were closed down by the military on May 15 although allowed to resume publication about ten days later. They were closed again on military orders on the day of the second coup and informed a week later that they could publish under 'military censorship'. The military also took control of the government radio stations and imposed censorship on news bulletins. Hundreds of foreign journalists flooded into Fiji to report on the crisis and many experienced first-hand acts of harassment from the military. These took the form of the arrest and brief detention of several journalists, expulsions, and numerous incidents involving raids on journalists' hotel rooms, confiscation of equipment and notes and jamming of telephone lines. It was also reported that the military attempted to censor the despatches of foreign journalists by stationing soldiers around the capital's main telex and telephone exchange.

The sensitivity of the Army to the presence of the foreign media is believed to have been in reaction to reports of the crisis presenting a negative image of Fiji and the military to the outside world. In the absence of free reporting at home, Fijians had to rely on external broadcasting stations for news of political developments. One journalist claims to have learnt from a reliable source that, as the military had no jamming equipment, it was at one point considering the confiscation of every short-wave radio in the country.

The military took action to silence its critics at home, principally by means of arrests and short-term detentions. According to Amnesty International, over one hundred people were arrested between the two coups under the emergency regulations, including members and supporters of the deposed government who favoured a return to constitutional government and had access to the media to express their views and opinions. Supporters of the 'Back to Early May Movement' were also targeted for arrest for distributing their material and seeking signatures on petitions.

**Fundamental Freedoms Decree:** The reasons behind the coups in Fiji are more complex than solely the issue of racial divisions in the country. However, some ethnic Fijians did perceive the danger of being a minority in their own country and losing political control to the Indian community, and sought to overcome this by denying the Indians their fundamental rights. The Fundamental Freedoms Decree of Oct. 14 has swept away the rights of all Fijians to political activity. Section 12 has 'suspended from the date of this decree until otherwise ordered in so far as those activities relate to political activity by whatever party, group or affiliation in the interest of public order and public safety' all guarantees of freedom of expression, thereby spelling out in very clear terms the basis for total censorship in the country. On Dec. 5, 1987, Brig. Rabuka announced that Fiji would be returning to civilian rule.

# THEMES AND ISSUES

This section is an initial effort at classification and annotation of the many themes and issues that arise from an analysis of freedom of expression and censorship on a global basis. It is neither comprehensive nor exhaustive. ARTICLE 19 intends to expand and develop this classification as a separate project. Nevertheless, this version allows a ready overview of the principal concerns raised in the book that challenge the full enjoyment of the unrestricted exchange of ideas and information as envisaged by the Universal Declaration of Human Rights. Entries are cross-referenced alphabetically in the Index at the back of this book, while the entries in this section themselves make reference as appropriate to the countries covered in the Country Reports.

We begin with INTERNATIONAL STANDARDS. The starting point of any analysis of freedom of expression and freedom of information as a global entitlement must be the international standards themselves, to which governments almost without exception claim commitment. These are set out as are the exceptions, restrictions and limitations which they acknowledge. Parts 2, 3 and 4 of this section look at CENSORSHIP: REASONS; at CENSORSHIP: METHODS; and at CENSORSHIP: TARGETS. Part 5 breaks down the theme of DEFENDING FREEDOM OF EXPRESSION: POLICIES AND PROGRAMMES.

## 1. INTERNATIONAL STANDARDS

Since its foundation in 1945, a major achievement of the United Nations has been the development of new universal standards for the protection of human rights. However, the major problem today is that of persuading states to implement these standards which are now contained in regional and global international human rights treaties. Each of the principal treaties has some mechanism of enforcement. The rights to freedom of opinion, expression and information are included in all of the international conventions. An effort to draft a separate United Nations sponsored treaty on freedom of information failed in the 1950s.

In addition to defining the positive right to freedom of expression, these international texts give the only grounds that a government may use to limit the right. The key issue is invariably the justification for such limitations. Their imposition should be judged, if contested, by a court and not by the executive power of the state. Any restriction must be demonstrated to be necessary in a democratic society. It is in the supervision of government actions and laws permitting restriction that courts play a crucial role in implementing both national and international legal guarantees on freedom of information.

**Universal Declaration of Human Rights**: Proclaimed in 1948, the Declaration is still the most powerful statement of the global aspiration of respect for human rights. Being a declaration it is not a binding treaty but is widely regarded as having achieved the status of customary international law. Its provisions have been adopted in many constitutions of the world. Article 19 of the Declaration reads: 'Everyone has the right to freedom of opinion and expression; this right includes freedom to hold opinions without interference and to seek, receive and impart information and ideas through any media regardless of frontiers.'

**International Covenant on Civil and Political Rights**: This major universal treaty (ICCPR) came into force in 1976 along with the parallel Covenant on Economic, Social and Cultural Rights. At the end of 1987 it had been ratified by eighty-six countries. States which ratify undertake to submit reports to the Human Rights Committee, established under ICCPR, on the state of human rights protection in the country. There is an optional provision whereby states agree to allow individuals to complain to the Committee over human rights violations by the state. Article 18 of the Covenant guarantees freedom of conscience, religion and belief; Article 19, freedom of expression.; and Article 20 deals with the duty to prohibit propaganda for war and racial incitement. Article 19 of the Covenant reads:

'1. Everyone shall have the right to hold opinions without interference. '2. Everyone shall have the right to freedom of expression; this right shall include freedom to seek, receive and impart information and ideas of all kinds, regardless of frontiers, either orally, in writing or in print, in the form of art, or through any other media of his choice.

'3. The exercise of the rights provided for in paragraph 2 of this Article carries with it special duties and responsibilities. It may therefore be subject to certain restrictions, but these shall only be such as are provided by law and are necessary: (a) for respect of the rights or reputations of others; (b) for the protection of national security or of public order (*ordre public*), or of public health or morals.'

**African Charter on Human and Peoples' Rights**: The African Charter ratified by thirty-five states (as of November 1987) came into force in 1986. The Charter is distinctive because of its emphasis on peoples' as well as individual rights. The African Human Rights Commission has been established to implement the Charter, and individuals will be entitled to complain to it. The Charter's text does not protect freedom of opinion nor, at least explicitly, the rights to seek and impart information and ideas.

Article 9 of the Charter reads:

'1. Every individual shall have the right to receive information.

'2. Every individual shall have the right to free association provided that he abides by the law.'

**American Convention on Human Rights**: Adopted in 1950, this Convention for the Americas follows the American Declaration of the Rights and Duties of Man. The Convention has not been ratified by the United States and Canada. Nineteen countries from Central and South America have ratified it. There is a Commission and a Human Rights Court. The Convention has an elaborate and strong formulation of the right to freedom of expression set out as follows in Article 13:

'Everyone has the right to freedom of thought and expression. This right includes freedom to seek, receive, and impart information and ideas of all kinds, regardless of frontiers, either orally, in writing, in print, in the form of art, or through any other medium of one's choice.

'2. The exercise of the right provided for in the foregoing paragraph shall not be subject to prior censorship but shall be subject to subsequent imposition of liability, which shall be expressly established by law and be necessary in order to ensure: (a) respect for the rights or reputations of others; or (b) the protection of national security, public order, or public health or morals.

'3. The right of expression may not be restricted by indirect methods or means, such as the abuse of government or private controls over newsprint, radio broadcasting frequencies, or implements or equipment used in the dissemination of information, or by any other means tending to impede the communication and circulation of ideas and opinions.

292

'4. Notwithstanding the provisions of paragraph 2 above, public entertainment may be subject by law to prior censorship, for the sole purpose of regulating access to them for the moral protection of childhood and adolescence.

'5. Any propaganda for war and any advocacy of national, racial, or religious hatred that constitutes incitements to lawless violence cr any other similar illegal action against any person or group of persons on any grounds including those of race, colour, religion, language, or national origin shall be considered as offences punishable by law.'

**The European Convention on Human Rights**: The most developed of the regional international human rights treaties, the Council of Europe Convention for the Protection of Human Rights and Fundamental Freedoms, embraces twenty-one Western European states. The Convention is enforced by a Commission, a Court and a political body, a Committee of Ministers from the member states. The European Court of Human Rights gives binding judgments under the Convention. In the field of freedom of expression its important judgments include the *Sunday Times* case and the Lingens case. The right to seek information is not expressly recognized. Article 10 of the European Convention on Human Rights provides:

'1. Everyone has the right to freedom of expression. This right shall include freedom to hold opinions and to receive and impart information and ideas without interference by public authority and regardless of frontiers. This Article shall not prevent states from requiring the licensing of broadcasting, television or cinema enterprises.

'2. The exercise of these freedoms, since it carries with it duties and responsibilities, may be subject to such formalities, conditions, restrictions or penalties as are prescribed by law and are necessary in a democratic society in the interests of national security, territorial integrity or public safety, for the prevention of disorder, or crime, for the protection of health or morals, for the protection of the reputation or rights of others, for preventing the disclosure of information received in confidence, or for maintaining the authority and impartiality of the judiciary.'

**Helsinki Final Act**: The Helsinki Final Act is the title given to the accord agreed after the Conference on Security and Co-operation in Europe (CSCE) in 1975. Thirty-five states participated— all of the Eastern and Western European states with the exception of Albania, and the United States and Canada. The accord is not a binding treaty, but has under its terms been reviewed in follow-up conferences, the latest in Vienna commencing in 1986. The Final Act adopted ten principles guiding relations between participating states, and three 'baskets' of more detailed promises including 'co-operation in humanitarian and other fields'. The pact includes a section on greater human contact, improving the dissemination of information of all kinds and the working conditions of journalists.

The Helsinki Final Act has been the springboard for the development of a network of non-governmental initiatives to monitor compliance by states. Members of the International Helsinki Federation publish regular reports and lobby at CSCE review conferences. Helsinki monitoring groups in the socialist states have suffered consistent harassment or suppression.

# 2. CENSORSHIP: REASONS

Governments invoke a variety of reasons or grounds to censor speech and publications or to justify secrecy, or for actions against individuals because of their opinions. Such grounds are often spurious and lack justification in the sense that they are not recognized as permissible restrictions in international law and have an illegitimate aim, such as the suppression of criticism or thought unacceptable to the authorities.

No interference whatsoever is justified with the holding of opinions. Nevertheless limits placed on freedom of expression and the availability of information can be justified in certain circumstances. The crucial test is whether restriction is applied so as to deny totally freedom of expression in the name of some competing interest or right. The general principle should be that 'freedom is the rule and its limitation the exception'. The onus to justify any restriction must rest with the authorities imposing it and it must be possible to contest any restriction through a procedure independent of the government, such as a court.

## The rights of others

Claims that freedom of expression should be limited in order to protect the rights of others is the most common general ground given for censorship in the various legal systems of the world.

**Defamation and protection of reputation**: Defamation is the general legal term for the act of damaging another's reputation or honour through words or publication. In many countries there are penal as well as civil codes governing defamation. In an important decision the European Court of Human Rights (Lingens, July 1986) endorsed the distinction between private personality and a public figure: politicians and celebrities ought to tolerate stronger comment on their activities than ordinary members of the public. However this distinction (accepted in the United States) is not widely recognized. Indeed the reverse is the case. People holding high office, such as presidents, monarchs, heads of state, the military and judges, are protected by laws that make it a criminal offence, and occasionally an offence meriting the death penalty, to voice criticism. In many countries defamation laws are a major constraint on reporting by the media. Offences such as *lèse-majesté* do not conform with international standards, including when the offence is extended to the dead. *See Australia, Canada, Chile, Denmark, Iraq, Morocco, Spain, United Kingdom, Zaïre.*

**Privacy**: Privacy as a general concept has given rise to difficulty of definition and is usually specified in such terms as the right to respect for a person's private life, home and correspondence. As such, it is recognized by international human rights instruments and in some national laws as a fundamental right.

Although frequently ignored by journalists, privacy is equally essential to journalists' research and investigation. For example, sources of information will often only speak to journalists if they feel secure that their identities will not be revealed. Similarly, when communications are intercepted, people will not converse or write freely for fear that their private writings or conversations are being read or heard by government agencies. In Britian, journalists can be compelled by courts to reveal sources of information, whereas journalists' privilege is fully protected in Sweden. *See Australia, Canada, Sweden, United Kingdom.*

## Public interest

There is no specific reference to public interest in international treaties. The 'public interest' is used both by censoring authorities and by advocates of freedom of information respectively to connote overriding considerations of public policy. Disclosure of information 'in the public interest' consists of new and important matter for public debate. Such information may only be suppressed, according to the European Court on Human Rights, where a 'pressing social need' for its suppression is demonstrated; see the *Sunday Times* case, 1979.

Scepticism often follows official justifications given for the suppression of any information. Information that is often simply embarrassing to individuals in the government may find itself deemed 'against the public interest' when disclosure is threatened. *See Australia, Canada, Denmark, Mexico, United Kingdom, United States, Zambia.*

294

## National security

National security is the most commonly used excuse for censorship and secrecy. Strictly defined, national security is the safety of the nation from threats by other nations to its political and economic independence, its territorial and judicial sovereignty, its cultural heritage and way of life. When other nations pose a threat or, it is feared, might pose such a threat, secrecy surrounding the nation's defences against enemy attacks or interference and its secret service personnel is often justified on grounds of national security.

However, those elements of a nation considered to be most fundamental to its continuing identity and independence are often open to wide differences of opinion.

National security has been cited to prevent or delay publication of material potentially embarrassing to government officials but which may not be related to the defence of the nation state.

The effects of national security legislation may be far-reaching and affect fundamental freedoms. Exit visas may be denied to citizens seeking to emigrate, for example, when previous knowledge of state secrets is used as a pretext. National security is also cited as a reason to prevent indigenous populations making contact with foreigners (especially journalists) on the grounds that they might inadvertently pass on information useful to enemies of the state. National security grounds have also been used to deport or deny re-entry to non-nationals on the grounds of the quality of their political opinions or affiliations.

The increasing difficulties many governments face in maintaining control on information that has been classified for national security reasons has led to highly restrictive classification systems. The National Security Administration in the United States imposes controls through classification on the exportation of high-technology goods. An attempt by the agency to assume power to reclassify documents formerly in the public domain and to edit public domain databases without the permission of authors was foiled after public outcry. *See India, Israel, South Korea, Malaysia, Nicaragua, Poland, Romania, South Africa, Soviet Union, Sweden, Taiwan, Turkey, United Kingdom, United States, Yugoslavia.*

**State security**: In contrast to national security, state security is a term used to refer to the safety of a particular form of state or government. The perceived threat may originate from internal as well as external sources. State security is frequently invoked to justify censoring opinions and maintaining secrecy over information liable to discredit or embarrass members of the government. State security laws, for example, are used to prevent 'slander' of the head of state or the head of armed forces. Internal Security Acts provide the legal basis to repress critics of the government. *See Chile, India, Israel and the Occupied Territories, Malaysia, Nicaragua, Romania, South Africa, Sweden.*

**Sedition**: It is everywhere a crime to plot the overthrow of a government or state. However, there is a distinction to be made between efforts to overthrow government unlawfully through violence, and peaceful efforts to advocate reform of government. In many countries, this distinction is ignored. Anyone who by word or deed propounds reform can be made subject to severe penalties, including detention and imprisonment or even death. Legal definitions of what may or may not be considered seditious are often dangerously vague. There are instances in which the possession of publications deemed seditious can result in imprisonment. A political system violates respect for freedom of opinion and expression where it denies the possibility of lawful advocacy of its alteration. *See Ghana, Kenya, North Korea, South Korea, Indonesia, Iraq, Zaïre.*

## Public order

'Public order' in the English language denotes absence of disorder, but the French legal term *ordre public* denotes the wider concept of the principles which underly an entire social structure. Maintenance of public order is evoked to regulate rioting and civil disturbance but may often be used arbitrarily to block peaceful demonstrations or manifestations of political opinion. Reporting restrictions are often placed on the media and justified as being necessary to protect public order. *See Chile, Israel, South Korea, Kuwait, Malaysia, Nicaragua, South Africa, Spain, Uganda, Zaïre.*

## Public health

The protection of public health is often invoked in constitutions as a limitation clause to the right to freedom of expression and to guarantees of other fundamental rights and freedoms. It is a recognized restriction in international treaties. Controls on advertising of tobacco and alcohol are well known examples. Compulsory warnings of health hazards of specific products (pharmaceuticals) or activities (AIDS) and the provision of information concerning ingredients, secondary effects of drugs, food products, toys, etc. represent a form of manipulation of information by the state that might be considered to be in the public interest. *See Ireland, Kenya, Rwanda, Turkey.*

## Public morals

Concern for public morals, morality and *bonnes moeurs* is accepted in international human rights standards as a justifiable restriction. However, such restrictions should only be such as 'provided by law' and as 'necessary'. No restriction should be imposed to suppress freedom of expression of minorities, or to 'encourage and uphold prejudice against minorities, even if their opinion is insulting or shocking to the majority' (the Handyside case, 1976).
Typical examples of limitations are 'obscenity' and 'blasphemy' and as such figure in many countries' legislation. The protection of youth is a prime concern. Differing cultural perceptions are, however, used to justify and sometimes excuse a wider application of censorship than 'necessary'. In France in March 1987, the Minister of the Interior insisted that administrative authorities rather than judicial authorities should oversee public morality. In East Germany, a group of youths were charged in the autumn of 1987 with 'hooliganism' and offending public morality. In India in 1987 state television banned 'winking' by women in commercials as part of a campaign to 'improve the nation's morals'. Reference to public morals is often used to restrict the import of foreign publications.
Evidence shows that in a number of countries governments use the reference to public morals to restrict freedom of political expression and opposition views. In particular, in countries with strong single political philosophies the distinction between offending public morals and questioning the political system becomes vague. In Zaïre, the application of *bonnes moeurs* defined as good standards of behaviour has been used extensively to suppress opposition views and thinking. The insistence on 'authenticity', or cultural identity, by the state in the same breath as *bonnes moeurs* is used to justify further pressure on dissidents. *See France, Honduras, Iran, Iraq, Ireland, Kuwait, Malaysia, Pakistan, South Africa, Turkey, Yugoslavia, Zaïre.*

**Obscenity**: Obscenity is used here to embrace offensive, indecent and pornographic material. In the 1964 US Supreme Court Mr Justice Stewart confessed his inability to define obscenity but claimed 'I know it when I see it'. This remark points to an abiding difficulty in aligning legal and ethical definitions of the word 'obscene' and its cognates. What is 'lewd', 'filthy', 'disgusting', 'perverse' in one culture may be accepted as part of everyday life in another. Definitions of the obscene have proved notoriously and dangerously vague as well as being legally unworkable. Obscenity laws can provide a false remedy for an undefined and constantly changing area of moral consensus.

In the United Kingdom, the Williams Committee commented (1976): 'To specify what we regard as representing the level of offensiveness against which the law should act involves fixing a standard relative to our conception of current reactions. But that standard may no longer be valid when legislation comes to be enacted: and once it is enacted it will become an extremely inflexible standard which will tend to attract even more ridicule and odium to the law.'

In 1987 in the United Kingdom, a proposed bill to extend obscene publication laws to television defined obscenity as 'being grossly offensive to a reasonable person'. The loose wording of the formulation (when does offensive material become *grossly* offensive?) led to fears that news and current affairs could be doctored if certain images were deemed offensive.

In many countries reference is made to the 'reasonable' or 'civilized' person as the best judge of matters obscene, yet there can be no clear consensus on what is meant by 'reasonable' or 'civilized'. One of the first victims of obscenity law in many societies is art. An artistic representation of Adam and Eve may be considered obscene according to the ethos and ideology of one nation yet hang as an aesthetic masterpiece in the galleries of others. Similarly, a book on eroticism in India may pass unnoticed on the bookshelves of one country whilst all copies of it are burned in another. Protection of minors is acknowledged by the American Convention on Human Rights as a ground for prior censorship of public entertainment.

Increasing interest is being shown in West Germany and the UK in the efforts by certain feminist thinkers and groups in the United States to have obscene or pornographic material suppressed. See *Australia, Canada, India, Ireland, Pakistan, South Africa, Turkey, United Kingdom.*

In November 1987, the American Federal Communications Commission (FCC) ruled that radio and television stations could broadcast 'indecent' programming between midnight and 6.00 a.m. The FCC's ruling clarified a decision made the previous spring which defined indecency as 'material which depicts or describes in terms patently offensive, as measured by contemporary community standards for the broadcast medium, sexual or excretory activities or organs'.

The concept of 'offensiveness' can be given a political interpretation by governments. By declaring the material 'offensive to the government' or 'offensive and dangerous to public interests', political opposition may be gagged. See *Nicaragua, Pakistan, Mexico, United Kingdom, United States.*

**Violence**: A link between public morals and the depiction of violent actions is made in many countries. Yet, in the debate on whether the representation of violence on television and video leads to greater violence in society, arguments have centred on limited statistical surveys or conflicting expert reports. Demands to ban violence from the media, including violence depicted in news reporting, often arise as a 'panic' reaction following instances of mass murders, riots or violent demonstrations. Recently, a UK government advertisement urging support for the security forces in Northern Ireland was required to be shown late in the evening on local television because of its violent content.

In some countries political violence is interpreted by the authorities so broadly that it in fact includes the non-violent expression of dissenting views. In Chile, journalists who accused the military of repression have been prosecuted under legislation which broadly defines slander as a violent political offence. A number of Yugoslav laws create 'verbal crimes' (*délit d'opinion*). It appears no distinction is made between violent and non-violent advocacy or expression of opinion. Similarly, in Zaïre opposition leaders have been sentenced under a law which deals with 'attempts to overthrow the constitutional order' in disregard of their non-violent expression of dissenting political views. *See Australia, Chile, Colombia, Singapore, Yugoslavia, Zaïre.*

## Linguistic and cultural hegemony

All forms of cultural oppression contravene Article 27 of the ICCPR which states: 'In those States in which ethnic, religious or linguistic minorities exist, persons belonging to such minorities shall not be denied the right, in community with other members of their group, to enjoy their own culture ... or to use their own language.'

In a variety of countries, linguistic and cultural dominance of ethnic or linguistic groups is maintained through censorship and the deprivation of language rights. This can lead to the systematic destruction of individual communities' linguistic or cultural integrity. In some countries languages and dialects may be curtailed in school teaching and access of all ethnic groups to the mass media denied. In Turkey, the use of the Kurdish language can be a criminal offence; at the same time Turkish authorities have consistently blamed Bulgaria for enforced 'Bulgarization' of Turks to the level of non-identification of individuals through name changes. Official histories taught in schools may deny the claims of such groups' own interpretations. A study of book censorship by Israeli authorities in the Occupied Territories noted that prohibited titles were those that fostered Palestinian national feelings and national heritage. *See Canada, Iran, Iraq, Israel, Romania, Soviet Union, Turkey.*

## Racism

Racism is regarded in international law as an area of permissible limitation on freedom of expression as it constitutes an infringement of the fundamental rights of others. Racial groups are any group of persons defined by race, colour or ethnic origin. Article 20 of the ICCPR requires states to prohibit 'any advocacy of national, racial or religious hatred that constitutes incitement to discrimination, hostility or violence'. Some states have entered a reservation over this article because of its conflict with freedom of expression.

Although condemnation of racist expression is part of international human rights standards included in many constitutions and outlawed in national legislation and press laws, the censorship debate on racism continues. Rather than deny the right of an individual or group access to the media to express a racist message, some would argue in favour of stiff penalties subsequent to breach of the law as opposed to prior censorship. However, although racist expression may be a punishable offence under criminal law, a colloquium held in France in June 1987 to take stock of fifteen years' application of the law against racism there demonstrated how difficult it is to prove the offence, and to compensate its victims. *See Australia, Canada, Denmark, South Africa.*

## Sexism

Sexism may be considered as any discriminatory practice against women or men on the ground of sex. Such discrimination is often made manifest in depictions of the role and status of sexual groups in the media and through other communication channels. The UN Convention on the Elimination of Discrimination against Women (1981) seeks 'the elimination of prejudices and customary and other practices which are based on the idea of the inferiority or the superiority of either of the sexes or on stereotyped roles for men and women'. As with racism, many would argue that the elimination of sexist material (now said to include the obscene or pornographic) constitutes a valid ground for censorship and self-regulation in the media, whilst absolute supporters of freedom of expression argue that such censorship may, in the end, advance the cause of continuing sexism. The issue remains controversial. *See Canada, Ireland, United States.*

## Religious intolerance

Freedom to believe or not to believe in a religion involves freedom to practise or express any faith or lack of faith. The UN Declaration on Religious Intolerance (1981) recognizes that an important aspect of such freedom is to propagate the dogma, aims or beliefs of a religion. In this context, censorship can be said to affect orthodox religious, dissenting and non-religious individuals or groups when they are formally proscribed or otherwise prevented from manifesting in whole or in part their beliefs or objection to beliefs and practices, for example through the dissemination of religious artefacts and publications. Persecution and discrimination on the grounds of religious belief remains a serious world problem.

In the United States censorship of books and public school curricula on religious grounds has increased considerably over the last few years. In Pakistan, the content of teaching materials must conform to political and religious dogma endorsed by the government. In Mexico, members of religious orders are prohibited from criticizing state institutions and government actions, nor are they permitted to participate in the electoral process. In Czechoslovakia, the state controls the activities of the Catholic Church through licensing: without the licence, a priest may not publicly say mass or engage in any pastoral activity. *See Argentina, Australia, Canada, Czechoslovakia, Ecuador, Egypt, France, India, Indonesia, Iran, Iraq, North Korea, Kuwait, Malaysia, Mexico, Nicaragua, Pakistan, Singapore, South Africa, Soviet Union, Turkey, United States, Yugoslavia.*

**Heresy and blasphemy**: Heresy is a theological doctrine or system of religious thought rejected as false by official ecclesiastical authority. It is defined as a dangerous deviation from orthodox faith. In countries where religion and the state are merged, heresy is considered as a civil offence punishable under criminal law. In Iran, for example, the Bahai sect are considered to be 'heretics'; some 300 Bahais are reported to have been executed. In late 1987 in Egypt, forty-eight adherents of the Bahai faith were fined and imprisoned on charges of 'holding ideas that run counter to the divinely revealed religions on which the system of government in Egypt is based' and of belonging to an 'apostate religion'.

Blasphemy is any oral or written reproach contemptuous or insulting to God or religion. In many countries blasphemy is a criminal offence and refers only to the dominant belief—Christianity in the UK or Islam in Pakistan for example. In Argentina a judge banned the showing of the controversial 1986 French film '*Je vous salue, Marie*'. The Church considered it blasphemous and an unknown group threatened to bomb the cinema where it was due to be shown. The distributors withdrew the film. A similar controversy concerning censorship of this film arose in France. *See Argentina, Egypt, France, Indonesia, Iran, Pakistan.*

## Propaganda

**War propaganda**: Article 20 of the ICCPR states among other things that 'any propaganda for war shall be prohibited by law'. There is, however, no agreed definition of propaganda either in international law or in different legal systems. As the expert committee for human rights of the Council of Europe has commented, without such agreed definition legal prohibitions can lead to abuse.

**Government propaganda**: Propaganda is a term sometimes applied to all information produced by a government and is appropriate where the information is supplied in a biased form. Governments have a duty to inform the public about their activities and policies, and about matters of general

concern such as public health.
Government propaganda usually expresses the official political or religious ideology, and divergent or dissident views are described as 'anti-government' propaganda, as in the offence of 'anti-Soviet agitation, slander and propaganda', contained in Articles 70 and 190-1 of the RSFSR Criminal Code. A Department of Propaganda is a feature of many governments; often it is attached to the ruling party's own structures and has the role of propagating the ideas of the party through the organs of governmental authority. In the United States, the Foreign Agents Registration Act requires that any film produced under the auspices of a foreign country be labelled propaganda unless the film is 'not serving a predominantly foreign interest'. *See Egypt, Paraguay, South Africa, United States.*

**Media bias**: The conscious manipulation of news and information to serve the interests of a government, racial group, ideology or individual may take the form of restrictions on access to the media of political, social or ethnic groups; or an imbalance of coverage to stress or understress certain events or factors and pressures exerted upon journalists which jeopardize impartial reporting. Accusations of bias are often levelled at television coverage of events, since television has become both the least easy medium to monitor and the most powerful tool for governments to manipulate public opinion through censorship without incurring too much adverse publicity. Alternatively, many governments become particularly sensitive when opposition views are given too much airtime and will often employ their own media bias monitors.
In the UK, the IBA was required by the 1981 Broadcasting Act to ensure 'due impartiality on the part of persons providing the programmes as respects matters of political...controversy or relating to current public policy'. Most media organizations, however, have no statutory obligation to be impartial.

Particular indignation was felt in Spain in 1987 concerning the state-controlled television network's uneven coverage of a referendum concerning the country's entry into NATO. In Ireland the opposition party *Sinn Fein,* due to its links with the IRA, is excluded from access to the broadcasting media. This is justified on the grounds that any appearance of a *Sinn Fein* representative would incite violence.
On the international level, countries will often accuse foreign broadcasts of imbalanced reporting. The Malaysian government for instance claims that its own news agency, *Bernama,* the sole distributor of news from foreign agencies, aims to combat the imbalance of news from developed nations and 'biased' reporting of events in the Third World. The same rationale lay behind restrictions by the authorities in Singapore on *Time* and the *Asian Wall Street Journal* in 1986 and 1987. See *El Salvador, Ireland, France, Malaysia, Spain, United Kingdom.*

**Disinformation**: Disinformation is the deliberate dissemination of false or misleading information in order to manipulate or influence people's perceptions or opinions regarding certain situations or events and to create a climate of assent, fear or mistrust as a pretext for taking certain action. Disinformation techniques are used by agents wishing either to maintain or change the status quo, by governments and legal or illegal opposition groups. Since the abortive coup attempt in November 1986 in the Philippines, radio station *DYLA* on Cebu has been maintaining a systematic disinformation campaign against the central government in favour of the rebel military. After the incidents in August 1987, the vice-president of the House of Representatives demanded the withdrawal of *DYLA's* radio licence. In 1986 the French authorities proposed the establishment of a research institute to investigate alleged disinformation strategies in reports by journalists writing on military matters. *See Honduras, North Korea, United States.*

## Copyright and intellectual property

Copyright is an internationally protected legal right, under the International Copyright Convention of 1971, to control copying and other commercially significant exploitation of authors' works (writings, art, music and drama), certain manufactured works (sound recordings, cinematograph films, published editions of books and other literary works) and electronic phenomena (broadcasts, cable programmes and computer software). Each type of work protected by copyright can usually be used or copied in accordance with laws which tolerate certain forms of 'fair dealing' and non-commercial unauthorised use of another's work. In the United Kingdom for example, no court will restrain an alleged copyright infringement if it is felt that the public's interest in gaining access to the information outweighs the copyright owner's interest in suppressing unauthorised use. Other forms of intellectual property include patents (which protect inventions) and trade secrets law (a refined branch of the law of breach of confidence). *See India, United Kingdom, United States.*

## Confidentiality

The development of a principle of confidentiality covering information received or learned through public or private employment is a major new challenge to freedom of information and of the press, and is a central element in the United Kingdom 'Spycatcher' controversy.
Contractual obligations to secrecy and confidentiality are frequently imposed on civil servants, as well as on certain employees in the private sector. The obligation not to transmit information to unauthorized bodies relates to the knowledge obtained through the position as an employee, e.g. about policies, activities, plans, supplies, inventions, contracts under negotiation, finances and personal files concerning employees. The reasons for requiring contractual secrecy vary, depending on the nature of the parties involved. Civil servants may be bound for 'national security' reasons or the need for a public authority to have the citizens' trust that personal files and applications will be kept confidential. Depending on the individual contract, the obligations are likely to last after the resignation of an employee. The need for confidentiality will in some cases conflict with what is claimed to be in the public interest. This was another theme in the 'Spycatcher' litigation in Australia and the UK. Courts in both countries recognized that the public interest in disclosure of crime outweighs a duty of confidentiality in some cases. 'Whistleblowing' laws in the USA which protect private employees from reprisals for disclosing illegal activities in private businesses are now firmly established. *See Australia, Denmark, Sweden, United Kingdom, United States.*

## Corruption

Censorship is frequently used to prevent journalists investigating topics which expose corruption and vested interests in government or in financial institutions. Defamation laws may be invoked against journalists to block investigations, and a frequent motive for the killing, detention and expulsion of journalists is investigation of the abuse of public office to accumulate personal gain. Two Australian journalists were expelled from Indonesia in April 1986 after the *Sydney Morning Herald* published a report on alleged corruption at the highest level. In November 1986 three issues of the *Asia Wall Street Journal* containing a similar analysis were banned by the Indonesian authorities. *See Australia, China, Colombia, Ecuador, Honduras, India, Indonesia.*

## Special situations

**States of emergency and wars**: The international standards recognize that, as with other rights, international armed conflict may justify a country imposing a regime of censorship. This can extend not only to control of the media but also to the censorship of other forms of expression and even to all correspondence. Freedom of expression and opinion are often the first victims subjected to special regulations under states of emergency and states of siege.

A serious concern arises that, in the states of siege or emergency frequently declared by governments, censorship is designed to facilitate repressive measures by removing any monitoring or control of the actions of the security forces which otherwise result from independent press reporting on clashes, arrests, treatment of civilians etc. A declared state of emergency is recognized under international law as a special circumstance in which the curtailment of certain rights is permissible, but these should be clearly speficied by law and should not infringe on basic human rights. However, such measures are often taken simply to minimize opposition to government policy. States of emergency may not always automatically involve the introduction of formal censorship powers, however. In Northern Ireland, for example, a state of emergency which was withdrawn in 1984 was not accompanied by formal censorship of news coming from that region.

States of emergency may continue long after the circumstance that provoked them has disappeared. In Egypt, state of emergency powers, including the power to censor letters, publications, or drawings, to confiscate or close printing facilities and houses, or to break up mass meetings and rallies, are still available to the Egyptian President. The legislation was enacted in 1981 following the assassination of President Sadat. During declared emergency periods, governments often revise legislation according to the level of unrest they deem exists in the country. In South Africa, state of emergency regulations allow for draconian powers of censorship, including detention without trial, the harassment of journalists and a virtual news blackout on matters concerning 'unrest

situations'. Commenting on the expulsion of foreign correspondents from South Africa, the Foreign Correspondents' Association stated that the government intended to end independent coverage of South Africa's social conflict 'because it believes secrecy will help it win'. In Chile, between November 1984 and May 1985, reporting prohibitions were imposed on all news which might 'create alarm' whilst six weekly newspapers were shut. In 1987 in Fiji journalists were arrested under sweeping emergency regulations. In many countries states of emergency lead to the creation of 'emergency zones' where reporting is restricted or prohibited. *See Chile, Ecuador, Egypt, Fiji, Honduras, India, Israel and the Occupied Territories, Nicaragua, Paraguay, Peru, South Africa, Taiwan, Turkey.*

**Election periods**: During election periods ruling parties are most apt to react most sensitively to the exercise of the right to freedom of expression guaranteed to opposition parties. Access to broadcasting and radio stations is often curtailed or denied and the allocation of time given to parties can be disproportionately favourable to the ruling party. The European Commission of Human Rights agreed that there was no 'general and unfettered right' for any particular political party to have access to broadcasting time but also noted that 'the denial of broadcasting time to one or more specific groups or persons may in particular circumstances, raise an issue … for instance if one political party was excluded from broadcasting facilities at election time while others were given broadcasting time'. *See Ireland, South Korea, Paraguay, Spain.*

# 3. CENSORSHIP: METHODS
## Press laws

Press laws refer to that body of legislation which defines the rules pertaining to press, publishing and the electronic media. Such laws frequently determine

302

the rights and responsibilities of journalists. The existence of laws on the press does not *per se* constitute infringement on freedom of expression. The international standards specifically include a concept of responsibility in the exercise of freedom of expression. However the abuse of laws on the press ostensibly to promote press freedom is widespread in the world.

Press law content varies from country to country. In Czechoslovakia the 1950 Press Law proclaimed that among other things it was the mission of the media to help educate the people for Socialism; the 1978 amended press laws in Romania exercised tight control in all aspects of writing and publishing—among the stated duties of journalists was the duty to 'foster love for the Party'. Honduran press laws require all journalists to belong to a professional guild, whilst in Turkey the press laws require that all journalists are certified. Certification of journalists who have been convicted in Turkey is refused—a frequent occurrence in a country where journalists are often persecuted for their writing. In Egypt the 1980 Press Law makes it an offence to challenge the truth of divine teachings or advocate opposition or hatred to state institutions, whilst in Zaïre, press laws state that prior authorization is required for all newspapers and periodicals. *See Czechoslovakia, Egypt, Honduras, Malaysia, Romania, Turkey, Zaïre.*

## Prior restraint

The classic form of censorship entails prior authorization to publish, and is known widely by the American constitutional term, prior restraint. Prior restraint covers all procedures formal and informal whereby publication is vetted; it is contrasted with post-publication responsibility under the ordinary law for the contents of a newspaper, book or programme. Prior restraint as practised in many countries is incompatible with the ordinary application of freedom of expression and of the media.

An important form of prior restraint is the issuing of guidelines by governments to publishers, editors etc. These may vary from mandatory to discretionary documents, or be simple requests or warnings delivered by telephone or in person.

Informal and consultative methods are used in countries where members of the government make personal contact with editors with a view to influencing content and perspective. In many countries, official coverage requirements are backed up by the requirement of licences or permits to publish, or government control of newsprint and advertising: supplies of both can be cut off if papers do not comply with 'press advice'.

Lists of the exact nature of prohibited matter (other than state or official secrets) are often not publicly available, and so editors often find it difficult to determine what may or may not be inadvisable to publish. Such prescriptions concerning content normally relate to a perceived state duty to foster allegiance to the ruling party. Formal official guidelines are issued in the UK, Australia and Canada through bodies such as the 'D' Notice Committee. These guidelines usually apply to any category of information which the government deems to relate to national security. This information is normally listed, and publishers and editors are requested not to publish from it. *See Chile, Kenya, Indonesia, Malaysia, Peru, Romania, South Africa, Soviet Union, United Kingdom, United States.*

## Post-publication censorship

Post-publication censorship covers the stages from the initial publication or broadcasting of matter (be it oral, visual or in print) to its dissemination or transmission. This may include any legal action taken against matter already in the public domain, leading to the banning, burning, reclassification or confiscation of books, or of visual material (paintings or photographs, films, videos), or the confiscation of the technical means by which any of the above are produced (through typewriters, photographic and video cameras, sound recording apparatus, and so on). It can also include the oppressive or arbitrary application of defamation and other laws against writers, journalists and others. *See Chile, China, Fiji, France, Nicaragua, Turkey.*

**Closures**: Action taken against radio and television stations, printing houses, or newspapers leading to closure following dissemination of material may constitute both post-publication censorship and prior restraint. According to the Committee to Protect Journalists, in 1987 more than thirty-five media organs were ordered to be closed by authorities in fourteen countries, either temporarily or permanently. *See Israel, Nicaragua, Paraguay, South Africa.*

**Banning of organizations**: Freedom of association involves the liberty to join with others for the pursuit or furtherance of any of a wide variety of ends, whether for social, artistic, literary, scientific, cultural, political, religious, or other reasons. This freedom is complemented by freedom of assembly whereby people may peacefully assemble in private or in public. Both rights are protected in the ICCPR (Art. 21, 22) and may only be restricted for reasons of national security, public order, public health or morals and the protection of the rights of others.

Organizations are often banned when they are deemed to constitute a challenge to the government or the status quo, and frequently without reference to whether the opposition is violent or non-violent.

Prohibited organizations may be denied access to the media; media reporting regarded as sympathetic to such organizations may be censored and journalists punished for 'condoning terrorism'. *See Congo, Czechoslovakia, Iran, Iraq, Ireland, Israel, Paraguay, Poland, South Africa, Spain, Turkey.*

**Banning individuals**: Banning orders denying the individual freedom of expression and preventing his or her right to exercise a profession is an extreme censorship measure not infrequently resorted to. Bans on individuals may be accompanied by prohibitions on quoting them in any way, or prohibitions on their meeting other individuals. Prevention of terrorism laws often enable governments to impose restrictions or prohibitions on persons in respect of their movements or activities in relation to any political organization, association or body of which they are a member; they may be banned from taking part in any political activity, or from addressing public meetings. Banning orders are frequently linked with internal exile. *See Chile, South Africa, Soviet Union, Turkey.*

## Economic pressures

Economic pressures on the media exerted by governments or private interests are a serious and persistent form of interference. Most independent newspapers, radio and television stations rely heavily on revenue from advertising for their survival, so that threats by governments or private advertisers to withdraw such funding will produce compliance with pressures or the collapse of such ventures.

Government monopolies on newsprint and other materials essential to media production can be used effectively to force closure of media bodies. *See Colombia, France, Honduras, India, Mexico, Nicaragua, Paraguay, United States.*

## Media concentration and ownership

There is an increasing concentration of both printed and electronic media ownership world-wide. The United Nations Human Rights Committee has commented on this development with concern for freedom of expression. A few powerful organizations may have shares in both national and international markets; private ownership of media organizations is restricted in some countries to allow smaller publications ventures to compete. The burden of proving that such concentration might be against the public interest generally falls on the opponents of concentration. Media concentration is often defended on the grounds that it is the only commercial way that can secure the continuing progress and development of media ventures. The possible dangers involved in contraction of ownership are that a narrower range of opinions is available to the public; that those opinions may reflect the proprietorial interests; that journalistic values may be compromised by commercial interests; that standards might fall in the absence of competition. At greatest risk is the level, variety and quality of debate on issues of public concern.

In certain countries, leading newspapers exist under the ownership of a select number of politicians or influential families closely aligned with political parties.

Similar dangers exist with state or single party ownership of all or the bulk of the media. Control varies from subtle or open 'guidance' to the use of media outlets as mouthpieces for ruling individuals or parties, and as a source of biased but influential versions of events. Debate on public and political issues is either stage-managed or one of 'nuance' rather than real issues. *See Australia, Colombia, France, Honduras, India, Iraq, Poland, Soviet Union, Spain, United Kingdom, United States.*

## Self-regulatory methods

**Self-regulating bodies**: In many countries press or media councils or committees have been established with the objective of preserving freedom of the press, through encouraging self-regulation. Among the tasks of such bodies are to promote and ensure high professional and commercial standards, to consider complaints, and to monitor restrictions on the supply of information of public interest or importance. The success of such bodies depends on the credence given to them by governments, the public, journalists, management and owners of national press bodies alike. In countries where such bodies do not exist, self-regulation can still takes place. In single-party states it is often the case that membership of the official media is restricted to members or partisans of the ruling party; this entails establishing common objectives for the profession, thus reducing the need for open government interference with the media. In Poland, for instance, a meeting of officially-recognized publishers in 1984 resolved not to publish any writers critical of the government. In Iraq, entry to journalism courses is restricted to members of the *Ba'th* party. *See France, Poland, South Africa, Sweden, United Kingdom, Zaïre.*

**Self-censorship.** The term 'self-censorship' is used to describe the various reasons why journalists, writers and publishers suppress or withhold information themselves which might otherwise be deemed suitable matter for publication. When an editor or journalist with the opportunity to choose feels obliged not to publish, or not to act in accordance with his or her own convictions or sympathies, self-censorship is in operation. It must be considered as an important and pervasive category of censorship. It operates at various levels and is often difficult to identify or monitor. In many countries, press reporting is based on the understanding that coverage of sensitive issues is minimized or dropped and criticism moderated. Such compliance may be secured by threats of dismissal, detention, closure or, in the case of the foreign press, expulsion or refusal to renew a work permit. Low pay contributes to self-censorship. Journalistic sympathies may be fostered by salary increments and gifts from the government. *See China, El Salvador, Ghana, Honduras, Kenya, South Korea, Kuwait, Mexico.*

## On seeking and receiving information

**Control of the supply of information to media**: Control, constraint and suppression of the supply of information to journalists and other researchers seeking information from public or private authorities is exercised through a number of methods, including the following: control of official press releases and authorized briefings; classification or reclassification of information; subjection of government officials to a duty of 'lifetime' confidentiality; restriction of the importation and exportation of publications and films; denial or restriction of visas and accreditation for travel within and between countries, access to official or independent sources, availability of independent local assistance; and restriction on information to main news agencies and bureaux.

**News agencies**: The five major international news agencies, *Associated Press, United Press International, Reuters* and *Agence France-Presse* and *TASS*, the Soviet news agency, account for the bulk of the gathering and dissemination of international news. A sixth agency, *Inter Press Service*, has consciously responded to the criticism levelled at the larger agencies that they emphasize information and ideas that are of concern principally to the developed world. Through the use of mainly local correspondents *Inter Press Service* provides information and news concerned with economic and social development. Regional news agencies include *Xinhua* (New China News Agency), the *Pan African News Agency*, the *Organization of Asian News Agencies*, the *Union of Arab News Agencies* and the *Caribbean News Agency*.

National news agencies are often close to the government and may restrict reporting on domestic affairs to the outside world in compliance with overall government policies. *See China, Kenya, North Korea, Mexico, Zaïre.*

## On imparting information

Dissemination and distribution of information materials is in many countries hampered not only by legal restrictions put on citizens by their governments but also by the cost of dissemination. Information may be concentrated in capitals and large towns and not available in rural areas. Modern technology not only gives many opportunities for distribution of information; it also, through its sheer complexity and cost, puts control of such distribution in the hands of few countries and their corporations. It is only recently that aid to developing countries has taken the form of strengthening information technology resources.

**Newsprint**: Authorities enjoying monopoly control on newsprint and machinery who wish to restrict publications will often try to do so through control of the raw materials or machinery required by publishers. In Ghana, for instance, the Ministry of Information has control over the supply and allocation of almost all media equipment and facilities from newsprint to telephones and typewriters. This renders all journalists dependent on government approval. Supplies can easily be cut to any critics of government policy. In Mexico the Ministry of the Interior has the monopoly on the production of newsprint; it oversees the printed media—newspapers, magazines and books—through the *Comision Calificadora de Publicaciones y Revistas Ilustradas* and issues printing certificates. All import of relevant machinery is licensed. The genuine shortage of paper in some countries in Africa has been used to justify non-publication of the text of national laws such as the Constitution relevant to the protection of human rights. The control of paper supply in sufficient quantity and at the right time means that many newspapers, big and small, faced with the danger of closing down due to lack of paper, prefer to apply a form of self-censorship. *See Congo, Ghana, Mexico.*

**Typewriters:** In the pursuit of the aim of silencing unwanted opinions government have put restrictions on the use of typewriters. In Romania, for example, a 1983 decree gives the authorities power to decide who may or may not possess a typewriter. A register is kept of all those owning typewriters, and repairs to individual typewriters can only be carried out in special workshops. No-one with a police record is allowed to own a typewriter. In Iraq, importing typewriters (and also printers attached to computers) is allowed only after obtaining permission from the General Security Directorate. Foreigners entering Iraq have their typewriter number stamped on to their passports.

On Feb. 20, 1987 the Vienna CSCE Conference dealing with the implementation of the Helsinki Accords discussed a call to abolish all restrictions on the possession and use of typewriters in any of the thirty-five countries party to the Accord. *See Ghana, Iraq, Romania.*

**Photocopiers**: Since the introduction of the photocopier, duplication and therefore distribution of written materials has become much easier for those with access to such a machine. Often photocopies of material escaping the censor circulate extensively through the use of photocopiers. In Hungary, for example, the Ministry of Industry handles all licences for photocopiers and duplication machinery. In some countries such licences are hardly ever given to private bodies.

Sometimes the photocopier is the only and crucial means by which the world is informed about human rights atrocities. Such was the case in Kampuchea where massive killings were documented by the perpetrators themselves and photocopies of these documents (made on the spot under extreme circumstances and with a sporadic electricity supply) formed important evidence of the atrocities. *See Iraq.*

**Restrictions on circulation**: When the actual production of a publication is not hindered or made impossible, authorities may still control and limit its distribution. Circulation figures of books or newspapers are of course affected not only by government measures: national literacy rates or poverty are more important factors.

In some countries clauses referring to the importance of free distribution are included in their constitutions. In Honduras for example the law states that 'those who by direct or indirect means restrict or limit the communication and circulation of ideas shall be liable before the law'. In practice, such guarantees are often ignored.

Prior censorship of newspapers, as for example when copy must be sent to the censor before publication, can substantially delay publication and distribution deadlines. The delaying tactics of censors cost newspapers (especially dailies) crucial time and money and can lead to a collapse of sales figures.

In many countries the circulation of foreign publications is restricted. Without recourse to judicial proceedings, ministers can prohibit the sale and distribution of publications and issues of periodicals. *See Honduras, Malaysia, Singapore, Taiwan, Zaïre.*

# 4. CENSORSHIP: TARGETS

**Speech**: Freedom of speech has come to stand for freedom of all types of expression through any media including the printed word, yet strict censorship of oral communications is still commonplace. In many countries speech that is allowed in small private circles is not allowed as part of the content of public speeches. Public speech may be denied to an individual altogether, temporarily or permanently, or doctored to accord with official policy. In the United States federal employees are required to submit for pre-publication review speeches that could refer to intelligence data. In Yugoslavia the law provides for prosecution of those who commit 'verbal crimes', including the spreading of 'false news'. Under Kenya's sedition law, individuals may be prosecuted for single utterances. In South Africa, any reference to members of banned organizations in public speech constitutes a punishable offence. *See Czechoslovakia, Kenya, Morocco, South Africa, United States, Yugoslavia.*

**Correspondence**: Interception of mail is a violation of the right to privacy, as stated in Article 8 of the European Convention of Human Rights and in Article 12 of the Universal Declaration of Human Rights. It is reported that all mail sent to the USSR from outside the socialist bloc is monitored through one post office. In India, the 1986 amendment to the Indian Postal Act gives unlimited powers to both central and state government to intercept, detain or dispose of all postal articles. In Denmark, the Constitution prohibits any such violation of privacy, unless under special circumstances, in which case a judge needs to approve the measures being taken according to strict criteria. *See Denmark, India, North Korea, Morocco.*

**Telephone communications**: Opponents of government policy are countered through surveillance methods, a means of censorship through the creation of an atmosphere of fear and suspicion without direct preventive actions such as arrest and imprisonment. In Malaysia, for example, the Special Branch enjoys unlimited powers under the Internal Security Act (ISA) to investigate and tap the telephones of those deemed 'subversives'. In Argentina fears were recently expressed that members of the armed forces were responsible for bugging the telephones of politicians and union leaders. In the USA in 1981 under President Reagan orders were issued to expand the authority of the CIA and FBI to conduct domestic surveillance. Evidence of illegal surveillance of political groups in previous years in the United States has already come to light under Freedom of Information Act legislation. *See Argentina, Ireland, North Korea, South Korea, Malaysia, United States.*

**Prisons and other places of detention**: The European Court of Human Rights has come to the view that a prisoner's right to privacy concerning his or her correspondence and writings is the same as that of a person at liberty, and the Court envisages a free flow of such communications, even if they are intended for publication. Any interference in these communications must be justified specifically under Article 8(2). In 1975 the European Court on Human Rights observed that impeding someone from initiating correspondence constitutes the most far-reaching form of 'interference' in the exercise of the right to respect for his correspondence. Similarly, denial of access to newspapers and other media is deemed a violation of prisoners' rights. *See Morocco.*

**Meetings and demonstrations**: One aspect of the right to freedom of association as guaranteed by Article 20 of the Universal Declaration of Human Rights is the right to meet in private, or in public, for purposes connected with the objects of the association in order to propagate its aims and win support. On several occasions in Czechoslovakia during 1987, meetings of members of the Charter 77 human rights organization held in private homes have been broken up.

Political meetings or press conferences may be banned or directly disrupted by government security forces or pressure may be put on the media not to report or to play down these sensitive events. In 1987 in South Korea for example, anti-government demonstrations fell into a category of events on which newspapers were instructed to show caution in reporting. In Haiti and South Africa, if demonstrations are allowed to take place at all, journalists and particularly cameramen have been prevented from covering them by means which include arrest, assault and prosecutions. *See Czechoslovakia, South Korea, South Africa.*

## Media workers

**Editors and producers**: Editorial decisions and policy play a crucial role in determining what issues are covered in the press and by which journalists. Editorial policy will normally reflect a certain political or economic stance or viewpoint, and so editorial discretion is often confused with covert censorship.

There are, however, many examples of direct proprietorial or state interference in editorial policy which in turn determines overall policy. This is particularly evident when the state controls appointments to editorial boards. *See China, India, Romania, Yugoslavia.*

**Journalists**: Many countries regulate journalists' access to information through registration, accreditation and licensing. Codes of ethics exist to maintain professional and ethical standards. Often included in such codes is the obligation of journalists to defend the principle of freedom and independence of the press.
By the very nature of their work, journalists are a prime target for censorship, and a whole range of measures and action is employed against them which could be characterized as censorship.

**Dismissals**: There are numerous examples of journalists being denied employment and employment opportunities as a result of the exercise of their professional duties. Journalists have been dismissed for expressing political views, for views critical of the government, for questioning the official account of events, for trade union activity, and for deviation from the official line. Between 1975 to 1980 in South Africa, between 600 and 700 journalists lost their jobs as a result of their demands for greater press freedom. In Poland in the 1980s over 1,000 journalists lost their jobs and as many were demoted in the aftermath of the introduction of martial law. *See China, Ecuador, France, Poland, South Africa.*

**Dangerous missions**: There has been increasing recognition that journalism has become a dangerous profession and that journalists place themselves in life-threatening situations when covering armed conflict situations such as wars, terrorism and civil strife. Attempts to provide journalists with greater protection have been made both at the level of international law

and guarantees, and through non- governmental initiatives. Article 79 of the Geneva Convention's Protocol No. 1 on Measures of Protection for Journalists was adopted by the Diplomatic Conference of June 8, 1977. In 1985 the International Committee of the Red Cross (ICRC) established its 'hot line' to assist journalists on dangerous missions. The International Press Institute (IPI) has produced a manual to help journalists on dangerous assignments to 'avoid death, injury, jail, expulsions and other perils'. *See Colombia, El Salvador, Peru.*

**Warnings, threats and harassment**: Journalists are susceptible to warnings, threats and harassment. Such actions are usually taken against journalists in order to influence their reporting. The effect is usually a degree of self-censorship. In Colombia there is evidence that the increasing incidence of threats against journalists has led to greater co-operation between journalists in order to prevent attacks on particular individuals within the profession. Sweden has attempted to build legal safeguards into its Press Act to protect individual journalists from harassment. More extreme forms of intimidation include the publication of death lists of named journalists. *See Colombia, Honduras, Iran, Sweden.*

**Investigative journalism**: Investigative journalism has emerged as a separate and specialized mode of journalistic inquiry. It involves the investigation and exposure of corruption, misconduct and mismanagement in government, bureaucracy, the military, etc. with the purpose of checking this behaviour through informing public opinion. It came to the fore during the Watergate scandal in the United States but has long been a feature of German journalism as exemplified by *Der Spiegel*. Investigative journalism extends the limits of public debate and political participation. The emergence of investigative journalism in other countries such as the USSR and Spain may be viewed as a sign of increasing demands for more openness in government. Such investigations are often seen as hostile activity. In other countries, investigative journalism is an alien concept. *See Australia, China, El Salvador, Mexico, Paraguay, Sweden.*

**Restricted movement and expulsions**: Freedom of movement is essential to journalistic activity. However, both domestic and foreign journalists have often been barred from zones of war and emergency, for example, in the North and Eastern provinces in Sri Lanka. The Israeli authorities have placed Palestinian journalists under house or town arrest, thereby preventing them from performing their duties effectively. The Indonesian authorities prohibited journalists from travelling to certain rural areas during the election campaign in 1987. South African journalists have been denied passports to travel abroad. Numerous foreign correspondents are expelled from countries each year, and there appears to be an increase in such expulsions. According to the Committee to Protect Journalists, in 1987 alone more than thirty journalists were expelled from ten countries; in addition fifteen foreign journalists were expelled from Tibet, and more than twelve journalists left their countries of work under threat. Another common practice is the refusal to issue or renew visas and work permits. This often constitutes *de facto* expulsion. *See Indonesia, Iran, Iraq, Israel, North Korea, South Africa.*

**Bribery and corruption**: Corruption is common in countries where journalists are poorly paid and the acceptance of bribes from politicians and businessmen has become routine. *See Honduras, El Salvador, Mexico.*

**Kidnapping and missing persons**: Under many military regimes, journalists may be abducted or 'disappear'. There are many examples of missing journalists whose fate has never been explained. Journalists can also be a target of groups in opposition to the government as a means of attracting media attention, and have also been used as a bargaining tool to gain political concessions, as in the case of the Lebanon. *See Ecuador, Honduras, Peru.*

**Attacks, torture, killings**: Assassination of the writer is the ultimate censorship. Unfortunately physical attacks such as beatings, bomb attacks, torture and killings of journalists are not rare. According to the Committee to Protect Journalists, there were nine journalists murdered in 1987 in seven countries, apparently in connection with what they wrote, broadcast or filmed (not including journalists killed in crossfire or for reasons unrelated to their journalism). More than sixty journalists were assaulted (i.e. fired upon, beaten, had their house bombed, etc.). These incidents are intended to serve as a warning not to investigate or expose certain practices such as government corruption and drug trafficking, and to observe self-censorship. In Mexico and Colombia the assassination of journalists has mobilized media workers who have called for greater preventive government action. During 1987 journalists were killed in Colombia, Nigeria, Japan and Peru. *See Colombia, Mexico.*

**Arrest, detention and imprisonment**: In 1987, according to the Committee to Protect Journalists, more than 200 journalists were arrested in thirty-eight countries. Some were held only for a few hours, others are still in prison. Short-term detentions are often used as a means of intimidating journalists and preventing them from reporting on a current crisis. Long-term detention without trial and fear of long-term imprisonment effectively silences dissent within a country. Journalists are arrested for expressing views critical of the authorities, views of proscribed groups and organizations, views contrary to the interests of national security, or likely to incite public disorder or violence. *See Fiji, India, Malaysia, South Africa.*

## Printed matter

**Books**: Many countries have an official Censorship Board or equivalent which scans new publications for content. Some countries publish lists of banned books. Penalties may often be incurred for the possession of certain types of proscribed literature. Post-publication censorship may allow for limited unofficial editions to circulate yet the costs incurred by publishers whose works are later censored makes independent publishing a precarious business in many countries.

The classic censorship measure of book-burning did not die with the medieval Catholic Church's list of prohibited books, the *Index Librorum Prohibitorum*. The method is still in use today, although less extreme methods of post-publication censorship are more usual. In 1986 in Turkey, books weighing a total of thirty-nine tons were pulped following the publication of a list of books banned by the Minister of Justice. The public burning of books is recorded to have happened in Argentina in Cordoba in 1976, in Chile in 1986 (14,000 copies of a book by Gabriel Garcia Marquez were set alight) and most recently in France (March 4, 1987). As part of the campaign against 'bourgeois liberalization' in China, the authorities in 1986 were reported to have seized seven million books and magazines specializing mostly in martial arts, romantic and erotic themes. In 1986 in Israel a book exhibition organized by Palestinians was raided, resulting in the confiscation of 1,000 books and the arrest of three of the exhibition's organizers.

The importation of books may be circumscribed for reasons of sexual, political or religious content. Censorship of textbooks is common in many countries. Following the Islamic Cultural Revolution in Iran, educational books were replaced with Islamic texts. In Poland, 650,000 copies of a history textbook, 'Modern History', were shredded for making reference to taboo historical subjects. Censorship in Poland can be extended to censorship of book reviews of émigré literature. The protection of state secrets often leads to the screening of books; in the Soviet Union, officials of *Glavlit* screen books for names and events relating to state secrets.

Censorship of books will often stimulate a thriving unofficial publication network. In Czechoslovakia, a 'counter-press' *samizdat* regularly circulates officially censored printed matter. In Indonesia, post-publication censorship allows for the circulation of photocopied editions of books. In Pakistan, Salman Rushdie's book 'Shame', despite official proscription, is obtainable through pirated editions in major bookshops. The phenomenal sales success of Peter Wright's book 'Spycatcher' in 1987 proves that book censorship may often be counter-productive. In Kenya, for example, exiled writers sell well in the streets, and in Ireland book banning can result in a boost in sales through importation across the border from Northern Ireland. *See Chile, China, France, Iran, Israel, Pakistan, Poland.*

**Newspapers and journals**: Freedom of the press is often given a central position in broader constitutional guarantees related to freedom of expression. The phrase 'freedom of the press' is used to refer to freedom of the print media but is often extended to refer to the freedom of all media. It is a fundamental clause in the First Amendment of the United States for instance, and is a notable omission in the Indian Constitution, where, however, it has been held to be implied. Despite the ascendancy of electronic media in most countries, the historic position of the independent press as an institution has led to a recognition that it is in the arena of independent newspaper publishing that the most publicized battles for freedom of expression are fought. It is not surprising therefore that the issue of press freedom (in the sense of daily or weekly circulation of printed matter) is a central theme in every country entry in this book. Magazines and small circulation journals are often targets for censorship, especially in countries with few or no independent newspaper outlets. The 'counter', unofficial or semi- official press organizations in many countries may be the main source of reliable information on national issues. *For particulars on press freedom, see also separate entries on editors, journalists, newsprint, restrictions on circulation, etc.*

## Film and cinema

In many countries, film censorship has become the last remaining example of classic pre-censorship. Although they have been abolished or weakened in an increasing number of countries film censorship bodies still remain in one form or another as an institution.

In its fullest form, film censorship stipulates that public exhibition and/or hire of films requires examination and grant of a certificate by a film censor, or more usually, a board of film censors consisting of officials and/or representatives of society. A refinement sometimes adds a censorship requirement for the export of films to prevent the country of production being shown in a bad light. Films may be either banned or passed subject to cuts being made. In some countries a censorship certificate must be obtained (and paid for) for each print of a film, but more often only a single certificate is granted and is valid for all prints struck from the master.

An early development was a primitive form of classification into two categories for showing respectively to adults only or to both adults and children. Latterly this has been developed into a more sophisticated system with several age-steps (pre-puberty, post-puberty, post-adolescence) and non-binding guidance indications.

There is a tendency for many censorship boards to convert into classification boards, with or without backing powers; but in such cases there is usually a residual control over films shown to children (which may be defined as non-adults or even as a younger age group). Some countries, such as Belgium, never had universal film censorship but merely a restriction on the entry of children into cinemas. Control of censorship boards is either central or municipal. In some countries where censorship powers are local, unofficial central boards have been set up by the film industry to provide a degree of unity in the decision-making process. In the United States a scheme was introduced to prevent the development of local powers and was therefore enforced not by law but by private cartel-like sanctions.

In very recent years the private (as opposed to public) showing of films has been brought into the censorship net in the form of video-censorship. In the UK, which in its Video Recording Act (1985) pioneered this new form of film censorship based on the sale of copies of the film rather than their exhibition, a new separate pre-censorship system has been introduced by statute. Ireland is following the British model. Scandinavian countries are following a different path by linking video censorship to existing film censorship certificates. Developments in other countries are still at an early stage.

Reasons given by the authorities to legitimize film censorship differ, depending on the religious or ideological basis of the society. (In Pakistan, for instance, all sexual matter in films is censored according to the laws of Islam.) However, film censorship may also be motivated by national security considerations. In Egypt criticism will not pass the censors, who have to approve every film produced in Egypt. In South Africa the government has recently granted the commissioner of police wide-ranging film censorship powers. The new regulations state that the commissioner may 'prohibit any ... film recording or sound recording containing any news ...' for the purpose of the safety of the public and maintenance of public interest.

## Electronic Media

**Radio**: World-wide, radio is the most important form of mass communication and the primary source

312

of news and information for people, especially in countries with low literacy rates or newspaper circulation. In some countries, radio operates under the same laws that constrain the press, but in addition it is regulated by a series of specific rules and guidelines which aim to define its objectives and regulate its programmes. These rules and guidelines differ from one political system to another, and are conceived by independent authorities or by the State itself.

All radio stations must acquire a licence, as well as a specific frequency from the State distributed under international agreement. Often, a licence is accompanied by conditions, and can be revoked.

In almost all countries, censorship bodies prohibit the broadcast of certain subject matter. In North Korea, most household and workplaces are equipped not with radio but with installed speakers, which are tuned to the national and local networks. Dials are fixed to prevent reception of external broadcasting.

Radio jamming is often used by governments either against radio stations within a country which relay opposition views, or against foreign broadcasts which are thought to carry propaganda hostile to the country concerned. Whilst defence against and control of propaganda is often cited as a rationale for radiowave jamming, this measure is more often used to gag and suppress reception of a plurality of ideas and opinions within a country. Jamming of internal broadcasts may take the form of sustained interference of frequencies or of sporadic interruptions of programmes with musical or other recordings. The ceasing of the Soviet jamming of the BBC Russian and Polish Services and *Voice of America* in 1987 was both a landmark in the reduction of international jamming and a tacit acknowledgement that jamming is expensive and fails to prevent millions from tuning in to foreign radio broadcasts. See *East Germany, North Korea, Nicaragua, Paraguay, Poland,*

*Romania, Soviet Union, United States.*
**Television**: In countries where television broadcasting is established, it is the most popular and powerful medium and is at the same time the most difficult medium to monitor in terms of censorship practice. Rapidly changing programmes and images, expensive recording techniques, behind-the-scenes production and editing procedures and difficulty in accessing original tape material combine to make 'watch-dog' activities a specialized task. Scenes may therefore easily be excised or altered or programmes censored or dropped without public knowledge. Television, where it is not overtly state controlled (as it is in the majority of countries), may be subject to codes outlined by government or independent regulatory bodies which issue guidelines to broadcasting organizations. In many countries these guidelines are very rigid and must be adhered to, in others they are routinely ignored. In many developing countries, radio is allowed to be privatized far in advance of television—a tacit acknowledgement of television's centrality as a government control mechanism. Opposition parties are often not given television airtime, or coverage sufficient to express their views fully. This is especially the case during election campaigns.

The rapid development of multinational and multilingual channels transmitted by satellite makes it possible to receive foreign television broadcasts in individual homes through cable television or through satellite dishes. In the United States alone there are an estimated two million 'backyard earth stations'. The advent of satellite television signals the possibility of wider choice in terms of television's cultural content. On the other hand, the sale and operation of satellite dishes may be subject to government monopoly and authorization.

Satellite broadcasting has been seen as a source of conflict between national laws on television broadcasting (governing obscenity for example) and multinational corporations, operating international commercial channels for global mass markets. Conflicts can arise for example from the advertising of alcohol, tobacco, firearms and drugs through satellite channels in countries where such matter may not be broadcast under national law. *See Denmark, France, Ireland, Mexico, Poland, Soviet Union, Spain, Sweden, United Kingdom, United States.*

**Computers**: Computers, from the simplest to the most sophisticated models, are able to store, analyze, code and decode information to a degree that makes them increasingly the most powerful and at the same time the most vulnerable instruments of information collection and dissemination. Computers can be linked together via telephone links or other dedicated channels and the information or the result of the analysis process can be exchanged. Development in computer technology and general access to computers is limited mainly to industrialized countries due to the high costs for developing countries. World-wide availability is further limited by the attempts mainly by the USA to prevent sophisticated computer equipment from reaching Eastern European countries. Domestic and international legal principles concerning the use of computers, such as the right to communicate, copyright on unpublished works, the right to privacy, are all as yet underdeveloped, not being formulated at the same pace as the much faster development of high technology. Although the possession of computer equipment is often restricted and subject to licensing laws, there are few censorship laws which specifically mention the dissemination of information via computer networks. *See France, Iraq, United States.*

**Databases**: Databases and other computerized information stores allow for huge amounts of data to be processed and made widely accessible. Through technological advance, information in such data banks can be retrieved in an infinite combination of search terms. This potentially unlimited accessibility and compilation of data has led to concerns for sensitivity of data and information. In addition to privacy issues, commercial and political interests have resulted in restrictions or proposals for restricting access and use of databases. Some databases in the United States cannot be accessed by anybody outside the country. Also, there are regulations designed to prevent technological information and know-how from being exported to the Soviet Union and Eastern Europe. This has also led to restrictions preventing Western European users, in West Germany for example, from accessing specific categories of databases in the USA because of potential 'unauthorized' third-party users. A new category of sensitive information which requires protection was created in the United States in 1986: 'potentially sensitive'. This refers to unclassified, non-sensitive data which through compilation and matching can turn into 'sensitive' information. Access to scientific information is in danger of becoming unduly restricted. *See Denmark, United Kingdom, United States.*

**Transborder communication**: Article 19 of the Universal Declaration makes specific reference to the right to communicate '...through any media regardless of frontiers'. In the age of electronic and satellite technology, communication and flow of information are no longer restricted by national boundaries. The technological developments have taken place so rapidly that the legal systems for the protection of freedom of information and the regulations protecting privacy, copyright and intellectual property have been lagging behind. The balance between freedom of information and government power to control information are being reappraised and redefined. Transborder communication and its specific technologies have highlighted an imbalance between 'information-rich' and 'information-poor' countries.

314

Countries without legislation on 'transborder dataflow' (TDF) have been termed 'data havens', and countries with such legislation may restrict information flow into those countries. On the other hand, concern about uncontrolled use of data by users based in other countries has led to extensive restrictions and controls for economic and state security reasons. While regulations are in preparation in the USA to restrict the use of satellite-sensed photographs in the media, the Soviet Union is reported to offer remote-sensing images for sale to the media (except that no such images are offered of Soviet territory). The European Communities have been concerned with researching access limitation problems, particularly as applied by the United States. The findings have not been published to date. Some countries, in particular in Africa, face enormous financial and also political difficulties in developing these technologies and their applications.

**Satellite communications**: Satellites provide a way of transferring information over long distances and to a large geographical area. The relayed information can be telephone and telex communications, radio or television broadcasts, or a wide variety of data relating to specific purposes such as weather information, financial markets or company information, often collected by computer databases on both ends of the link. The enormous scope of satellite communications can be summarized as being able to transfer voice, data, text and image without regard to frontiers.

Since the introduction of satellites in the 1960s, a number of new issues have been raised concerning their ownership and operation, including:
—the high costs incurred in purchasing the technology associated with maintaining satellites, and the virtual monopoly a few rich countries have on the control and use of satellites;
—the limited number of satellites that can be launched into a geostationary orbit (GSO) to act as television transmitters for certain areas;
—the absence in international law of rights which allow for all countries to have at least one such GSO;
—the fact that satellites know no frontiers, which means that it is quite possible for neighbouring countries to receive information broadcast to a specific country;
—the potential use of satellites for secret intelligence gathering, including photographs and telephone tapping;
—the need for common technical standards designed to allow easy exchange of information between different satellite communication channels. A current concept involves the creation of the Integrated Services Digital Network (ISDN), able to relay all telecommunication services.

Among the organizations that deal specifically with world-wide satellite issues are the World Administrative Radio Conference (WARC) and the International Telecommunications Union (ITU). *See Denmark, France, Mexico, Soviet Union, Spain, Sweden, United Kingdom.*

## Artistic expression

Article 19 of the ICCPR guarantees freedom of expression 'in the form of art' or through any other media. This clause in the Covenant is a recognition that art has been a classic target of censorship practice. Organizations such as International PEN Writers in Prison Committee and Index on Censorship who publish the work of censored writers are involved in defending the international right to artistic expression. In this sense, artistic expression has long had a special status conferred upon it by those who defend freedom of expression.

Censorship of art is usually based on dangerous (or simply impoverished) assumptions about artistic substance and intention. The messages and the manner in which ideas embodied in art become popular lead to high degrees of distrust between authorities and the artistic community. It is often the fact that art is capable of expressing more than one thing at a time that makes artists vulnerable to the misapprehensions of their censors.

This is not to deny that many works of art are often produced with the firm intention of defying authorities or established moral codes. The division between political and artistic expression may indeed be very slim; protest poems and protest songs have become a recognizable genre; *avant-garde* art may be purposefully designed to shock or to disgust. Yet even in the case of the protest singer, the artist's self-proclaimed intentions will not exhaust the possible interpretations that can be bestowed by those who censor art. This is why, long after an artist's death, censors continue to censor artistic works just as critics perennially renew debate on an author's artistic message. More commonly, a work of art is censored in anticipation of or as a response to popular reactions to art and the uses that the public might make of it.

Censors, like bad art critics, take liberties or ride roughshod over any artistic conventions in order to pass judgment only on sections of works which are subsequently divorced from the ambience of rich connotations that distinguish them in the uncensored work. Often it is poor quality art that is censored with the least difficulty, since the margin of error on the censors' part in abstracting simple 'messages' from such matter is reduced. All art, from paintings to music to literature, is censored regardless of the autonomous quality of its form.

One of the most chilling aspects of art censorship is not only the suppression of the work of art itself but the manner in which it becomes bureaucratically possible to criminalize the imagination. This strikes at the heart of freedom— the freedom to imagine. Ironically, however, censorship may create the conditions in which art is at least taken seriously. A banned book or author may enjoy a wider audience following censorship (provided the suppression is not total) than he or she could have

expected otherwise. Artists in many cultures, particularly writers and poets, are properly elevated to the position of spokesmen for their society—largely because they speak for it with precise and articulate energy. Poets may well be considered cultural ambassadors in Latin America; musicians in Czechoslovakia may well articulate the frustrations of a generation. Yet the power of art to alter society is limited. 'Poets are not legislators' writes the British poet Geoffrey Hill, 'unless they happen to be so employed, in government or law.'

**Theatre**: In many countries public performances are subject to pre-censorship. In Czechoslavakia the Main Administration of Press Supervision (HSTD) has powers to censor any public performance, cultural or artistic activity. In China the National Censorship Commission can impose censorship on the media, on the theatre and on artists. In Indonesia anyone planning to stage a play, poetry reading or short-story reading must first obtain permits from the local police. Fringe theatre groups staging controversial plays in Indonesia perform to restricted audiences only in private homes. In Egypt a censor is expected to monitor performances and check that actors do not deviate from the written text. In countries such as Kenya, with a strong oral tradition, excessive measures have been taken against the performance of plays that have gained mass popularity. The Israeli Board for Film and Theatre Review supervises all films and plays. In December 1986 a play, 'The Last Secular Jew' was banned because it was 'liable to stir up hatred against all religious people'. A Palestinian theatre in East Jerusalem, *Al Hakwati,* has been closed over thirteen times since it opened in January 1986 for allegedly fostering 'illegal meetings'.

Banning of a play may also entail a banning order on the playwright, as in the case of the Congolese playwright, Guy Menga, who continues to be banned even though the ban on one of his plays has been lifted. Distinctions can be made between staged and televised versions of plays. In South Africa a play by Athol Fugard could be staged but television screenings were not permitted.

Exile can face those involved in theatrical productions. In November 1987 death threats were issued to seventy-eight actors, actresses, playwrights and theatre directors in Chile by members of *Acción Pacificadora Trizano*. The actors were accused of being 'spearheads of international Marxism' and were given thirty days to leave the country. They declared their intention not to leave the country and called on the authorities to protect them.

One effect of art censorship can be a cultural 'brain drain'. In East Germany many actors and theatre directors and producers have left the country as a result of restrictions on artistic expression. The satirical political cabaret *Die Distel* is state-funded in the East Germany and scripts are censored by the Ministry of Culture. *See Chile, Congo, Czechoslovakia, Egypt, East Germany, Israel, Kenya, Soviet Union.*

**Poems and novels**: Poetry is censored if it is judged to convey ideas hostile to government policy or to public morals or taste. One of the sources of strength in poetic language—ambiguity—is often the source of censors' disaffection with the medium, since it is suspected of carrying 'covert', 'confusing' and therefore dangerous messages. In Yugoslavia a collection of poems was withdrawn, as they could be 'interpreted as having a number of meanings and their content ... bring ideological confusion to the readers'. In Pakistan, translations of love poems by the English poets Robert Browning and D. H. Lawrence are among works deemed offensive to Moslem sensibilities. In Iran, following a purge of artists unsympathetic to the current regime, Soraya Montaza, a twenty-three-year-old poetess, was executed after being found guilty of 'advocating sexual freedom'. The inconsistency of much South African censorship of art is exemplified in its treatment of poetry. A collection of poems by a black South African poet can appear in book form yet a periodical which contains one of his poems can be banned for printing it. As part of the policy of *glasnost* in the Soviet Union, once proscribed writers, including the poet Nikolai Gumilev, are now being published.

Novels are similarly censored for moral purposes or because of their sustained artistic dramatizations of political-historical movements. In early 1988 the first instalment of Boris Pasternak's novel 'Dr Zhivago' was published in a Soviet magazine. Similarly, in 1987, Anatoly Rybakov's novel on the effects of Stalinism, 'Children of Arbat', was published. *See Iran, Pakistan, South Africa, Soviet Union, Yugoslavia.*

**Art**: Pictorial representations, from sketches and drawings to paintings and sculpture, are censored, or the range of subject matter that can be treated in such works is controlled, through the direct interference of authorities or, in some countries, through the compliance of artists' unions with government policy. In January 1988 in the Soviet Union, reformers attending a congress of the Union of Artists mounted an open challenge to traditional leadership, stating that despite an explosion of interest in art in recent years, 'the union leadership chooses who is to be and who is not to be in artistic life, who is allocated a studio or a workshop, who is allowed to give an exhibition, who should become known through reviews of books'. Pre-censorship through institutional control of art avoids some of the problems involved in overtly censoring something as physically cumbersome as a painting, involving, for example, its removal from galleries. In Turkey authorities removed paintings by a Polish artist, Jan Dubkowski, following a judgment from Turkish President Evren that the painting was obscene. In Pakistan in January 1987 the editor of *Frontier Post* was prosecuted for publishing a photograph of a painting of Adam and Eve by the Renaissance artist Lucas Cranach, considered sacrilegious to Moslem ideology.

**Music**: On first thought, music and song might be thought to be immune from censorship. In fact, this is far from being the case. In some countries music is perceived by the authorities as such an important medium for the dissemination of ideas that special laws on performance and recording have been made. In Zaïre, laws prescribing censorship of music are in the Penal Code. The Censorship Commission has to ensure that the songs are not of a nature to 'provoke racial or tribal hatred, nor to include anything that contains insults, strong dislikes, slanderous or damaging claims'. Popular music and musicians have always attracted censorship. Current campaigns over the lyrics of pop music and performances by pop groups in the United States are but the latest example. Since *glasnost*, music by hitherto proscribed songwriters can be performed and publicly disseminated in the Soviet Union. *See Czechoslovakia, Zaïre.*

## Education and research

**Libraries**: Libraries and librarians perform a vital role in protecting freedom of information and the right to know. They have the professional duty to provide access to materials covering the widest range of expressions and opinions. In many countries, therefore, governments influence or interfere with the operation of libraries. In Iraq, for example, all libraries are directly supervised by the authorities. Access to certain collections of books and periodicals held in major libraries in East Germany is limited to specific categories of users.

The restriction of access to materials held in libraries on political, moral, aesthetic, or religious grounds can operate on various levels. Pressures can be exerted by government authorities, employers or users. A decision to introduce monthly booklists for the acquisition of children's books in French public libraries in October 1986 resulted in strong opposition from members of the library profession who subsequently launched a campaign against such a censorship measure. At another level, librarians may exercise 'self-censorship' through selective acquisition or restrictive dissemination procedures. At the same time, professionals at both national and international level have become more active in monitoring and opposing censorship in libraries. *See Iraq, Romania, United Kingdom, United States.*

**Academic and scientific freedom**: Academics and scientists face limitations on the freedom with which they can exercise their profession, and can find themselves dismissed from posts, blocked from publishing, denied funding for research or the opportunity to travel abroad to international congresses and meetings. Research findings are often of a sensitive nature and are restricted by use of classification rules in the interests of national security. Academics and scientists are also denied contact with foreigners for reasons of state security. Total ideological control can be exercised over intellectual and scientific life on political or religious grounds. The dangerous boundary between academic or scientific opinion and political opinion and the freedom to express matters of conscience can bring severe penalties leading to, for example, psychiatric abuse in the Soviet Union. *See East Germany, Iran, Iraq, Soviet Union, United States.*

## Advertising

The ICCPR Article 19 defines freedom of expression as including 'freedom to seek, receive and impart information and ideas *of all kinds*'. This language is clearly wide enough to cover advertising. Advertising as a mode of conveying ideas and information need not have a commercial motive alone. Advertisement for political purposes or to promote knowledge of rights and entitlements is commonplace for example. Advertising is subject to censorship and regulation. The European Commission of Human Rights has recognized commercial speech as within the human rights guarantee of freedom of expression (Wiljenberg, 1983; Barthold, 1985). The argument that commercial speech is entitled to lesser protection has not been finally determined at the international level. In the USA the Supreme Court has held that there is no First Amendment protection for false advertising or unlawful products, but that otherwise restriction on commercial speech must be justified by a substantive state interest and be the least restrictive method to advance that interest. The World Federation of Advertisers campaigns for self-regulation of advertising, now the policy of the US Federal Trade Commission. Consumer groups have expressed concern that misleading advertising, comparative advertising, advertising time limits on television and sponsorship of television programmes by commercial groups should remain controlled. A developing area of importance is transborder television advertising.

## Health information

The right to health is protected by a number of international instruments, and recognized in Article 12 of the International Covenant on Economic and Social Rights (ICES) as 'the right of everyone to the enjoyment of the highest attainable standard of physical and mental health'.

The provision or denial of information concerning the right to health covers a broad range of issues. There are obvious controls on this information such as the prohibition on advertising of alcohol, cigarettes and other drugs (in 1987 France banned alcohol advertising on television, for example) in the interest of protecting the health of the nation. However, there are numerous examples of the restriction and suppression of information on health issues where it is argued that the public

has a right to know. These include: family planning and information on abortions and contraceptives (in 1987 it became illegal in Ireland to provide referral information on abortion clinics in the UK); AIDS and other sexually tranmitted diseases (there has been considerable sensitivity on the part of some governments of African countries to the attention given by the international media to the spread of AIDS); the safety and purposes of nuclear installations and the link between health and radiation leaks (suppression by the UK government of information about Sellafield nuclear plant events following the 1986 Chernobyl disaster); the dumping of banned pharmaceuticals and hazardous products in Third World countries where information on their danger is not available. Information with implications for public health is also frequently restricted under official secrecy laws. *See Ireland, Poland, Soviet Union, Uganda, United Kingdom.*

## Nuclear information

Although the subjects of nuclear arms, nuclear energy and nuclear safety are much discussed, the general public knows very little about them, concealed as they are in a maze of technicalities, propaganda and secrecy. It has gradually emerged that the utilization of nuclear energy as a source for generating electricity was accompanied by rigorous censorship and systematic disinformation. All governments introducing nuclear industries have denied full information concerning the real risks involved. In 1987 it was disclosed that the UK government had suppressed information for thirty years about the effects of serious fire at a nuclear reactor at Windscale (which is today known as Sellafield). At least one reason was to deny the information to opponents of the government's nuclear policies.

Three recent cases have brought to a head the extent to which the nuclear industry surrounds itself in secrecy: the nuclear 'accident' at Chernobyl; the revelations of Mordechai Vanunu about the state of the nuclear industry in Israel; and the alleged illegal export of plutonium by a nuclear waste company from West Germany via Belgium to Pakistan and Libya. When the Chernobyl accident occurred the Soviet authorities failed to supply information for forty-eight hours, and for the first week almost all newspaper information about the accident could be found only in foreign news sections. In the absence of full information on the accident from the the Soviet Union after the initial announcement, the US and other Western news media filled the information vacuum with often unsubst atiated reports. Soviet secrecy was seen as a prime cause of defective coverage of the Chernobyl accident.

In Israel, Mordechai Vanunu is being tried *in camera*, charged with treason and espionage after revealing that Israel has a large independent stockpile of nuclear weapons. As members of his family stated at a press conference in early 1987: 'The policy of utter secrecy adopted by the Israeli government in all aspects of the Vanunu affair is a direct outgrowth of the policy of secrecy and deception of the whole nuclear issue.' The scale and ramifications of the West German plutonium export scandal will only full emerge in 1988. Pakistan, Argentina, Brazil and South Africa are widely believed to have the technological capacity to produce their own atomic weapons. The West German magazine *Der Spiegel* reported that by April 1987 the International Atomic Energy Agency had received more than 250 'hushed-up' reports of nuclear power plant accidents around the world.

## Historical information

Official archives are generally subject to a rule whereby they are not made available to the public before a certain period; the judgment as to when it is permissible to release them varies (twenty-five years in the USA, thirty in the UK and fifty in Greece, for example). Information deemed to be sensitive is subject to a longer or indefinite restriction, chiefly for reasons of national security and public order.

This restriction has been criticized for allowing official 'cover-ups' of embarrassing or damaging information, and for lending currency to inaccurate or partisan versions of history in the absence of source material and 'hard facts'.

Where access to official sources is absolutely denied, the official version stands as the only version available in reference books, school and university textbooks, documentaries etc.. This enables the suppression of facts detrimental to the status quo, and the presentation of a single self-justifying interpretation presented as irrefutable fact.

Books containing conflicting versions of history are sometimes subjected to banning. *See Iran, Kenya, South Korea, Romania, Turkey, United Kingdom.*

# 5. DEFENDING FREEDOM OF EXPRESSION: POLICIES AND PROGRAMMES

## Non-governmental bodies

All major institutions from governments to trade unions to church organizations are duty bound to protect those they speak for, and to secure their fundamental rights. Yet conflicting interests may lead to a reversal of this role, and freedom of expression is often the first right to be curtailed. In this sense, international, non-governmental organizations have over the years played a significant role in working directly or indirectly to combat censorship.

Among such organizations are those with membership or affiliated bodies in several countries, such as Amnesty International, International PEN, the Committees to Protect Journalists, the International Helsinki Watch committees, and the International Commission of Jurists.

Other relevant international organizations include the International

Press Institute, Index on Censorship, International Federation of Journalists, International Organization of Journalists, World Press Freedom Committee, International Publishers' Association, International Federation of Actors, the Association for the Promotion of the International Circulation of the Press, and the Commonwealth Press Union.

On the national level there are an increasing number of human rights and other organizations who see it as part of their work to monitor and document the performance of their government in the field of freedom of information and who try to mobilize public opinion in support. Many such organizations are little known and struggle to exist under extreme pressure. Some examples may be found in the country entries of this book.

## Intergovernmental agencies

The mandate of most intergovernmental agencies impinges on some aspect of freedom of expression and information. Under the international and regional conventions related to human rights the responsibility for monitoring and implementation is vested in intergovernmental bodies such as the United Nations Human Rights Committee and the Council of Europe. Among the UN agencies, UNESCO has particular responsibility for the protection and promotion of rights in the field of education, science and culture. Other agencies, such as the International Labour Organization (ILO), are concerned with upholding the right to freedom of association. Outside the UN system the Intergovernmental Bureau of Informatics (IBI) has taken specific responsibility for the development and promotion of informatics and telecommunications around the world.

**New world information and communication order**: This concept was mentioned for the first time in a resolution of the UN General Assembly in 1978 and subsequently referred to UNESCO. In 1980, UNESCO began to debate the implementation of policies based on the conclusion of the MacBride Commission's report, 'Many Voices, One World'. The UNESCO General Conference stated that a 'new world information and communication order' could be based, among other things, on: '(i) elimination of the imbalances and inequalities which characterize the present situation; (ii) elimination of the negative effects of certain monopolies, public or private, and excessive concentrations; (iii) removal of the internal and external obstacles to a free flow and wider and better balanced dissemination of information and ideas; (iv) plurality of sources and channels of information; (v) freedom of the press and information; (vi) the freedom of journalists and all professionals in the communication media, a freedom inseparable from responsibility; (vii) the capacity of developing countries to achieve improvement of their own situations, notably by providing their own equipment, by training their personnel, by improving their infrastructures and by making their information and communication media suitable to their needs and aspirations; (viii) the sincere will of developed countries to help them attain these objectives; (ix) respect for each people's cultural identity and for the right of each nation to inform the world public about its interests, its aspirations and its social and cultural values; (x) respect for the right of all peoples to participate in international exchanges of information on the basis of equality, justice and mutual benefit; (xi) respect for the right of the public, of ethnic and social groups and of individuals to have access to information sources and to participate actively in the communication process'.

The conference also stated that this new world information and communication order should be 'based on the fundamental principles of international law, as laid down in the Charter of the United Nations', and that 'diverse solutions to information and communication problems are required because social, political, cultural and economic problems differ from one country to another and, within a given country, from one group to another'. The history of international interpretation of UNESCO's policies on information has since been characterized by much heated debate and controversy, and was one of the grounds given for the withdrawal of the United States and the United Kingdom from UNESCO.

## National law

Freedom of expression requires legal protection. This should be based on the fullest implementation of international standards governing this right. Where a country has a written constitution, freedom of expression should be protected within it and in other national legislation. There can be a great variety of legal means designed to promote freedom of expression, freedom of the press, and the right to have access to information. Equally, various institutions can encourage the concept of media responsibility. In the United States, for example, newspapers are increasingly appointing an inhouse ombudsman with the duty of properly responding to the complaints of readers. In all measures taken to promote freedom of expression at the national level the international principle that 'freedom is the rule and limitation the exception' should be adhered to.

**Access to information:** Freedom of expression as defined in the international standards is not only the right to impart ideas and information but also the right to seek information. This 'right to know' requires greater recognition and protection, and is fundamental to ensuring open and accountable government. In some countries 'freedom of information' is defined as the right of a citizen or a group to have access to information held in private and public authorities' files.

The right of access to files can be regulated in order to keep certain information secret or confidential.

Where public access to information is a working principle at all, it may be said that countries fall into two broad categories: those which have specific laws governing rights of access (the United States, Canada, France, Sweden and Australia, for example), and those which adhere mainly to the principle of discretionary secrecy in the release of information (the United Kingdom, for example). *See Canada, Denmark, France, United Kingdom, United States.*

**Freedom of Information Acts:** The aims of the various Freedom of Information Acts that exist have been to increase the flow of information between government and individuals both quantitatively and qualitatively. Among the many difficulties involved in the effective implementation of such acts has been the pressing need to reconcile existing secrecy provisions with the terms laid down in the Acts. Intelligence agencies, for example, often have the right to deny compliance for the production of documents, or sections of documents, on the grounds of national security. Many journalists in Canada, not having access to information on vital government policies of public interest because of absence of such legislation in their own country, can discover details of such policies only through referring to documents available under the United States Freedom of Information Act. *See Australia, Canada, United States.*

**Data protection:** Data protection is an abbreviated term to describe the individual's right to access to his or her personal files held by public or private 'data users', with a view to ensuring that the personal data is accurate, up-to-date and relevant for the purpose for which it is kept and that no unauthorized person can get access to the information. Data protection is therefore also related to the privacy of information.

Concerns about data protection were first enshrined in Scandinavian and West German legislation in the early 1970s, and developed as a result of the concern over the increasing power of computer systems to manipulate data without individuals knowing what data is kept and how it is used. The European Convention on Data Protection provides an international legal framework for countries to adopt. The Convention is open for ratification internationally and came into force in October 1985. The majority of countries who have signed the Convention so far are Western European, with interest increasing among countries in other parts of the world.

Most national legislation defines rights of access and rights to correct personal information stored separately concerning public and private data users. Although dealing mainly with information stored on computers, the law extends in some countries to records kept manually. Concern has been expressed in some countries where the right to access to personal records excludes those held by public offices such as police, social security, and immigration authorities. *See France, United Kingdom.*

**Right of reply**: The 'right of reply' is enshrined in law particularly in countries with legal systems based on French, Spanish and German law, and an international convention on the Right of Correction is in force since 1962, with however only eleven ratifying countries. Countries with legal systems based on English law do not usually provide a 'right of reply' and rely rather on non-legal protection of principle through self-regulatory measures. Article 14(1) of the American Convention on Human Rights allows to anyone injured by inaccurate or offensive statements the right of reply in the same communications outlet in which such statements were made. The application of this right requires the media to publish the injured party's reply free of charge. At the end of 1987 a Private Members' Bill on 'Unfair Reporting and the Right of Reply' was due a second reading in the House of Commons in the United Kingdom. The Bill's supporters argued that suing newspapers in court for damages was too expensive a remedy for the majority of the population. In some countries, the right of reply has been extended to include government officials and departments. This has led to an abuse of the right by imposing on the media an obligation to publish extensive government reports and even propaganda in response to alleged misrepresentation in the media. *See Australia, France, India, Paraguay, Singapore, United Kingdom.*

# SUGGESTED FURTHER READING

## General sources: serials

*Amnesty International Newsletter*, London, Amnesty International
*ARTICLE 19 Bulletin*, London, ARTICLE 19
*Consideration of reports submitted by States Parties under article 40 of the International Covenant on Civil and Political Rights*, Geneva & New York, Human Rights Committee of the United Nations
*CPJ Update*, New York, Committee to Protect Journalists
*Direct Line*, Brussels, International Federation of Journalists
*Human Rights Watch*, New York, Watch Committees & Fund for Free Expression
*Index on Censorship*, London, Writers & Scholars International
*IPI Report*, London, International Press Institute
*Mass Communication Media in the World, excerpts from the press*, Prague, International Journalism Institute
*Media Law and Practice*, London, Frank Cass & Co.
*Pen Freedom-to-Write Bulletin*, New York, Pen American Center
*Persecution and Protection of Journalists: news clippings*, Prague, International Journalism Institute

## General sources: books and reference

*Amnesty International report*, Amnesty International, London, 1987
*Country reports on human rights practices for 1986*, US Department of State, Washington, February 1987
*Global journalism: a survey of the world's mass media*, Merrill, J.C. (ed.), London, Longman, 1983
*The international law of human rights*, Sieghart, P., London, Clarendon Press, 1983
*Journalists on dangerous assignments: a guide for staying alive*, Falls Montgomery, L. (ed.), London, International Press Institute, 1986
*Libel and Slander*, Carter-Ruck, P.F., & Walker, R., London, Butterworth, 1985
*World press encyclopedia*, Kurian, G.T. (ed.), London, 1982

## Africa

*Censorship in South Africa*, Rooyen, JCW van, Johannesburg, Juta & Co., 1987
*Freedom of information and expression in The Congo*, ARTICLE 19, London, 1987
*Freedom of information and expression in Rwanda*, ARTICLE 19, London, 1988
*Freedom of information and expression in Zaïre*, ARTICLE 19, London, 1987
*Freedom of information and expression in Zambia*, ARTICLE 19, London, 1988
*Government restrictions on the press in South Africa: the state of emergency and international law*, Roadstrum Moffett, M., Washington, International Human Rights Law Group, March 1987

# SUGGESTED FURTHER READING

*Journalists and international humanitarian law: seminar final report*, Union of African Journalists & International Committee of the Red Cross, Geneva, December 1985

## Americas

*IAPA News*, Miami, Inter American Press Association

*Latinamerica Press*, Lima, Latinamerica Press

*The News Media and the Law*, Washington, Reporters Committee for Freedom of the Press

*Annual report of the Inter-American Commission on Human Rights, IACHR*, Washington, Organization of American States, 1987

*The Central-Americanization of Colombia? human rights and the peace process*, New York, Americas Watch, January 1986

*Chile: no news allowed*, Committee to Protect Journalists, New York, May 1985

*Honduras: a journalism of silence*, Committee to Protect Journalists, New York, January 1984

*Mexico: a country study*, ARTICLE 19, London, 1988

*The right to know*, Data Center, Oakland (California), 1985

*Survey of press freedom in Latin America*, Council on Hemispheric Affairs & Newspaper Guild, New York, 1987

## Asia

*Korea Weekly report*, Washington, North American Coalition for Human Rights in Korea

*TAPOL Bulletin*, London, Indonesia Human Rights Campaign

*Human rights in Taiwan*, Asia Watch, New York, 1987

*Newspapers in Asia: contemporary trends and problems*, Lent, J.A. (ed.), Heinemann Asia, 1982

*People's Republic of China: the human rights exception*, Cohen, R., in *Human Rights Quarterly*, vol 9 no. 4, November 1987

*Violation of freedom of the press*, Press Council of India, Indian Law Institute, Bombay, 1986

*Zia's law: human rights under military rule in Pakistan*, Lawyers' Committee for Human Rights, New York, July 1985

## Europe

*Uncensored Poland News Bulletin*, London, Information Centre for Polish Affairs

*Assignment Eastern Europe: the working conditions of foreign journalists in Bulgaria, Czechoslovakia, Poland and Romania*, International Helsinki Federation for Human Rights, Vienna, July 1987

*Freedom of information and expression in Poland*, ARTICLE 19, London, 1987

# SUGGESTED FURTHER READING

*Freedom of information and expression in Romania*, ARTICLE 19, London, 1987

*Independent peace and environmental movements in Eastern Europe*, Helsinki Watch, New York, September 1987

*Is there censorship in the Soviet Union? methodological problems of studying Soviet censorship*, Golovskoy, V., Washington, Kennan Institute for Advanced Russian Studies, 1985

*Reinventing civil society: Poland's quiet revolution 1981–1986*, Toch, M., New York, US Helsinki Watch Committee, December 1986

*Romania: human rights violations in the eighties*, Amnesty International, London, July 1987

*Free Press: journal of the Campaign for Press and Broadcasting Freedom*, London, CPBF

*Black book on the militarist "democracy" in Turkey*, Info-Türk, Brussels, June 1986

*Freedom of information: the law, the practice and the ideal*, Birkinshaw, P.J., London, Weidenfield & Nicolson, 1988

*Lingens case (12/1984/84/131)*, European Court of Human Rights, Council of Europe, Strasbourg, July 1986

*Media law: the rights of journalists, broadcasters and publishers*, Robertson, G., & Nicol, A.G.L., London, Sage Publications, 1984

*Official secrets: the use and abuse of the Act*, Hooper, David, London, Secker & Warburg, 1987

*Censoring "the troubles": an Irish solution to an Irish problem*, International Federation of Journalists, Brussels, May 1987

*Violations of the Helsinki Accords—Turkey*, Helsinki Watch, New York, November 1986

## Middle East and North Africa

*Newsletter*, Cairo, Arab Organization for Human Rights

*Les droits de l'homme dans le monde arabe: rapport annuel 1986*, Association des droits de l'homme et libertés démocratiques dans le monde arabe, Paris, 1986

*Censorship of the Palestinian press*, ARTICLE 19 & Committee to Protect Journalists, New York, 1988

*Excessive secrecy, lack of guidelines: a report on military censorship in the West Bank*, Falloon, Virgil, West Bank, Al-Haq, 1986

*Freedom of information and expression in Iraq*, ARTICLE 19, London, 1987

## Oceania

*Communications, law and policy in Australia*, Armstrong, Grey & Hitchens, Sydney, Butterworth (looseleaf)

*Fiji*, Minority Rights Group, London, October 1987

*Guilty secrets: free speech in Australia*, Pullan, Sydney, Methuen, 1984

*Media law in Australia*, Armstrong, Blakeney & Waterson, Melbourne, Oxford University Press, 1988

# INDEX